LAW & DISORDER

LAW & DISORDER

The Chaotic Birth of the
NYPD

BRUCE CHADWICK

THOMAS DUNNE BOOKS
St. Martin's Press
New York

THOMAS DUNNE BOOKS.
An imprint of St. Martin's Press.

LAW & DISORDER. Copyright © 2017 by Bruce Chadwick. All rights reserved.
Printed in the United States of America. For information, address
St. Martin's Press, 175 Fifth Avenue, New York, N.Y. 10010.

www.thomasdunnebooks.com
www.stmartins.com

Designed by Kathryn Parise

The Library of Congress Cataloging-in-Publication Data
is available upon request.

ISBN 978-1-250-08258-9 (hardcover)
ISBN 978-1-250-08259-6 (e-book)

Our books may be purchased in bulk for promotional, educational, or business
use. Please contact your local bookseller or the Macmillan Corporate and
Premium Sales Department at 1-800-221-7945, extension 5442, or
by e-mail at MacmillanSpecialMarkets@macmillan.com.

First Edition: April 2017

10 9 8 7 6 5 4 3 2 1

For my late and beloved wife, Marjorie,

who was everything to me

Contents

Contents

Acknowledgments

The pleasure in writing a book about history is meeting so many history lovers along the way who help me with my task. They are as interested in the American story as I am, and it has been a joy to work with them. I thanked each of them at the time I met them, and I happily thank them again here for helping me to complete this book.

First and foremost, I owe a great debt of thanks to all the librarians I met in my journey: In New Jersey, thanks to Tom Glynn and his associates at Rutgers University; Head Librarian Fred Smith, Tim Stuckey, and all of their able assistants at New Jersey City University; and the folks at the Morris County Free Library, the Randolph Library, Drew University, and the Morristown–Morris Township Library. In New York, thanks to the librarians at the John Jay College of Criminal Justice, the New-York Historical Society, and the New York Public Library. In Washington, D.C., many thanks to the librarians at the Library of Congress.

Many thanks to my agent, Jonathan Lyons, and his assistant, Sarah Perillo, and, at Thomas Dunne Books, to publisher Tom Dunne and his assistant, Will Anderson, to editor Emily Angell and her assistant, Lisa Bonvissuto, and to copy editor India Cooper.

Author's Note

In the decades prior to the Civil War, the crime rate in New York was about four times what it is today, and the murder rate was five or six times the current rate. Three times as many people were arrested in New York each day as the total number of those arrested in London and Paris combined. The crime wave that engulfed New York was perhaps the biggest in the history of the United States.

And there was no one there to stop it.

It [New York] is constantly changing, growing greater and more wonderful in its power and splendors, more worthy of admiration in its higher and nobler life, more generous in its charities, and more mysterious and appalling in its romances and crimes. . . . Its magnificence is remarkable, its squalor appalling.

—New York City journalist James McCabe Jr.

LAW & DISORDER

CHAPTER ONE

Riot!

If the riots which have disgraced our city for the few days past
are to be often repeated, we shall soon cease to have any claim
to the character of a decent and orderly community.

—Editor of the *Evening Post*, July 9, 1836

Some New York residents called 1834 "the riot year" because of the
dozens of civil disturbances that took place in the city. There were
riots against the Irish immigrants, political parties, churches, and African Americans. The ever-growing megalopolis of nearly half a million people seemed ready to explode as angry groups of thousands of
people swarmed through the darkened city streets intent on confrontation and destruction.

Summer was always sweltering hot in New York. Everyone kept their
windows open so that air could circulate through their homes. Men
wiped their sweating foreheads with rags. The temperature often
climbed into the nineties and sometimes soared over one hundred
degrees. The sun seemed to stay high in the sky all day. The city was
always humid, and millions of pesky mosquitoes, who could not be
killed, flew through the city air. When heavy rainstorms hit in summertime they flooded all the cellars in town. "Stifling," wrote one

New Yorker of the heat in the summer of 1836. "Wall Street, always a purgatory, has this day become a pandemonium: clouds of dust flying, chippings of granite whizzing in volleys like grapeshot."[1]

The canyons of tall buildings held the hot air close to the earth and made it even hotter, no matter the summer. Wealthy New York lawyer George Templeton Strong, who traveled the city extensively and kept a mammoth diary filled with thousands of pages of notes on people and events, wrote of a July day in 1841, "Let this day be infamous to after ages as the hottest a New Yorker ever perspired under. . . . There will be nothing left of me by tomorrow morning."[2]

The oppressive heat seemed to increase the anger that city dwellers felt in general, and the whites' deep rage against blacks in particular. Whites seethed against blacks, and blacks feared their wrath, as they had for quite some time.

The abolitionist movement in New York City had grown rapidly by the summer of 1834, fueled by the early successes of the Underground Railroad and the brand-new abolitionist newspapers. Several slave revolts in the South had been reported and attracted even more New Yorkers to the abolitionist banner. Black-and-white tensions in New York had mounted since the 1820s, with the end of all laws legalizing slavery in the state ("the awful curse of Negro slavery," said one New York mayor).[3] All of the former slaves in the city were now free, and at times they numbered as high as thirteen thousand. That number grew throughout the 1830s as thousands of black freedmen and -women from other northern cities and villages immigrated to the city. The tension increased considerably from April through June.[4]

On July 7, a group of black men planned a large meeting at the Chatham Street Chapel downtown. They had the use of the chapel because another civic group had given it to them. Not all members of the other group knew this, though, and some of them arrived and heatedly demanded to use the building. The black group refused, and a riot commenced in which six black men were arrested. This kicked off five days of disturbances.

The editor of the *New York Courier and Enquirer,* James Watson Webb, wrote that it was all the fault of the abolitionists, who were led by Arthur and Lewis Tappan. On July 9, a group of them met at the church. Without any warning, the gathering was attacked and broken up by an angry mob of more than two hundred antiabolitionists who had arrived with little interference from the city's weak law enforcement agents, the constables. The raucous rioters drove the abolitionists into the city streets with chains and sticks, forcing them to run any which way they could to save themselves.

Undaunted, the abolitionists reconvened at the same church the next night, and the assembly was broken up yet again by a fuming white mob. The mob chased the abolitionists away and continued to riot all night and for two entire days and nights more, fighting abolitionists and New York's badly outnumbered, outgunned, and weary constable force. The mob broke down doors, shoved passersby on the streets, shouted down anyone they saw, and tossed rocks through numerous business and residential windows. The uncontrolled horde wrecked part of the Bowery Theater and nearby buildings and destroyed the homes of several of New York's abolitionist leaders, including the large mansion of the Tappans, the wealthy patrician brothers who were the ringleaders of the antislavery movement in New York. Mayor Cornelius Lawrence and a band of constables tried to stop the rioters at the Tappan home but were driven away by the mob. A dozen more large homes were set on fire, and others were partially damaged. Seven churches were burned down, and a school for black children was destroyed. Thick billows of smoke rose from the city streets and drifted through the air for days. The damage from the riot was well over $50 million in today's money.

The surging crowd of rioters, mostly unruly young men, had at first been driven back by the local constables, who threw stones and bricks at them and sometimes fired weapons, if they had them. That effort did not succeed, though, and after two long days of confrontation in the streets, the losing constables simply gave up; the mayor had to call in the three-hundred-man state militia, armed and on horseback, to disperse the crowd. After a few loud warnings, the militia opened fire into the crowd. Several people were killed, and dozens were wounded. Friends tried to bind up the wounds of those shot down with ragged sleeves torn off their shirts. The wounded were rushed to city hospitals and doctors' offices. The dirt in the street was dotted with puddles of blood. A half-dozen black men were captured in the uprising and badly beaten; one nearly died.

The violence thus ended, the mayor supplemented the militia presence by putting all the city's constables on alert and adding hundreds of "temporary constables" from the citizenry, many of them armed. The sheer size of the force helped to prevent any more riots or protests for the moment. However, "the diabolical spirit which prompted this outrage is not quenched and I apprehend we shall see more of it," said former mayor Philip Hone, who was there.[5]

The rioters represented "not only the denunciation of an insulted community, but the violence of an infuriated populace," wrote the editor of the *The Boston Post.*[6]

The New York Times wrote that the events were "disgraceful riots, originating in the hatred of whites for the blacks."[7]

People said that the riots were brought about by a social chain reaction, that one disturbance fed on the others, and that all exploded in a society living under incredible confusion and stress in a year, in a decade, when the nation was experiencing lightning changes everywhere. "The scene . . . was more disgraceful than anything we have witnessed in our city," editorialized the *New York Journal of Commerce*. Most residents blamed the ineffective constables for the collapse of law and order.[8]

There was something deeper, though. The antislavery movement was gaining ground, and quickly, in the 1830s, and the police had no idea how to handle it and the furious reaction of the people who opposed its champions. "Abolitionism . . . may play the devil with our institutions," predicted George Templeton Strong, and "grow greater and greater until it brings the whole system into a state of discord and dissension." From 1831 on, it seemed that one of the dominating conversations in New York was the rebellion of slave Nat Turner and other insurrections. At one party in upstate Saratoga Springs, in the summer of 1831, crime was all anyone could talk about.[9]

New Yorkers were fearful not only of the tensions between blacks and whites over slavery. The abolitionist riot was just the surface of the river of savagery that flowed throughout the city. Riots were commonplace in that era. There were clashes over street gangs, political clubs, elections, drinking, gambling, religion, and even dog licenses. New York City had become a carnival of violence. Any dispute seemed to trigger a riot, and the frustrations of the people were deep. In the antebellum era, civil disturbances were not only expected but seemed a part of the landscape.

Constables, along with a small force of night watchmen, had been policing New York City since 1658 and were supposed to preserve law and order. The New York constable force was the second in the United States. The first was formed in Boston in 1636, the third in Philadelphia in 1700. None was particularly effective. As early as 1732, Benjamin Franklin was denouncing the constables and calling for a professional, trained, and armed police force in Philadelphia, but few listened to him.

The American constable system was based on the Asian and European constable institutions that had flourished for several thousand years. There were constables in China and Greece in 2000 B.C. *Vigiles* (from which the American term "vigilante" was derived), a thousand of them, served as police, along with soldiers, in Rome during the reign of Augustus Caesar in 40 B.C. In the 1500s, Spanish cities were protected by organized "brotherhoods" of several hundred men who worked as constables. Napoleon created a national constable force of five thousand men in France in 1805. None of them were trained, all owed their jobs to politicians, and few were armed. Most were ineffective, as were their American counterparts.

The abolitionist riot was the biggest riot that year of 1834 in New

York, but a close mayoral election, the first in the city's history (prior to it, the city council members chose the mayor), started another three-day riot in the spring of 1835.

"If the riots which have disgraced our city for the few days past are to be often repeated, we shall soon cease to have any claim to the character of a decent and orderly community," wrote the editor of the *Evening Post*.[10]

The riots shook everybody, and many New Yorkers questioned the future of both the city and the country. Was this chaotic, criminal landscape the result of American democracy? Was it republicanism run amok? Former president John Quincy Adams, then a congressman from Massachusetts, shook his head. "My hopes of the long continuance of this Union are extinct. . . . The people must go the way of all the world, and split up into an uncertain number of rival communities," he wrote.[11]

City mobs, pumped up by emotion, took on a life of their own during the riots. In one instance, a mob stormed a house of ill repute in New York where a man had fled after being acquitted of raping a New York girl. The mob tore down the entire house, littering the streets with boards, window frames, and furniture, chopped up by axes. "The excess did not stop there for the mob, once excited, continued its riotous proceedings several successive nights and many houses of ill-fame in other parts of the city were destroyed and their miserable inmates driven naked and houseless into the streets," wrote enraged former mayor Hone in his detailed diary.

At forty-three, Hone, a tall, thin, handsome man with curly brown hair and full cheeks who lived in a large, well-appointed two-story mansion fronted by huge white columns, the Colonnade Houses, at 714–716 Broadway, near the rolling lawns of City Hall Park, had been one of the city's social lions for years. He had made his fortune as a merchant and by about 1820 was effectively able to retire. As one of the richest people in New York, he was sought after by all of the social lionesses of the city and spent most nights as a guest at some lavish party or hosting his own. He and his wife went to the theater, served on the boards of charitable organizations, and dressed in the finest clothes; he usually wore a light blue swallowtail coat, tight gray trousers, a choker collar with projecting points, and a flowered white stock on his daytime trips around the city.[12]

Early on, he was sought after by both political parties and became a Whig. (He would continue to be an active member of the Whig Party all of his life and would frequently travel to Washington, D.C., meeting with presidents and greeting foreign diplomats.) He was elected an assistant alderman in 1824, and in 1826, when the two parties were unable to agree on a mayor, he became the compromise head of the city for a single year.

He also became one of the most illustrious men-about-town in New York history. He loved the stage and became close friends with stars such as Junius Booth, writers, directors, and producers. Famous authors dined with him regularly and frequently traveled with him. Actors joined writers, politicians, artists, and professors at his dining table, set in a lavish room with windows that overlooked Broadway. Later, in the early 1840s, Broadway became a wide avenue lined with four- and five-story-high stone and brick buildings, jammed with shoppers, pedestrians, omnibuses, and carriages. It was already one of the great streets of the world.

Hone lived in high society but traveled all over town in elegant sleighs in winter and carriages in summer and observed everything and everybody. An eyewitness to the history of the city and its riots for a generation, he was vitally interested in crime in the city because his party's livelihood depended on running the city in an orderly manner. The general breakdown of law and order troubled him greatly. Hone's lengthy, colorful, and carefully written diary offered an insider's look at crime and police in New York.

After his term as mayor, since he no longer worked, he had plenty of time to volunteer, and people began to call upon him in emergencies, such as the 1831 riot at the Park Theater, when they noticed him in the crowd. "His address to the crowd on the street . . . was so characterized by the feeling of a good citizen and a reflecting man that hundreds left the grounds immediately," said an observer.[13]

When the recession of 1833 hit, the city and Hone's finances took a beating. He and others did not just fear death and injuries to rioters and the destruction of property; they feared getting hurt themselves in the general melee. "One can't look out of his window without the risk of being knocked down by some stray bullet or other that was intended for somebody else entirely, or fired on speculation without meaning anything against anybody in particular," wrote George Templeton Strong.[14]

Riots and unruly crowds were not new in New York City. Rowdy crowds roamed throughout town in the 1820s, smashing windows with wooden clubs, kicking over cans, shoving people on the sidewalk, and generating enormous noise that unsettled all of the residents in the neighborhoods through which they roamed. In 1827, one crowd of workers surged up Broadway, and a troop of constables appeared in the street to stop them. The crowd yelled and screamed and pushed forward. The constables, mostly unarmed and all nervous, gave way and let them wreak havoc as they paraded uptown and disappeared, noisily, into the night.[15]

Riots were easy to start.

Those interested in stirring up some mischief in New York City merely had to distribute paper handbills telling citizens to gather in one of the city parks at a particular hour to begin the rampage. The riot mongers all had a similar pitch, defined in one handbill connected to the flour riot in the late 1830s. It was, like many riots, aimed at what appeared to be an onerous scheme by business to defraud the public. The producers of flour, one of the most necessary ingredients for cooking, had doubled the price of a barrel from $5.50 to $11. *The New York Sun* told its readers that there did not seem to be any reason for the price hike except excessive profits. Many agreed.[16] "All friends of humanity, determined to resist monopolists and extortioners are invited to attend," the handbill read.

At that rally at 4:00 P.M. on a chilly day in February 1837, amid
controversy over rising flour prices, Hone wrote, firebrands told the
crowd that the owners of the Eli and Hart store had fifty thousand barrels of flour that they would sell to enrich themselves and keep from
the hungry poor. They got rich "while the city was starving," one of
the speakers said. Hone listened to it all. Then he wrote that "away
went the mob to Hart's store near Washington and Cortlandt Street,
which they forced open and threw 500 barrels and large quantities of
wheat into the street, and committed all the extravagant acts which
usually flow from the unlicensed fury of a mob."[17]

People even rioted over dogs. One summer in the 1830s, city fathers
ordered the constables to round up and slaughter fifteen hundred
dogs. The summer-long killing of dogs inflamed citizens, who pro-
tested often. "The poor creatures are knocked down on the street and
beaten to death. It is exceedingly cruel and demoralizing,"[18] wrote Lydia
Maria Child, the editor of the *National Anti-Slavery Standard* newspaper
and author of several books (she wrote the famous poem "Over the
River and Through the Wood") who left her troublesome husband at
home in Massachusetts and moved to New York in the early 1840s, and
followed city events closely. Child had spent her life deploring violence
against African Americans and saw New York as the capital of that practice; she kept a close eye on racial riots, women's issues, and other civil
controversies. One of her favorite pastimes in the city was to walk the
streets on routes that carried her through all kinds of neighborhoods.
She remembered everything that she could to include in her well-written
and well-read columns in the newspapers. She also wrote about what she
saw, the bad as well as the good, in her numerous and lengthy letters to
friends. Her friends back in Boston, especially, were fascinated by the
view they had of New York and its savagery. She arrived at the height of
the rising crime wave and the debate over the inept constable force.

Anything and everything seemed to cause a riot, because aggravated crowds realized that they could create a ruckus and wreak havoc
and not suffer any dire consequences from the badly trained police
force of constables. Commenting on a local stevedore strike, Philip

Hone wrote that "an immense body of the malcontents paraded the wharves all yesterday and attacked the men who refused to join them . . . several officers were attacked by the rioters, one of whom named Brink, had his skull fractured by the rioters."[19]

No one believed that the constables could halt anything. The early cops "were subject to very little discipline, and were anything but imposing or athletic. Should one attempt to make an arrest, he was either very roughly handled, or led [on] a long and fruitless chase, in the course of which he was sure to meet with many and ludicrous mishaps. He was, in fact, unable to protect himself, let alone guarding and protecting citizens and property," said George Washington Walling, who would become the city's police chief in 1874.[20]

During the nation's first two hundred years, the small urban areas and little villages that dotted the countryside relied on a trained militia and lowly paid, or volunteer, watchmen and constables for protection. The lawmen considered it a service to their city. Residents of New York did not think much of the puny constable force, but with little crime it sufficed. The New York militia units stationed in the city backed up the constables in times of trouble and worked for free. New Yorkers liked that idea because it kept down the cost of protection while the city was battered by financial crises, such as the depressions of 1819 and 1837 and the recessions of the early 1780s and 1833. As the city grew, though, problems arose.

The early New York constables had little supervision. They reported to police headquarters and then went out into their assigned neighborhoods to conduct patrols, alone. There were no rules against drinking, and many spent the night imbibing to pass time. They often slept on park benches. Many worked as constables as a second job and were already exhausted when they reported to their posts. Almost all just carried a "billy club," or thick wooden nightstick, for protection. Few used them. They had a charge to arrest criminals they literally saw committing a crime and to provide some sort of police presence to deter crime. They rarely did this. They avoided street patrols in high-crime areas for fear of being a victim themselves. They all avoided working in the slums because that was where many of the criminals lived, and they did not want to encounter them. Consequently, crime in the high-crime areas such as Five Points and in the slums increased.[21]

The cops spent most of their time trying to recover stolen goods for citizens. In order to employ them without pay or at low wages, New York's Common Council gave them rewards for collecting both private and public debts, collecting rents, foreclosing on mortgages, and serving court orders. Constables refused to investigate cases of stolen property unless they were given a bonus. To get property back, victims often gave one reward for the apprehension of the criminal and a larger reward for the return of the property (leading police and thieves into a profitable arrangement). The constables supervised no one, and no one supervised them.[22]

Many crimes were never solved. Constables, working with a coroner, were asked to appoint a street crowd to help them investigate a crime, usually an assault or a murder. These public investigations, by randomly selected amateurs who had not seen the crime, usually turned up no suspects and resulted in no arrests. These ad hoc investigations usually lasted only a few hours.

The city courts were one place where the constables were used often. Judges had them quiet down unruly crowds at trials. The constables, handfuls of them, would at first plead for quiet, then scream at courtgoers, and then, exhausted from all that, take out their billy clubs and pound them against the tables in the courtroom. Few paid any attention to them.

They were the descendants of an early constable force known as the "rattle watch." These groups of watchmen, who worked the streets of New York in the mid-1600s, spent most of their time rattling a chain of keys as they walked down city streets, looking for mischief-makers and, from time to time, loudly announcing the time of the evening to residents of their neighborhood by shouting and pounding their billy clubs on the sides of houses or barns. The "rattle watch" constables also carried a green lantern on a pole as they walked so residents could identify them. When they returned to their watch house, they put the lantern outside it; this is why all old precinct houses in the city today have green lanterns beside their front entrances. The men were under strict orders not to fall asleep or engage in fist-fights with each other. The *New-York Gazette* said of them in 1757 that they were a "parcel of idle, drinking, vigilant snorers, who never quelled any nocturnal tumult in their lives (nor as we can learn, were ever the dis-coverers of any fire breaking out), but would, perhaps, be as willing to join in a burglary as any thief in Christendom. A happy set, indeed, to defend the rich and populous city against the terrors of the night."[23]

That half-asleep, half-drunk, and completely inept persona of the constable, then, was set in stone by 1757. In 1788, the watch force was increased to include a captain and thirty men. Crime increased that year, though, so thirty additional men were hired. A year later, when crime ebbed, the thirty new constables were all let go. That level of watchmen was not to be reached again for years.

The next generation of constables learned from them and behaved badly, too, as did the next generation, and the next and the next. By the time constables walked the beat in the 1840s, they were just the lat-est generation of slovenly law enforcers who really did not care how good a job they did.

Constables had "sentinel boxes" where they could store goods and keep warm on frigid nights; they were assisted by a half dozen or so marshals, who mostly worked as court officers and helped collect debts for the city. One resident complained that it was dangerous "to walk the streets at night or be in a crowd in the day."[24]

The city's pyramid of police authority was troubling, too. The mayor, not elected by the people but chosen by the aldermen, New York's version of the city council, oversaw the police in riots. The day-to-day operations of the force were run by High Constable Jacob Hays for nearly fifty years, but by the troubled 1830s and 1840s Hays was an old man. Like the mayor, all of the police were appointed by city alder-men. After Tammany Hall swept the Federalists out of office in 1816, that corrupt political organization helped pick all of the city's watch-men and patrolmen because they controlled the aldermen. That was clear in an 1842 motion passed by the board to name new patrolmen for two wards. The language of the motion was that the new cops were "under the direction of the Aldermen and Assistant Aldermen of the above wards," and they were all named by Tammany.[25]

Civic disturbances could be brutal regardless of the presence of the constables. A reporter at one disturbance wrote that "the mob exhibited more than fiendish brutality, beating and mutilating some of the old, confiding and unoffending blacks, with a savageness surpassing anything we could have believed men capable of."[26]

New York riots that started out small always grew in size and intensity because onlookers joined any melee that lasted several days. Many New Yorkers watched a riot and joined the rabble-rousers. They could be entertained and punish people they did not like. They also knew that the chances they would be arrested by the beleaguered constables were small. Organizers of riots who planned on a thousand participants soon had two or three thousand, through no extra work of their own.[27]

One of the most frequent riots in New York was the election riot, which took place just about every Election Day. You had an election? Someone had a riot for it. The Election Day riot was planned by one political party to ensure that its rival party did not collect votes and win offices. The goal was not destruction of a neighborhood, although that often occurred, or punishment of a group of people, although that often transpired, too. Rioters made the area around the polls so destructive, and harassed potential voters so badly, that they stayed home, fearful of venturing near the polling place. That meant that your party won its standard, say, forty thousand votes, but the other party, which might have won, say, forty-five thousand, received only thirty-eight thousand because of low voter turnout. The result—victory for your party.

Election Day riots were a joint venture between a political party, especially New York's massive and well-oiled political machine, Tammany Hall, and a street gang. The street gang would stage the daylong riot, and the political party would direct it. The street gang would not be paid for its work, but throughout the year the ruling party in office would restrain law enforcement from cracking down on the gang members as they engaged in their criminal activity. The Election Day riot consisted of tearing down broadside posters, destroying opposition party newspapers and literature, forcing speakers off their platforms, and haranguing people not to vote for the rival party. Polling places in that era were not secret voting booths such as those we enjoy today. Most were open-air tables on a sidewalk in a town square. People surged around them all day. Everybody surrounding the table would shout at you when you arrived to convince you to vote for a particular party. It was here, in the few yards around the polling-place table, where the election riots and their leaders created the most havoc, sending panicked potential voters scurrying home without casting a ballot. The neighborhood around each polling place was full of overturned tables and chairs, torn-down posters, and garbage.

Some political parties staged their own riots on Election Day. One of the more infamous parties was the Know Nothings, who thrived in the 1850s, particularly in cities and especially in New York. They hated foreigners, Catholics, and blacks. Its members would surround polling places and hand out printed ballots with Know Nothing candidates' names already checked off. Anyone who did not take, and use, his printed ballot was shoved, punched, or beaten up. "What we have here is the demon of democracy," said one urban resident in that era.[28]

Few of the rioters were caught, because they knew how to run and hide in the city's landscape of myriad narrow, crooked streets, which were filled with tiny, dark, twisting alleys. There were a thousand places to hide, and the rioters knew all of them. The police who tried to chase them? Their skills were so low that in 1841 the New York City Common Council officially described them as men who were charged to "prevent the running of swine in the public street." What could be expected of them?[29]

New York had been crippled by riots for years. In the 1830s, New York was plagued with laborer riots against employers; the biggest was the stonecutters riot of 1833. Marble contractors and stonecutters were scheduled to put all of the marble into a new New York University building, but the university learned that it could buy marble cheaply, and get free labor, at Sing Sing prison, in upstate New York. The university turned down the stonecutter members of the Manufacturers of Marble Mantels Association. After several fruitless meetings, 150 stonecutters stormed the store of the NYU marble works contractor, destroying much of it with rocks and brickbats in a daylong riot. The National Guard had to be called in to put down the disturbance. In 1835, constables failed to hold back a wave of looters who descended on lower Manhattan following a terrible fire that wiped out one-third of the area, and the militia had to be called in to curb the trouble-makers. In the mid-1830s, constables were unable to contain crowds in antislavery riots, and again a militia unit was called in.[30]

Many people laughed at the militia, too. "Neither the officers nor the men have got the necessary pluck for anything but marching round a puddle," sneered George Templeton Strong as he watched them saddle up for an encounter in 1839.[31]

Riots were not uncommon in other cities in the era either; in fact, they were the norm. Historian Richard Maxwell Brown counted thirty-five in Boston, New York, Baltimore, and Philadelphia alone. According to historian John Schneider, "at least seventy per cent of American cities with a population of twenty thousand or more by 1850 experienced some degree of major disorder." Abolitionist leaders, who kept close tabs on civil disturbances, counted 209 riots in the 1830s and 1840s. Abraham Lincoln, then a state legislator in Illinois, said that there were too many, and in every part of the country. They were, he said, "the everyday news of the times."[32]

Still, New York had become, by the mid-1830s, the largest city in America, with more than 400,000 residents. It was a bustling city that was a vision of beauty to the eye, an American Athens. The town was an expanding metropolis of thousands of buildings, businesses, warehouses, churches, tenements, and theaters, packed in tightly between Fourteenth Street and the Battery, with the Hudson and East

Rivers on each side of it. Most buildings did not rise higher than four stories because of fire regulations, and a long, necklace-like string of bustling docks filled with tall oceangoing vessels stretched around the city to service the growing shipping industry.

The city had become the banking, entertainment, and publishing capital of America. It was the nation's chief manufacturing center and the heart of America's shipbuilding industry. It was filled with fascinating museums, gorgeous mansions, and lovely parks. But beneath its glimmering exterior was a dark and sinister interior. New York had too many people and too few jobs, forcing thousands into poorhouses, and other thousands to live in poverty in rancid tenement hovels with little warmth in winter, oppressive heat in summer, and starvation all year long.

In the 1830s, there was still no substantial running water in town, and people had to haul heavy wooden buckets of imported water up four or five flights of stairs in order to wash dishes or take a bath. Dozens of people, rich and poor, died in summer from heat exhaustion. Transportation, on congested dirt streets, was a mess. British author Charles Dickens, who toured the city in 1841, said of the city's overcrowded neighborhoods that the buildings there "were hideous tenements which take their names from robbery and murder; all that is loathsome, drooping and decayed is here."[33]

Thousands of street urchins, many of them pickpockets, roamed the town. Street gangs flourished, and the crime rates were far higher than they would be later, at the dawn of the twenty-first century, when the city was home to eight million souls. Prostitution, drinking, and gambling were causing the crime rate to soar. The city was home to over four thousand bars, seven thousand prostitutes, five hundred gambling casinos, and hundreds of daily and weekly lottery, or "numbers," gambling parlors. Burglary was so common that newspaper editors called the coming of winter "the burglary season." One distraught woman said that New York was "the criminal capital of the world." More than thirty thousand arrests were made each year, more than the number in London and Paris combined. Among the city's estimated seven thousand prostitutes were hundreds of eleven- and twelve-year old girls. "One cannot walk the length of Broadway without meeting some hideous troupe of ragged girls, from 12 years old down, brutalized beyond redemption by premature vice clad in the filthy refuse of the rag pickers, obscene of speech, the stamp of childhood gone from their faces," wrote George Templeton Strong in his diary.

The riots that threatened to ruin city life had many causes. The city was jammed with young, headstrong men who had no work and nothing better to do than cause trouble. Most disturbances took place in the summer, when, in oppressive heat, tempers flared. One riot in mid-August was remembered by participants as taking place on "the hottest day of the year."[34]

The signs of trouble and riots were in the faces of the poor and those out of work. The population of downtown New York City was tired and angry. The economy of the mid-1830s was shaky, and the masses, uncertain why that was so, turned their anger on institutions and racial targets.

New York had become a grim place to live. Critics said the growing city was too crowded and that its hundreds of buildings were blotting out the sun and creating a perfect dark, sinister setting for crime and public disturbances. "Commerce is devouring inch by inch the coast of the island, and if we would rescue any part of it for health and recreation it must be done now," argued William Cullen Bryant, editor of the *New York Post*.[35]

Public events often drew huge crowds in which people pressed against each other, argued, engaged in fistfights, shoved others, and constantly threatened riots. In 1830, tens of thousands of New Yorkers participated in a memorial parade following the death of President James Monroe. Military guards protected the speakers' platform, but those in the front line of the parade pushed them away and threatened to overrun the stage. The main speaker at the event, pleading and waving his arms, had to calm down the entire group to prevent what all thought was going to be a riot. This pressure was continual.[36]

A decade earlier, observant novelist James Fenimore Cooper (*The Last of the Mohicans*) had predicted problems because of the rapid and uncontrolled growth of the city, which was not anticipated by anyone. It was a growing city with no plan.[37]

Many New Yorkers used the Boston Tea Party of 1773 as an example of the need for good, noble citizens to use violence to achieve a deserved goal denied them by the system. The Tea Party riot had worked for the colonists, so why not continue the practice? Many city residents argued that no one in the system would acknowledge their presence in it, that they (for "they," choose any ethnic group) were invisible in public life. Excluded, they felt that staging riots would bring attention to them and give them a place in the world. Dissidents suggested that rioting expressed "people power" and that it was the truest way to define Americanism.

The extremists, the vigilantes of the era, cited that idea often. "We are the believers in the doctrine of popular sovereignty, that the people of this country are the real sovereigns, and that whenever the laws, made by those to whom they have delegated their authority, are found inadequate, to their protection, it is the right of the people to take the protection of their property into their own hands, and to deal with these villains according to their just deserts," wrote one vigilante leader.[38]

Huge waves of immigrants had arrived in New York, trudging down the gangplanks of a thousand ships, eyes wide open, intent on populating a new world. Their dreams died fast, and they were forced to live in overcrowded buildings in run-down, congested neighborhoods. Unable to get jobs that paid well, or any jobs at all, they took to the streets to protest their conditions. On the streets marching and shouting amid hordes of people and vendor carts, too, were native New Yorkers who resented the new immigrant arrivals. Americans had a fear of anybody who spoke a foreign language or still had a foreign accent. "The day must come, and, we fear, is not too far distant, when most of our offices will be held by foreigners—men who have no sympathy with the spirit of our institutions, who have done aught to secure the blessings they enjoy, and instead of governing ourselves, we shall be governed by men, many of whom, but a few short years previously, scarcely knew of our existence," said one city dweller in the 1840s.[39]

By the 1830s, the Protestants and Catholics living in New York had begun to hate each other. These antagonisms erupted into religious riots and the wholesale burning of churches and neighborhoods where large percentages of religious groups lived. Many New Yorkers trembled as they saw the Irish Catholics, who arrived in droves, taking over jobs, schools, and political clubs; they feared that the Irish would take over the entire city and the country. In a few short years, they assumed, Washington, D.C., would be replaced by an Irish Catholic city as the nation's capital. They had to be driven out.[40]

An example of that intense dislike of Catholics took place April 12, 1842. A Roman Catholic church had its windows broken when a mob attacked it. Later that evening, Bishop John Hughes's home was partially destroyed in an attack. "They were like the no-popery riots of old," said George Templeton Strong.[41]

Rioters were not warned to curb their actions, but encouraged in their work by important members of the community. Several prominent Bostonians led an anti-Irish riot in Massachusetts. Rioters were urged on by ethnic newspapers, dozens of them, which were read by tens of thousands in New York. "The bloody hand of the Pope has stretched forth for our destruction," roared the *Native American* in 1844.[42] In Utica, New York, in 1835, a grand jury ruled that the upcoming antislavery convention there was not only wrong, but criminal sedition, and implored locals to "put it down." A Utica newspaper said locals had to use the law of the land or the "law of Judge Lynch" to stop it. One Utica newspaper editor, Augustine Dauby, said that he would stop the convention "peacefully if I can, forcibly if I must," to the roar of a crowd. A riot followed.[43]

There was unbridled anger in the hearts of tens of thousands of disenfranchised and frustrated people. That resentment grew deeper each year in the 1830s and '40s. "We have evidence too strong to be either doubted or denied that if the great among us are growing better, the bad are growing worse," wrote one newspaper editor then.[44]

Rioters had no respect for the law. "There is an awful tendency towards insubordination and contempt for the law and there is reason to apprehend that good order and morality will ere long be overcome by intemperance and violence," argued Hone, who added sadly, "My poor country."[45]

Riots were also seen as a way to celebrate something via destruction. Many said that riots were summer parties. One man wrote after a race riot in Cincinnati in 1843, "The mob in Cincinnati must have their annual festival—their carnival—just as at stated periods the ancient Romans enjoyed the Saturnalia."[46]

All of America's cities found that they had the same problems in the 1830s and '40s. None were immune. In Philadelphia in 1838, the evening session of an abolitionist society meeting at Pennsylvania Hall was attacked by weapons-toting whites in a crowd of some twenty thousand angry city residents. Much of the hall was destroyed and the abolitionists were forced out of the building as hundreds of constables stood by and did nothing. Several people were seriously wounded in the melee. White women and black men walking arm in arm in an earlier protest march ignited the fury of the whites in the attacking crowd. In Baltimore, large mobs of depositors inflamed over the collapse of a bank attacked the bank and wrecked it. Then they went on a lawless spree, burning down the homes of several bank employees and marching on the home of the city's mayor. They forced him to resign his office. The city's replacement mayor, who hurried from his home to the scene of the disturbance, promptly called up a posse of three thousand volunteers, all armed, who attacked the rioters and put down the rebellion.

In Charlestown, Massachusetts, now a part of Boston, a mob of over two thousand anti-Catholic men insisted that a novice Ursuline nun be released from a convent. They had heard a rumor that she had been physically abused there. This followed a series of newspaper articles by a former novice who had left the convent and claimed the nuns tried to make her accept strident religious views that were against her wishes. When the novice was not turned over to the men, they stormed the building, injuring several nuns and burning it to the ground, the flames lighting up the night sky. Bostonians were horrified. "If the wishes of the lowest class that suffer in these long [Boston] streets should execute themselves, who can doubt that the city would topple in ruins?" wrote Ralph Waldo Emerson.[47]

These riots targeted specific groups. There were few riots in New York in which a general melee erupted. Riot organizers selected groups to victimize, such as blacks, Irish, a street gang, or a political party.[48]

Many believed that rioting would destroy the foundation of American democracy. Writing after yet another riot in Philadelphia in the late 1860s, Philadelphia resident Sidney George Fisher said that the United States was "destined to be destroyed by the dark masses of ignorance and brutality which lie beneath it, like the first of a volcano."[49]

All New Yorkers trembled at the thought of a riot. "Every fresh event should remind our citizens that we are in the city over the crust of a volcano. . . . There is in every large city, and especially this one, a powerful, 'dangerous class' who care nothing for our liberty or civilization . . . who burrow at the roots of society . . . and only come forth in times of disturbances, to plunder and prey," said one New Yorker of an 1830s riot.[50]

New Yorkers always seemed ready to riot, though, especially in situations involving large crowds. At an opera performance in New York in 1848 the audience began to boo singer Sesto Benedetti as soon as he walked onstage. The hissing and booing was so loud ("a hurricane of sibilation," said a man in the theater) that he could not sing and walked offstage. That brought on more boos. An opera official took the stage to calm the crowd and Benedetti returned, to quietude. It was typical of crowd responses in New York and how heated feelings became in a large theater filled with people. Back in 1830, the crowd booed lustily at a British actor, Anderson, who everybody thought had insulted America in a newspaper article. He was hissed off the stage several times and then a riot broke out. Philip Hone, who was there, said that "apples, eggs and other missiles were showered upon the stage." To quiet the mob, the theater manager announced that a different play would be held the next night, and it was. Two nights later the play with Anderson was brought back again and another riot ensued and lasted through morning with damage to the theater, neighborhood windows broken, and a shabby police force failing to control the protestors.[51]

All had different views of who the rioters were. Hezekiah Niles, publisher of *Niles' Weekly Register,* wrote that "sober and peaceable individuals are called upon to defend their own personal rights, or those of their neighbors, by force . . . instead of relying upon . . . the law." Philip Hone was more to the point. He said the rioters were all "a set of fanatics."[52]

Each riot built on the last, and there was little law enforcement to stop them. There seemed to be only one villain. Everyone in the public and the press blamed the spineless constable force for the riots and predicted more, and worse, public disturbances if the force was not discontinued and a new police department installed—and quickly.

There were many reasons why riots started and could not be controlled in New York City, but without a doubt the greatest was the lack of professional police. The city was defended by a small six-hundred-man force of inept constables, who were little more than security guards, in a huge city. They were spread woefully thin. Broken down into three daily shifts, there were roughly two constables for every 2,500 residents (today there is one cop for every 150 people).

The stumbling constables, political party appointees, often were not paid a salary. They were paid for services rendered or received bonuses for work well done, but not for arrests. As an example, they were given fees for the delivery of legal papers on behalf of the city. They were also given bonuses for finding stolen property. Consequently, the constables had little interest in maintaining law and order and putting themselves at risk without any reward. Constables in New York usually flinched when asked to make an arrest or break up a fight. Many declined to do so. If they were reluctant to do that, how could they possibly handle a mass riot?[53]

They were often made fun of by New Yorkers; in his diary, Hone always added, after an entry about their arrival somewhere, that they'd come "tardily." Newspapers ran cartoons of them sleeping on the job and running from a confrontation. Constables and watchmen were the worst possible choices to defend a city and its residents in the middle of a ferocious riot filled with fires, explosions, hails of musket balls and bullets, and fistfights along the streets.

There was universal disapproval of the constables. Hone wrote after a riot that "the police came after some time, but they have no energy and want courage to resist an army like this. They are appointed as a reward for party services performed at the polls, not to quell riots created by the very fellows who assisted to place the men in office from whom they derive their support."[54]

Rioters knew that and had no fear of the constables. Hence, one riot followed the other, each longer than the last, with little chance that the constables could stop any of them. An example was a fracas started by thug Yankee Sullivan and his mob in the spring of 1842. Sullivan and his men beat up a dozen or so Irishmen in the bar of the Sixth Ward Hotel, fearing interference from the constables, and getting none. The bloodied Irish retreated to their neighborhood, recruited more than a hundred men, all armed, and went looking for Sullivan and his men. They found them and launched an all-out attack, clubs bashing heads, fists flying, and blood flowing. The Sullivan men fled, recruited their own small army, and descended on the Irish neighborhood, beating up anybody they could find, with no one arrested.

New York newspapers reflected the citizenry's attitude toward the force. James Gordon Bennett had arrived in New York from Scotland ten years earlier and in the mid-1830s had become the editor of the *Herald,* one of the first truly sensationalist newspapers in New York, which routinely covered riots and crime. He disdained the constables, often referring to them as the "corps of leather skulls,"[55] and said that they were cops who had no right being cops. His newspaper rival, the oddly dressed Horace Greeley, was so involved in riot and crime coverage that by the early 1850s he was running a complete column of murder stories from across the United States along with lengthy riot stories and frequent complaints about the constables.

Public figures and citizens all argued that the police had two jobs, not one. They not only had to put down riots when they started, but had to work to make certain that there was enough law enforcement in place, trained law enforcement, to prevent riots from happening at all. Police had to establish a preventative law enforcement framework that included informers, liaisons, and community contacts to prevent riots and ease the public's fear of them. In the 1830s and '40s, that was not in place.

Another reason why a police force made up of constables was ineffective was that the law enforcement agents were untrained and too few in number to establish any kind of intelligence-gathering ring to thwart a riot. It is hard to pick up intelligence on the activities of mob leaders in a small town, but much more difficult in a city. To do that in an extremely large city like New York with such a small force was nigh impossible.[56] The constables did not have a network of contacts within the public realm to stop riots when they began, either. Today, all big-city police departments have dozens of local civilian leaders, men and women they can get in touch with immediately and work with to stop a riot. In the 1830s, constables did not know any local leaders; when public disturbances started, there was no one they could contact to quell the trouble. It put law enforcement at a distinct disadvantage.

The last resort, and the best at the time, was the heavily armed state militia. The problem there was that since they were not called until after the New York constables had put up a fierce battle and then fled, they were often quite late. A full day of rioting might have taken place before they rode into a town square and loaded their rifles and fired on demonstrators.[57]

Riot organizers traditionally planned activities in areas where they believed the police to be neutral and not predisposed to harass them. In New York, the police were simply missing from the riot neighborhood completely. This knowledge that there were very few police to put down their riot greatly encouraged the leaders of civil disturbances. Crowd organizers want to create havoc, but they do not want to get arrested. In New York City, with its bumbling police, that was easy to do.[58]

Why were New Yorkers so reluctant to hire a new, armed, trained, and professional police force to quell the city's riots and patrol its streets?

The British army had occupied several American cities prior to the American Revolution and continued to do so during the conflict. The people hated the British for doing that. That sour feeling continued to be felt for generations, and the people saw the proposed police force as another occupying army, loyal to the mayor and not the residents. New Yorkers, and people throughout the country, also feared the enormous cost of a large and professional force. The country had just staggered through two recessions and the financially catastrophic Panic of 1837; citizens were careful with every penny of public expenditures, and a police force would cost a lot of money. Americans also believed that the troubles of the 1830s and '40s would end and peace would be restored to the streets.

That restrictive attitude would soon change. For a number of reasons, not least the long chain of fatal and destructive riots, by the early 1840s the people of New York, fed up with chaos and havoc, finally would begin a strong push for the dismantling of the ragged force of constables and call for professional, trained police. The streets would be covered with rivers of blood by the time they did that, though.

CHAPTER TWO

The Gruesome Murder of Helen Jewett

Our city was disgraced on Sunday by one of the most foul and premeditated murders that ever fell to our lot to record.

—James Gordon Bennett, editor of the *New York Herald*, April 11, 1836

It was clear and chilly on the night of April 9, 1836, in New York City in the middle of a spring that did not arrive until quite late on the calendar. It was so cold that in just a few days the city streets would be filled with six inches of snow from an unexpected storm. Men pulled their coat collars up tight around their necks as they trudged through the cold night air. It was too cold to think that on this night one of the most horrid murders in the history of New York City would take place.

Until the spring of 1836, crimes did not occupy a large amount of space, or editorial attention, in New York City newspapers. The editors did cover spectacles, such as the Great Fire of 1835, and the numerous riots that plagued the city for years, but they stayed away from crime, especially serious crimes like murder, rape, and robbery. The larger, five- and six-cent journals (they cost a hefty ten dollars a year on subscription) would never descend into the basement of journalism to write about street crimes, but neither did the scandal-tinged penny sheets that seemed to chase every sensational story they could find. Crime stories were taboo. "It is a fashion that does not meet with our approbation on the score of either propriety or taste," wrote the editor of the *Statesman*. "To say nothing of the absolute indecency of some of the cases which are allowed occasionally to creep into print, we deem it of little benefit to the cause of morals thus to familiarize the community, and especially the younger parts of it, with the details of misdemeanor and crime."[1]

Some of the murders had been lurid, too. In the winter of 1830, the crew of the merchant ship *Vineyard,* bound from New Orleans, mutinied, murdered the captain, stole $100,000, and scuttled the ship. They put the money in two separate longboats, but one sank. The men then crowded into one boat and made it to a Long Island shore, where they were captured. On September 4, 1835, two sailors, Richard Jackson and John "Little Jack" Roberts, took a room together at a downtown boardinghouse. The matron of the house, Harriet Shultz, who showed them the room, climbed into one of the two beds there and pretended to be asleep. Another woman arrived and got into bed with Harriet. Roberts joined them and began to have sex with Harriet. Jackson, enraged, pulled out a gun, aimed at Roberts's head, and fired, point-blank, but missed. He fired again and hit him. Roberts fell dead, blood covering the floor. The *Sun* jumped on the story. Its star crime reporter, Richard Locke, spent hours talking to Jackson in his cell and then wrote a twelve-part series on the slaying, which occupied *Sun* readers from November 14 until just after Thanksgiving. The story received only scant notice in the other newspapers, though. The lack of news stories about crimes kept the spotlight off the shoddy work of city constables, whose ability to solve crimes, many charged, was severely limited.[2]

All of that changed on Sunday morning, April 10, 1836, when the body of the beautiful, sophisticated prostitute Helen Jewett was discovered, hacked viciously by an ax and charred by a fire, in her room at Rosina Townsend's upscale brothel at 41 Thomas Street, just off Broadway in the high-end prostitution neighborhood of the city. The high-class whore, who made so much money that she had her own servant, had been killed, allegedly, by Richard Robinson, a client who was deeply in love with her. On the surface, it was just one more brutal act against prostitutes, one more name on the list, but *Herald* editor James Gordon Bennett, like a hound on the scent of prey in the forest, jumped on the case and quickly turned it into the story of the century.

It had all the elements necessary to make it a sizzling tabloid story that would be read and discussed not only by all New Yorkers, but by newspaper readers as far west as Texas.

Helen was no grimy, back-alley fifty-cent street hooker. She was a gorgeous, well-dressed intellectual who had her own library of books in her room, subscribed to literary magazines, and was a regular theatergoer. She had arrived in New York from Maine, via a stint as a hooker in Boston, and represented the new wave of single men and women from far away who had started to call the city their home. Many men in the city knew her and had succumbed to her charms.

Her assailant was a descendant of a prominent Connecticut political family, the kind of spoiled rich kid who always evaded justice through money and connections. Robinson lived at a boardinghouse in Manhattan, as did so many of the new wave of bachelors who crowded the city, working hard at business during the day and even harder at debauchery at night.

The apparent killer professed his innocence, and speculation swirled that perhaps another prostitute, or Townsend, jealous of Helen's popularity and wealth, might have killed her.

Beyond all of that, though, the slaying represented the bloody end of a new story that was moving through New York like a moralistic tidal wave—what happens to women just trying to make a living, especially the forty thousand or so single women in the city who had to pay all of their own bills? That saga, spread far and wide by all of the moral reform societies and their bands, parades, and banners, and embraced by hundreds of thousands of women, was that women could not get jobs, or if they could find them they were menial and low paying. As an example, streetwalkers earned approximately eight times as much money as garment workers and five times as much as public school teachers. Unable to work, or make enough money to meet their rent, they were forced into prostitution. No woman wanted to be a prostitute, the moral reform leaders argued, and it was society's failures that forced some women to join the ranks of those who made love for money.[3]

Many domestic servants became hookers, but not just because they could make far more money. They crowded into employment offices and argued hard to get jobs. Many failed. Those who did land jobs hated them because they were treated poorly. "The unnatural and degrading position she occupies—forced to beg or even pay for the chance of being selected for somebody's domestic slave . . . and often to endure the vulgar insolence of some sister woman who happens to have a house and a husband, only to be told at last, in grating and harsh terms, that 'she won't do,' or her 'references are not satisfactory,' or 'I don't like your looks' and to go back . . . heart-broken to resume her seat on the pine bench of the Intelligence Office, until some other Mrs. Arrogance sends for a servant. . . . Who can wonder that she thus in time becomes hardened and indifferent," wrote journalist George Foster, who added that when those girls did get jobs, they hated their employers. Many of them sought out pimps, brothels, steady work, and a lot more money.[4]

A report of the reform-oriented New York Magdalen Society said that women's decisions to enter prostitution and engage in all of its crimes "were the result of sheer necessity, poverty rather than will-consenting."[5]

Women also outnumbered men in New York at a ratio of 120 to 100,[6] making it harder for single women to attract husbands or get jobs.

They were all victims, and Helen Jewett represented them. Her death symbolized the deaths of any of them and those deaths represented the death of the American dream. It was a powerful argument. Some men were just as angry about women forced into prostitution as the prostitutes themselves. George Templeton Strong read in the *Herald* that a man in Maine had seduced Helen, sending her into a career in prostitution. "He deserves hanging as much or more than her murderer," said Strong.[7]

The woes of prostitutes put forth by some citizens did not make prostitution a subject for loud public debate, though. James Gordon Bennett did that. The *Herald* editor, always sniffing about city streets for a story, found out about this one from a tipster on the morning after it happened. Bennett went to the brothel at 41 Thomas Street, still smoking from the fire on the second floor started the night before, and walked into the parlor on the first floor where women partied happily with johns before going to their bedrooms with them for sex. There Bennett met all of the prostitutes in the house as well as the madam, Rosina Townsend, well dressed as always. To his surprise, he also met New York mayor Cornelius Lawrence, in the middle of a reelection campaign. The mayor said he was there out of concern over crime in the city (it was rumored that Lawrence had been a client of Townsend's brothel).

Bennett then decided, for the first time in American journalism history, to interview them all. He saw, right away, that he had a great story and that the interviews, full of drama and color, would bring it to life. He realized, too, and quickly, that this kind of a torrid, sexy story could be strung along in his paper for months, until the trial and verdict, whenever that was, selling more and more copies of it each day, breaking city, state, and national circulation sales records. It was the story for which he had been looking for years, the story that would make his newspaper the most important in the city, perhaps in the nation itself.[8]

It was a story, too, that underscored editor Bennett's loathing for the city's constable force, which he had often criticized for its weak record on preventing crime or making arrests when the law was broken. Indeed, the city's lazy police force was criticized by everyone, and that chorus grew louder throughout the Jewett case as the press and public learned how dim-witted the constables were.

The next morning, the newsboys who hawked the *Herald* stood on top of their wooden boxes and shouted out the headline about the murder of the lovely young prostitute. Readers found not the usual one-paragraph item about the killing but a huge story, full of interviews, and were, on the spot, completely mesmerized by the bloody, sordid tale.

"Our city was disgraced on Sunday by one of the most foul and premeditated murders that ever fell to our lot to record," the story began, and with each paragraph and each sentence, all dripping in tawdry sex and violence, it soared.

Bennett wrote that according to madam Rosina Townsend and several prostitutes, the handsome Richard Robinson, one of the slender, busty whore's clients, went to see her with an ax concealed under his cloak. He tried to talk her into giving up her other clients and staying only with him, and she refused. He demanded that she return to him love letters and presents, and she again refused. Furious, Bennett wrote, Robinson then pulled the ax from under his cape and hit Helen across the back of the head. She fell to the floor, and blood started to ooze from the rear of her skull. Then an enraged Robinson took the ax and slammed it against her skull two more times. In a hurry to cover up the crime, he pulled Helen's body over to her bed, rolled it onto the mattress, and set the sheets around her on fire. The blaze began, and thick black smoke rolled out of her window as Robinson fled down the back stairs and through the small yard at the rear of the brothel.

Townsend, who had earlier brought the pair a bottle of wine, noticed in a late-night inspection that the back door of the establishment was unlocked. She went to Helen's room to check on her because Robinson had been a late arrival. The door was ajar, and she opened it, falling back when billows of thick smoke belched through the doorway. Townsend ran back to her own room, opened her window, and looked out into the streets for one of the town's constables but found none. Upset, the madam then screamed for one. None came. Not until she shouted numerous times did a policeman finally emerge from the darkness of the streets. It was a "horrible" crime, Bennett wrote. He said that Robinson's "conduct upon this occasion must stamp him as a villain of too black a die for mortal. Of this there can be no doubt."

The police who investigated the case went no farther than the backyard of Townsend's brothel, where Robinson's cape and his ax were found conveniently lying on the ground near each other. It never dawned on any of the constables that Robinson might have been framed. They never considered another suspect, and never started a second investigation. They had their man, even though the case had seemed far too easy to solve. The constables would look like fools in a few weeks. Robinson was arrested and, Bennett said, was clearly guilty.

The journalist was just getting started. On the second day, he wrote another, longer story filled with interviews and anecdotes that gave New Yorkers a behind-the-scenes look inside the bawdy house and explained where everybody lived and how business was conducted. Bennett was, of course, the hero of the story, walking from room to room with the constables to dig up information for his eager readers to devour.

He wrote gushingly of Helen, as one might have written of Helen of Troy. He chose to overlook the fact that her head had been cracked open by three blows from an ax and that a medical examiner had already opened up sections of her body for examination and then sewed the skin back together, badly disfiguring the appearance of the girl. Bennett instead used his pen to scribble an outline of pristine glamour, a vision of beauty. He wrote that "the body looked as white, as full, as polished, as the purest Parian marble. The perfect figure, the exquisite limbs, the fine face, the full arms, the beautiful bust, all surpassed, in every respect, the Venus de Medici."

Then Bennett looked about the room and described it to readers, carefully chronicling all of the lovely dresses, the books, and a picture of the poet Lord Byron in an exquisite frame on the wall. His story went on and on. Bennett talked about the "mob" that he said surrounded the bawdy house and threatened to attack it. He wrote of all the handsome young men, the best of the city, whom he found lurking, half dressed, in the rooms of 41 Thomas Street with the prostitutes. "In what a horrible condition is a portion of the young men of this devoted city," he said.

In a beautifully written story, filled with tension, he explained how the murder had stunned all. "This extraordinary murder has caused a sensation in this city never before felt or known," wrote Bennett.[9]

Bennett tried to produce as many newspapers as possible, anticipating the public's lust for stories about the grisly murder. "We could have sold 30,000 copies yesterday," he told a worker.[10]

The mystery grew. Helen Jewett was not Helen Jewett at all, but originally Dorcas Doyen (reported as Dorrance by Bennett). She changed her name to Helen Mar when she moved to Boston and then to Jewett when she arrived in New York. Tidbits of information on her mysterious background were fed to the public each day as circulation climbed and the clamor for news about the slaying intensified.

- She had lived with different men in the city, including a Kentuckian in disguise.
- She had been the star of parties at which large groups of young men gathered.
- It was she whom everyone remembered as the strikingly beautiful young woman who paraded up and down Wall Street the previous summer.
- Richard Robinson often wrote her letters under the code name of "Frank Rivers."

Bennett also went to great lengths to paint a portrait of her as an intellectual and a philosopher. He wrote that police found a hardbound and elegant copy of Lady Blessington's *The Flowers of Loveliness* lying between the bloodied sheets of her bed. In another article, he wrote that police found a cache of some seventy letters between her and dignified men of New York and other cities. All of the letters were of the highest moral tone, and there was not a word on sex in them, showing that Helen really was a splendid, high-class woman, cut down in the prime of her youth by a deranged suitor.

"Her way of life in New York has corresponded with the terrible state of society in this city," Bennett wrote.[11]

Day after day, somewhere in his story, Bennett would proclaim that Helen was the victim of a city full of crime and sin that had run amok. Her death was "the natural result of a state of society and morals which ought to be reformed altogether in unhappy New York," he wrote in one of his stories that week.[12]

The circulation of the *Herald* tripled that week, even despite the surprise early-April snowstorm, and continued to climb even higher the next. The other editors in New York, of mainstream papers and penny sheets alike, all jumped on the story. Every editor in the city realized that this was not the typical monstrous, inebriated men grabbing, raping, and killing a ragamuffin street whore, but the passionate, romantic killing by a social playboy of an intelligent courtesan.

The *Sun* understood why the killing was a sensation right away. "The excitement throughout the city in relation to this melancholy business continues unabated," its editor wrote of the "cold blooded, deliberate and savage . . . massacre" of Jewett.[13]

That someone as debonair as Robinson, who came from such a fine suburban background and was an employee of the prestigious Hoxie store, could commit a murder, much less the murder of a prostitute, was impossible for many New Yorkers to believe. Within a week, pro-Robinson "fan clubs" started forming, and hundreds of his supporters began to wear special "Robinson hats" to signify their belief in his innocence.

Pretty soon, letters turned up revealing that Helen had had many lovers with whom she kept in touch regularly. Could one of them have killed her?

Then there was the evidence. The watchmen found a cloak that appeared to belong to Robinson at the crime scene. They also found the ax, the murder weapon, covered in dirt, in the backyard of Townsend's establishment. A piece of twine used with buttons on his cloak was attached to the ax. Robinson's attorney asked all in the courtroom why a man who had just murdered someone—whose miniature portrait, by the way, was in his possession—would leave his cape and the weapon behind, in a spot where they would be found near each other, and right away. Had he been framed? Why did the watchmen finish their investigation and make an arrest so quickly?

Could one of the hookers have killed her out of jealousy? Had one of the prostitutes, or Townsend, been having a lesbian affair with her and killed her in a jealous rage?

And was she really so refined after all? The Boston newspapers began printing stories about her, using sources in her hometown in Maine, that said she rarely read books at all and did not appreciate the theater. She was, like so many other young women, a tramp who sold her body to make money and live well. Who was right?[14]

The crime caused the circulation of the *Sun*, the *Daily Transcript*, and all the other New York papers to soar. Other newspapers throughout the country copied *Herald* stories and ran them in their own pages. Shopkeepers in New York, and throughout America, spent hours each day talking about the case to their customers, as did bartenders and casino bosses. "Everyone talking about the murder committed on Saturday night," wrote George Templeton Strong in his diary. Strong, like so many others, promptly walked over to 41 Thomas Street, stood across the street from the brothel, and gawked, tracking all of the watchmen and hookers coming in and out of the building.[15]

At the end of the week, Bennett began to think that Robinson might not be the culprit after all. Then he easily pointed the finger of guilt at Townsend, claiming that an odd painting on the wall of the living room showed someone with an ax, and that meant Townsend was the killer. This assertion started a whole new spate of stories, and circulation grew even more.

Bennett then pressured Townsend to tell him her side of the story, which he reported in a long news article filled with direct quotes from the madam. It was loaded with color and detail, and Bennett wrote it like a great detective writer. The story was published on April 17. At the end, he told readers that Townsend was owed money by Jewett and indirectly suggested that she might have killed Helen in an argument over it. Bennett said Jewett had owned a lot of jewels, which had all disappeared. Who else but Townsend, who ran the house of ill repute and had the keys to each room, could have taken them?

Benjamin Day, editor of the *Sun,* then printed letters from Robinson that showed he was the killer, the *Sun* charged. Bennett roared back with accusations that the police had leaked the letters to the *Sun* and charges that the *Sun* was defrauding the reading public. The *Sun* answered back that it was the *Herald,* not the *Sun,* that was doing the defrauding. Someone suggested that Bennett had flirted with the whores at 41 Thomas Street on the day he interviewed Rosina Townsend. Bennett, stung, refuted the charge and went into a long printed diatribe against hookers that had all of New York chuckling. Other editors joined in the rumble of newspaper chiefs. Circulation climbed.

Philip Hone was one of the many New Yorkers who did not think the case was an open-and-shut affair. He had a dim view of prostitutes and believed that many other New Yorkers did, too. Who would believe the testimony of any of them against Robinson? And the defendant looked innocent. "He is young, good looking and supported by influential friends. He certainly looks as little like a murderer as any person I ever saw," Hone said. "There are good reasons for public sympathy."[16]

And there was the lingering suspicion that the police had not performed well in the case. They made the arrest too quickly, made uncertain assumptions, and had no real evidence to back up their murder charges. The Robinson trial in New York at the beginning of June was wild. Six thousand people rushed toward the courtroom in City Hall each morning, pushing and clawing at each other for the few available seats. The rush was so great that on one morning the crowd knocked over the wooden railings in the courtroom. Those who could not get in crowded around on the lawns outside the building, beneath open windows, to hear the proceedings. There were police at the courthouse to keep order, but they did a poor job, and it further reflected badly on the entire police department's performance in that case and in many others. Many of the spectators were certain Robinson would hang. Other spectators looked forward to Robinson's acquittal, not believing that the prosecution could convict him. "There is no doubt of the guilt of the wretched youth, but it is to be feared he will escape punishment," said Philip Hone.

The judge was Ogden Edwards, one of the most respected in the state. He was the grandson of the famed preacher Jonathan Edwards, one of the leaders of the Great Awakening religious movement. The district attorney was Thomas Phoenix.

Phoenix's case was simple: A number of prostitutes had seen Robinson go into Helen's room with her. Later, after the murder, an ax from his store had been found along with his cloak, and a piece of string on the ax was said to be from a tassel on that cloak. There were love letters between the two, and talk that Robinson was insanely jealous of her other clients. In addition to all of that, he had testimony from a druggist's clerk who said that prior to the murder, Robinson had talked to the druggist about buying a bottle of rat poison (by implication, to use on Helen).

The defense's case was just as simple: Someone else killed Jewett and framed Robinson, who as a jealous suitor could be seen as a likely victim for the plot. The defense also had a grocery store clerk, Robert Furlong, who testified that Robinson was in his store, smoking cigars, at the time of the murder.[17]

In a series of stunning decisions, Judge Edwards ruled that the jury should not pay much attention to the testimony of the women who testified against Robinson because they were ladies of the evening. He added that the love letters between Robinson and Jewett were not admissible and that her diary could not be introduced, either.

Hone felt that the case against Robinson relied on too much circumstantial evidence and that it would be easy for his lawyers to prove that any number of Jewett's numerous lovers might have killed her.

The trio of defense lawyers did a fine job. They tore apart Rosina Townsend's testimony and skillfully suggested to the jury, aided by the judge, that prostitutes could not be believed. The defense delivered a detailed three-hour summation of the case.

Robinson was acquitted after the jury had deliberated for just twenty minutes.

Hone, who through his connections got to sit in the courtroom during the trial, had yet another reflection, and it weighed heavily on the depth of crime in New York. "I was surrounded [in the courtroom] by young men, about his own age, apparently clerks like him, who appeared to be thoroughly initiated into the arcana of such houses as Mrs. [Rosina] Townsend's. They knew the wretched female inmates as they were brought up to testify, and joked with each other in a manner illy comporting with the solemnity of the occasion."[18]

Those young men, and others in the courtroom, roared their approval at the jury's verdict. Bennett wrote that "the cheering and huzzas were tremendous—in vain the court assayed to stop them. . . . They might as well have tried to choke the current of a river with sand, as to put a stop to that hearty outburst."[19]

Law enforcement received all of the blame for the acquittal. The district attorney was criticized for not calling a number of men caught in the house at the time of the murder. He was protecting his male buddies from scandal, right? He was blamed for not having corroborating witnesses to back up the testimony of the prostitutes. He should have realized that the judge would discount the hookers' testimony. He should have had a better attack than just that all the evidence found at the scene of the slaying was connected to Robinson. It did look like a frame-up to many.

The judge was blamed for not emphasizing the testimony of eyewitnesses—the prostitutes—and the constables were heavily criticized for arresting a man who turned out to be the wrong one and was acquitted. Because they focused only on Robinson, they let the real killer get away. They had no investigative skills and did a very poor job in the case against Robinson. One of the four was so dumb, people said, that when he was summoned to 41 Thomas Street he believed the call was not to solve a murder but to break up a fistfight.

The not-guilty verdict did not seem to solve anything. Many always believed Robinson killed Helen. Five books were written about the case, along with dozens of magazine articles and hundreds of newspaper stories. The New York press kept up its landslide coverage of the trial for nearly two weeks after it ended, pages and pages filled with analysis of the verdict. The penny press howled about the outcome. Why couldn't law enforcement do its job? And, equally important, how did a group of watchmen all standing within a block of 41 Thomas Street allow not only a murder to take place, but a fire as well? And, if that wasn't enough, how had they stood by while the killer fled? And how was it that law enforcement was so feeble that anyone could plan, and carry out, a vicious murder right in the middle of a brothel right in the middle of one of the busiest neighborhoods in town? What was the city, the world, coming to with law enforcement like this?[20]

Almost all the newspapers that covered the trial were unhappy with the verdict and some, like Thurlow Weed in the *Albany Evening Journal,* believed that it made a fool of the legal system.

There were charges that Robert Furlong lied when he testified that Robinson was with him on the night of the murder, and he later killed himself. Others accused Robinson's employer, store owner Joseph Hoxie, of bribing the jury (never proved). His lawyers were accused of chicanery and the jurors of prejudice against the hookers who testified.

"The acquittal of Robinson on the charge of murdering Helen Jewett was the foulest blot on the jurisprudence of our country," snorted Philip Hone.[21]

George Templeton Strong, who had followed the trial carefully in the newspapers, thought that Furlong lied to protect Robinson. "I have no doubt whatever that Furlong is a perjured man . . . and perjured himself for Mr. Hoxie's cash. No matter—time will show—and if it should not, that will make no difference in the final punishment of either perjury or murder."[22]

There was some benefit to Helen's murder, though. Surely, everyone believed, the incompetence of the constables in solving the murder, and in law enforcement in general, plus the unprecedented press coverage of the case, would finally bring about the end of the constables and herald a new era with a trained, competent police force.

Or would it?

CHAPTER THREE

Extra! Extra! The Penny Press
Chases Crime

Everywhere is their influence felt. No man can measure it, for
it is immeasurable.

—Walt Whitman

Nobody understood what had happened to the New York media
because of the Helen Jewett murder and trial better than James
Gordon Bennett, the truculent, cross-eyed Scotsman who was editor
of the *Herald*. Right from the minute that he walked into Jewett's
bedroom and looked down at her charred body in the early spring of
1836, Bennett knew that the slaying was a turning point in both press
and American history. Following the killing of the gorgeous prostitute, Bennett worked tirelessly, with his editors and reporters, to re-
shape the *Herald* to make it the first and most successful tabloid in the
United States. It became a newspaper whose pages overflowed with
both domestic and international news and opinion, but a newspaper
full of sordid crime, lurid sex, and juicy scandal, too. He was one of
the editors who would change the look of city newspapers, and American journalism, over the next twenty years. And, over those two decades, nobody in the United States worked harder than a fed-up
Bennett to bring about the creation of a paid, professional police

force in New York. He was joined by other editors. The penny press led the war on crime and the war to get a professional police force.

A professional police force was necessary to replace the bungling, stumbling constable force, he told everyone—at parties, in street-corner conversations, and in the pages of his paper. The changing times demanded changing policies. New York was no longer a city of quiet streets and lovely views of the water in the harbor. It had become, sixty years after the Revolution, a hustling, bustling, and very congested and overcrowded city. One in every twenty-five Americans lived there.[1] It was also a city reeking with sin. It had become an ugly city, too, infested with rats, garbage, whores, and drunks.

And it had become a city full of criminals.

The flamboyant Bennett, whom his reporters referred to as "the Emperor," more than anyone else, pushing and prodding the politicians and civic leaders, would become responsible for a new look at crime and criminals in the city and in all of America. New York was changing. The United States was changing. The police might not have been necessary when George Washington took office and only twenty thousand people lived in the twisting, winding streets of the town, but they were certainly needed now, when blood flowed in the streets, people feared for their lives, and killers escaped unscathed.

All of the criminal mayhem was wonderful grist for the sensational new "penny press," and its editors made the most of it. The editors of the titillating penny sheets revolutionized American journalism. The penny press editors were the first to employ street-corner newsboys (the city had about three hundred of them) shouting out to passersby to purchase a paper. They shouted out more crime-story headlines at the top of their lungs than any other stories because crime sold newspapers.

The newsboys, ragamuffin heroes of stories, movies, and plays for a hundred and fifty years afterward, stood on top of wooden crates with a thick pile of freshly printed papers at their feet on chilly February mornings and steamy July afternoons. They all wore slouched cloth caps, wrinkled jackets, and breeches, went barefoot, and possessed, one man said, "a dirty face with hands to match." The newsboys seemed to live in their own world. "Tom Newsboy . . . swears, we know, freely; drinks, fights, and very often stays out all night. . . . [He] indulges too in games of Chance, and is scarcely ever without dice, small cards, and other implements of hazard in his pocket," said one observer. They waved the newspaper in the air and shouted out the headlines to sell the papers. Whether it was a murder, a fire, or a circus elephant run amok, the ten- and eleven-year-old kids screamed out the headline for all to hear— "Extra! Extra! Read all about it—banker slays wife!"[2]

The newsboys popped up anywhere there was a chance to sell a newspaper for a penny. They jumped onto omnibuses without paying a fare and badgered people to purchase a paper until the harried omnibus conductor chased them off the vehicle. The newsboys stood outside of theaters, or baseball fields, and shouted out their headlines about murder and mayhem as long and loud as they could to draw a crowd. They were generally a grimy lot of ragamuffins who had little money and came from poor families. Some were so destitute that Bennett and other editors allowed them to sleep in the offices of the newspapers. In the 1850s, one paper opened up a boardinghouse just for newsboys. Some newsboys fell in love with the venues where they sold their papers. Barney Williams, as an example, sold papers outside of a theater, was entranced by the entertainment he saw inside of it, and became a professional Irish jig dancer.[3]

The penny press editors hired boats to take their reporters out into the harbor at dawn to greet newly arriving oceangoing ships bobbing in the water to gather news from Europe and interview politicians and entertainers. Anything that anybody said in those interviews was blown up into a gargantuan story the next morning. Newsboys would shout out the headlines gleaned from shipboard interviews, and people would get the news first on street corners. Hundreds of New Yorkers waited eagerly for shipboard news from Europe during the Crimean War.[4] The penny papers did not rely on the financial support of the city's political factions, as the other newspapers did, but instead courted large department stores and other businesses to advertise, guaranteeing them huge lists of readers. Beholden to no one, the journals could comment on everyone, sometimes viciously.

And, best of all, they were affordable to everyone. "The object of this paper is to lay before the public, at a price within the means of everyone, all the news of the day," wrote Benjamin Day in the inaugural issue of the first penny sheet, the *Sun.* Five years later, after considerable success, he wrote that "the *Sun* has probably done more to benefit the community by enlightening the minds of the common people than all the other papers together."[5]

Poet Walt Whitman saw the penny press as extraordinarily power-ful in New York. He often said that the candid, fiery penny press was to American reading what the public school was to education. Whit-man was a reporter for several papers and then became an editor. He filled the columns of his paper with crime stories and stories in which he and his writers quoted critics of the erratic city force of constables.[6]

It was the *Sun* that started regular crime reporting. Soon after it opened its doors in 1833, shortly after a cholera epidemic claimed the lives of thirty thousand New Yorkers (including Horace Greeley's son), the *Sun*'s reporter George Wisner began to cover the proceedings in the city's police court on a regular basis. His reporting was printed in a regular crime column entitled "Police Office." The very first edi-tion of the *Sun* featured a string of crime stories, from armed robbery to petty domestic disputes. The *Sun* not only ran as many murder sto-ries as it could find in New York but reprinted homicide stories from other newspapers around the country. In one early edition it had tales of murder from Florida, Pennsylvania, and Ohio.[7]

Wisner and other reporters, especially those from the *Herald,* loved crime stories tied to divorce cases. There was always some woman in front of a judge charging that her husband had thrown a pot at her or hit her with a broomstick. The judge made fun of both of them, and so did the police reporters, which spun the crime proceedings into lengthy, sarcastic stories that amused readers.[8]

Newspapers of that era generally sold for a nickel or six cents, but the heads of the penny press believed that if they sold their sheets for only a penny they could sell so many of them, targeting the general public and not the well-to-do, that the profits would surpass those of publishers who sold their newspapers for more. To sell that many papers, they naturally turned to sensational stories. Crime led the list. Bennett wrote in 1842 that crime had caused all of the disorder and confusion in the city, and other editors in New York heartily agreed with him.

Along with all of his stories about crime and murder, Bennett ran numerous pieces and editorials on the hapless and hopeless police force of unskilled constables and insisted, from the Helen Jewett murder onward, that the city had to get rid of its constables and hire an all-new, trained police force. He constantly criticized the constables and the government that seemed to love them.

New York was home to eleven daily newspapers by the late 1830s, some published in the morning and some in the evening, most with circulations of around three or four thousand, and their number grew to thirty-five by the early 1840s. In 1830, the United States had 857 papers, but by 1840, that number had doubled and total circulation of newspapers climbed from 68 million to 196 million.[9]

This was made possible by an exploding population and the development of the Napier steam printing press, which could publish twenty times as many copies as the old wooden hand presses. The new presses did not use single sheets of paper, like the old hand presses, but continuous rolls of paper that could be fed through quickly to produce an enormous amount of copies. All of the penny presses in New York began with small staffs, usually just an editor and a printer, but by the mid-1840s papers like the *Herald* had a dozen reporters and editors and twenty or so compositors.

The cheap papers had a willing audience for their crime stories and tawdry features. By the 1840s, thanks to increased public education, America's literacy rate was high, and almost everybody could read the newspapers. Tens of thousands preferred reading the penny press because the stories were written for the average person and were colorful and short. Horace Greeley of the *Tribune* advised his reporters that "a half column has ten chances [of publication] where two columns have one and three columns none."[10]

The editors knew how the readers liked to peruse a paper and delivered that compact four-page paper into their hands—and for just a penny. They also knew that readers loved their daily stories of crime, sex, scandal, and corruption because they found the subjects titillating and because New Yorkers feared crime in the streets and were overly anxious about the ever-growing city in general and the terrors that it posed to them. The new, urban mass entertainment world was perfect for New Yorkers, too, and so was the penny press that covered it.

The journals also thrived because the United States had undergone a financial recession in 1833 and then a depression four years later, the Panic of 1837. People had little income, so the one-cent newspapers were far more attractive than the five- and six-cent sheets they competed against.

The *Herald,* the *Sun,* the *Express,* and the *Transcript* were some of the leading pennies. The penny sheets were financially independent and not tied to Tammany Hall and other political organizations, as were most of the five- and six-cent sheets. Bennett wrote that he "found out the hollow heartedness and humbuggery of these political associations and political men."[11]

The penny press, in its crackdown on crime, led by Bennett in the Jewett case, pioneered the practice of interviewing people for stories, which was never attempted by the more expensive sheets. The penny bosses theorized that the people who read their papers wanted to know what the people in the stories, heroes and villains, had to say. The success of the interview stories enabled Bennett to get the very first newspaper interview of President Martin Van Buren in 1839, a real coup for any journalist.

The penny press impressed foreigners. British writer Edward Dicey, after having spent six months in America, wrote, "I admit feely that the American press, if you judge it correctly, is a tolerably fair—probably the fairest exponent—of American opinion."[12]

Another thing that the penny press did was build enormous pride in their city for New Yorkers. Bennett argued for twenty years that it should not only replace Albany as the state capital but replace Washington as the national capital. He constantly referred to it as "our noble and moral city" and treated New York as the center of the universe.[13]

The stories that the *Herald* ran about crime emphasized murders and robberies as an ever-growing menace that needed to be curbed. The media attention made crime a major topic of conversation in city streets, taverns, and parlors. Along with their coverage of crime itself, the penny sheets wrote about the inability of the police to stop it.

In its crime coverage, the penny press highlighted murder. Readers loved murders; they could not get enough stories about them. It was the most compelling and titillating kind of story the penny papers could run, and they ran every murder story they could find. Husband slays wife. Wife slays husband. Robbers kill victims. Poor carpenter kills rich banker over woman. The pages of the *Sun* and *Herald* were filled with salacious tales from the front page to the last. The stories were sexy, bawdy, tawdry, and sizzling—and they sold. The *Herald* ran so many of these crime stories that a YMCA in Buffalo banned the newspapers from sale there in order to protect its members. The masses loved the penny papers; the upper classes said they hated them, but many read them secretly. "They lie upon magnificent center tables and are met with in the parlors of the wealthy and proud," wrote Walt Whitman in 1842.[14]

New Yorkers knew what was within the pages of the *Herald*. "It is equally intended for the great masses of the community—the merchant, mechanic, working people—the private family as well as the public hotel—the journeyman and his employer—the clerk and his principal," said Bennett.[15]

Almost all of the penny sheets were located on congested Nassau Street, in lower Manhattan, parallel to Broadway and just south of City Hall. Others were on Anne Street, a few blocks from a police precinct and another few blocks from Tammany Hall's massive stone headquarters. The penny press editors genuinely believed in their causes. They crusaded against the sins of the city, championing the reformers, splashing stories about the antiprostitution and temperance parades across their pages, and urging their readers to rise up in rebellion against the killers, whores, and drunks that infested the town, as well as the bungling constables who never seemed to be able to catch the crooks.[16]

The penny press hated crime and loathed criminals. Bennett despised lawbreakers so much that he even urged the residents of the city to ignore the lazy constables and shoot down any rioters they saw in the streets "like so many mad dogs, as pests to the community, whose deaths are a common blessing."[17]

Bennett, a tall, well-built man with a rather solemn face, arrived in Canada from Scotland in 1819 at the age of twenty. He started contributing stories to papers in 1824, covered politics in Washington, D.C., for one, and gained a solid reputation as a reporter and as a hustler in the nine years prior to his arrival as the new boss of the *Herald.* Like archenemy Horace Greeley and others, he came to the editorship of his paper after many long years of working in journalism, years in which he gained invaluable experience. He had already worked as a reporter and columnist for seven different newspapers in America. "He had made journalism a science," said his managing editor, Frederic Hudson.[18]

One of Bennett's contemporaries, Lambert Wilmer, like many, understood that Bennett's newspaper was one for the masses that flooded the streets of New York, and also the denizens of high society. "This journal is read by people of all classes and its power and influence are universally acknowledged. Although the *Herald* is denounced from one end of the country to the other as the most corrupt and profligate in existence, its opinions on almost every subject are often quoted as indisputable authority," Wilmer wrote.[19]

With the *Herald,* Bennett had created a middle-of-the-road, non-political paper. It was not a journal for those who had much, but for those who had little. The great middle class and working class had no newspaper until Bennett gave them the *Herald.* He quickly realized that the great masses made up 95 percent of the population of New York City and the nation and that all of the increases in population in New York were from the working class, not the rich. Those people had a new voice in the city, and Bennett knew what they wanted, such as crime stories. In the pages of the *Herald* he gave it to them.[20]

Many penny editors, like Walt Whitman, hated the sophisticated six-penny papers even more than they loathed their rivals. "They assume a position of pompous dignity and they affect a sovereign contempt for their little contemporaries," Whitman wrote in 1842. He despised Bennett and called him "a reptile marking his path with slime wherever he goes and breathing mildew at everything fresh and fragrant."[21]

The rivalry between papers, especially in crime coverage, was intense. The *Herald* trained a flock of pigeons to carry notes tied around their legs from reporters in the field to the home office, and Greeley hired marksmen who stood on the roof of the *Tribune* and shot down the pigeons.[22]

Many in town chuckled at the word duels between the editors of the penny press. Philip Hone hated Bennett and delighted in any attack on him. He called Bennett an "ill-looking squinting man . . . now editor of the *Herald*, one of the penny papers which are hawked about the streets by a gang of troublesome ragged boys, and in which scandal is retailed to all."[23]

News editors around the city acknowledged, though, that the penny sheets had been successful because of their coverage of crime and their crusade against the police. In 1845, George Wilkes and Enoch Camp, certain that there was an audience for an all-crime paper, founded the *National Police Gazette*, which in just a few years, with its nonstop crime coverage and wonderful illustrations by some of the city's most skilled artists, became one of the most successful newspapers in American history.

Bennett was oblivious to all of the many lawsuits filed against him, by everyone from farmers to opera house managers to merchants. "He is the great ogre of the *Herald*," complained showman P. T. Barnum.[24]

Politician Albert Ramsey complained to President James Buchanan that "Bennett is the vainest man that has lived since Boswell and his vanity makes his friendship or his enmity equally injurious." President Buchanan said that if he could find any small reason to do so, he would have Bennett indicted. Buchanan had been mad at the *Herald* for years because it had opposed him during all four years of his term and while he was secretary of state. He was not happy with *Tribune* editor Horace Greeley, either, because Greeley opposed many of his policies.[25]

The feisty *Herald* editor did have his supporters among rivals in New York. George Wilkes, one of the founders of the *National Police Gazette*, said that "the *Herald* is the only journal I care about reading, and is, according to my notions, the best specimen of a newspaper I ever saw." Bennett had champions around the country, too. One editor in Natchez, Mississippi, wrote that "no writer in the union is so universally quoted and relied upon by the standards of both sides of the Atlantic. This is the triumph of genius."[26]

One of Bennett's strongest supports was Senator William Seward, whose votes in Congress and policies he frequently attacked. Seward had no complaints about Bennett, or any other editor. To him, they were all just doing their job. "The press is not despotic," said Seward. "The sweeping allegations brought against the press are not in any way just. . . . It reflects in all things the character of the country."[27]

Crime, and the *Herald*'s crusade for professional police, became an important issue because the *Herald* was growing into the highest-circulation newspaper in New York in the 1840s and '50s. By the outbreak of the Civil War, it would boast the largest circulation in America, and Bennett would be one of the most powerful men in the country. All of the penny sheets succeeded, not just the *Herald*. They became so popular that in the mid-1850s, 70,000 New York residents, out of a population of some 300,000, read a penny newspaper each day. On one day in the late 1830s, crime stories filled all the penny papers. Four penny outsold all of the other papers in town. Other publishers across the country began to scrap the six-cent sheets and publish penny papers. "The penny papers are rapidly increasing through-out the country," said Bennett; "the large papers will sink in a few years."[28]

Bennett always moaned about the city's watchmen, who he thought were powerless to prevent the city's going to "perdition and pestilence." Bennett understood, however, as did the other editors, that corruption in the city's court system was just as responsible for the crime wave as inept police officers. In the summer of 1841, the *Herald* published numerous stories on city and state investigations of the corrupt courts and crooked judges and lawyers.[29]

Reporters regularly visited police courts, a special judicial division started in the mid-1830s when crime began to overwhelm the city. They sat on benches and covered all kinds of criminal cases before the police magistrate. Press people also met at Butter Cake Dick's, a sleazy all-night coffee shop located in a basement near City Hall. There reporters mingled with police, lawyers, and Tammany Hall workers and picked up numerous stories. Butter Cake Dick's became famous because journalists hung out there. It was just one of several dozen such coffee shops.[30]

There was plenty of crime to complain about, too. Here are some stories published just in the *Herald* in one month in 1841:

Two sons of deceased millionaire John Stuart tried to have their mother incarcerated in the lunatic asylum on Blackwell's Island so they could seize all of their father's money and estates, leaving Mom penniless.

Boxing champion Yankee Sullivan killed a man in the ring, and the *Herald* made the fight a murder story and supported all of Sullivan's critics in a short series of articles.

A member of one of New York's blissful utopian colonies was savagely murdered.

A local politician shot a congressman dead in the middle of a street in a duel over a woman.

The son of a millionaire, seen arguing with his girlfriend at a party after both had consumed much champagne, was later fished out of the East River, dead.

A vast prostitution ring composed of bored New York housewives trying to make a little extra spending money for themselves was broken up.

A man was arrested for sexually molesting his two teenage daughters.

A ring of prostitutes who routinely robbed their clients of their jewelry and turned the loot over to a second ring of prostitutes who turned it all over to very grateful department store managers, who sold it to customers, was smashed.

Two sisters from a quiet town in Connecticut who spent the summer in a New York apartment working as prostitutes to make extra money on their "vacation" were arrested.

Two New York sisters counterfeited money and had others use it to buy goods, which they then sold to stores for cash, thus turning a huge profit, were arrested.

The beautiful, flirtatious daughter of a boardinghouse manager was stabbed to death after spurning one of the boarders who lusted after her.

The *Police Gazette* went a step further than Bennett. Its editors created a column they entitled "Lives of Felons" and in it drew colorful pictures of wicked criminals who were out not only to steal whatever they could or batter whomever they chose but to disrupt the social life of New York City and its inhabitants. In these long portraits, the *Gazette* writers brought in hundreds of crimes to paint a disparaging picture of city criminals, adding to what Bennett called the Shakespearean aspect of crime and the success of criminals because of the incompetence of the police force.[31]

Journalists believed that crime was not only news that sold but news that the people needed to help them reform the city. "The worst symptoms of social disease would be manifested were the crimes and offenses of the day unheeded or passed by with trivial notices by the journalists," said Whitman.[32]

The *Herald,* the *Sun,* and other papers routinely ran notices that warned readers about pickpockets and burglary rings and preached against gambling and drinking on their editorial pages. The warnings were frequent. Writing in *Life Illustrated,* Whitman, the poet and full-time journalist who would work for eight New York papers in his life, warned visitors to the city of "sojourners robbed, swindled, and perhaps beaten." He told them to "deposit your money in a bank; with a trusty business acquaintance; in the safe of the hotel, through a clerk, retaining only your pocket money. It is neither safe to leave it in your room, nor to carry it about your person."[33]

If not for the anticrime and antipolice crusades by Bennett and the other editors, the public would never have been aroused as it was and never driven to protest to the government that a new police force was needed. The penny sheets reminded the public, every day and in every column, that New York had spun out of control and needed help—and fast.

CHAPTER FOUR

The Magnificent City and the Malignant Crime Wave

The city itself seems clear and bright in the distance—its deformations hidden and its beauty exaggerated, like the fame of far off heroes. When the sun shines on its steeples, windows and roofs of glittering tin, it is as if the fine spirits had suddenly created a city of fairy palaces. And when the still shadows creep over it, and the distant lights shine like descended constellations, twinkling to the morning music of the sea, there is something oppressive in its solemn beauty. Then comes the golden morning light, as if God suddenly unveiled his glory!

—Social reformer Lydia Maria Child, 1841

By the early 1840s, New York was the largest city in the United States, surpassing longtime rivals Boston and Philadelphia with nearly half a million residents. By 1870 the population would grow to nearly one million, more if you add the 250,000 residents of Brooklyn, then its own separate city, and another 400,000 or so people who lived somewhere else but worked in the city or visited it. There were also about 50,000 people who were transients and moved in and out of the city at an uneven pace. Seventy percent of all the hundreds of thousands of foreigners who came to America as part of the great wave of immigrants in the first decades of the nineteenth century arrived in New York. The city had over forty times the population of the 1790s, when it served as the nation's first capital.[1]

Many New Yorkers had arrived from inland America. "The crowd in Broadway . . . seems to have come from out of town," wrote George William Curtis. "It has a strange wondering air. And the population of the city itself is so incessantly reinforced by those who come from the country that the city has always a little air of novelty in its own citizens."[2]

That population boom was already under way when Spaniard Ramon de la Sagra visited the town in 1835. He was "astonished" at the rapid growth of the city. "Everywhere they are building houses, repairing whole sections, constructing superb hotels, opening large squares, and as if to second this activity, laying out new streets and embankments. . . . The whole length of the wharves, there rises up a forest of masts belonging to the vessels of many nations and steamships engaged in trade among the various states of the Union. On the North river, the bay and its eastern arm, magnificent steamboats cross and recross without ceasing," he wrote.[3]

A British writer had a wonderful description for the sprawling growth of New York. He said that it was "Jack the giant killer's beanstalk."[4]

New York was gorgeous in winter, when residents sped through the streets in large, colorful horse-drawn sleighs, whose runners cut through the newly fallen white snow, and icicles hung from fifth-story rooftops. It was even prettier in summer. Social reformer Lydia Maria Child, dazzled by its vivaciousness, told her friends that it was "Babylon."[5]

New York was a magical place to all who saw it. Poet Walt Whitman, who would later use it as the landscape for his book *Leaves of Grass,* loved it. He remembered vividly the sights and sounds of New York Harbor. "The river and bay scenery, all about New York island, any time of a fine day the hurrying, splashing sea-tides—the changing panorama of steamers, all sizes, often a string of big ones, outward bound to distant ports—the myriads of white-sail'd schooners, sloops, skiffs, and the marvellously beautiful yachts . . . as they rounded the Battery . . . what refreshment of spirit such sights and experiences gave me," he scribbled in one of his notebooks.[6]

On a trip back later in life, Whitman wrote that "I find in this visit to New York, and the daily contact and rapport with its myriad people, on the scale of the oceans and tides, the best, most effective medicine my soul has yet partaken.—the grandest physical habitat and surroundings of land and water the globe affords—namely, Manhattan island and Brooklyn, which the future shall join in one city—city of superb democracy, and amid superb surroundings."[7]

For better or worse, New York was a colossus. "Here are people of all classes and stages of rank—from all countries on the globe—engaged in all the varieties of avocations—of every grade, of every hue of ignorance and learning, morality and vice, wealth and want, fashion and coarseness, breeding and brutality, elevation and degradation, impudence and modesty," said Whitman.[8]

In many ways, the city was the jewel of America. Residents bragged of their numerous mansions, museums, and gardens. It was the banking capital of the country and the nation's chief manufacturing center as the Industrial Revolution took root in America. It boasted the greatest number of newspapers, plus literary magazines, political pamphlets, and the publications of the many social and political movements with headquarters in the city. It had the most lawyers, engineers, doctors, and architects in the country. Twenty-seven percent of all the mail in the United States passed through the New York City post office, and 60 percent of all foreign mail was sent from there. Three-quarters of all the books published in America were produced in New York City. If you wanted something, New York City had it. Journalist George Foster joked that every great country needed an intellectual center, just as a person needed a brain. New York, he said, was that for America.[9]

The city had the biggest stores, such as Lord & Taylor, Arnold Constable & Co., James McCreery & Co., and A. T. Stewart, the enormous discount store, a six-story-high shopping mecca so big that it had its own telegraph office.[10]

The owner of Stewart's, Alexander Stewart, one of the wealthiest men in the world, became famous for a crime thirty years later. Grave robbers stole his body from a church cemetery in the Bowery in 1878 and demanded a $200,000 ransom for it. New York detectives launched a massive investigation and finally arrested two men. The district attorney said there was not enough evidence for a trial, though, and released them. The family did get Stewart's remains back, or believed they did, in 1881, when their attorney paid unknown body snatchers $20,000 for a bag of bones said to be Stewart's. The family buried the bones in a church they built in Garden City, Long Island, in the department store titan's honor, and they remain there today.[11]

New York had begun to compete with Paris as a shopping and fashion capital. The stores that lined Broadway and Fifth Avenue were among the finest and most expensive on earth, and wealthy residents paraded up and down those avenues to show off their newly purchased and expensive suits and elegant dresses. "The shops of Broadway are world famed," wrote Whitman. "A man can edify himself for hours by looking in the shop windows of Broadway."[12] And by the early 1850s, Fifth Avenue had become "the most magnificent street on this continent," according to a guidebook.[13]

The sweet-smelling bakeries could rival those in any fabled European kingdom. "Cakes were of every conceivable shape—pyramids, obelisks, towers, pagodas, castles, &c. Some frosted loaves nestled lovingly in a pretty basket of sugar eggs; others were garlanded with flowers, or surmounted by cooing doves, or dancing cupids," gushed Lydia Child, who loved to frequent them.[14]

And then there were the dozens of quaint, narrow ice cream parlors, whose chairs and walls were painted with every color of the rainbow. Brightly dressed young women stood behind counters full of tubs of different-flavored ice cream and surrounded by counters of fruits, candies, cookies, and other delicacies whose aromas filled the air. Men, women, and children sat at wooden tables in these shops long into the afternoon finishing the best ice cream the world had to offer. The emporiums opened in early April, when the snow started to melt, and stayed open until the first shadows of winter quietly crept across the city in late November.[15]

New York was the capital of both shipbuilding and shipping. Hundreds of sleek, handsome, tall-masted oceangoing ships and the brand-new, fast-moving, colorful steamships were berthed at the congested docks that ringed Manhattan like a shining necklace. The heaviest concentration of ships, with the largest horde of shipworkers, was at South Street, on the Lower East Side, where tall-masted vessels were berthed, or being repaired, as far as the human eye could see. In addition to merchant shipbuilding, the New York docks were home to dozens of companies that built and repaired warships for the U.S. Navy and for foreign countries such as Greece, Turkey, Russia, and France.[16] The completion of the Erie Canal in upstate New York in the early 1830s brought steady boat traffic from the Midwest to the Hudson River and then to New York, with millions of pounds of additional cargo each year. By the early 1840s, more than five thousand ships a year docked in New York City. Several new railroad lines brought into Gotham boxcars full of produce that was then put on ships by thousands of stevedores who worked the busy, loud docks and sent to ports around the globe. The tragic crop failures in Ireland in the late 1830s made the demand for American crops, piled high on the wide decks of those ships in large wooden crates, nearly insatiable.

The city was a base for the nation's young literary lions, such as Walt Whitman, James Fenimore Cooper, Henry Wadsworth Longfellow, and the morose, angry poet Edgar Allan Poe, just arrived from Philadelphia in 1844 and living downtown on Greenwich Street. People formed clubs to toast famous writers and public figures. Philip Hone founded the Hone Club, which held dinners for the famous, such as Daniel Webster. Half a dozen writers formed the Bread and Cheese Club. Noted public figures formed the Union Club in 1836, and it still has an active membership today.

New York surpassed all other United States cities in entertainment, with dozens of music halls that presented some of the finest orchestras in America and touring symphonies from Europe. Its theater district had exploded and was home to American productions, not just touring British shows, and New York's homegrown singers, actors, and comedians were gaining fame throughout the world.[17]

Beneath that level there were theaters that featured Negro minstrel shows, heavily attended small concert halls that hosted orchestras, singers, and prominent lecturers, and small baseball fields where new city amateur teams played. Part of the rainbow array of entertainment meccas was P. T. Barnum's Museum, admission just twenty-five cents, where the iconic showman offered patrons numerous large rooms of bizarre exhibits, such as a dog with two legs and a cow with four horns ("to gratify a morbid taste for the horrible," said one visitor), a 3:00 P.M. comics showcase, and, if all that were not enough, a melodrama in the evening.[18]

Inordinately popular with all New Yorkers was the circus building on Fourteenth Street, whose interior was designed like the large tents the circus moguls set up outdoors in cities and villages where they stopped on their many national tours. Nearby was the huge Amphitheater, where colorful animal shows were produced. The Amphitheater often had hundreds of patrons inside and hundreds more outside, clamoring for tickets and pushing and shoving each other. Police were often called in for crowd control on the streets in front of the building and to prevent a riot by raucous fans who were unable to get tickets. One reason for the heavy demand was that city newspapers, especially the penny sheets, not only ran ads for theaters but, as a gesture of goodwill, ran columns of free space in which the newspapers let readers know what attractions were being staged in town each day.[19]

The Broadway neighborhoods were loaded with restaurants. One visitor from Great Britain, Basil Hall, was astounded at the number of eateries and how busy they were. He and a friend found the last table in one restaurant whose tables were separated into boxes by low wooden walls and could not get over the hum of noise in it or how efficient the waiters were. "[They] were gliding up and down, and across the passage, inclining their heads for an instant, first to one box, then to another, and receiving the whispered wishes of the company, which they straightway bawled out in a loud voice, to give notice of what fare was wanted. It quite baffled my comprehension to imagine how the people at the upper end of the room, by whom a communication was kept up in some magical way with the kitchen, continue to distinguish between one order and the other," he said.[20]

And then there was the city's carnival, the Bowery, the Las Vegas of its time. The Bowery was an avenue that ran north and south between Chatham Square and the Cooper Institute at Eighth Street on the city's southeast side, parallel to Broadway and twice as wide. Broadway had its first-rate entertainment, and the Bowery had its third-rate entertainment. Broadway was where the city's elite gathered at night, and the Bowery was where the most despicable congregated. It was anchored by a first-rate stage, the Bowery Theater, a cavernous edifice that could seat over a thousand people. It featured some classy actors, such as Edwin Forrest, and some touring British shows but made most of its money on lowbrow extravaganzas filled with acrobats, singing groups, jugglers, and horse acts. Ticket prices at all the venues were low. They were low at the Bowery Theater, too. That emporium sat, with its large entrance and thick velvet curtains, in the middle of the Bowery. Around it were whorehouses, bars, boardinghouses, stores, stables, and ever-present omnibuses, rambling along all day and all night. Peddlers, vendors, and out-of-work drifters filled its streets, which were also lined with pickpockets.

Ironically, the Bowery, cluttered with hundreds of organ grinders and their trained monkeys, as well as other street musicians, gypsies, fortune-tellers, and outrageously dressed men who sold questionable bottles of medicine, was developed on land that for decades served as pig farms or cattle slaughterhouses.

You never knew who you would see on the crowded streets of the Bowery or other avenues in New York in those years. Teenager Walt Whitman was walking through town one morning in 1832 and spotted a very rich man leaving his home. He was "a bent, feeble but stout-built, very old man, bearded, swathed in rich furs, with a great ermine cap on his head, led and assisted, almost carried, down the steps of his high front stoop, a dozen friends and servants, emulous, carefully holding, guiding him, and then lifted and tucked in a gorgeous sleigh, enveloped in other furs, for a ride. The sleigh was drawn by the finest team of horses I ever saw."

The man Whitman was watching was said to be the richest man in the world—John Jacob Astor, worth between $50 million and $100 million.[21]

New Yorkers loved their town. " 'Our city' is the great place of the western continent, the heart, the brain, the focus, the main spring, the pinnacle, the extremity, the no more beyond, of the New World," Whitman wrote in 1842.[22]

The buildings were magnificent, the avenues inviting, and the crowds, buses, and carriages on the streets a waterfall of majesty. "All the walks here are wide, and the spaces ample and free, now flooded with liquid gold from the last two hours of sunshine, . . ." wrote Whitman of Manhattan. "A Mississippi of horses and rich vehicles, not by dozens and scores, but hundreds and thousands—the broad [Fifth] avenue filled and cramm'd with them—a moving, sparkling, hurrying crush, for more than two miles (I wonder they don't get block'd, but I believe they never do). Altogether it is to me the marvel sight of New York. I like to get into one of the Fifth avenue stages and ride up, stemming the swift-moving procession. I doubt if London or Paris or any city in the world could show such a carriage carnival as I have seen here . . . these beautiful May afternoons."[23]

Yet at the same time, the metropolis's raging success, beauty, size, and prosperity threatened to ruin it, just as the success and prosperity of old Rome brought it down with a thunderous roar long ago.

"The din of crowded life, and the eager chase for gain, still runs through its streets, like the perpetual murmur of a hive. Wealth dozes on French couches, thrice piled, and canopied with damask, while poverty camps out on the dirty pavement, or sleeps off its wretchedness in the watch-house," wrote reformer Lydia Child after walking through the congested and dirty streets in the early 1840s, peering at all the laundry hung outside the windows of the grimy five- and six-story-high tenement houses to dry. "New York is a vast emporium of poverty."[24]

The press of people in New York was at times overwhelming. The density of people living below Canal Street leaped from 94.5 per acre in 1820 to 163.3 in 1850, and the average block density rose from 157.5 to 172.5. In the Seventh and Tenth Wards, overloaded with newly arrived Irish, the average block density climbed from 54.5 in 1820 to 170.9 in 1840. Tenants had to pay between $3 and $13 per "apartment" per month and $1.25 per week for single rooms. The number of people in each block and building was so high that hundreds were forced to live in damp, barely lit, and horribly ventilated cellars; neighbors started to call them "cellar dwellers." By the late 1840s, tenants held antirent rallies, started to form associations, and received wide support from newspapers in their struggle for lower rents. Angry tenants repeatedly charged that high and unmonitored rents were criminal acts, but their assertions were ignored in the yearly crime statistics.[25]

Work was scarce and wages were low for white workers and recently arrived immigrants, but they were very low for African Americans. One, Willis Hodges, a recently arrived black laborer from Virginia, found he could land only low-paying jobs, first as a maintenance man at the docks, where he swept up dirt in the summer and chopped up ice in the winter, and later as a cartman. He worked pushing carts for years and made some money, but then he lost his job and nearly lost everything. "I did not like New York any way it could be placed before me," he said.[26]

And, too, low wages meant that hordes of workers had to live in the same neighborhoods as their jobs, because they could not afford more expensive housing or the omnibus commuter fares. This created hopelessly overcrowded streets and residential living zones. One problem was simply piggybacked on top of another. These people did not live in squalor, but they had none of the refinements of the wealthy, who lived uptown. The working class had no indoor privies and had to use chamber pots. Light was brought into their homes at night in cheap, badly made lamps. Their firewood was not purchased or secured by servants but cut from jangled clusters of fallen spruces and oaks in city forests.

The crowded tenements in which the working class was forced to live had been built by profit-hungry developers in the wake of the Great Fire of 1835, which destroyed one-third of the city and thousands of housing units, to handle the growing population of New York, especially the newly arrived immigrants from Europe. Some four-story-high brick buildings contained as many as ninety tenants, all jammed together and battling for fresh air and some peace and quiet, living their lives as the sounds of others living theirs loudly resonated through the thin walls of the building. Most tenements were 25' by 100' and had eighteen rooms per floor. Just two of those rooms received direct sunlight. Men trudged out each day to work for little money in factories, and women either went to someone's home to work as a domestic servant or used their own home as a shop to wash or mend clothes for others; the piled-up dirty laundry often took up the entire living room and a bedroom.

Many residents of the working-class neighborhoods of New York had a garbage problem. Municipal garbage pickups were few and far between, and most refuse ended up being tossed, or accidentally pushed, into the streets. There, it became a problem for the street-cleaning crew, whose members had to toil harder than any other street cleaners in urban America to keep their city presentable.[27] The city smelled not only from garbage but from sewage. In the late 1840s, only one-fourth of New York City streets had any sewage lines. City health inspectors and beat patrolmen did little or nothing to improve sewage and garbage conditions.[28]

New York was, Philip Hone scoffed in 1832 and reiterated through the 1840s, "one huge pigsty."[29]

Nearly every available building in the city was teeming with people. In the mid-1850s, there were 161,000 families in town, residing in 60,000 buildings. Only 15,000 occupied single-family residences. The rest were jammed into any edifices they could find. Some tenements downtown housed more than 200 people; another was home to 112 families. A large old warehouse in Five Points was rumored to have a thousand people living in it. One tenement house was worse than another. Until laws were passed in the 1840s limiting their number and forcing them to obtain a city license, "immigrant runners," hundreds of them, met families from Europe as soon as they arrived on the docks and, for a fee, hustled them off to tenement houses, where they promised lavish living at low prices. The agents took their fees; the immigrants opened their dwelling doors and stood in shock. Life went on.[30]

Hone was not the only aging public figure worried about overcrowding and crime in New York. Former president Thomas Jefferson had long been reluctant to promote the growth of cities. He wrote from Monticello, his Virginia plantation, that the city seemed swamped with problems. "A city life offers you . . . painful objects of vice and wretchedness. New York . . . seems to be a Cloacina [anus] of all the depravities of human nature," he wrote a friend in 1823.[31]

New York's problems seemed endless. The sanitary scene in the city was deplorable. One cop, officer William Bell, told his superiors about a depression on a Lower East Side lawn filled with stagnant water and carcasses of dead dogs. "This pond is not only detrimental to the public health, but is dangerous to the lives of our citizens. Within the last year, five persons have drowned in it. . . . The water is on a level with the sidewalk and a person walking down the sidewalk at night is liable to walk in it and drown before assistance could reach him," he said.[32]

Poverty reigned, and many people had it worse than the tenement dwellers. Estimates were that between forty thousand and fifty thousand people were living in "almshouses," or poorhouses, run by the city at an enormous cost. They were deplorable. "It was badly ventilated and badly lighted," wrote Charles Dickens when he visited one. "Not too clean and impressed me on the whole very uncomfortably."[33]

Still others eked out an existence in the streets and slept on park benches at night, often clearing off snow from the wooden seat. Thousands of "bummers" spent their day panhandling for money in city streets and in parks, begging for food scraps near restaurants, and telling visitors to the city that they could develop a business if they only had money—from them. They were badly dressed, depressed, and a nuisance to all.

Hundreds of poverty-stricken people became ragpickers. They walked through city streets early in the morning as the sun rose with large bags slung over their shoulders and picked up jars, vases, string, boards, pieces of garbage, and anything else they could find, all left on the streets the night before. The ragpickers made a living out of selling the debris they gathered to middlemen who then sold the materials to early-day "recyclers" who used them to create utensils, plates, and other things that they could market. One thirteen-year-old girl earned ten cents a day picking up and selling animal bones that were later turned into combs by manufacturers. The ragpickers helped to create a whole cottage industry of junk shops, pawnshops, secondhand stores, and a version of today's "dollar stores." Ragpickers were usually paid two cents a pound for the rags they collected that were recycled into clothes by small factories. The ragpickers earned only a half dollar or so a week, but it helped them to get by. Other street people made a living by collecting as much old rope as they could find and selling it to stores or to new or refurbished ships. Many women searched the streets for old nails, or stole them, put them into kegs, and sold the kegs to stores for their subsistence. Others prowled neighborhoods where restaurants and bars were located to scavenge for old bottles that they sold to junk shops.[34]

The ragpickers were admired by many New Yorkers who felt they were at least trying to make a living, even if it was on the edge of squalor. "The little muddy, dripping girl, with her rough hair and torn dress, who is sweeping the walk and flying about with her broom in the storm, like an ugly little sprite, may be just keeping herself and an old mother from the alms-house," wrote Reverend Charles Loring Brace in a newspaper column.[35]

Other poor people were taken in by homes founded by several moral reform societies to house the needy. Thousands of squatters took over abandoned buildings, making small fires to keep warm and stretching sheets over doors and windows to ward off cold winter winds that blew in off the harbor with regularity in winter. Smelly slums abounded. A reporter for *The New York Times* later said of the squatters that they "prefer dwelling rent free amid filth and squalor to paying a landlord's agent monthly dues for the enjoyment of similar privileges conferred upon the lodgers in a tenement house." New York City was "one of the most crime-haunted and dangerous cities in all of Christendom," railed Whitman.[36]

The city was a mess. Whitman said of it in 1842, "Imagine all the accumulations of filth in a great city—not merely the slops and rottenness thrown in the streets and byways (and never thoroughly carried away)—but the numberless privies, cesspools, sinks and gulches of abomination . . . the unmeasurable dirt that is filtered into the earth through its myriad pores" and added that the city's drinking water was practically "poisoned" by the unsanitary conditions he found just about everywhere.

He wailed even more about crime. In the winter of 1842 he became so despondent about it that he warned young men from the country not to move to New York. "Every kind of wickedness that can be festered into life by the crowding together by a huge mass of people is here to be found," he said.[37]

Race was a growing problem in that era. New Yorkers may not have realized that their hatred of African Americans in a slave-free city was far more virulent than the hatred of southerners for blacks in a region where there was slavery. It was noticed immediately by Tocqueville and Beaumont on their visit to New York. They said it was one of the main causes of problems in the northern states and cities. This odd social contempt in the slave-free North drove the animosity toward all antislavery supporters, especially the abolitionists.[38]

Nativists despised African Americans. Black men were murdered in cities by nativists because they landed jobs that white men believed they themselves should have been given. Black men who married or courted white women were badly beaten. Blacks who committed crimes, or were merely suspected of committing crimes, were beaten or even lynched. In parts of New York and other cities, the homicide rates for blacks crept far past those for whites.

The city government was corrupt, too. The Tammany Hall political machine controlled the city, and bribery was a way of life. Tammany Hall appointed the judges, who were often as corrupt as the men who gave them their jobs. Just about anything could be bought for a few hundred dollars. One briber was so bold that he knocked on the front door of the sheriff's office and, when it was opened, handed the sheriff an envelope with $1,000 in cash in it.[39] Tammany Hall candidates were usually elected, though, because its leaders hired street gang toughs to disrupt the political rallies of opposing candidates and to prevent opposition supporters from voting on Election Day, sometimes using baseball bats and chains to do so.

And if all of those woes were not enough to demoralize New Yorkers, they were, in the early 1840s, face-to-face with the greatest crime wave in the history of the United States. All of the triumphs of New York in business and culture were endangered by a crime epidemic perpetuated by an army of sordid criminals that threatened to topple the magnificent metropolis. Newspaper stories, Board of Aldermen reports, and state investigations showed that crime had been climbing at an alarming rate from the end of the War of 1812 into the early 1840s and that the city remained very badly policed. An 1843 Board of Aldermen report charged that "the criminal department was designed exclusively and only for arrest, trial and punishment of offenders and was not calculated efficiently to prevent crime or to suppress the licentiousness and vices which lead to it." The crime wave seemed unstoppable, and New York City was completely unprepared for it.[40]

CHAPTER FIVE

Crime Everywhere

The Devil's work is done here on a gigantic scale.
—James McCabe Jr.

New York was a city of immediate danger and a city of intoxicating, sordid sin and crime in the 1830s, '40s, and '50s. The metropolis boasted 4,567 bars, 769 of them unlicensed (the Five Points/Paradise Square neighborhood alone had 270 saloons), and several hundred houses of prostitution (some said as many as 600) that were home to anywhere from 6,000 to 10,000 hookers (depending on who was counting). There were nearly 600 legal gambling emporiums where fistfights over gaming debts and cheating were routine. It was the era in which the numbers racket was born, and many in the city bragged that it was home to over 1,000 numbers shops and 3,000 numbers operators, who took in over $2.5 million a year (about $500 million in today's currency) in the two-a-day numbers lotteries.

Crime ruled in pre–Civil War New York City. More than 30,000 people were arrested each year, most for drunkenness, disorderly conduct, and assault. Three times as many people were arrested in New York each day as the number arrested in London and Paris *combined*. New York had the highest crime and murder rate in the country. Lawbreaking continued to rise, too. In the 1830s, there had been more than 10,000 arrests in New York each year. In the 1840s, the number climbed even higher, and in the late 1850s, nearly 50,000 people a year were being charged and incarcerated in the notorious Tombs prison and other city jails.[1]

There was always someone stealing or someone beating up someone else in every neighborhood. From 1845 to 1853, one study showed, there were 257,738 arrests made, or some 32,000 per year. Some of the biggest arrest totals were for drunkenness (82,000), assault and battery (27,000), disorderly conduct (34,735), fighting in the streets (4,131), insanity (2,873), petit larceny (24,298), vagrancy (21,155), grand larceny (4,190), and pickpocketing (670). There were 270 people arrested for insulting females and 344 arrests of "runaway apprentices." There were also a number of arrests for carrying a slingshot, which men used to wound their enemies in street fights, and detentions for staging dogfights and cockfights. Men were even arrested for talking badly about their girlfriends in public. Within just eight more years, that 32,000-per-year arrest total would soar to 87,682. That would mean that given today's New York population, the number of arrests would be about 911,000, and about 1.1 million including Brooklyn, or nearly quadruple actual current totals (the 2012 arrest total in New York City was approximately 338,000). There were so many people arraigned that it was estimated that by 1860 one in every ten New Yorkers had a criminal record. The crime rate kept climbing, too. As an example, it jumped nearly 25 percent in just one year, from 1852 to 1853. New York led the nation in murders, robberies, and assaults, and no other city came close to its criminality. In 1858, for instance, there were 22,634 arrests, 20 of them for murder, in Philadelphia. Comparatively, that would mean 47 murders per 700,000 or so people, New York's population, but New York had 88 homicides that year, nearly double Philadelphia's projected total. The total number of people charged with crimes in Philadelphia in 1858, extrapolated to 700,000 people, would be 52,000, but New York had 81,000, or 60 percent more.[2]

Statistics in that era were not well kept. There were 86 murders in the city in the year 1857, according to the Board of Aldermen. Another

study, published by the National Science Foundation in 2015, showed
that New York City murders in that same year totaled 98. A third
study, by police historian Eric Monkkonen, showed about 110 murders in 1860. Those numbers, given the population differences between the 1850s and the contemporary era, translate to a contemporary
number of murders of about 1,400, or nearly five times today's actual
New York City homicide rate (328 murders in 2014).[3] The number
of murders had risen exponentially from the early 1830s to the 1850s,
too. In the 1830s, the murder rate was about 4 per 100,000 residents of New York, but by the 1850s, it had climbed to 13 or 14 per
100,000, extraordinary rates rarely seen again in U.S. history. In addition to all of the slain New Yorkers, there were several hundred
men and women who simply were "lost" and never found each year,
many believed to have been killed. Some were executed and then buried or thrown into a river with weights tied to their bodies. There
were so many "missing" city dwellers that by the late 1850s the New
York police even formed an official Bureau for the Recovery of Lost
Persons. Many of the missing eventually turned up at the city morgue
in Bellevue Hospital, where autopsies by the city coroner showed that
many of the 200 "missing" persons delivered there each year had signs
of violence on their bodies, indicating that they had been murdered.
So many dead were discovered that later the police set up a Bureau
of Information to help them find the families of the missing dead.[4]
Bodies were found everywhere. A little girl playing in a wooded area
in the Williamsburg section of Brooklyn stumbled upon the completely
nude body of an attractive twenty-five-year-old woman who had been
slain and left to the elements and animals.[5] One unknown man whose
well-dressed, purplish body had been fished out of the East River was
discovered to have been stabbed in the side by a wide-bladed knife and
killed.

    Hundreds of abortions were performed each year in New York
City, all of them illegal in that era. They were never included in the
murder or crime rates, either. One estimate was that there was one

abortion for every four live births. The doctors who performed them and women who underwent them did not say a word to anyone about the operations. Many married women, as well as single women, had them, and police hinted that many of those married women were wealthy wives.

There was so much murder and violence in New York City that Davy Crockett, the legendary frontiersman, swore he would never return to the city after one frightening visit in 1835. "I thought I would rather risk myself in an Indian fight than venture among those creatures after night," he said.[6]

New York City not only led the nation in murders but was first in suicides, too. A man who took an informal survey of suicides nationally, using newspapers as his source, reported that there were 63 suicides in the first three months of 1841, and 32 of them took place in New York. The second-place city had only 8.[7]

Some of the suicides were drab throat-slitters, but some were unusual. A downtown man put on his sleeping clothes, lay down in bed, pulled the covers up to his chin, and was still for two hours. Then he rose, opened the third-floor window, and leaped to his death. His body plummeted down into an alley at the side of the tenement house and was not discovered until the early-morning watchman saw it in a crumpled heap. Another man took a ride on one of the Hudson River ferries on a chilly January afternoon, climbed to the very top of the boat, looked left, looked right, and then jumped off, landing in the waterway and promptly drowning.[8]

Crimes against property were a problem, too. Large, organized burglary rings thrived, and some perpetrators were so brazen that they took out newspaper advertisements to let residents know that their stolen property would be sold to the highest bidder at mid-nineteenth-century "Tupperware" parties at the homes of local women.

By the early 1840s "fences," men who would buy stolen goods and then sell them somewhere else at a profit, emerged. Gustavus Reed stole a number of items from a store one afternoon with the intention of selling them to a fence but was arrested at midnight at a grocery store before he could do so. There was so much stolen property to be had in New York, and in other cities, that globally minded fences set up offices to buy goods in one city and sell them in others. Joe Erich, as an example, became the number one fence in New York City by 1855 and set up an operation that dealt goods to other communities. Ephraim Snow set up shop in Philadelphia and sold goods that he had purchased from middle-level fences in Manhattan all over the country. In 1860, newspapers claimed that New York fences had put together a network in which they sold goods from the city to points as far west as New Orleans.[9]

The overall crime rate of the 1840s and 1850s, as reported by the police and city officials, while staggering, was not even the true crime rate. Journalist Edward Crapsey, of *The New York Times,* said in the 1850s that there were far more crimes than the records showed. "The police commissioners of New York have never had the courage to inform the public of the number of burglaries and robberies annually committed in the metropolis," he said, "but enough is known in a general way for us to be certain that there are hundreds of these crimes committed of which the public is not told. The rule is to keep secret all such affairs when an arrest does not follow the offense, and hardly any police official will venture to claim that the arrests occur in more than a [minority] of the cases. There are hundreds of such crimes every year in which the criminal is not detected."[10]

The criminals began to stop just stealing unprotected property, too, and started attacking people themselves. The New York Prison Association reported that during the 1840s, crimes against property increased about 50 percent over the 1830s but that there was an alarming 129 percent jump for crimes against people, with beatings and murders connected to robberies always on the rise. Thousands of New Yorkers began to carry the new Colt revolver, invented in 1839, for protection. In one *New York Herald* newspaper survey of readers, 80 percent admitted to carrying a gun when they left their home or apartment.[11]

All of these various slayings might have swelled the murder rate to six or seven times the current level, or perhaps even higher. The crime rate was so high that historians later noted it was as bad as in the raucous cattle towns of the Wild West of the 1870s and 1880s, places such as Dodge City, Tombstone, Denver, and Deadwood. Those communities were so terrified of their criminals that many formed a "Law and Order" league to combat crime. That fear was not necessary, though. The murder rates in those Wild West communities were actually much lower than in New York City, an average of 1.5 murders per year for each of them, compared to New York's 8.8 or so.[12]

"The Devil's work is done here on a gigantic scale," moaned one New Yorker.[13]

Every time reporter Crapsey or some other journalist would write a story about crime, others would denounce the sensational press for scaring the public. "The penny press is an unmixed evil," complained the staid, six-cent *New York American.* "It panders to the worst passions and lives upon the fears, the credulity and the crimes of the community."[14]

Editors of the penny papers were enraged by those attacks and suggested that the problem was not the vicious crime stories that the penny sheets published. "The worst symptom of social disease would be manifested were the crimes and offenses of the day unheeded or passed by with trivial notices by the journalists," Whitman countered.[15]

Many crimes were never reported. There were undoubtedly more rapes committed than admitted in those years, since many victims of rape feared being socially ostracized if they reported the assault; hundreds of women on the thousands of immigrant ships additionally feared being prevented from disembarking and forced to return to Europe.[16] Other crimes were often not counted in the criminal statistics, such as infanticides, the murder of infants by mothers who did not want them. Midwives who were clearly guilty of negligence in the deaths of women giving birth, usually in grimy boardinghouse rooms with dirty sheets and polluted water, were usually not charged. Coroner's juries rarely did in-depth investigations of murder-suicides, and the two dead bodies were often not counted as homicides. Many bodies discovered washed up on a riverbank were dismissed as accidental drownings and not murders.[17]

One glaring omission in crime reporting was the activity in the Five Points neighborhood. The area was so riddled with dangerous criminals and street gangs that the police refused to patrol there, so the hundreds of crimes committed in Five Points regularly, from prostitution to illegal gambling to pickpocketing to assault and murder, were never reported.

In Five Points, too, less threatening but also unreported, was what went on within the community that would become Chinatown. In the 1840s and 1850s, only a few hundred Asian immigrants lived there, but they had already established an enclave with a mostly Chinese population that by the 1860s would grow to seven thousand. It was an independent area that ran itself and oversaw its own law enforcement. "That the majority of [the Chinese] are incurable gamblers and beings of a low moral tone is unfortunately true, but they mind their own business as they understand it and are never guilty of ruffianism. . . . They never appear in police courts except as complainants against ruffians who have damaged their property or brutally assaulted them," said officer George Walling of them.[18]

Criminals whose actions went unreported or undetected also included pickpockets, johns who frequented illegal houses of prostitution, illegal gamblers, counterfeiters, fake charity workers who fraudulently solicited funds for the poor, unscrupulous train conductors who convinced immigrants who could not speak or read English that they had the wrong train tickets but would be allowed to ride for a small fee, salesmen who dealt in watches that were made to look expensive but were not, thieves who stole silver and gold watches for immediate and highly profitable resale, swindlers who sold fake sports tickets or land deeds or identification papers, fraudulent clothing salesmen who collected money from wealthy people but never delivered the orders, and forgers of checks, money orders, and bank withdrawal slips.[19]

In addition, there were the transgressions of the wealthy on Wall

Street and the men who preyed on them. Many white-collar money crimes were never reported. An example was the theft of $1.8 million in bonds in the late 1850s. Detectives had no idea how to conduct their investigation, so they offered a $25,000 reward. Queries for the reward led them to a suburban thief who had some of the bonds. He told them that a British liquor dealer, in New York on business, had returned to London with the rest. The police then negotiated with London bobbies for his prosecution but settled for the return of the bonds. The Wall Street moguls had little interest in criminal prosecution; they just wanted their money back. In the end, none of the more than half a dozen men involved in the theft were prosecuted for the crime, and just about all of the bonds were recovered, less the reward. It was one of many such crimes for which no one was arrested as long as the money or property was recovered. The wealthy did not care about prosecutions, and neither did the police.[20]

The police, under severe criticism for not cracking down on so many criminals, fought back by making thousands of detentions of poor people, usually immigrants, to pad their annual arrest statistics. Any slight transgression or misdemeanor committed by an immigrant, which would be ignored if committed by a wealthy or middle-class resident of the town, was met with an arrest, and often police arrested immigrants merely on the charge of "suspicion." If an amount of money was stolen from a boardinghouse, an immigrant who lived there might be arrested on suspicion; an immigrant standing in a store when a robbery took place was arrested on "suspicion" of knowing something about the robbery. They were often released, but all such detentions greatly increased crime numbers at the end of the year and showed that the police were working hard.

They were not.[21]

The 1840s and 1850s were also the era of extremely lenient juries, whose members were often not certain that the inept police force had gathered enough evidence, or legitimate evidence, against those charged with any crime and acquitted suspects. In many urban areas with over-crowded legal calendars, grand jurors dismissed about one-quarter of all violent-crime charges on various grounds. Trial juries might acquit or simply refuse to bring back any verdict from their deliberation, causing the judge to declare a mistrial. In Chicago, just one-quarter of all those charged with murder were convicted by juries. Overall, a comprehensive state study showed, New York City trial juries convicted only two-thirds of those brought to court from 1845 to 1870. There were many cases, in New York and in other cities, in which juries believed there was a fine line between homicide and self-defense, especially in the many street fights in which someone was charged with a killing. What should a man do when attacked? If someone is killed in the resulting melee, is it really homicide? Many New York juries did not believe that it was. So the real crime rate was even higher than the already alarming rates reported by the police.[22]

"Public opinion now requires that the utmost leniency shall be exhibited towards criminals—that the lightest punishment shall be meted out to them, and that they shall have the benefit of all doubts, flaws or deficiencies in the chain of evidence," wrote one reporter. Leniency in criminal cases was so great that after one man was given a harsh sentence for fraud, a newspaper reporter said that he should have committed murder because the sentence would have been even less.[23]

Thieves wandered the streets unchecked.

A reformer, Dr. Henry Bellows, charged that thirty thousand professional thieves lived in Manhattan alone in the 1850s.[24] The police put the number of thieves at about three thousand for those same years, broken down into burglars, bank sneaks, forgers, store robbers, safe blowers, and sneak thieves. The police said most male criminals lived with female criminals and that couples often hatched plots together. Burglars often worked in clusters of four or five men. Safe blowers wrapped safes in thick wet blankets to mute the blast and then drilled holes into the walls of the safe. Dynamite was forced into the holes and lit. Windows were left slightly open so that the blast would not shatter the glass and make an excessive amount of noise.[25]

Did constables chase all of those criminals? No. They wasted their time chasing men and boys swimming in the East River, usually in

desolate areas so they would not be seen. New Yorkers were astonished, and some exploded at the arrests of the men in their wet pants.
"We cannot at all commend the mock vigilance of the policemen, who
pounce upon parties of young men and boys—arresting them and
carrying them to the station houses, for the frightful crime of bathing!"
wrote Walt Whitman.[26] This was done in the middle of the most violent
and crime-ridden era in both New York City and American history.[27]

New York's slide into criminality was in many ways due to its success. As an example, the city expanded quickly in population, and that
attracted businesses whose proprietors hoped to profit off the large
revenue from a much greater number of urban residents. That also
meant, though, that criminals now had many more stores to rob. The
bigger the stores, the more attractive their cash registers and shelves
filled with expensive goods became to the denizens of the underworld.
The meteoric growth in businesses, and businesses usually concen-
trated in a specific district, meant a smaller and easier target area for
thieves and, an unintended consequence, faster escape routes.

The growth of stores meant more shoppers, and that meant more
victims for robbers. The increase in overall population also meant
many more citizens walking the streets of residential neighborhoods
who could be held up. The growth of the city also meant more men who
could pursue prostitutes, drink at taverns, and gamble away their weekly
wages. The surging metropolis also attracted tens of thousands of men
from other, smaller cities and towns. No one in the city knew who
they were, and many feared they might be criminals drawn to the
community by its newfound wealth. Criminals not only created direct
problems for New York City; the fear of them significantly com-
pounded the apprehension of residents. "The morals and manners
of youth are neglected and . . . corrupt society is poisoned at the
fountain and all its channels and branches will soon become infected
with the deadly taint," argued a big-city mayor. The city's increasing
magnetism for out-of-towners also meant its social decline.[28]

Anyone who visited New York saw immediately that it was, at the
same time, dazzling and treacherous, populated by the very rich and

the very poor, the highly moral and the despicably immoral. It was a "dirty, smoky, noisy, busy, great and animating emporium," wrote one man from Virginia who vacationed there in the 1840s. It had "the princely dwelling, the costly equipage and the splendid appearances; and on the other hand, the squalid hut of poverty, of filth, of extreme misery and degradation." It was filled with "eddying throngs, gathering and whirling, scattering and hurrying hither and thither."[29]

Many of those who lived there hated it, mostly because of the crime threat. "What an immense vat of misery and crime and filth much of this great city is," wrote Charles Loring Brace, the head of the Children's Aid Society, after he had lived in New York for several years. "I realize it more and more. Think of ten thousand children growing up almost sure to be prostitutes and rogues."[30]

Everybody knew what Brace was talking about because hundreds of abandoned children were found each year, often brothers or sisters, barely clothed, huddled together in the snow, left there by their poverty-stricken parents. Some were taken in by House of Refuge; some were cared for by families who pitied them. Others grew up on the streets and wound up in careers as young thieves or twelve-year-old whores.

Many New Yorkers saw their troubled city as a magnet for killers and thieves. "The enterprising, the curious, the reckless, and the criminal flock hither from all corners of the world, as to a common centre, whence they can diverge at pleasure. . . . Great numbers here live with somewhat of that license which prevails in times of pestilence. Life is a reckless game, and death is a business transaction. Warehouses of ready-made coffins stand beside warehouses of ready-made clothing," said Lydia Child, who had been shaken when she had witnessed dozens of coffins sold at auction to the families of those who had died of diseases or been slain. So many coffins had been made for the victims of crime, cholera, yellow fever, and other epidemics (75 percent of all children under the age of two died from some disease) that flowed through the city in the 1830s and '40s that they sold at retail for just four dollars.[31]

Reformers in town bemoaned the seemingly endless pestilence and told city officials that the filth and grime in the city, in neighborhood after neighborhood, caused health epidemics such as cholera and yellow fever. If the environment was brought under control, so would epidemics be brought under control. Child was as upset with living conditions in Manhattan as her fellow reformers.[32]

One of those coffins had been taken by the wife of Edward Coleman, a local robber. She was one of the city's pretty "hot corn girls" who wore beautiful clothing and sold ears of hot corn from buckets as they glided through the streets of the city. Coleman lived off her earnings. They had a fight because her earnings were not enough. Coleman killed her and became famous—he was the very first man hanged in the city's brand-new jail, the "Tombs," a huge, forbidding-looking granite building. He was hanged on January 12, 1839.

The lovely hot corn girls had a dramatic effect on men. Years later, men would remember encountering them on the streets with great fondness, a treasured memory of their youth. On a chilly night in January of 1854, George Templeton Strong reminisced about "sultry nights in August or early September, when one has walked through close, unfragrant air and flooding moonlight and crowds, in Broadway or in the Bowery, and heard the cry rising at every corner, or has been lulled to sleep by its mournful cadence in the distance as he lay under only a sheet and wondered if tomorrow would be cooler. Alas for some far-off times when I remember so to have heard it!"[33]

The Tombs, a mammoth stone mausoleum right on the street, was a miserable prison. It was built to hold about two hundred prisoners but usually was filled with four hundred or more. There was an inner prison for males connected to an outer prison that ringed it for females and boys. The two prisons were connected by what inmates called the "bridge of sighs," representing your sighs as you were taken into it. The buildings, which took up an entire city block, were damp all year long and badly ventilated. Prisoners often suffered from illnesses brought on by the cold and stale air. The male prison was an ill-designed, narrow jail with four stories of cells, one on top of the other, badly ventilated, with a single small window filled with iron bars to bring in minimal light. The cells overlooked a high atrium.

The outer prison, for women and boys, also contained a dozen or so spacious, well-appointed cells with large windows that overlooked the streets and had far more light. These were rented to convicts who could afford to pay extra money for more comfort and relative quiet and separation from the coarser general population. These usually contained corrupt politicians, counterfeiters, and merchants convicted of business fraud or the wealthy convicted of any number of crimes. The Tombs also contained a "Bummers' Room," which was a very large holding cell for those tossed into the jail for drunkenness and public disorder. They usually stayed but one night. Several police courts, with judges, were in the Tombs for the administration of rapid justice to the hordes of overnight convicts.

It was, those incarcerated there claimed, a monument to the collapse of the city. Journalist George Foster, who once spent a month there, called it "a redhot furnace of corruption, bribery, theft, burglary, murder, prostitution, and delirium tremens [where] the very air is rarefied with crime." He added that it "was filled with drunken men and women, found helpless in the street, with night-brawlers and disturbers of the public peace, and with young boys and girls who have been caught asleep on cellar doors or are suspected of the high crime of stealing junk bottles and old iron. The very lowest and most brutal form of human depravity may here be seen in all its horrors."[34]

Charles Dickens was an authority on rotting prisons from his days in London, but he was thunderstruck when he was taken to the Tombs. "Do you thrust people into holes such as these?" he asked. "Do men and women against whom no crime is proved lie here all night in perfect darkness surrounded by . . . noisome vapors . . . and breathing this filthy and offensive stench? Why, such indecent and disgusting dungeons would bring disgrace upon the most despotic empire in the world!"[35]

Many Americans agreed with Dickens. Senator William Seward was appalled by the jails of the city and state. "New York penitentiaries often exhibit scenes revolting to humanity; and many a youthful prisoner, instead of being subjected to salutary discipline, becomes more depraved," he wrote.[36]

One area of law enforcement that irked all was the sentencing of young boys and girls, some just ten and eleven years old, to the Tombs. One boy who beat up the owner of the *Atlas* was sent there for thirty days. More usually, judges sent children off to the House of Refuge for a few weeks or months. An example was Joseph Solomon, who stole a collection of India rubber goods from a downtown store and was caught by the proprietor. A magistrate sent him off to the House of Refuge.[37]

Many reformers saw the Tombs, and other jails, as useless. "Society . . . seek[s] to protect itself from [crime] by the incalculable expense of bolts, bars, the gallows, watch-houses, police courts, constables, and 'Egyptian tombs,' " complained Lydia Child in the *Anti-Slavery Standard*.[38]

Men and women hated being locked up in the Tombs, and many attempted to escape, some using complicated schemes. One man used a bent utensil to remove several stone blocks from the wall of his cell, but the noise he made on the final block awakened the man in the cell below him, who alerted the guards, who stopped the escape.[39]

The Tombs itself was a cauldron of corruption. Constables who found money stolen from people returned it in a court inside the Tombs, but only half of it. They pocketed the other half. Many of those taken to the Tombs complained that they not only had to pay fines but had to pay fees for the constable who arrested them, and usually a bribe to a constable for a good recommendation to the sentencing judge. These prisoners who had committed a single crime were forced into a string of them.

Women who were not prostitutes but committed a crime of some sort were dumped into jail with whores and had to listen to the "drunken, bloated, diseased white and black women cursing and blaspheming," wrote George Foster.[40] The Tombs and other, smaller city jails were so overcrowded that jailers put dozens of women in the hallways, where they slept curled up next to each other, leaning against the cold bars of jail cells. Guards tiptoed through their sleeping bodies to reach other parts of the prison. It was not until 1841 that the Common Council voted to clear out two large rooms where debtors had been held and turn them over to the women prisoners so that they could enjoy some comfort.[41]

The massive overcrowding and poor health conditions caused the city to institute the Prison Association of New York in 1844. It was a reform organization that sent its members to visit prisons to ensure proper care for inmates and to investigate inmates' claims of unfair imprisonment. They conducted investigations and interviewed prisoners. By the late 1860s, the Prison Association had obtained releases for over six thousand prisoners and convinced judges to free more than seven thousand others jailed on a first offense. The members of the association also helped prisoners who were released in obtaining food, housing, and a job. Between 1844 and 1869 they aided 156,000 inmates or ex-inmates.[42]

The city's newspapers campaigned for prison reform, too; the *Sun* was the first, calling for improvements at and eventually the closing of Bridewell, a City Hall Park prison for local debtors.[43]

Within ten years of the Tombs' opening, prison administrators admitted that it and other city jails had failed in their goal of rehabilitating the incarcerated. They did punish people who had committed crimes, but these men and women were just released and drifted back to a life of crime in the city. Recidivism rates were high, too, and the idea of reforming the great mass of criminals through jail time and facility programs failed and failed badly.[44]

All New Yorkers despised killers, whether men in bare-knuckled fights or men with knives or guns. One wrote that a murderer "must have had a heart seared and blackened by the fiercest fires of hell, and an arm nerved to steady firmness by the most infernal hatred and revenge." Walt Whitman said that "there sometimes occur cases of murder so horrible, that the universal indignation of humanity rises up against them and cries out for the blood of the homicide." Editors at the *Sun* made the same charge.[45]

The rapid increase in crime and murder in New York City defied the reduction of murder and mayhem that was sweeping much of the world in the 1830s, '40s, and '50s. The countries of England, Germany, and Italy all experienced significant drops in crime and murder rates from 1830 to 1865, but the United States did not, and in New York City they soared. The difference, some have said, was the bolstering of political democracy in Europe in those years, more opportunities for formerly disenfranchised people to vote, and stronger state, regional, and central governments. Citizens of those countries were pleased that the governments responded to their plights, and that sense of security and faith toned down their anger, and that toned down criminal activity. People in those countries had their faith in their nations not only restored but strengthened by far-ranging sets of laws that gave all the people more power and control in the governmental system.

Just the opposite happened in America. The government of much promise under Presidents Washington, Adams, Jefferson, Madison, and Monroe had been badly battered by huge land acquisition and ever-exploding growth in population, especially in the cities and especially in New York. The federal government could not keep up with it, and neither could the cities.

And by the 1840s, America had entered a new and very different era. By the end of the 1830s, all of the heroes of the American Revolution had died (President Monroe's death in 1830 was cause for mass funerals and somber ceremonies throughout the land). The founding era was over, and the next era, an era of land expansion, transportation development, hordes of immigrants, and lots of crime, had begun. No one in New York, or the United States, knew how to manage that new era, and people were scared.

Many believed the crime wave would be halted if more criminals were hanged. One writer in the *Tribune*, "T.L.," said to be a university professor, insisted that people who killed had been taken over by the spirit of witches. He then noted that the killing of witches had been authorized by the Bible. Therefore, he insisted, all found guilty of murder had to be hanged.[46]

Public hangings had been held in New York for nearly two hundred years, always with deterrence as a goal, but it never worked. Murders kept increasing, not decreasing. What would stop the murders? And when?

People also wondered about criminal sentences. New York judges were overly harsh in sentencing felons. They believed that long terms of incarceration would deter others from committing crimes and end the interest in crime of those jailed. American and New York prison sentences were generally two to three times as long as similar sentences in England. Sentences varied, too. Ed Thompson was sent to prison for two years for a third-degree burglary in the spring of 1841, but just an hour later that same judge gave a woman, Ann Sharp, only six months in jail for beating up and attempting to kill Charles Kelley. One judge gave an Irish defendant forty years for the theft of six cents, but an hour later he released a man charged with felonious assault. Emma Francis was sent to the Tombs for three long years for attempting to kill a man. Henry Henecker was sentenced to prison for six long months just for stealing a pair of boots; a week later another man stole a pair of shoes but was put in jail for only thirty days. Two teenagers were jailed for thirty days for stealing two geese from a neighbor. A neighborhood butcher's dog bit a child. The child's father went to the police, and the police put down the dog. The butcher, furious at the death of his beloved pet, found the father, pulled out one of his long butcher's knives, grabbed him by the neck, and slit his throat with the knife, nearly killing him. The butcher received only a five-hundred-dollar fine. Others were sent to the Tombs after committing unbelievable thefts, which they clearly believed they would get away with. One man appeared in court in the spring of 1841 charged with stealing a four-foot-high barrel of oil and brazenly rolling it through the middle of city streets until he was finally spotted by a constable. A New Yorker named Christopher Brennan was sent to jail for stealing the same watch twice. He stole it from one man and sold it to another. A short time later, he trailed the second man and stole it from him, too. Steve Gordon and Alex Stewart were sent to jail for selling brass watches as gold ones.

One man stole a fireman's coat worth four dollars and was sent to jail for three years. George Thomas stole two coats worth a total of fifty-six dollars and was sent to prison for two years. Henry Gilliam was given two years for stealing a half ton of coal. George Cisco was given six months for stealing a single set of iron castings. Ben Reynolds stuck his hand into his boss's money drawer and pulled out a small wad of bills; the judge gave him six months. And then there were strange thefts, such as the one by Nicolas Davis, who was jailed in 1852 for stealing fifty pounds of butter. There were even stranger defenses. A man was arrested for sneaking into the backyard of a woman and examining a dozen or so shirts drying on a clothesline. He picked one out, shoved it under his coat, and ran away, only to be arrested a short time later. His defense? "I only stole one!" he told the officer.[47]

There were bizarre crime stops. One elderly, well-dressed dandy stood on a Broadway street corner and, in broad daylight, made sexual remarks to every woman who passed him. The police, alerted by several incensed women, arrested him on charges of making lewd comments.

Thieves hid stolen goods in the strangest places. One man looted a jewelry store and shoved a necklace into his boot so that no one would see it. Later that night a suspicious cop asked him to remove his boots, and the necklace tumbled out. Another man slit open the lining of his pants and shoved wads of stolen bills inside, carefully sewing the pants back up. Police noticed that the bottom of his pants seemed loaded with something and arrested him; they quickly found the slit.[48]

Criminals stole odd items. Teenager John Pigret was sent to the House of Refuge for stealing one hundred ornate plates with stanzas of an elaborate "Philosophy of Marriage" painted on them.[49]

Did some harsh sentences deter crime? Over the next twenty years, crime soared.[50]

The hordes of criminal cases that tumbled into the courts were often interspersed with unusual delights, such as the case of Isaac Steinberg. He had romanced Delia Phillips for months and promised to marry her, but refused to set a date. Tired of being put off, she sued him for breach of promise, probably hoping that the prospect of going to jail would get him to marry her. The judge did sentence him to jail, but Steinberg still steadfastly refused to marry Delia and went off to one of the city prisons. She and her relatives visited him there several times. As her impassioned pleas for marriage grew, Stenberg's ability to put up with life in jail diminished. He finally gave in, and they were married—by the judge who threw him in jail and in that same courtroom.[51]

On some days no arrests were made. On those days James Gordon Bennett joked that "the police offices yesterday were as quiet as could be desired by the public and the magistrates."[52]

The rapidly rising crime rate, the street gangs, and the hordes of street urchins who worked as pickpockets convinced many New Yorkers that there was evil in their streets. "Every fresh event . . . should remind our citizens that we are in this city over the crust of a volcano. . . . There is in every large city, and especially in this, a powerful 'dangerous class' who care nothing for our liberty or civilization . . . who burrow at the roots of society, and only come forth . . . in times of disturbance, to plunder and prey," wrote one New Yorker.[53]

Charles Loring Brace called New York's street people "young burglars and murderers, the garroters and rioters, the thieves and flash-men . . . ruffians." He said that all of them, from twelve-year-old pickpockets to forty-five-year-old killers, were the worst criminals in the world. Comparing them to European lawbreakers, he wrote, "They rifle a bank, where English thieves pick a pocket; they murder, where European *prolétaires* cudgel or fight with fists; in a riot, they begin what seems about to be the sacking of a city, where English rioters would merely batter policemen, or smash lamps," and added that "the murder of an unoffending old man . . . is nothing to them." He might have added, too, that New York had the youngest killers in the world; the number of killers between the ages of fourteen and seventeen was five times as high as the national average.[54]

So many people believed in the "dangerous class" of criminals that they were afraid to do much of anything. They were so afraid that *Harper's Weekly* published a cartoon of a crowded city omnibus, with a woman and her daughter reluctant to get on it. It was a "car crowded with murderers and thieves," the cartoonist wrote derisively. The city ordered a study of the crime rate and found that not only had crime risen, but so had the fear of crime.[55]

Visitors to the city seemed to be fascinated by the omnibus, the horse-drawn carriage that held twelve to fifteen people and followed planned routes. "Carriages may go two miles. Take all of these stages, west, north and east and they exceed 70, & from the cheapness of the fare are always filled," said John Pintard in 1833.[56]

The ferries that left the Battery for Brooklyn, Staten Island, and New Jersey intrigued people, too. They drew enormous crowds of people that created traffic jams. About forty-four million people rode them each year. A foreigner visiting New York said that the crowd on the shore around the ships was immense. "Troops of friends, assembled to take leave, were jostled by tradesmen, hotel keepers and hackney coachmen, urging the payment of their accounts, and by newsmen disposing of papers wet from the printing press squeezing among carts, wagons and wheelbarrows filled with luggage," said one man. Silently slipping throughout the crowd were dozens of professional pickpockets, who treasured large, tight, noisy crowds like that.[57]

Many of the cartmen, easily lost in the sea of people, were delivering stolen goods in their carts, hidden under blankets or boxes and unnoticed by anyone. The cartmen were often part of a ring of seven to twelve people that operated twenty-four hours a day to steal, store, and sell stolen property.[58]

George Templeton Strong loved to walk the streets of the city at

night, after the sun drifted over the horizon, but was appalled at the
sights of the evening. He smirked at the rivers of New Yorkers he found
standing in front of saloons or shops and filling the intersections.
"Whores and blackguards make up about two-thirds of the throng,"
he snorted.[59]

Some city dwellers fled to the country. One man who moved to
Connecticut, fed up with crime and the bungling police, complained
about "the increase of crime, the ferocity and frequency of assaults on
private citizens at night in this city" and said that his friends were
buying guns for protection.[60]

Those who stayed in the city complained that *anybody* could be the
victim of a grievous crime. Ask Catherine Burns. Eight months pregnant, Burns was nearly beaten to death by William Johnson, an
acquaintance, who repeatedly hit her over the head and shoulders
with a large hickory stick.[61]

The invention of the Colt revolver resulted in an increase in
crime and a change in the way it was conducted. Surveys show that by the
mid-1840s about 30 percent of all murders were committed with the
new handgun, sold to the public for just twelve dollars (today guns figure
in about 65 percent of all murders). Ironically, the new guns provided
local newspapers with thousands of dollars in revenue from Colt and,
later, others who manufactured the guns and sold the weapons through
newspapers not only for protection but as symbols of both masculinity
and success in New York City and America generally.[62]

The guns were dangerous for several reasons. Men determined to
kill themselves now had an easy method to carry out their wish. Others
were accidentally killed or badly wounded when guns misfired. The
poet John Greenleaf Whittier was standing on a street when a gun in
the hands of a small boy nearby went off. The bullet hit Whittier in
the face and exited through his neck, knocking him to the ground and
nearly killing him. A middle-aged man in Manhattan was showing his
young lover how to load a gun in his bedroom. The gun went off accidentally, and the bullet hit the woman in the chest, killing her.[63]

Social trouble contributed to the galloping crime rate. One of the anomalies of life in New York in the era was the disproportion of young, single men with little to do with their free time. In the era, about 40 percent of men were still single by the age of thirty-five. They had no wife to discipline them and keep them home at night, no children to whom they owed a responsibility as a parent. Without traditional marital and family responsibilities, they had no ties to traditional community life, and many of them tumbled into the streets of the city and wound up at whorehouses, bars, and gambling casinos where they drank heavily and added to the huge numbers of men arrested for drunkenness and disorderly conduct. They also plunged into fights inside saloons or in the streets and alleys nearby, becoming the perpetrators or victims of assault-and-battery crimes.

Many men went looking for trouble, armed with a rock or bottle or bludgeon. Walter Hunt accidentally encountered a man with whom he was angry on the staircase of a building. He was carrying a cane, so he looked at the man, looked down at the cane, raised it, and proceeded to thrash the man with his cane for several minutes, knocking him to the floor. The man bled all over the staircase and nearly died.[64]

The 1840s and 1850s were an era when men, particularly young men, saw fistfights as a defense of their honor and a symbol of their manhood. Beating up someone was a badge of honor in New York.[65] Fisticuffs were common among older men and even among distinguished older men. All New Yorkers remembered the day that the famous stage actor Edwin Forrest, angry at the attention the poet Nathaniel P. Willis paid to his wife, rushed up behind Willis on a busy street and attacked him. Forrest knocked him to the ground and then proceeded to beat him senseless with his cane, pushing off anyone who tried to interfere. The public was disgusted with the masculinity fights. Walt Whitman said that they did not build manhood; they just brought about injuries and bleeding for no good reason.[66]

The teenage boys, especially the immigrants, were worse than the men. Crowds gathered around men and boys fighting, but no one broke up the brawls. All just watched for entertainment. People who saw a fight as something noble were doubly prone to engage in one if they were drunk, and did. The city rapidly became a cesspool of unattached young men, drinking and fighting and winding up in the crime statistics, which grew as the years went by.[67]

The onslaught of crime, starting with the Jewett murder in 1836, was not quiet. Murders were extremely violent, rapes brutal, and robberies messy and raucous. As the 1830s rolled into the 1840s, the settings for a criminal world in the streets of New York grew—more prostitutes, worse gambling, prolonged drinking and drunken bar fights, pickpockets, and extreme poverty. These sins invaded other cities, too. A writer at the *Chicago Tribune* wrote of "the proximate incitements to theft and violence . . . [namely] drinking, gambling and prostitution."[68]

The relentless rise in crime in these years helped to break down the citizenry's historic reluctance to embrace a standing army or a police force. No one supported a new police force more than Walt Whitman.

People listened to Whitman, even though many had mixed feelings about him. Some thought him crude as a writer, as crude as many of the ruffians he wrote about. One critic said that he showed "the quality of the celebrated New York 'rough' full of muscular and excessively virile energy, full of animal blood, masterful, striding to the front rank, allowing none to walk before him, full of rudeness and recklessness, talking and acting his own way, utterly regardless of other people's ways." Others saw the tall, thin, bearded writer who always kept his shirt collar open and wore a slightly floppy, dark-colored hat as not just a penny scribbler but a deep thinker and street-corner philosopher who found remarkable ways to write about city life.[69]

None saw him as clearly as he saw himself. "Tall, large, rough-looking man, in a journeyman carpenter's uniform. Course, sanguine complexion, strong, gristly, grizzled beard; singular eyes, of a semitransparent, indistinct light blue, and with that sleepy look that comes when the lid rests halfway down over the pupil; careless, lounging gait," he wrote of himself in *Leaves of Grass*.[70]

When he became the editor of the *Aurora* in 1842, he started wearing a more formal frock coat and tie, used a cane, switched to a high hat, and sported a boutonniere. He arrived at the newspaper office around 11:00 A.M., stayed until shortly after noon, and then strolled lower Broadway and the Battery for an hour or so. He loved that area of New York. "The crowd and the jam were tremendous. Hundreds of splendid women and fashionable men filled the pave, and between the curb stones whirled one incessant clang of omnibuses, carriages and other vehicles," he wrote in the spring of 1842.[71]

William Sutton, a printer for Whitman in 1842, said that he would write his editorial in "a beautiful hand, plain as a pikestaff, punctuating it all the way through, so that the compositor only had to follow copy." He added that if anybody changed a single comma of his work they would be chastised severely by Whitman.

Whitman had an unshakable faith in newspapers, which he saw as the great defenders of freedom, and once wrote that he wished for "a newspaper-ruled people." He earned the praise of the people and rival newspaper editors. The editor of the *Brooklyn Evening Star* said the *Eagle* under Whitman had "a brilliant lot of editorials," and the *Tribune*'s Greeley snorted that it "was well got up." Charles Eliot Norton said of him that he was "a compound of New England transcendentalist and New York rowdy."[72]

By the time his *Leaves of Grass* was published in 1855, Whitman had served as the editor of eight New York newspapers, written for twenty, and put together small collections of fiction writing based on his newspaper work.

The poet/journalist had written a few short sentimental stories for the *Long Island Patriot* when he was twelve. Then, a few years later, he wrote some short stories for the *New-York Mirror* and was thrilled. "I remember with what half-suppress'd excitement I used to watch for the big, fat, red-faced, slow moving very old English carrier who distributed the 'Mirror' in Brooklyn; and when I got one, opening and cutting the leaves with trembling fingers. How it made my heart double-beat to see *my piece* on the pretty white paper," he wrote in his journal.[73]

He spent several years as a schoolteacher on Long Island before moving to Manhattan in 1841 to work as a reporter. Whitman wrote for the *Democratic Review* (he was a rock-hard Democrat) and the journal *Brother Jonathan* in 1841 and 1842 and then in the spring of 1842 became the editor/writer of the penny sheet the *New York Aurora,* where he really established himself as an observer of the city—and of its crime and constables. His bosses there said he was a bold and original writer.

Fired from the *Aurora* in a dispute with the owners, he went to New Orleans and spent two years as a crime reporter for the *Crescent* and then returned to New York. He moved back to Brooklyn in 1846 and worked for several years as editor/writer for the *Brooklyn Daily Eagle*. He toiled as a journalist by day and as a poet and fiction writer at night. Whitman churned out four pieces of fiction, including the novel *Franklin Evans,* and nineteen poems, plus keeping a near-daily journal of his life. His hardscrabble, authentic journalism helped him become the original poet he was always praised as being, and many of his newspaper stories became part of his poetry later, as did his journal notes. Sometimes he reprinted his newspaper work word for word, or paraphrased it, in his poems. As an example, his newspaper stories of fires and firemen turned up in the lines beginning "I am the mash'd fireman with breast-bone broken. . . ." Another penny press story about how butchers' helpers in the city celebrated at night after a hard day at work was rewritten into a poetic stanza.[74] "If it had not been for his journalism years, Whitman would not have become the Whitman of *Leaves of Grass,*" said one scholar.[75]

Whitman contended that nothing was as beautiful as New York's new tree-filled parks that were sprinkled throughout the city. "It is a pleasant thing to see well-dressed crowds of men and women with smiling faces, promenading our streets or pubic grounds. And the little children! The fat, fresh, clean little children—it is better than splendor to look at them and their gambols. . . . A man may look a few rods about him and his gaze not be intercepted by brick walls and chimneys and fences," he wrote.[76]

New Yorkers made it a point to spend as much time as possible in the city's parks, such as the Battery and City Hall Park, to get away from the overbearing stench of city life. The streets were teeming with people and horses, crushing into each other. Hundreds of food vendors filled avenues such as Broadway and the Bowery, peddling their exotic-smelling foods to anyone with enough money to buy them. The air smelled of the foul breath of drunks who had just been thrown out of crowded saloons, of thick, wet horse manure dropped here and there, of the black, cloudy pollution spewed forth from the new steamships, of the garbage stacked up high in bags in front of stores and in alleys, its decaying food smells wafting through the air, nearly poisoning it. The parks, with thick forests of green trees, gently rolling hills, deep ponds, streams and walkways, and long and lovely gardens, was an escape from all of that, a paradise of fresh air and fresh feelings. They were, many said, the "lungs of the city," and through them people could breathe God's clean air. "More than a million lungs are hard at work day and night," wrote someone for the *New York Daily Times*, "respiring the city's air, many of them in lanes crowded to excess and buildings bursting with repletion. We have no competent breathing place." The triumph of these parks over congested city life led to the planning of Central Park in the 1850s and its opening in 1873.[77]

And what was the very first problem city planners and officials encountered in Central Park lands, and then within the park when it opened? Crime. Ruffians and thieves accosted park visitors, day and night, and became such an ugly presence and danger that when the park was officially opened it employed a security force of trained "policemen" entirely separate from the New York City police force, which the park's managers did not trust.

Moral reform leaders argued that it was not enough to continually help the victims of crime and sin—the drunkards and card players— but that the city had to build a new world in which they would not fall prey to temptation. Reformers were sick of funding almshouses and wanted a world in which there simply were no poor who needed them. Thomas Eddy was one reformer who embraced that feeling. He said of the poor that he was "tired seeing them in their distress, and it appears to me more wise to fix upon every profitable plan to prevent their poverty and misery."[78]

To achieve that goal, and to wipe out sin and crime, churches and civic organizations, old and new, flooded New York. The city was home to dozens of churches and synagogues and a number of new missionary groups funded by the established ministers of the "New Light" evangelical churches. Reform groups included the Society for the Prevention of Pauperism, the American Bible Society, the New York and American Religious Tract Societies, the Female Moral Reform Society, the Hebrew Benevolent Society, the Roman Catholic Orphan Asylum, the American Sisters of Charity, the Episcopalian New York Mission Council, the American Home Mission Society, the New York City Temperance Society, the New York Magdalen Society, and others.

The leaders of the moral reform societies, such as Lydia Finney, argued that the foundation of crime in New York was drunkenness. Men became inebriated and engaged in rowdy bar brawls or went home, stumbling all the way, and beat up their wives and children. Drunkenness was a persistent problem. The study mentioned earlier that tracked crime in New York from 1845 to 1853 showed that of 257,738 arrests, 63,944, or one-quarter, were on charges of intoxication. Another 18,217 charges were filed for men and women who were intoxicated and were also guilty of disorderly conduct. Altogether, arrests for being drunk totaled 82,161, or 31 percent of all the arraignments in town. (The drinking deluge was not endemic to New York; in 1858, two-thirds of Philadelphia arrests were for drunkenness and disorderly conduct.) If men did not drink, then these crimes would not take place. It was a strong argument, and it fueled the various temperance societies in the city. Reverend Leonard Bacon, of the New York Temperance Society, said that "more than 10,000 men will be made drunkards in one year."[79]

Drunks were everywhere. Unruly, lawless crowds full of them

surged through the city every day, paying no attention to the constables and roaming wherever they pleased. Dozens of men arrived at the traditional New Year's Day public reception at the home of Mayor Cornelius Lawrence in 1837 intent on stirring up trouble. "The rabble . . . use his house as a Five Points Tavern," complained Philip Hone, who was there. "Every scamp who has bawled out 'Huzza for Lawrence!' or 'Down with the Whigs!' considers himself authorized to use him and his house and furniture at his pleasure; to wear his hat in his presence; to smoke and spit upon his carpet; to devour his beef and turkey and to wipe his greasy fingers upon the curtains and get drunk with his liquor." Indeed, the men rushed the tables and liquor cabinets as soon as they swept into the home. They shoved each other and argued loudly. A furious Mayor Lawrence had to summon constables to help him chase the brigands out of his home and lock all the doors and windows so they could not return.[80]

Mayor Lawrence was popular. When he was elected, he rode into the city across New York Harbor from Perth Amboy on a large steamboat festooned with flags and red, white, and blue bunting. An exuberant band played for him when his ships docked. Lawrence led a parade of hundreds of well-dressed followers through the streets of New York past large and cheering throngs. It was a glorious day.[81]

Everybody had a solution for drunkenness. Close all the bars. Enforce the drinking age limits. Attach surcharges to drinks. Get ministers, priests, and rabbis to give more sermons denouncing drinking because it leads to crime. One popular proposal was to make sure all bars were licensed (one-sixth were not) and to indict any bartender who served alcohol to men who were already obviously drunk. None of these worked, though.[82]

Later, a disgruntled Hone said that the city government of his friend the mayor and the entire electoral process had no future because of the decline of the city. "Scenes of violence, disorder and riot have taught us in this city that universal suffrage will not do for large communities," he wrote, telling friends that in country villages a "black sheep" is easily spotted, but in huge metropolises they never are—and are not stopped.[83]

Hone told people, too, that the night constables not only seemed powerless but were. For years, a law prevented night watchmen from conducting investigations or making arrests for any crime except one that they saw committed right in front of them. The day watchmen, however, could make arrests and conduct investigations. The irony of it was that the only exception to the rule was that a night watchman could make an arrest if he could get a day watchman to make the arrest with him.[84]

Outside, as the dark night deepened around ex-mayor Hone's neighborhood, all was quiet. A few blocks away on the Bowery, the bars were full, and people drank everything in sight.

CHAPTER SIX

Lydia Child, Crime, and Chaos

There arrived at this port, during the month of May, 15,825 passengers. All Europe is coming across the ocean; all that part at least who cannot make a living at home; and what shall we do with them? They increase our taxes, eat our bread, and encumber our streets, and not one in twenty is competent to keep himself.

—Former mayor Philip Hone, June 1836

One of the most fervent crusaders against crime was Lydia Child. The reformer was thirty-eight when she joined many other new arrivals in New York City. She was a plain-looking, conservatively dressed lady with an angular face and square chin. She wore her hair in a tight bun, as did most of the female reformers, and had thin eyes. She came from Boston, where she had become one of the most revered women writers in the country and a leader of both the antislavery and the women's movements.

The *National Anti-Slavery Standard,* based in New York, was looking for a new editor, and Child, a prolific writer of essays and novels and familiar to all, came highly recommended. She became the first woman to serve as editor of a national antislavery publication.

. . .

Child was just one of dozens of hardworking reformers who had moved to New York.

Another was John McDowall, a Princeton divinity student who became a missionary. He and his followers formed the New York Moral Reform Society and attacked the depravity in the city in an organized way, day by day, week by week, month by month.

Reformers like McDowall said that hookers paid off police officers with sex or money not to arrest them, and johns paid them off, too. The constables, he charged, were just as guilty as the hookers and johns in committing so many crimes due to prostitution. In one of his columns, McDowall even suggested that the brothels and their madams were responsible for murders in the city and that they "ought to be executed" themselves.[1]

He was later backed up by Police Commissioner Joel Erhardt, who wrote in 1879, speaking of the 1840s and 1850s, that police captains had received many "contributions" from the heads of brothels, and that in 1879 it was still an ongoing practice. Officials on a police corruption panel that sat in 1894 and 1895, the Lexow Commission, agreed. Speaking of the pre–Civil War era, Clarence Lexow wrote that prostitution was "fostered and protected by the police of the city" and that the police had "a partnership . . . in the traffic [of prostitutes] resulting in the largest part of the resulting profit." Reformer Frank Moss told the Lexow Commission that the police knew everything about prostitution and gambling and simply, for a bribe, looked the other way. "It knows every prostitute, it knows every house, and no prostitute, no gambler, can live for a moment in any place in the city without being known and his haunt being known. The police are just as competent to put their hands on a disorderly person in a flat as they are in a whorehouse," said Moss, adding that police were paid off to protect whorehouses. Around the turn of the twentieth century, many reformers testified and wrote that the corruption of the police in the 1880s and 1890s followed a long pattern that extended back to the pre–Civil War era.[2]

Madams who ran houses of prostitution in the 1880s and 1890s testified that they had to pay an initiation fee of several hundred dollars for each brothel to a police captain or patrolman, then begin monthly fee payments of from twenty-five to fifty dollars. They did this, they said, because their predecessors going back to the 1840s had done the same thing. The managers of lottery shops and gambling casinos gave the same testimony and said it had been the cost of doing business since the early decades of the nineteenth century.[3]

Reformers had support in the press, where editors believed not only that prostitutes were victims of society but that prostitution caused significant crime in the city. "If the object of the New York authorities were to increase prostitution and depravity, they could not better accomplish it than by their present policy towards the unfortunate class that everybody endeavors to ignore, but who suffer and cause more guilt, crime and misery than even bad rum can justly be held accountable for," wrote Walt Whitman, who added that the police arrested whores and then tossed them into the Tombs with the thieves they serviced.[4]

One of those women sent to the Tombs, and then transferred to a different jail, was Amelia Norman, an attractive young working girl arrested for the attempted murder of a wealthy man who had seduced her, promised marriage, and then abandoned her. She stabbed him in a rage. She seemed to be just like all the city's other prostitutes, everyone said.

Many of Amelia's fellow hookers were furious about the arrest, and so was reformer Lydia Child. To the editor of the *National Anti-Slavery Standard,* Amelia was symbolic of the sexual plague that had attacked New York and all of the United States. She saw this as a typical case of men being able to do anything and women having no chance to protect themselves. Any woman who struck out against a man who sexually abused her was not comforted but bounced off the streets into a cold, dank prison. Child visited Norman often in jail, got her friend John Hopper to find her a good lawyer, started a committee to raise money for her legal defense, and covered her trial in the pages of the *Standard*. In all of her writing about the case, Child explained what the prosecution always did in trials like Norman's—paint the woman defendant as a whore in order to deprive her of any sympathy from the jury. Ergo, Child said, all women who ever had sex with a man, for love or money, had to be whores, which was not so. It was Amelia who was the victim in this case, not the man she stabbed.[5]

"I had no doubt that if all deeply injured women were to undertake to redress their wrongs in this bad way, there would be a huge pile of dead citizens. I even thought it not impossible that some of the honorable court themselves might be among the missing," she wrote in one of her several incendiary "Letters from New-York" columns.[6]

Thanks to the hard work of the lawyer Child obtained (she gave him themes to use in the case, too), her public writing about the case, and her defense of oppressed women, the jury ruled in favor of Amelia and freed her. The editor did not stop there, though. She took Amelia home with her, nursed her, fed her, gave her some new clothes, and let her stay for a few months. Then she found her a job in New England and paid for her transportation there. Later, she wrote letters of recommendation for her to obtain other jobs.

Amelia was an example, Child told friends, of how badly "criminals" were treated by the law enforcement and justice system. The rich go free, and the indigent, no matter how innocent they might be, go to jail. "When I look at this poor, misguided girl, now so useful, and improving daily in her view of things," she wrote later of Norman, "and think what she would have been, had they sent her to Sing Sing, my feelings with regard to society's treatment of criminals grow stronger and stronger."[7]

Child and many other reformers, especially anticrime advocates, did not believe that the city government of New York was committed to their goals, and so they went to Albany to lobby for changes in New York City laws through the state legislature. This well-intentioned campaign backfired because the new state laws often conflicted with city laws, and city fathers resented both the reformers and state legislators for meddling with city business.[8]

"The world would be in a happier condition if legislators spent half as much time and labor to prevent crime as they do to punish it," a frustrated Child wrote after one of her many prison visits.[9]

Amelia Norman was freed in the middle of yet another tidal wave of immigrants that arrived on ship transports in New York and stayed in the city. The surge of immigrants arriving daily scared most New Yorkers. Hone, who had watched them walk down the gangways of hundreds of ships during his lifetime, was angry with the relentless hordes. As an example, in the 1830s, four times as many immigrants arrived in the port of New York as had arrived during the previous decade. By the early 1850s, more than 300,000 immigrants a year would arrive in New York City. The increases in immigrants in other seaports and river ports, such as Philadelphia and Richmond, Virginia, were the same. "There arrived at this port, during the month of May, 15,825 passengers. All Europe is coming across the ocean; all that part at least who cannot make a living at home; and what shall we do with them? They increase our taxes, eat our bread, and encumber our streets, and not one in twenty is competent to keep himself," New Yorker Hone complained in June 1836.[10]

Added a French visitor, Jean Ampère, "The flood arrives without interruption."[11]

The new arrivals were of all shapes and sizes. "The pavements present men of every land and color, red, black, yellow, and white, in every variety of costume and beard, and ladies, beautiful and ugly, richly dressed," noted a woman.[12]

Hone and Ampère were angry not only at the arrival of so many immigrants but at their attitude. "They are scarcely a year in the country before they pretend to be equal to our born citizens. I should have no objections to their coming here, provided they would remain content

to become servants—the only condition, by the by, they are fit for: but
when they come without a cent in their pockets, pretending to enjoy
the same privileges as our oldest and most respectable citizens, my
blood boils with rage," one man said.[13]

Many New Yorkers felt that the endless wave of immigrants from
Europe caused the crime wave, that European states bundled up their
most notorious criminals and sent all of them to New York, just as
the British had done back in the early years of the eighteenth century.
In the 1840s, people often stumbled upon dead bodies, sometimes
dismembered, near the docks or in lower New York alleys. Men were
murdered for pocket change by cliques of robbers. One German immigrant was killed by robbers as he walked through Battery Park late
one winter night. The murderers then went through his pockets and
collected a total of twelve cents. Angry at their paltry haul, they threw
the man's dead body into the river, where it did not sink but landed on
the ice. "It remained upon the ice, and those who passed along the
battery wall early the next morning saw glaring at them the fixed eyes of
a frozen corpse," said Officer George Walling.[14]

The press called the corpses "raw heads and bloody bones" and
used the expression to underscore the violence of crime. Many of the
dead were immigrants. Many of the people who killed them were
immigrants, too. One study showed that nearly 65 percent of all of
the men arrested for crimes in the 1840s were immigrants, and that
shocked people, as did the previous criminal history of many in their
home countries. The fever to stop the importation of immigrants
who had any kind of criminal record was so high that Whig congressman Henry Seaman introduced a bill in Congress to give city officials
the right to scrutinize the record of all new arrivals and to deport
them back to their homeland if they appeared to be a security risk.

No other immigrant group was despised as much as the Irish
Catholics. Protestants hated them, and the Catholics returned the
favor. New York was ripped apart by a general anti-Catholic feeling,
spurred by Bishop John Hughes's endless speeches insisting that the
Catholics would soon take over the city, and the rough, tough, and

dirt-poor Catholics newly arrived from Ireland, driven to America by the potato famine in the 1840s, would be the army to do it. Hughes and his cadre had a flood of new arrivals—angry Irish arrivals—to join their ranks.

Most native New Yorkers hated the Irish, who seemed to arrive in never-ending boatloads. Between 1845 and 1881, three million Irish fled to America following the potato famine. One million Irish who remained home died during that period of time. To establish the size of that migration, consider that there were three times as many Irish as all of the immigrants that came to America from every other country in the world between 1830 and 1845. Their numbers grew each year. In 1850 alone, 117,000 of them arrived in Gotham. That number grew to 204,000 by the end of the 1850s.[15] City dwellers did not simply fear the Irish but were afraid that as their numbers grew, to about 40 percent of the city population by the late 1850s, they would take over the city government and run the social world. The police saw them as a crime problem. Close to half the prisoners in New York—city and state—were Irish. They would get out of jail and return to their criminal lives, city officials worried. So many Irish were being arrested and tossed into police wagons that the cops soon started calling the vehicles "paddy wagons." Few wanted to help them, either. In the late 1850s, help-wanted signs in store windows and ads in newspapers began to specify "No Irish Need Apply." One job that Irish women did get was that of the domestic maid in homes and apartments. The job was considered lowly and well beneath native women, so they let the Irish do it. The women they worked for, and their husbands, all disdained the Irish. "Thieving rascals . . . who have never done a day's work in their lives," snorted one New Yorker about them.[16]

Hughes and his parish priests did not help matters by telling everyone within earshot that the Catholics wanted state and city taxes to pay for their private parochial schools, but did not want to pay taxes themselves because they chose not to use the public schools. They wanted the lands that churches sat upon given to Holy Mother Church in Rome.

Protestants who believed the preachings of Bishop Hughes genuinely feared the Irish and created as many roadblocks as they could to
deter their success in America. Protestant ire was easy to ignite. They
attacked and desecrated Catholic churches, beat up parishioners,
burned rectories and convents. The Catholics, of course, then retali-
ated. The constables stood by and did little.[17]

The African Americans in New York detested the Irish because
the newly arrived residents from the Emerald Isle worked cheaper
than they did. The Irish laborers eventually drove the blacks out of
New York. The number of African Americans living in the city
dropped from 16,358 in 1840 to 12,472 in 1865.[18]

City fathers did not know how to handle the varied ethnic groups,
just as they did not know how to manage growth or control law enforcement. They should have. Cities in Europe had dealt with those
same problems, especially newly arrived ethnic people who spoke a different language, for hundreds of years, back to ancient Rome and
Athens. New York paid no attention to how those urban areas confronted their problems. They had few studies or histories to read, but
they still could have interviewed hundreds of new arrivals about how
life was in their former cities; they never did so.[19]

The feelings of those who hated the Irish Catholics, or any ethnic
group, were scorned by Whitman and others who saw immigrants as
the strength, not the weakness, of America. "Let them come and welcome!" Whitman said of the new arrivals, noting that the city was already full of poor immigrants. "The more the better. . . . [New York]
wants the wealth of stout poor men who will work."[20]

By the 1840s, too, there was a growing resentment toward the
rich of the city among the working-class laborers and the poor. The rich
glided through town in their lavish horse-drawn carriages, dressed in
the best suits and dresses money could buy, and were often seen in
public with some of their many servants, as the wretched poor on the
streets watched them with resentment in their eyes. That class war
continued into the courts, where the people of New York felt that
they could not get a fair hearing in any dispute with the wealthy or

powerful. The judges there not only sided with the rich but were corrupt to the core as well.

The poor were disliked, too. The downtrodden, many insisted, were responsible for the epidemics of cholera and other diseases that swept through New York in the pre—Civil War period. "Cases are confined as yet to our disgraceful tenement houses and foul side streets," wrote George Templeton Strong. "We are letting [the poor] perish and . . . they will prove their . . . common humanity by killing us with the same disease."[21]

Many blamed the collapse of the churches for crime. People had lost faith, no longer relied on God, and turned to killing and stealing. Others blamed the diminished role of the previously stern father in family life. Dads were no longer just farmers, either. The "new" father of the 1840s and '50s had to work outside the home, in factories and shops, usually six days a week, and was no longer home to discipline his children, who, unsupervised and lured by the temptations of the big city, turned to crime.[22]

What would happen to all of these different classes of criminals? To the people? Where was the future? Where were the tough police that the city needed to combat these multiple crises that all cascaded through the town at the same time?

CHAPTER SEVEN

Faith in the Constables Frays
as the City Implodes

The undeniable imbecility and inefficiency of the police is creating great alarm in the decent and orderly portion of our inhabitants.

—*New York Tribune*, July 10, 1852

The New York police force was a mess. The entire chain of command of politically appointed, untrained, and lazy watchmen was overseen by politicians, who also paid them low wages, making a fee system for chores accomplished necessary. Watchmen, day and night, worked for about 90 cents a day or about $300 a year (that pay would rise to about $1,200 a year twenty years later); captains earned $1.87 per day (this fell to $1.75 for constables and rose to $2.25 for captains). The watchmen were then paid fees on top of their salary. The fees were so high that one group of watchmen signed a petition that stated they did not want a pay increase; they made their money on fees. Fees could mount up, too. The constables were given 25 cents for every warrant they served, 19 cents for each summons, 12 cents for taking a defendant into custody, 25 cents for questioning someone on unpaid bills, 12½ cents for summoning a jury, 12½ cents for each mile traveled for work, 12 cents for notifying a defendant of a trial date, 37 cents for arranging a bail bond, and 12½ cents for each subpoena issued.[1]

The fees amounted to so much extra cash that when the watchmen finally did lobby for a basic daily salary increase in 1831 the Common Council promptly turned them down.

Daytime constables could function like modern policemen, but nighttime constables could not. They could arrest someone for a crime only if they saw him or her commit it. They could conduct an investigation to make an arrest, but only if they did so with a daytime constable; the difficulty was getting one of them to work without a reward or work at night or assume some physical risk. That limited all police work.

The state legislature created another hurdle. It had control over just about all New York City operations and the budget and had retained that power since 1811. Under that authority, it controlled the size of the New York force and, to save money, continually kept it small. No matter what the city wanted to do, it required the approval of a state legislature that met nearly two hundred miles away. At the time that system was put in place, the federal government was just forty years old and still trying to bolster its strength in determining national policies while leaving other powers to the states. The states, in turn, wanted to control government within their borders, and that included control of the cities. That left little control of local government to cities. Control of the cities also increased the power of the political party that was dominant in the state legislature and enabled it to institute more taxes to use for state programs, not city purposes. That lack of home rule made it difficult for cities to function properly. The New York legislature kept power over New York City. Most other state legislatures in that pre–Civil War era gradually gave power to the cities, though, making the governing of them, especially in law enforcement, easier. New York lawmakers did not, and held out against power sharing until it was too late.[2]

Another problem in law enforcement was the public's continued bizarre reluctance to obey orders from the police. A police magistrate,

Charles Christian, wrote an anonymous pamphlet on police reform in 1812 in which he told readers that the residents of New York saw themselves as good Republicans who could supervise themselves and did not need any brutish policemen to tell them what to do.

The city grew to 123,000 inhabitants by 1820, but the numbers of murders and robberies were low. That was because the great invasion of immigrants had not yet started, the street toughs had not risen, poverty had not washed through city streets, the revolver had not been invented, religious and racial hatreds were still at a low boil, the factories had not opened in large numbers, and tenement slums had not yet developed.

By the 1830s, the constables remained an organization of mostly unarmed law enforcers who had no professional training and were physically weak and unable to grapple with criminals. They were unwilling to put down disturbances, too. One watchman tried to do just that in an anti-Catholic riot in 1806, and the rioters killed him. It was a lesson for all.

Everyone made fun of the constables. They wore long, dark coats and leather helmets for protection that looked foolish. The press soon started calling them "leatherheads" or "leather skulls." They were advised to varnish their helmet brims, which were on the back, and the hats became hard and heavy and difficult to wear. Public officials wrung their hands over the constables, the press laughed at them, and the residents of the city feared for their lives because they had such weak protection from the forces that lurked in the night.

They were correct. In the early 1830s, a mob of thieves targeted the police for some late-night mischief. A city council Watch Committee report in that era stated that "the lower part of the city is infested with a gang of robbers who have recently entered at night several watchhouses, committed depredations on the property of the occupants, and succeeded for some time in eluding the vigilance of the police and watch departments."

The inability of the constables to protect themselves, or the town, was obvious to all and a reminder that during the past generations law enforcement had been lax. "Our city has been so long exempt from the horrors of midnight robbery that it is feared that the citizens have relaxed in those precautions necessary for the preservation of their property, and without which, any efforts made by this board must be ineffectual to correct the evil complained of," the report that involved the watch houses concluded.[3]

Yet, despite this overwhelming criticism of the constables, the mayor and his staff seemed quite pleased with them. "The persons so engaged," said the mayor on June 18, 1832, "had always constituted a highly respectable class, with few exceptions, and under the judicious arrangement of their captains, the Watch were becoming constantly more useful, and were entitled to confidence and encouragement." That view, of course, was a major part of the problem.[4]

Constables were more comforters than law enforcers and reveled in caring for those whom they did not protect. A good example was an 1841 incident in which a very drunk old woman, dressed in rags, staggered down a street toward one of the city's small watch houses, or one-man guardhouses, where watchmen sat rather than walking the streets. She fell into the watchman's arms, and he held her tightly as he looked around the neighborhood for assistance. "Thank you kindly, sir, for I should like to go home," she said. A woman who lived on the quiet residential street, her bedroom window open to catch evening breezes, heard the conversation. She saw "the dreary image of the watchhouse, which that poor wretch dreamed was her home. It proved too much for my overloaded sympathies. I hid my face in the pillow and wept," she wrote.[5]

The untrained and rarely supervised constables often acted in amateurish fashion. In an 1836 court case, a judge told a group of constables to go outside the courtroom, open a particular door, and admit six gentlemen who were witnesses for a trial. The constables opened the wrong door, and about sixty ragamuffins ran into the courtroom, shouting loudly, and began to jeer at the judge.

One frustrated man said that "the undeniable imbecility and in-efficiency of the police is creating great alarm in the decent and orderly portion of our inhabitants."[6]

In short, the New York constable was a joke.

New York in the late 1830s, after the Jewett murder and at the start of the great crime wave, was chaotic. It was a city still reeling from the economic distress of the Panic of 1837, the infusion of immigrants, and the antics of the roughnecks in the city's street gangs. The setting was rife for an explosion of lawlessness. "The times are certainly hard. Money is scarce and provisions are dear. Goods won't sell and cus-tomers don't pay, the banks won't discount, stocks are down to nothing and real estate unavailable," wrote Philip Hone, who lost half his for-tune, and real estate value in New York depreciated about $40 million in just six months.[7]

Captain Frederick Marryat, a naval officer from England, was in New York at that time. He was a jovial visitor. "My appearance in New York was very much like bursting into a friend's house with a merry face when there is a death in it," he wrote of the fatalistic feelings of New Yorkers in 1837.[8]

There were many killings in that era, but to many the saddest of all was the murder of the usually homeless and yet quite popular Mc-Donald Clarke, who slept on the lawns of the city's parks. He was an irate, rambunctious, garrulous, probably autistic man who had fallen in love, only to have his lover's mother kidnap her and forbid her to ever see him again. It broke his heart. He roamed city street corners greeting all in an overly friendly way and, wherever he could, spout-ing his poetry. He did so happily, a big smile on his face, eyes wide, his hands always gesturing, inside the salons of the rich and in the alleys of the poorest neighborhoods. Everybody in New York City seemed to know him and love him, and pity him.

"He was as innocent as a child," said reformer Child, who met him twice on the streets, as did just about everybody else. "Often, when he had nothing to give, he would snatch up a ragged, shivering child on the street, carry it to the door of some princely mansion and demand to see the lady of the house. When she would appear, he would say 'Madam, God has made you one of the trustees of his wealth. Take this poor child. Wash it, feed it, clothe it, comfort it—in God's name.' "[9]

Child, like all, was crushed when she learned that Clarke had been put in jail, a common event for the poet, and then killed under mysterious circumstances (the jailers said he drowned in a large puddle of water in his cell; friends said the jailers beat him to death). Even further angered was Walt Whitman, who as a poet knew Clarke well. He was moved to write a poem about Clarke after his strange death that was published in a newspaper. Whitman called him "the poor poet, the eccentric and unfortunate McDonald Clarke."[10]

The high numbers of crimes and the murders of hundreds in New York brought about depression in many residents. None was more morose about all the killings than reformer Child, who saw all the deaths as symbolic of the poisoning of life in New York City. She was especially frazzled after she walked with John Hopper past a pauper's cemetery and a Catholic cemetery on the same afternoon, both across the street from busy neighborhoods. Her emotions were triggered by the rows of tombstones in them. "Bright lights shone through crimson, blue, and green, in the apothecaries' windows, and were reflected in prismatic beauty from the dirty pools in the street. It was like poetic thoughts in the minds of the poor and ignorant; like the memory of pure aspirations in the vicious; like a rainbow of promise, that God's spirit never leaves even the most degraded soul. I smiled as my spirit gratefully accepted this love-token from the outward; and I thanked our heavenly Father for a world beyond this."[11]

Saddened by her barren love life, and despite the close friendship with reform writer and fellow intellectual Margaret Fuller, Child turned more and more of her energy to fighting law enforcement in New York. She was certainly not alone. At the end of 1842, the Common Council voted to form a special committee to study a reorganization of the police force and to solicit suggestions from the city police

magistrates in connection with the idea. That came just a few weeks
after the council restored patrolmen pay cuts that had been voted a year
before.[12]

In 1843, a special report turned in to the Board of Aldermen by a
board subcommittee mentioned the new criminal class, "a large number of persons who are wicked and debased," but put the blame for
chaos in the city squarely on the police force. It said that the police
were inefficient, commanders were ill-prepared for their posts, the
justice system was almost inoperable, and the entire force, appointed
by city officials, was loaded with untrained and ineffectual men who
merely knew the right people. The police in New York, the report concluded, were an absolute disaster, and had been for many years.[13]

One large problem in New York City law enforcement was leadership. High Constable (Chief) Jacob Hays was a big, burly man always
dressed in black pants and a frock coat. He wore a black hat and tied a
white kerchief around his neck. Hays was partially bald and had the
dress and look of a wealthy patrician. He joined the force at the end
of the previous century and continued leading it almost until his death
in 1850. He plunged into daily police work with a passion. Hays not
only solved bank robberies but personally arrested the robbers. He
walked the streets of the city looking for criminals and arrested them
wherever he found them. He once charged off a platform where the
mayor was giving a speech and arrested someone in the crowd whom
the police had sought for months. Hays outdetected the detectives,
outfought the good fighters, outsmarted the smartest constables. He
was a diligent administrator, and he held his job for decades during
the administrations of several mayors from different political parties.
The men who ran Tammany Hall loved him, and so did the people.

The drawback, though, was that Hays was all legend. He was a
lawman in the East like Bat Masterson was in the West—famous, mercu-
rial, brilliant, and known throughout the land. He was no reformer,
though. He was so venerated by officials and the people that no one
pushed him to improve the force. Hays was just Hays, hailed by all.
He could have done a lot to change the nature of the police force as

RICHARD P. ROBINSON.
(From a Photograph.)

Richard Robinson was acquitted in the murder of sophisticated prostitute Helen Jewett. *(From* Recollections of a New York Chief of Police, *George Washington Walling, New York: Caxton Book Concern, Limited, 1887)*

The 1836 murder of gorgeous, sophisticated prostitute Helen Jewett kicked off the mammoth crime wave that swamped New York in the middle of the nineteenth century and highlighted the incompetency of the police. *(From* Recollections of a New York Chief of Police, *George Washington Walling, New York: Caxton Book Concern, Limited, 1887.)*

HELEN JEWETT
(From a Photograph.)

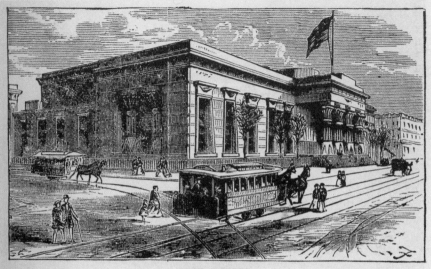

THE TOMBS.

The mammoth Tombs prison, that later became one of the longest used jails in America, filled up an entire city block. It was so large that it not only had separate wings for women and men, but even had courthouses inside of it for arraignments and trials. *(From* Lights and Shadows of New York Life: or, the Sights and Sensations of the Great City, *James D. McCabe, Jr., Philadelphia, Chicago [etc.]: National Publishing Company, 1872)*

A FIVE POINTS RUM SHOP.

The notorious Five Points neighborhood was home to numerous street gangs, houses of prostitution, and large "rum shops" such as this one, where residents went to drink at all hours of the day and night. *(From* Lights and Shadows of New York Life: or, the Sights and Sensations of the Great City, *James D. McCabe, Jr., Philadelphia, Chicago [etc.]: National Publishing Company, 1872)*

A FIRST-CLASS GAMBLING HOUSE.

This first-class gambling emporium with numerous gaming tables and bars was one of many lavish casinos that dotted lower Manhattan in the 1850s. They were rarely raided by the police, who were usually paid off to keep their distance. *(From* Lights and Shadows of New York Life: or, the Sights and Sensations of the Great City, *James D. McCabe, Jr., Philadelphia, Chicago [etc.]: National Publishing Company, 1872)*

George W. Walling

Resigned June 9, 1885.

George Walling, joined the police force as a young patrolman in 1847 and eventually became a captain and, later, the chief of police. *(From* Our Police Protectors: History of the New York Police from the Earliest Period to the Present Time, *Augustine Costello, New York: C. F. Roper & co, 1885)*

Police putting down one of the dozens of riots that plagued the city in the early days of the nineteenth century. *(From* Our Police Protectors: History of the New York Police from the Earliest Period to the Present Time, *Augustine Costello, New York: C. F. Roper & co, 1885)*

Escaping Rioters Surprised by the Police.

Police at a downtown precinct house interrogate a prisoner accused of burglary. *(From* Our Police Protectors: History of the New York Police from the Earliest Period to the Present Time, *Augustine Costello, New York: C. F. Roper & co, 1885)*

On Post.

This patrolman's uniform was typical of those on the streets of New York in the 1850s. He has his "billy club" in his hands already. *(From* Our Police Protectors: History of the New York Police from the Earliest Period to the Present Time, *Augustine Costello, New York: C. F. Roper & co, 1885)*

Woman's Prison: A Mutual Recognition.

Thousands of women were incarcerated at the Tombs. They lived in crowded quarters, though, not like the one sanitized in this drawing. *(From* Our Police Protectors: History of the New York Police from the Earliest Period to the Present Time, *Augustine Costello, New York: C. F. Roper & co, 1885)*

Blackwell's Island and East River

Blackwell's Island was home to one of the nation's largest asylums for the mentally ill and many criminals were also held there. *(From* Our Police Protectors: History of the New York Police from the Earliest Period to the Present Time, *Augustine Costello, New York: C. F. Roper & co, 1885)*

FERNANDO WOOD.
(From a Photograph.)

His Honor, the flamboyant New York Mayor Fernando Wood. *(From* Our Police Protectors: History of the New York Police from the Earliest Period to the Present Time, *Augustine Costello, New York: C. F. Roper & co, 1885)*

Five Points in 1829. *(From an old print.)*

This is a drawing of the notorious crime district Five Points, completed in 1829. By the mid-1850s, Five Points was far more crowded, home to dozens of rowdy street gangs, and riddled with crime. Police were afraid to visit it. *(From* Our Police Protectors: History of the New York Police from the Earliest Period to the Present Time, *Augustine Costello, New York: C. F. Roper & co, 1885)*

COLT TRAGEDY.—THE DISCOVERY

The body chopped up and stuffed into this trunk found in the hold of ship docked in the East River was placed there by John C. Colt, brother of famed gunmaker Samuel Colt. Colt killed the man because he did not pay his rent. The homicide was one of the most publicized in New York City history and the incarceration of Colt was bungled by police. *(From* Recollections of a New York Chief of Police, *George Washington Walling, New York: Caxton Book Concern, Limited, 1887)*

Bill Poole, the noted boxer and well-dressed man-about-town, was gunned down by Lewis Baker, with whom he had feuded for over a year, at the bar in Stanwix Hall, a midtown hotel. *(From* Recollections of a New York Chief of Police, *George Washington Walling, New York: Caxton Book Concern, Limited, 1887)*

POLICE PARADE, BROADWAY

MADAM RESTELL.
(From a Photograph.)

Madam Marie Restell ran a string of abortion clinics in New York. She was often arrested but rarely convicted and served little time behind bars. *(From* Recollections of a New York Chief of Police, *George Washington Walling, New York: Caxton Book Concern, Limited, 1887)*

Officers staged dozens of "police parades" each year to showcase the department's force and to let the members of the public know that in the hands of these men they were safe. Mayor Fernando Wood often led the lengthy parades, waving and bowing to the substantial crowds that filled the city sidewalks to watch the festive events. *(From* Recollections of a New York Chief of Police, *George Washington Walling, New York: Caxton Book Concern, Limited, 1887)* he saw the crime rate soar, but did not. No one asked him to lead a reform of the department, either, and so he rested on his law-and-order laurels. As far as High Constable Hays was concerned, all was well. All was not.

Work was often hard to find in big cities, especially New York. Huge factories and stores hired large labor forces, but most jobs were menial and low paying.[14] In addition to that, many jobs in the mid-nineteenth century, such as shipping, were seasonal. Much work was outdoors, despite the growth of factories and large stores. When winter set in, outdoor jobs were cut back and unemployment in New York rose. The thousands of men who had no jobs had little to do and, with idle time on their hands, became involved in petty crime or, hanging out in the streets, fell prey to crime.[15]

Workers in New York felt a great sense of emptiness, too, because few worked for themselves anymore. Self-employment, whether running a farm or a city store, had been a marked part of American tradition. That historic feeling of making your own way in the world and providing for your family or relying on yourself had been lost, and people resented it. They felt that the ambiguous "city" had snatched something precious from them, and they were angry. As employees of someone else, the people felt their strength being drained away, and that gave them a sense of insecurity and made them feel like they were victims. Chaos and crime were a result.[16]

Everything seemed to bring out the worst in New Yorkers. Men engaged in fights over lost card games, dogfights, and bets. If there was a fight to start, New Yorkers would be there to start it.

In New York City in the early 1840s, too, there was a general feeling of the loss of self-respect that brought about alienation. Men fought with anybody who disrespected them. Many men felt exiled from all of society, in an emotional corner, and knew of no other way to get out of that corner than with their fists. It was an era of manliness, and many men strutted around town, challenging others to a

fight. Some walked brazenly down city streets with swords at their
sides, or revolvers tucked into their belts. Some dressed as pirates
and tied colorful bandanas around their heads. They looked for confrontations and enjoyed them, knowing that the constables with no
weapons and no desire for a fistfight were not going to stop them.
Some brawlers forgot about each other and lay in wait for constables.
Two young men beat up a watchman in front of a public house on
Grand Street just for fun one night in 1840. Sometimes people were
killed in these brawls, and at other times they escaped with just a bad
beating. These midnight marauders were feared by the populace.[17]

Although there were not a lot of murders of wives by their husbands,
those that did occur scared everybody. Men in a rage over something
picked up any weapon they could find and assaulted their spouse. On
New Year's Day 1842, Thomas Tappan became angry at his wife. There
was no gun or wooden club in his house, so he ran to the kitchen
and grabbed a knife and fork from a drawer near the sink. Tappan
rushed back into the bedroom, held his wife down on her back, and
stabbed her to death with the utensils.[18]

People were afraid, tense, and anxious about everything in New
York City and were unable to get help from the town's government,
which they believed to be both inept and corrupt. They felt that they
had no other way to obtain fairness, justice, and a chance at a good
life than through violence. Brawls took place on the streets, and in
some of them people were killed. Robbers ransacked houses, street
urchins seemed to pick everybody's pocket, and twelve-year-old girls
sold their bodies for pocket change. The preteen whores, twelve-year-
old pickpockets, and kids who worked for the street gangs lived on the
streets or in old vacant warehouses and were called "street Arabs."
They were rarely arrested because the police and city magistrates felt
sorry for them, never quite understanding how they were carving out
a small criminal empire for themselves. By 1845 there were just over
ten thousand of them, and they scared all. New Yorkers lived, many
of them said, on the edge of an earthquake of political, social, cul-

tural, racial, and emotional pressure that appeared ready to erupt and ruin them and their city.[19]

Many crusaded against the unruly rabble that threatened to devour the town. James Gordon Bennett of the *Herald* conducted lengthy campaigns to reform not just the police but the magistrates, too. In 1841, his efforts resulted in the impeachment of one. It was charged, Bennett reported in the *Herald,* that the judge routinely took payoffs from pickpockets to give them probation and not jail terms. He was charged with exacting a $400 bribe from another man to give him a suspended sentence. Bennett was happy about the impeachment but would not stop, demanding a citywide probe of police magistrates and their rather lax attitude toward criminals. Many constables believed that judges threw out charges they brought against gamblers because the detainees contributed money to political clubs to which the judges belonged. After a few years of these practices, constables simply delivered their own justice, with a beating or crack on the back of the head with a nightstick, instead of bringing lawbreakers to court for a pointless appearance. Bennett wrote that the entire police magistrate system was corrupt. He was not alone. Mike Walsh, editor of the penny *Subterranean,* called another judge "one of the human stink weeds which are nurtured by the moral slime and putrefaction of that sink of inequity . . . the Halls of Justice."[20]

A much-cited joke of the era was that a man who was robbed of $1,000 could obtain $500 of it back easily by paying a judge to get it from the man who stole it.

The crime wave seemed never ending to Bennett and others, as did the ineptitude of the constable force. At the beginning of each year, frustrated New Yorkers promised themselves that things would get better. Philip Hone did that on New Year's Day 1840. He refused to let the routine law enforcement breakdown in 1839 depress him. His finances had improved somewhat since the Panic of 1837 nearly ruined him. Revenues at his family's auction house had increased. He woke up on New Year's Day 1840 bright eyed and determined to make it a good year for himself and hoped it would be a good year for the entire city. The day began well enough as Hone finished his breakfast and put on some of his finest clothes for required visits to his friends on the annual holiday.

A recent snowfall still covered the city, and sheets of ice had formed on the streets. Long, clear icicles hung from the roofs of residences and stores. A northwest wind howled. New Year's Day was a special event in New York City in the 1840s. Residents invited friends to receptions and parties at their homes that lasted from roughly 10:00 A.M. until midnight (receptions at the homes of the super-rich never began until noon). Invitations were sent out on elegant cards. People like Hone would receive dozens of them. The receptions were often lavish, so elegant that people hired bartenders just for the day, along with special waitstaffs. Receptions at the more elegant homes always had a three- or four-piece orchestra on hand to play music for the guests. All tried their best to keep out roving bands of young men with invitations of some kind, often stolen or counterfeited, who crashed parties and, inebriated, disgraced themselves. Partygoers on New Year's Day enjoyed the best of food, such as pheasant and woodcock, along with the finest imported wines and liquors.[21]

George Templeton Strong went to many of these parties. At times he enjoyed himself, and at other times he was angry at all of his friends who tried to play matchmaker and introduced him to various single women, all of whom he found either dull or manipulative. Some were "supernaturally ugly," he said, and "wooden in their stupidity." He loathed the gold diggers who were only interested in "an Elizabethan mansion, fifty feet by ninety-five, with furniture and establishment to match, on . . . Fifth Avenue."[22]

Guests at these nighttime receptions would drink the most expensive wines in the world and sample the carefully made appetizers. Dancing to music provided by the orchestras would begin around 11:00 P.M., and around midnight the dining rooms were opened and people would have dinner. That was followed by more dancing until the evening ended around 3:00 or 4:00 A.M. Soirees at these elegant ballrooms were expensive, up to $1 million a gala in today's money. The reward was great, though. Partygoers enjoyed themselves, and, even more important, the party elevated the hosts in the esteem of the rich.[23]

The grandest parties were on New Year's Eve and the following day. If a New Year's Day fell during a snowstorm, partygoers traveled the city streets in sleighs that slid noiselessly through the neighborhoods (every year, several people were killed when they were catapulted out of sleighs in fabled "sleigh races" in city neighborhoods). Hone walked out the door and down the stone steps of his stoop to the street. It was so chilly that he felt like he was at the "north pole," but he paid the weather no mind as he walked, bundled up with a top hat and thick wool scarf tied around his neck, to visit friends and neighbors on his traditional parade through the city on New Year's Day. The former mayor ignored what was left of the refuse left on the snow from the celebrants of New Year's Eve parties in the streets, despite the cold, the night before. Thousands of revelers gathered near his home in the Broadway and Bowery area to celebrate every year, causing considerable noise and leaving garbage strewn over the street. This morning, because of the snow, everything looked better than usual on the first day of the year. Hone spent nearly five hours trudging through the ice and snow to the homes of those he loved. He was in good spirits, too, because he had hit a milestone; he had turned sixty on October 23. ("As to health and strength and preservation of my faculties, I have great reason to be thankful," he wrote in his diary.)

His New Year's joy ended quickly, though, when he read the newspapers that morning. Not one but two murders kicked off the New Year in New York. A Staten Island butcher had seduced a local girl, and one of her friends had caught him and killed him. In lower Manhattan, a gang of street toughs broke into the home of a German man and his friends who were celebrating on New Year's Eve, assaulted them, and destroyed much of the house. The German and his friends drove them off, but the young men returned later, armed. The young people burst into his house, but the German, waiting for them, was armed with one of the new Colt revolvers. He started blasting. He killed the ringleader, a twenty-two-year-old man named John Armstrong, and badly wounded four others, who fled into the streets.[24]

Happy New Year . . .

CHAPTER EIGHT

Amateur Police Walk the Beat
of a Raucous City

Here are people of all classes . . . of every grade, every hue of
ignorance and learning, morality and vice, wealth and want,
fashion and coarseness, breeding and brutality, elevation and
degradation.

—Walt Whitman, *Aurora*, March 8, 1842

Philip Hone woke up the following morning and looked out the
window at a crisp and cold New York whose residents were growing angrier at the spurt of crime. From the Five Points to the docks,
from saloons to brothels, the city seemed about to be swamped by
crime—with no one there to save it except a bungling, comical force
of mostly unarmed constables.

Gotham was awash in problems. In addition to murders and
robberies, many New Yorkers felt that the exploding population
threatened to swallow them up in a tidal wave of filth, corruption, and
crime. Reformer Lydia Child was one of them. She said that life in
the city "has sometimes forced upon me, for a few moments, an appalling night-mare sensation of vanishing identity; as if I were but
an unknown, unnoticed, and unseparated drop in the great ocean of
human existence, as if the uncomfortable old theory were true, and

we were but portions of a Great Mundane Soul, to which we ulti-
mately return, to be swallowed up in its infinity." She added that, like
many others, she found herself "like the absent[-minded] man who
put his clothes in bed, and hung himself over the chair."[1]

New York was by far the most populous city hit with a crime wave,
but it was certainly not alone. Other urban areas suffered criminal epidemics just as Gotham did. Up and down the East Coast, and as far
inland as Chicago and on the West Coast, too, crime was the number
one problem for city dwellers. Its cure was their number one goal. Residents of other cities had been blind to the devastating effects of the
crime wave and should be made aware of them, argued many reformers. "It is a fact against which we ought no longer to shut our eyes,"
wrote one editor in Pittsburgh, "that we have in the very midst of us a
population of the most abandoned kind."[2]

Philadelphians, too, were targets of the new urban crime wave. "The
numerous acts of outrage upon the persons and property of our peaceable citizens and the boldness with which many of these acts are committed . . . are sure indications that we are infested at this time by an
unusual number of villains, of the boldest and most daring character," said Mayor William Milnor in the City of Brotherly Love.[3]

The number of constables in New York remained quite small in
the mid-1840s. The city only had about 850 constables, a ratio of 1
watchmen for every 805 residents, and they worked in shifts so that at
any one time, the city of nearly half a million people was supervised
by just 300 or so officers. It ranked only a sad sixth in the country in
constables per population. Tiny Richmond, Virginia, with just 27,000
residents, had 123 watchmen (projected against New York, it means
that New York should have employed 2,400 officers). London, as an
example, had 1 per 455 people.[4]

New York's employment of law enforcement officers did not keep
pace with the galloping increase in city population, either. While the
population of the town increased by more than 100 percent from 1840
to 1860, the percentage of constables increased by only 34 percent.

About 40 percent of all murders and assaults were committed in the streets of the city, and another 10 percent took place in saloons, usually connected to drinking. Constables were needed to prevent street crimes or arrest street criminals who murdered people, and yet they were hardly visible.[5]

The wave of murders scared everyone, rich and poor, and dominated all conversations. Mrs. William Seward, the wife of the New York senator, was badly shaken when a murder was committed in their hometown of Auburn, New York, in 1846. She wrote her husband in Washington that the slaying terrified everybody. The residents of the community did not feel safe in their homes. "The occurrence of that fearful murder has made me feel very much alone with the little ones. . . . Nothing else has been thought or talked of here for a week," she said.[6]

An exasperated Walt Whitman wrote that the city had to have a paid, professional force. "The broad fact is so glaringly evident that Brooklyn has a most inefficient police system . . . that no excuse can stave off the argument for reform," Whitman said. He complained bitterly about the unpaid watchmen who fell asleep on duty at night all over the borough. He asked "whether there should not be *good* watchmen, *paid a good price*; a man can't take a mere pittance, and work as though he had reasonable wages."[7]

The editor of the *New-York Commercial Advertiser* was furious about law enforcement, or the lack of it. He wrote that "it is notorious that the New York police is wretchedly inadequate to the arrest of offenders and the punishment of crime; as to prevention of crime, we might almost as well be without the name of a police, as we are all but without the substance. . . . Destructive rascality stalks at large in our streets and public places, at all time of the day and night, with none [i.e., no police] to make it afraid."[8]

The politicians who ran the city agreed. A special committee of the Board of Aldermen issued a blistering report on crime and the police. "The property of the citizen is pilfered, almost before his eyes. Dwellings and warehouses are entered with an ease and apparent coolness and carelessness of detection which shows that none are safe. Thronged as our city is, men are robbed in the street. Thousands, that are arrested, go unpunished, and the defenseless and the beautiful are ravished and murdered in the day time and no trace of the criminals is found," its authors said.[9] The savage report also charged that police only sought to arrest criminals after the commission of a crime but did nothing to prevent crimes from occurring. The protection of the people, it charged, required both the prevention of crime and criminal apprehension. The police were not successful at either.

Crime was so out of control, wrote an observer, that "there is not a day transpires but the citizens of New York hear of some disgraceful outrage of some kind, and everybody there must admit that there is something rotten in Denmark. In the police department, a great reformation is absolutely necessary there."[10]

One of those rotten somethings was the corrupt stolen-property recovery-fee system. Constables were paid fees to recover stolen property, so the lawmen made arrangements with criminals to give them property they stole so that they could collect the fee. In return, the constables would not arrest the thief. Sometimes constables would alert thieves who were their friends to where large sums of money or jewels were located so that their haul would be bigger and the constables' fee heftier. Sometimes police "recovered" most of the property and collected a fee and left the remainder to the thief, who sold it for his "fee." Police officials said that constables even kept careful records of thieves, and their homes and warehouses, not to make arrests but to make arrangements to collect fees when they recovered stolen goods from thieves whom they had previously let go.[11]

The size of the night watch did increase because the city's official boundary pushed northward from Fourteenth Street to Thirtieth Street on the East Side and Fortieth Street on the West Side. The city increased the number of watchmen over ten years. In 1843, when the city population was about 350,000, there were 1,095 patrolmen, 100 marshals, and 34 constables.[12] No administrative unit was formed to supervise the larger watch, though. The same system that had functioned badly for decades, with the mayor and/or aldermen in charge

of watch appointments and removals, remained in place. All watchmen continued to be hired based on political friendships and patronage, and most of them were highly unqualified for the job. All of the
mayors of New York, eager to solidify their own power, supported
this scheme. It was ingrained. The local street gangs, who worked for
political organizations, routinely nominated men for the watch, later
approved by the mayor, who were weak, ineffective, and useless, which
is just the way the street ruffians wished them to be.

Newspaper editors and civic leaders were relentless in their con-
demnation of both the mayor's power to select and fire police and the
ways in which various mayors went about the process. Horace Greeley
complained of Mayor Fernando Wood in 1857 that he was a "desperate political tyrant." The editor said "the autocrat of the police department [was] making the most of his vanishing power" and charged
that Wood hired and fired cops around 8:00 A.M., at his office, in
order to do it before newspaper reporters arrived.[13]

Police reporters did not learn much at Wood's office. They reported that Wood's police hiring and firing meetings were all held
behind closed doors and names were released much later. At these
meetings, dozens of cops were dismissed or hired at one time, usually
with no reason given for firings and no qualifications listed for those
who were hired. Reporters were not only barred from the meetings but
located by "scouts" from the mayor's office who kept them far away
from Wood all day. The mayor had total control of the force, hiring
or letting go lieutenants and captains as well as patrolmen. The reporters wrote acid stories about the appointments. In one story, a
reporter noted that the only qualification that one man named a captain had was that his previous job was as the owner of a downtown
liquor store.[14]

Young people continued to make fun of the watchmen and harassed
them. "Youthful and exuberant New Yorkers considered that an evening out was not spent in the orthodox manner unless they played some
rough practical jokes on the poor, old, inoffensive 'Leatherheads,'"
wrote police officer George Walling, a slowly balding man with a full

beard, mustache, and wide forehead, when he first started walking his
beat in 1847. One fellow "lassoed [a watch house] with a stout rope,
and with the aid of companions dragged it down Broadway, while the
watchman inside yelled loudly for help."[15]

Important people did try to reform law enforcement in the late
1830s, but their efforts met with failure. The first effort came after the
disgraceful looting that followed the Great Fire of 1835 and the Jewett
murder in the spring of 1836. During these two years, the city watch
force was increased, and extra watchmen were added for just Sunday.
The city built two new watch houses and repaired several. The number
of watch districts was increased. Watchmen were asked to patrol the
steamship docks, where hackmen and porters had engaged in numerous fights for years. It was hoped the constables' presence would dissuade arguments. One watchman was always posted in a booth in the
cupola high atop City Hall at night in order to spot fires in the area
and, with a swinging lamp, direct fire companies toward those blazes.[16]

Watch houses had been around since before the Revolution. They
were one-story, two-room houses, 28' by 18', with two fireplaces and
several windows, where watchmen could keep warm in winter and cool
in summer and have space to relax, as well as to store clothing and records. Sometimes criminals were held in the watch houses. They made
it possible for the constables to work in their districts without having
to trudge more than a mile to the police headquarters. They vanished
when large precinct houses were built in each section of the city.[17]

Hundreds of people stole clothing and other items during the fire
in 1835 that burned down hundreds of stores and residences. Watchmen at the scene did nothing to stop the thieves, and many charged
that the police were part of the scheme, rewarded with clothing for
their lack of effort. They were, one editor said, "rogues in pay."[18] Could
anybody else have stopped the looting? The fire companies were
there, but they were too busy engaging in fistfights with each other to
help the citizens and shopkeepers who were robbed.

Mayor Cornelius Lawrence was so incensed about the pathetic
state of law enforcement in 1836, especially after the Jewett slaying, that

he led a movement to reform the police. In September of 1836, he and police magistrate O. M. Lowndes sent a report to the Board of Aldermen that suggested the city form a new, physically capable, and trained police force with more administrators and more constables, and one that was paid better and did not collect fees as additional income. It was turned down by the Common Council (which did approve the plea for more constables, though). It seems that Mayor Lawrence knew the plan would be stymied by public fears of a "King's army" type of occupation force. The people did not need to fear "despotic governments," Lowndes and Lawrence wrote in the report, but the people did fear.[19]

Lawrence finished his term as mayor, Lowndes finished his term as police magistrate, and police reform died. Public worries over crime and the constables' inability to stop it continued, but there was not another heinous crime, or series of crimes, with which to connect that apprehension to a reform of the police department. The urgency over fee reform soon faded.

New Yorkers did not listen to Lawrence or anyone espousing an independent, decently paid police force. Foreigners visiting New York realized that necessity immediately. Frenchman Alexis de Tocqueville, who traveled through the United States in 1830 and 1831, wrote that what the city needed was "an armed force which, while it remains under the control of the majority of the nation . . . will be independent of the town population and able to repress its excesses."[20]

Mayor Lawrence did get the Common Council to approve, in a separate bill, the nation's very first detective force. Ninety-two men were hired as detectives, called roundmen, to work in each precinct of the city. Their job was to patrol the streets undercover, seek out and arrest wanted criminals, report on irregular behavior by constables, and try to solve crimes that had eluded the regular watch force. City officials said that "it had become necessary in every large town that there should be several intelligent and experienced men devoting their times and skill to the pursuit and arrest of . . . robbers, housebreakers, pickpockets and other felons."[21]

The early detectives may have been seen as highly skilled investigators, but there were no police academies to train them, and they had no real experience. They learned the job on the job. Actually, most of the beat cops did their own detective work. They ordinarily pieced together information, such as the color of shirts, style of pants or hats, footprints in the snow, eyewitness accounts, people who were left-handed or right-handed, descriptions of men with beards, the sounds of voices. Officer George Walling once broke up a robbery ring because he believed that one of the thieves had lost a coat button during a heist. A month later, a theater owner pointed out three men he believed to be working as pickpockets in his theater. Walling noticed that one of them had lost a button from his coat and the coat was believed to be the one worn by one of the men in the robbery. He and two other police followed the men from the theater and arrested them when they went to their homes. The one obscure coat button proved to be their undoing.[22]

In the early 1840s, following new and numerous public complaints, the New York state legislature conducted an investigation of New York City's police force and police courts system that shocked all. The report charged that constables made no arrests in criminal investigations and brought few suspects before the police magistrates. The report recommended that fifty additional officers be hired. Statistics show that police in Brooklyn, then a separate city from New York, made far more arrests per capita than those in New York, where police were involved in bribery schemes or looked the other way on potential arrests. In 1860, as an example, Brooklyn had 198 police officers who made 15,334 arrests. That same year, New York's 1,414 patrolmen made 65,809 arrests. Since New York had so many more patrolmen, its force should have made around 105,000 arrests, according to comparative statistics. The state investigation found that many criminals, prostitutes, pickpockets, and counterfeiters paid police bribes to drop all charges against them or not arrest them at all. As early as 1815, the court clerk for the city's Fifth Ward openly charged that police were taking bribes from prostitutes not to arrest them or lending the prostitutes money to pay fines ordered by local courts. "It seems that all connected with the police office get rich very soon," wrote the *Herald*'s James Gordon Bennett twenty-five years later.[23]

The police freely admitted that. Walling wrote that the partnership of the police with professional criminals was frequent and that the police often accepted bribes. He added that was common. "We are robbed and swindled right and left by the wealthy corporation which seizes upon our property with impunity and without reservation down through all the various grades to the thief with political influence who 'snatches' your watch while human life . . . can be taken with safety."[24]

Police were often bribed with goods and not money. A popular bribery scheme involved clothing. Street vendors and the proprietors of clothing shops whom police were investigating offered to buy any extra clothing that cops did not need. It was a purchase, not a bribe, but it was really a bribe.[25]

The state report prompted New York City to launch its own investigation, in which even more corruption was uncovered. Its report said that some police, through bribes, were earning $300,000 to $400,000 a year (in today's money). The report accused police of knowing about robberies days before they took place, sharing plunder with the robbers, developing friendships with criminals, protecting lawbreakers, and paying off judges to let their crooked friends go free.

The police covered over much of their lack of effort in arrests by heavily publicizing the good works that they did. As an example, statistics released for the year 1858 showed that while not as many arrests were being made as could have been, noble efforts were continually made to aid the citizenry. In that year, 121,597 disorderly or disoriented people were allowed to spend the night in precinct houses, 7,500 missing children were brought back to their parents, 58 abandoned infants and 751 sick or disabled persons found on the streets were taken care of, 134 persons were rescued from drowning, 180 fires were extinguished by the police, 1,724 stores with opened doors were locked, and some $160,000 worth of stolen property was recovered and returned to its owner.[26]

The idea of a "criminal class," heralded in major world cities as well as New York, grew dramatically in the early 1840s as crime spread not just in bad neighborhoods but in all neighborhoods. The Prison Association of New York even did a study a short time later that proved the theory. Its investigator, Richard Dugdale, visited numerous city and country jails and reported a clear class of dangerous men and women that should be eliminated. They were people who were "breeding like rats," said Dugdale, "in their alleys and hovels, [and] threatened . . . to overwhelm the well-bred classes of society." By the mid-1840s, too, novelists, short story writers, and playwrights embraced the idea of a "criminal class" being responsible for society's woes.

A considerable problem with the "criminal class" was that it was generally made up of young men, fourteen to thirty-five. They were a large group of people who were born and raised in poverty and were from broken homes. Fathers unable to support their families fled, as did mothers, and children grew up with one parent or none. They did not go to school. Their opportunity for advancement in the world was either through hard work and good fortune or committing crimes. Many chose the latter. These men and boys had other poverty-stricken members of that class as their friends, not middle-class students or young men who were brought up by two-parent, hardworking families. The support they had, and inspiration, came from other criminals.[27]

There was danger everywhere, even in celebrations. Revelers in the sprawling, eleven-acre City Hall Park got a jump on the Fourth of July in 1836 and began firing the latest firearms on July 3 at a nighttime celebration. It disgusted young lawyer George Templeton Strong, who lived nearby. "It was a shameful spectacle: the booths lighted up, the people as drunk as dogs, and such popping of squibs, rockets, pistols, etc. as I never heard. It did not look much like Sunday evening in a Christian country," he wrote in his diary that night.[28]

By the 1840s, Strong was six years into his career as a diarist covering the New York scene, from low taste to high society, gritty to gaudy,
and crinoline to crime. He lived in the rarefied world of the rich and
super-rich. He spent his days in his large mansion or at his high-
powered law office, but at night he gamboled through the congested
city streets on his way to extravagant balls and haughty receptions held
behind the doors of the most expensive homes in America. On the way
to and from his parties and balls and law courts, he observed New
York and New Yorkers very closely. Like former mayor Philip Hone,
Strong was a chronicler of the lives of New Yorkers in a frenetic era.
He wrote privately about the city, its street vigilantes and criminals,
its debutantes and politicians, much as Walt Whitman, James Gordon Bennett, and Horace Greeley did publicly.

Strong's father was a very successful lawyer who, in partnership
with others, had represented some of the city's and the nation's most
impressive corporations and individuals. His first wife died at twenty-
three, and his second gave birth to George in 1820. Young George
followed in his father's footsteps and became a successful attorney.
The Strongs lived in a large brick mansion on a tree-lined street near
Battery Park, an immaculately groomed park full of trees, shrubs,
and small, well-kept gardens overlooking the harbor where city dwellers strolled and listened to band concerts in the summertime. It was
home to Castle Garden, one of the country's largest entertainment
centers, where the sensational "Swedish Nightingale," Jenny Lind,
performed at the start of her national tour. The park and Castle Garden were gorgeous. "The city lamps surround you, like a shiny belt of
constellations," wrote Lydia Child. "And there stands Castle Garden,
with its gay perspective of coloured lamps, like a fairy grotto, where
imprisoned fire-spirits send up sparkling wreaths, with rockets laden
with glittery ear-drops, caught by the floating sea nymphs as they
fall."[29]

Castle Garden was joined in 1855 by the spectacular Crystal Palace,
made almost entirely of glass, which became home to huge concerts
and shows. People flocked to performances at the Palace, where Bryant

Park is today, and often arrived just to stroll around it and look at its magnificence. The showplace burned to the ground in 1858.

Strong was a very inquisitive child. As a teenager, young George told friends that one of his goals was to know about life in every neighborhood in the city. He wanted to know not just how the other half lived but who the other half was. What were their triumphs and tragedies, their problems? How did life in the ever-expanding city affect them? Why were the criminals running loose? Why did the government seem unable to keep up with the stupendous growth of the town? Why could the police not stem the tidal wave of criminality?

Strong was brilliant. He read his first complete book at four and a book on the American Revolution at ten, and he was at the head of his class at nine. As a child he learned to play the piano and organ. His father spent several hours each night studying with him. He started to write journals, as his father had done, and friends and family said that he wrote well.

More than anyone else, Strong was a representative of the upper crust of New York society, a group of high-toned, well-heeled people whose presence and importance in the city were often overshadowed by the wave of crime, prostitution, and drunkenness for which New York was famous. The city had a number of colleges, literary societies, parlor poetry readings, gardens, horse academies, debutante organizations, balls, and receptions that were supported by the rich. The upper crust, like Strong, kept homes on Long Island in the summer, where they maintained large staffs of servants and kept horses and carriages. They owned large yachts that were anchored either at harbors on the island or along the Manhattan waterfront. The wealthy did all they could to establish their colony of proper etiquette, literature, and fashion in a world around them that seemed to have gone mad.

Strong went to Columbia College, then just walking distance from his home, when he was fourteen and graduated with honors when he was eighteen, always jotting down things in his journal. He was a great lover of books and collected hundreds of them for his library. Strong often waited in wind and rain at the docks for the arrival of ships from

Europe carrying a shipment of new books that he had ordered. Soon after he became a lawyer, he joined a firm started by famed Canadian attorney Marshall Bidwell (it later became Strong and Bidwell), where he met all of the top legal people in the city and state and most of the politicians. He met even more when he was named a college trustee in 1853. Coming from a wealthy family, the successful young lawyer found easy entry to New York high society and its endless rounds of parties and balls. He did not find a woman to suit him until the late 1840s, when he began to court Eleanor Ruggles, whom he married.

He was a hopeless eccentric, constantly mixing together amateur medicinal treatments for his many ailments. He suffered from migraine headaches and to cure them used his own odd concoction of cayenne pepper and cream of tartar. Strong drank catnip tea when he had a cold. He was intrigued with any new medicine that came out and might become part of his own doctor's cabinet.

But Strong was even more intrigued by the wild life of the city, inheriting a love of the streets and rivers from his uncle, one of New York's most famous firemen. He was more entranced by the thugs and thieves than he was by the debutantes and men in perfect-fitting and superbly cut black dress suits. He rode through town in his carriage with his head always sweeping left and right and ears always open, taking in the sights and noises of the community—and the people. If there was a riot or a fire, Strong got there immediately to write about it. He sat in on court cases, passed hundreds of evenings at the theater, and spent days walking through parks and listening to firebrand speakers. He read many newspapers, in addition to his books, and had a comment on just about everything. He was, like Hone, a man of the people who lived in a castle. His world was not just the chime of a large clock in the study of his spacious and well-appointed home but the sounds of the street, the street gang howls, the firebells, the police whistles, the roars of the angry crowd. And, too, he walked through a lawless city that spun into disorder every day.

His writing was bold, descriptive, intuitive, beautiful, and, in a word, unique. He did not see rain as everyone else saw it. To him, it was "raining all day long like a collection of inverted Jets d'eau—the atmosphere penetrated by columns of descending water half an inch in diameter. . . . A very pleasant aquatic excursion it was." He did not merely watch fires consume houses and entire blocks but walked through the streets amid the hot blazes and recorded everything he saw. In the Great Fire of 1845, he wrote that he "came back to the scene of action, and seeing that all of Broad Street on both sides from about No. 20 down was one grand, solid substantial flame, most glorious and terrible to look at."[30]

CHAPTER NINE

Prostitution, Gambling, and Drinking: The Backbone of the Crime Surge and Downfall of the Police

The dives of New York are the hot-beds of its crime. . . . Vice germinates, grows, buds and yields its bitter fruit [there]. Every stage of crime is reflected in a true picture of these holes of viciousness.

—Captain George Walling, NYPD

George Templeton Strong walked through a city of sin. No matter what street, avenue, or alley he traveled on or through, or what tavern or store or theater or ferryboat he visited, somebody somewhere nearby was breaking the law. New York had become the Wild East.

No matter where he went, he always found himself face-to-face with the three biggest reasons for the soaring crime rate in his beloved New York—gambling, drinking, and sex.

There was more legal gambling in New York in the 1840s and 1850s than at any other time in American history until the establishment of legal gambling in Las Vegas a hundred years later. The heart of the gambling district in New York was Vesey Street, Barclay Street, and

Park Row downtown. Hundreds of small storefront gambling emporiums could be found nearby. The dozen or so big houses on those
streets were elegantly designed, with expensive rugs, imported satin-
and velvet-covered furniture, numerous bars, and small orchestras
that played music for visitors over the din of the tables. Sometimes
stars from music halls and the theater would entertain patrons. Liv-
eried servants were everywhere. Floor-to-ceiling mirrors filled some
rooms, and the walls of others were covered with expensive pieces of
art by fabled painters. Dinner was served in large, elegant dining
halls. Each diner had gold and silver plates and exquisitely cut crystal.

The gambling emporiums referred to their gamblers as "distinguished patrons," but the penny press referred to them as "despicable
characters." The *Herald* wrote that "many of these common gamblers,
compared with whom the skulking pickpocket is respectable, mingle
with the leaders of fashion in this city. They saunter along Broadway
in the mornings, drive out on the avenue in the afternoon, lounge at
the opera in the evening and cheat at Park Row and Barclay Street
until five o'clock in the morning." The *Sun* charged that the presence
of gambling casinos in the better sections of town was ruining the
neighborhoods.[1]

Part of the casino problem was that hundreds of them were illegal
and rarely monitored by the police. They were professionally run, and
the faro tables, dice pits, and roulette stations were packed with customers. In January of 1852, a Captain Taylor and six of his men burst
into an illegal casino and found a large operation. They arrested the
manager and thirteen workers.[2]

Thousands of men and women were addicted to gambling and
involved in many of the crimes associated with it, such as brawls, knife
attacks, robberies, and theft. They would do anything to get money to
toss onto a faro table. "The robber who stabs at a victim to get at his
pocket—the incendiary who fires a city in the hope of spoils—is not
more the slave of the lust for gold than that gray-haired sinner, or that
bright-eyed nervous youth, who stands leaning over the faro-table,

watching every card as if the destiny of his immortal soul hung—and so perhaps it does—upon the issue," wrote journalist George Foster.[3]

The police were deeply involved in gambling. Everybody knew that visitors just had to give a policeman a dollar and he would direct you to all of the gambling houses in the city, some illegal, some at the ends of snaking, narrow alleys that no one would be able to find without the expert help of the police, so eager to accept illegal money to aid the gamblers.

Critics of the faro tables and card games said they might be legal but were the foundation of lawbreaking. "Gambling is the synthesis of crime," wrote Foster, "and includes within itself the spirit of fraud, theft, robbery, and murder. The professed gambler is the most enormous pest ever engendered by a monstrous society."[4]

Gambling was prosperous in New York City. The gambling houses employed about three thousand workers, making the industry one of the largest in the city. Individual casino employees, particularly those who worked with teams in faro games, could earn twenty or thirty times as much money as the average city worker. Gambling exploded in New York in the mid-1830s because of the city's population jump and because of the fading popularity of gambling in the Southwest and the Northwest and on riverboats. Decades of cheating by fast-talking, suave gamblers had soured the public on pulling up a chair to play poker, and so the gamblers, and their games, moved to the growing metropolises. A new game, faro, appeared, and patrons thought that it was fair and that their chances of success were good. In faro, gamblers bet on cards from a deck imprinted on a green tablecloth, and then a dealer drew cards from a mechanized "boot" that could not be fixed (it was). Faro became a raging success prior to the Civil War.[5]

A lion of the gambling industry was "policy," or lotteries (in some ways the "numbers game" popular in the early twentieth century). The lottery started in America in the 1700s as a way to raise money for town governments and individuals who needed fast revenue to buy land or repair a barn. By the 1830s, lotteries had become wildly popular in all cities, particularly New York because of its population. In the 1850s, more than three thousand people worked in the lottery business, which was, like casino gambling, legal. The small lottery parlors, usually with two or three workers, sold sets of numbers to bettors for a lottery that was run twice each day to provide maximum betting opportunities. The buyers of lottery tickets were not the rich but working-class people and the poor. Those residents, people who lived in working-class neighborhoods and slums, would remain the base of the lottery system through the 1930s. The managers of the system designed it so that by the early 1840s numbers could be purchased for only three cents a ticket, making it a popular gambling game for many. The lotteries in New York alone took in close to $50 million a year in today's money. Lottery helped promote crime, as hundreds of people robbed someone, or a store, to get money to buy enormous sheets of lottery numbers or followed lottery winners home and robbed them.[6]

Horse racing, with small grandstands for seating at tracks and an amateurish ticket betting system, was starting to grow as a part of gambling in the 1840s but would not blossom until the 1860s, when wealthy horse lovers would build tracks at Saratoga, Pimlico, and Monmouth Park. After the Civil War, pari-mutuel betting became popular, and gamblers developed a huge off-track betting business in parlors set up in hotels. Some horse races were fixed.

Most gamblers who were brought to court by police were immediately released by the magistrates, who, it was said, had close relationships with the police in charge of rounding up gamblers. These police would take them to friendly judges for a bribe. The police were called "steers" or "ropers" because of the way in which they used the legal system to guide their gamblers to the "right" magistrates. Grand juries that did get cases involving criminality by gamblers often dismissed them. One grand jury released a group of men charged with running illegal parlors that sold lottery tickets. Many men on that grand jury had lottery tickets with them, all purchased at those same lottery parlors.[7]

One gambling house on Mott Street, just a block from police

headquarters, was reportedly populated by hundreds of the very policemen who were paid to monitor its activities.

The bloody slaying of hooker Helen Jewett in the spring of 1836 did
not end prostitution in New York City; it energized it. Five years after
Helen was butchered with an ax, anywhere from three thousand (city
number) to six thousand (reformer Ezra Stiles Ely's number) to ten
thousand (reformer John McDowall's number) prostitutes worked in
a community of whorehouses, on street corners, and even in the balconies of exquisite theaters, where they thought nothing of proposi-
tioning men in front of their wives. Numerous prostitutes saved room
money by servicing clients in their business offices. Many staked out
territories such as particular saloons or docks. One enterprising
fifteen-year-old girl became the prize hooker for men who worked on
a particular coal barge.[8]

Prostitution was very profitable. Women who worked in high-
end brothels in midtown New York west of Broadway, or in expensive
"parlor houses" such as the one on Thomas Street where Jewett died,
could clear, after fees to madams and room and board, close to $50 a
week, or some $300,000 a year in today's money. Even dirty street
urchin girls could earn 50 cents for quickie masturbations, or more
than $100 a trick in today's money. A girl who relieved three men a
day—not uncommon—could earn the equivalent of $100,000 a year.

The work was not easy for hookers, though, no matter the era in
which they worked. One study done in the early years of the twentieth
century showed that a woman in a slum whorehouse coupled with 19
men a day for a week and on one day slept with 28. Two other hookers in that house had sex with between 120 and 150 men a week, and one
day one of them had sex with 49 men. Some young girls would have
sex with 15 to 20 men in a three-hour period. Many of the girls were
twelve and thirteen and traveled the streets with a young sister, holding hands to ward off the chilly air and sometimes exchanging shoes
because one pair was cut up and cold.[9]

A whore's career was usually short-lived. Women who began selling their bodies at age twenty often stopped when they turned thirty
just because their looks started to fade. Men who had known them
for years tired of them. Younger hookers stole their business. The
biggest reason for leaving "the game" was that many women wanted to
become "normal," to marry and have a family, and could not do that
while living in a house of ill repute.

Madams' careers never ended, though, and were often prosperous. The high-class madams kept beautiful brothels. Johns entered
the home through a lobby and went to a large living room, where they
met the women of the house, chose one, and sat back to listen to a
woman play a piano. ("There is, however, no feeling nor expression
in what she sings," said one visitor. "All is cold as ice.")[10] Madams of
some of the more luxurious houses earned $1 million a year, in today's
money, and paid no income tax, either. Some, such as Maria William-
son, owned half a dozen houses of prostitution.[11] Others, like "Prin-
cess" Julia Brown, legendary for playing the piano at her brothel,
were frequent guests at parties and receptions hosted by the finest
families in town. Brown paid for pews at different churches in the city,
had season tickets to two different theaters, and contributed heavily
to local Bible societies.[12]

Sometimes the life of the hooker-turned-housewife was reversed.
Many working-class housewives in the pre–Civil War era moonlighted
as hookers to earn extra money that they thought was needed to run
their homes, buy groceries, and keep their children clothed. Some of
their husbands urged them to do so. Hundreds of them bought pro-
vocative dresses, walked the streets, procured johns, and took them to
rented rooms in boardinghouses for sex. Some women from other
states moved to New York temporarily, usually in the summer, and
rented rooms where they turned tricks for a month or two before going
back home.[13]

Ironically, hotel owners, even the managers of the most elegant
establishments in the city, did not mind having brothels nearby or

prostitutes walking their streets. It was good for business. Many out-of-town businessmen staying at the hotels sought prostitutes, and hotel employees provided them. The prostitutes were happy, and the hotel treasurer was happy. The police did not mind whorehouses near them, either. In the pre–Civil War era, four brothels were located on Greene Street, directly behind an early police precinct house.[14]

The police were part of the street hooker's life. She would pay police, possibly with money from her madam or pimp, to act as an escort to meet men recently arrived in New York and staying at hotels. The constable would meet men in the lobby and ask them where they wanted to go. They would talk about "fun," and the officer would take them to the Battery, or some other park, and introduce them to hookers he worked with. The officer would go with the john to the door of the hooker's boardinghouse and then leave the two alone, with a wad of bills in his pocket.

The constables also did a marvelous job of looking the other way when hookers and wild parties were involved. Whenever a watchman passed an illicit party at a brothel or boardinghouse, he would not stop to arrest the hookers or the gamblers running the illegal games that he found inside the loud rooms. Instead, he would merely rap on the door sharply with his wooden nightstick, as a reminder to keep the noise down, and move on down the street, blissfully ignorant.[15]

The parties in 1850 were bigger and louder and filled with more hookers and dandies than in 1840, and the saloons and theaters were more crowded than ever. The entire city was bigger and more bois-terous than ten years earlier. Broadway was a complete madhouse of people and traffic by 1850. "The crowd . . . pours along its turbid tide of life with a sullen roar and rushing, like the sound of the surf tram-pling upon the rocky beach. Before the theaters . . . the omnibuses are drawn up in solid phalanx, and at *the* place where the popular entertainment of the night is given, a row of carriages extends for a quarter of a mile either way," wrote journalist George Foster as he walked the streets of the city in 1850.[16]

People were constantly killed by the erratically driven omnibuses. In February of 1842 a ten-year-old boy was hit by one. The bus knocked his body to the ground and then the wheel ran over him, killing him instantly, to the horror of those on the bus.[17]

Lurking near each omnibus stop were the prostitutes, trying to solicit business. Prostitution was illegal in New York State, and had been for generations. Nothing stopped the world's oldest profession, though. During the Revolution, a mysterious fire wiped out a large section of New York City, including the area where most of the brothels were then housed. That did not set back the prostitution industry at all. Temporary houses, many with large, wide canvas ship's sails used as roofs, were constructed on Broad Street and opened for business rather quickly. They were "cheap and convenient lodgings for the frail sisterhood, who plied their trade most briskly in the vicinity of the shipping and the [British] barracks," chuckled New Yorker William Duer.[18]

Brit John Watt was enraged by the very public hookers in town during that era. New York was, he said, "the worst school for youth of any of his majesty's dominions, ignorance, vanity, dress and dissipation being the reigning characteristics of their insipid lives."[19]

The "whoreocracy," as many jokingly called it, prevailed after the city began its rapid population boom in the 1820s, and by the early 1840s New York was the prostitution capital of the United States. "New York is the Gomorrah of the New World," said Norwegian visitor Ole Raeder. The strumpets strolled Broadway in early afternoon or worked in packs of five or six and hung out in front of heavily populated restaurants or expensive hotels. Many had arrangements with hotels to use rooms frequently in order to get discounted quarters or, better yet, an hourly room rate.

They annoyed as many men and women as they pleased, but nobody seemed capable of getting rid of them. They were, Whitman said, "tawdry, hateful, foul tongued and harsh-voiced harlots." Reformer John Vose, as angry as Whitman, said that "our magnificent Broad-

way is rendered almost useless to our virtuous maidens by the courte-
sans who infest it."

"One is so accustomed to the sight of these gaudily dressed butter-
flies that the streets look very strange without them," wrote a *Tribune*
reporter.[20]

There were so many strumpets, and they were so open about approaching men for sexual assignations, that New York composers,
minstrel show musicians, and saloon band members wrote songs about
them. One, "The Bowery Girls," became one of the most popular
songs in American history:

> *De Bowery Girls dey come out at night*
> *Dey come out at night*
> *Dey come out at night.*
> *De Bowery girls dey come out at night,*
> *And dance by de light ob da moon.*

Most people know it by a later name given to it, "Buffalo Gals."

The constables paid no attention to the laws against prostitution,
and whores worked freely on the sidewalks and under the sheets. Any
time that a constable did admonish a prostitute, it was merely to remind her, or her madam, that she still owed him payoff money.

Hookers could be found everywhere. The city had used landfill to
create enormous new grounds just north of East Twelfth Street on
which to build even more new docks. Other large landfills on the Lower
East Side became homes for the workers who toiled on the docks all
day. These workers then became clients for the whores who moved to
the area or drifted in and out of it to meet men. The more successful
the waterfront became, the more profitable it was for the prostitutes.
Many lived alone in boardinghouses there.

All bemoaned the collapse of the city. Edgar Allan Poe and Herman Melville were two writers depressed by the city's growth and the
way it took shape. Poe, sailing in the harbor one day in the early 1840s,

groused about the explosive expansion of New York, where he had just moved. "I could not look upon the magnificent cliffs and stately trees, which at every moment met my view, without a sigh for their inevitable doom—inevitable and swift. In twenty years, or thirty at farthest, we shall see here nothing more romantic than shipping, warehouses, and wharves," he wrote gloomily. Of nearby Brooklyn, Poe added that "I know few towns which inspire me with so great disgust and contempt" and snarled that designing the homes that he saw in Brooklyn was like "cutting the throat of one's grandfather."[21]

Melville, the author of the classic sea tale *Moby-Dick*, shook his head negatively as he walked along the waterfront and encountered men and women who had lost the land under their feet to development and yearned now for the water's edge. "Here come more crowds, pacing straight for the water, and seemingly bound for a dive. Strange! Nothing will content them but the extremest limit of the land; loitering under the shady lee of yonder warehouses will not suffice. No. They must get just as nigh the water as they possibly can without falling in. And there they stand—miles of them—leagues. Inlanders all, they come from lanes and alleys, streets and avenues—north, east, south and west. Yet here they all unite. Tell me, does the magnetic needles of the compasses of all those ships attract them hither?"[22]

These authors lamented, as did many, that not only was the city growing too rapidly, but the growth was not planned. In many cities in Europe and America, particular areas were set aside for specific purposes—shipping, factories, residences, theaters, sports fields, finance—but in New York that did not happen. The wild, unpredictable growth of the segments of the city, with stores right next to row houses, and sports fields stuck in the middle of neighborhoods, bordered by streets and tenements, caused more problems, especially for law enforcement, whose members were battling criminals all over the city, not just in one area. Prior to the Civil War, city leaders in New York complained, too, that there had been very few studies done on urban problems and few books published on the history of the city in

America. Mayors and city planners had no blueprints to study and no footprints to follow.[23]

Illegal prostitution was on the waterfront and everywhere else, directly promoted by an odd assortment of new journals that plowed an unusual path into steamy sex and criminality—the "flash" newspapers.

The "sporting" or "flash" newspapers, such as the *Whip and Satirist of New-York and Brooklyn,* the *Libertine,* the *Weekly Rake,* and the *Flash,* printed long lists of brothels, and short reviews of them, for their readers, men about town who were referred to by all as "sporting men," or plea-sure seekers. These pages always included the address of the brothel, descriptions of its women and the services they provided, and, at times, what it cost to enjoy the feminine charms of the employees. The writers for these papers also wrote evaluations of the hookers they en-countered on the street and in city parks. The movement of a prosti-tute from one brothel to another was reported. There were columns on prostitute balls held in brothels, notes on prostitutes' fashions, and stories about seduction cases that landed in the city courts. The papers resembled today's *Fodor's Guides* for travelers. In Philadelphia, publishers produced guidebooks that devoted a page to each of the town's brothels with illustrations and descriptions of the girls. The New York papers and the sex guides in them were not a dirty little secret, either; they were sold openly at newsstands. They had no au-thentic news but just focused on the illegal sex trade conducted in brothels, boardinghouses, and back alleys. They wallowed in the world of illegal sex that had developed in New York at that time. They were designed for the man-about-town looking for a little tawdry fun, featuring lurid gossip columns and stories with advice on what to do for sex and where to go for it. They were illustrated with bawdy sex cartoons and illustrations that shocked many.[24]

There was a substantial difference between the flash papers and the mainstream papers, even the scandal and crime laden penny press, when it came to sex and criminality. The mainstream and penny press wrote about crime connected to prostitution, but the flash papers heralded prostitution itself and urged their readers to frequent illegal brothels and use the illegal services of streetwalkers. They encouraged breaking the law by consorting with prostitutes. The penny papers did not do that. The flash papers were a part of the criminal enterprise, and they knew it and reveled in it. Prostitution in all forms was illegal, even if the police wrapped their hands around bribe money and looked the other way. That did not bother the editors of the flash papers. In fact, with an ink-stained wink, the *Whip* promised "to keep a watchful eye on all the brothels and their frail inmates."[25]

The flash press did have one important influence on the mainstream sheets, though. It legitimized stories about cases of seduction. In 1842 the *Herald,* as an example, pressured by the flash papers, carried a lengthy and well-placed story of the seduction trial of Reverend William Van Zandt, charged with molesting an underage girl who was one of his religious students and took private Bible lessons from him at his home. The *Herald* and other penny sheets began to carry numerous stories about paternity suits.[26]

The flash papers were sold throughout New York City and in nearby suburbs. Writers in towns outside New York contributed columns on sin in their communities. This helped boost sales in the suburbs and increased the scope of sin stories in New York. Many suburbs banned the papers as obscene. An Albany newspaper covering a story about a fine levied against one paper wrote that "a man who will consent to pander to the vicious appetites of the low-minded and vulgar disseminating the blistering obscenity and filth which these papers teem with, and which poison the minds of hundreds of the young and virtuous, is far more guilty than the midnight thief or the highway robber."[27]

The first such paper, the *Flash,* was started in the early summer of 1841 by a vagabond writer from New England, William Snelling. His mother died when he was six, and his father was an alcoholic. He somehow got himself into West Point, but quit soon after he arrived to venture off into the badlands in the Dakotas. He returned, wrote a book castigating all poets, and then moved to New York. He wandered through the Five Points neighborhood on most nights, drinking heavily, and read flash-type British newspapers there. He decided that New York should have a newspaper just like that. The population was there, the bars and brothels were there, the whores were there, and the people he met said they would read it. He teamed up with George Wilkes, a legitimate writer, and they made journalism history, the tawdry kind.[28]

Wilkes, twenty-four, a tall, well-dressed man with a long neck and thick head of hair, was an alcoholic and midnight marauder who had spent years drifting in and out of the shadowy life that the *Flash* covered—bars, brothels, music halls, and cafés. He knew the nether side of New York better than anyone else in the publishing business.

Wilkes and the other *Flash* editors were pummeled by the penny press and six-cent press. "He has been a common loafer in groggeries and brothels, and actually spit in the face of a decent, hard-working woman in the public street, who was defrauded out of some money either by him or the person who fed him," wailed Mike Walsh of the *Subterranean,* who called the *Flash* "beastly, fraudulent, disgusting and obscene."[29]

The high-water mark of the sleazy flash papers came in 1842. There were four of them in town that summer, the *Rake,* the *Flash,* the *Libertine,* and the *Whip*. They had high circulations, and men grabbed copies as soon as they saw them sitting in high stacks on the counters at newsstands or on the boards set up on top of wooden boxes by street vendors. The papers, at six cents a copy, sold briskly. Their editors claimed they sold between four thousand and twelve thousand copies per week, figures high enough to rival some mainstream dailies. They were very profitable because they earned money in illicit ways in addition to circulation and advertising. They charged brothels fees to name them in their columns, and more money came in from readers, who paid a fee to be mentioned in their gossip columns in order to promote themselves. Still more revenue streamed into flash offices from people, usually married men caught with prostitutes, who paid them bribes to keep their names *out* of the pages of the paper. These men were usually named by initials that could identify them to many of their friends, relatives, and business associates—and their wives. The papers also threatened to send the names of men they identified in their columns to marshals for criminal prosecution, hoping they would pay them not to do so. The men did.[30] They often paid off their partners to keep quiet, too, adding a whole new wrinkle to the ever-growing crime wave.

The philosophy of the flash papers was simple: Men had the right to find sexual satisfaction wherever they could, whether or not their wives or girlfriends provided them with it. "Man is endowed by nature with passions that must be gratified," wrote the editor of the *Whip and Satirist,* "and no blame can be attached to him, who for that purpose occasionally sees a woman of pleasure."[31]

There were references to gay life in the publications, too, such as blind items (that is, mentioning no names) about half-dressed men dancing in clubs or on street corners, or discreet mentions of the nicknames of well-known gay prostitutes and where they had set up shop.[32]

A businessman who was said to have run a liquor business as a front for a house of gay prostitution was continually hounded by the *Whip and Satirist,* whose writers charged that he was using young neighborhood boys as male prostitutes. The *Flash* complained of gay predators, which its writers referred to as "man monsters." The paper said that "they are continually parading our streets of an evening watching for their prey, and hundreds of young boys, yes, sir, boys as young as twelve to eighteen, are victims of their foul and disgusting deeds." The papers had fun with oddball stories, too, like that of a man who fled the bedroom of a prostitute whose glass eye fell out during sex.[33]

In the early 1840s, the "flash men" started to appear in the streets and brothels. They were defined by an 1859 New York slang dictionary as men with no visible means of support or with a low income who dressed very stylishly and sported gaudy jewelry. One dictionary said that language in the sex world was the "language of thieves." Others simply defined them as rogues.[34]

The "sporting men" of New York, and all the readers of the "flash" papers, straight or gay, eager for the sex touted in the flash papers, often wound up victims of crime that night, robbed, beaten up, or knifed in sleazy neighborhoods where constables were nowhere to be found. When men were named in the flash papers as participants in hetero- and homosexuality, as providers or clients, they ended up in trouble.

The law? The law looked the other way. Few inhabitants of any of the gay brothels were ever arrested, and when they were, police magistrates let them go with nothing more than a warning (there were rumors, never proven, that some of the constables involved in supervising the neighborhoods were gay).[35]

The prostitution business, straight or gay, flourished, thanks to the flash papers. In late 1842, the *Whip and Satirist* editor wrote that the number of prostitutes was increasing rapidly in the city. "Very true," snapped the editor in his column. "So are thieves and burglars and the whole population."[36]

The woes of the flash papers continued. They were criticized relentlessly by the legitimate papers. "Their purpose . . . is to promote vice and crime—to point out the facilities for immoral practices, which are afforded in large cities—to propagate slanders—to blast character—to debate intelligence—corrupt the heart—and fill the paths to perdition!" wrote the editor of the *Philadelphia Journal*. A writer for the *Gazette Extraordinary* said that "the city is disgraced at home and abroad. The ribaldry and beastliness to which it gives utterance . . . calls forth the rebuke and reproach of sister communications, and all because our [New York] police are too imbecilic or too cowardly, or too wanton, to do its duty."[37]

The editors of the sex papers constantly fought with each other; important men in town who frequented brothels lambasted them; wives threw their papers out when they discovered them. The district attorney's office investigated them early and tried to find a way to put them out of business. Individuals who felt smeared by the flash papers filed numerous suits, chiefly libel, and sometimes succeeded.

Snelling, the co-editor of the *Flash* with Wilkes, spent a month in jail on libel charges in 1842, and the other editors spent much time in court defending themselves.

Many New Yorkers considered the attacks on the flash editors hypocritical. Lydia Child sat in on one obscenity hearing and smirked at the city's lawyers. "While I was there they brought in the editors of the *Flash,* the *Libertine,* and the *Weekly Rake*. My very soul loathes such polluted publications; yet a sense of justice . . . made me refractory. . . . They dared to *publish* what nine-tenths of all around them *lived* unreproved. Why should they be imprisoned while [others] flourished in the full tide of editorial success, circulating a paper as immoral, and perhaps more dangerous, because its indecency is slightly veiled? Why should the *Weekly Rake* be shut up, when daily rakes walk Broadway in fine broadcloth and silk velvet?"[38]

By the summer of 1843, armed with many editions of the papers and testimonials from dozens of complainers, the district attorney's office decided that the flash papers went too far and that they were obscene. The lawyers for the varied editors of the flash papers argued that they were protected under freedom of the press, but the juries, tired of their campaigns to support illegal sex in the brothels and on street corners, disagreed. By the fall of 1843, the flash papers that had debuted just two years earlier were all out of business, and they never returned.

Police magistrates saw sex cases as trivial, just part of the hooker landscape. Many were dismissed outright. Others were tossed after pleas from prominent madams who ran well-known whorehouses. Many district attorneys gave up on prosecutions of hookers and madams because of the high cost of trials and the low percentage of convictions. Magistrates and constables saw prostitutes as just one more group of entrepreneurs making money and left them alone.[39]

In addition to the "victimless" crime of soliciting, using, and paying prostitutes, violent crimes were committed against the women themselves. They were sometimes beaten, raped, or killed. Many were raped on orders of pimps and madams to make them submissive, to keep them in line, and to force them to work harder in the brothel. New York City's prostitution corps sustained dozens of brutal rapes in the 1830s and 1840s, some reported to the courts and most not.[40] Vicious crimes against prostitutes were not new. They had been attacked periodically since before the Revolution. In 1751, twenty-two hookers were arrested in raids on several houses of prostitution. Four were publicly whipped and ordered to leave the city. Groups of locals had prevented firemen from putting out a fire that destroyed a house of prostitution in 1761. In 1791, a mob destroyed several houses of prostitution that were built near each other, ending their trade for a few weeks.

A spirited Board of Aldermen report in 1812 warned the public that prostitutes were "alarming symptoms of the destruction of youth." But, as always, the problem caused by prostitutes ranked well behind those caused by unlimited drinking and unrestricted gambling. In the 1820s and 1830s, records showed that less than 2 percent of prisoners in New York's city jails or state prisons were behind bars for prostitution.[41]

The harlots all paraded into court to contest any criminal transgression against them and, often with lawyers, insisted on time-consuming trials. The beatings of hookers by angry clients climbed as the years went by, and each time a girl was hurt she went to court. Numerous prostitutes stood before judges with bumps and bruises to prove assault. They cursed and screamed and, in general, hopelessly tied up the court calendar and, every day, added to the list of crimes committed in Gotham (Helen Jewett herself had taken abusive clients to court in 1833 and 1835).[42]

And why should constables go after hookers? In 1826, one constable evicted a hooker from a theater where she was trying to solicit business. A crowd gathered outside the theater and hooted and jeered at the constable for doing his job.[43]

The ladies of the evening had some solid claims. In 1843, a hooker shoved by one of her clients on the steps of the Astor Hotel drew a sharp knife from the pocket of her dress and stabbed him in the chest.

Another prostitute fired a revolver at a drunken man in the parlor of her brothel when he tried to attack her. In 1841, one prostitute, Mary Ann Rogers, was sent to prison for beating up another prostitute on a street corner.[44]

More likely than not, the jury would agree with whores that they had been assaulted or maligned. In one case, a hooker went to bed with a sixty-five-year-old married man and another prostitute. She then emerged from the bedroom and yelled down from the top of the stairs that she had been sexually assaulted and the other woman was her eyewitness. The two whores provided a vivid description of the assault, and the man had a weak answer. The jury listened carefully. The woman had sued the married man for $10,000. The all-male jury agreed with her and ruled in her favor. Her award? Six cents and a loud guffaw from the jurors.[45]

Constables told judges and city officials that the force was not large enough to oversee the whores and robbers in a large city like New York. They also said that burglars and killers could disappear quickly into bad neighborhoods, where they were protected by the people who lived there. Those people did not like the police. In 1836, the editor of the *Journal of Commerce* wrote that "the people are not sufficiently in the habit of respecting the laws and obeying those appointed to enforce them."[46]

There were two criminal levels for streetwalkers, whether or not they were connected to constables. Almost all of the women charged with working for a madam in a high-end house of ill repute were let go, but most of the streetwalkers and teenage slum hookers were imprisoned. Incarceration was a regular part of their job, and many had spent months in jail (the usual sentence was sixty days). One woman was sent to jail eighteen times over the years that she worked the streets. Reformers visited hookers in the Tombs and other jails every Sunday to try to dissuade them from a life between the sheets. They were disturbed by the appearance of the prostitutes they met. The women were "worn out by drunkenness and dissipation," wrote one of the reformers, who commented on how young many of the hookers were and that they seemed much older because of their condition. The reformers noted in their reports, too, that the prostitutes who were in jail for the first time learned all they could about sex from the prostitutes they met there who had been incarcerated numerous times. Imprisonment turned out to be not a punishment but a "college" in which to learn how to be a better hooker and make more money through sex.[47]

The whores also told reformers that they lived in a caste system in which some were considered the upper crust of their profession and others the cellar dwellers. "The women who usually frequent the theater may be said to be of the second class of courtesan, in as much as they are looked down upon by the first rate women [hookers] who ride about in the carriage of rich protectors. Then the theatre-women think themselves degraded by comparison with those who do the excessively swellish on the *pavé*. The dashing Cyprian who treads the pavement of Broadway by day, scorns an alliance, in thought or name, with those who do the same thing at night; and the well dressed evening street-harlot looks even with pitiable contempt upon the ragged, low-life creatures who wander the street for the same purpose as herself," wrote the editor of the *Whip* in 1842.[48]

Many reform leaders concluded that the streetwalkers were condemned to a life of crime by the nature of their work and their isolation from mainstream society. "They had no home but a precarious one—that which the continued commission of crime procured. They had no character and could procure no service. They had no money but that which vice and theft had secured to them, and when they reformed, their means of living were gone. They were discountenanced, reviled and shunned by the chaste. Their courage was gone, and they had no friends whose timely interposition could rescue them," reformer McDowall wrote.[49]

On one visit a reformer noted that just about every hooker she spoke to, or prayed with, said that the only reason she had turned to prostitution was "bad company" and that she would never have sex for money again—once the reformer managed to get her out of jail.[50]

The varied Water Street neighborhoods near the docks had been filled with large mansions of successful shipowners and merchants until the early 1840s, but then the wealthy fled as the neighborhood was populated by thieves and hookers. The elegant homes were soon turned into brothels. It was said to be "one of the most riotous and disorderly localities in the city. The whole of these two blocks is . . . entirely occupied as houses of prostitution of the most degrading and infamous character," lamented one uptown resident.[51]

The police just nodded knowingly at complaints from New Yorkers about such houses of ill repute. One cop said that "as long as houses were not located in any neighborhood where they disturbed the peace I think it would be better for them to remain there than to be removed to a place where they would disturb the public."[52]

City residents were fed up with the prostitutes, the corrupt constables who refused to arrest the hookers, institutions that failed to rehabilitate the street urchins, and the city that would not shut down their illicit industry and stop all of the crime the hookers brought about. In 1843, a group of angry grand jurors wrote in an official report that "the conduct of female prostitutes promenading some of our principal streets in this city, especially Broadway, is not only reprehensible, but is an open violation of public decency. The gaudy and immodest manner in which they dress—the vulgar, obscene and profane conversation constantly made use of in a loud and impudent manner—the[ir] shameless and bold manner . . . the personal insults offered by them to our wives, sisters and daughters, call most earnestly for the strong arm of the law." In 1841, another grand jury had urged the city's hundreds of junk shops to stop buying things from urchins who walked in with sacks full of sheets of metal, small appliances, and old clothes that they stole from someone. All of these items could be purchased inside the stores or at the various sidewalk sales that were held regularly.[53]

In addition to the overt streetwalkers, New York was filled with hundreds of "saloon girls" and "dance hall girls." These were young women who worked as feminine attractions to draw men into the establishments and keep them there, eating and drinking, for as long as possible. The saloon girls worked at dirty, grimy, dark basement drinking holes in the Bowery or seedy second-story bars on Broadway. All of the bars had a run-down, beat-up look to them. They featured third-rate bands or off-key pianists who played all night long. The house girls lounged at the bar or at wooden tables, and one would approach every man who walked in and ask him to buy her a drink or dance with her. The girls were paid a percentage of money from the drinks (usually one-third) but no salary. It was to their advantage to get their "date" as drunk as possible to make money. Whatever else they did—robbery, prostitution—was their business. They were "abandoned wretches who were ready for any deed of violence or crime. They care for nothing but money and will rob or kill for it. . . . [The men] are drugged, robbed, murdered and then the harbor police may find their lifeless forms floating in the river at daybreak," the proprietor of one saloon told the *New York World*.

Many of the women were not good-looking, either. "They are beastly foul-mouthed, brutal wretches. Very many of them are half dead with consumption or disease," said one man.[54]

The dance hall girls were prettier, because they did not come from the city itself. Dance hall impresarios, always looking for new young girls to lure men onto the dance floor and into spending money, ran complex recruiting campaigns in the suburbs to dragoon young and innocent girls to their establishments, promising them hefty salaries, commissions, and good living conditions. Once there, many were drugged or threatened in order to get them to remain and dance the nights away with any lovesick mark who stumbled in from the street.[55]

The upper tier of the dance halls contained far more reputable establishments, such as Harry Hill's, where no girls were on staff and business was legitimate—sort of. Hill's dance hall was near the intersection of Houston and Mulberry Streets. You entered through a lobby and then moved to a large, high-ceilinged open room with a small orchestra playing well-known tunes. It was anchored by a huge, dark wood bar where drinks in small glasses were pushed hard in order

for Harry to make money. The middle-aged Hill, said to be one of
the richest men in New York, was a "short, thick-set man, with a
self-possessed, resolute air, and a face indicative of his calling. . . .
Sharp and decided in his manner, [he] exerts himself to maintain
order among the guests," according to a historian of the 1840s.[56]

The men who danced the night away with the attractive girls at the
dance halls, or "dives," as the rowdier ones were called, were from all
walks of life—judges, lawyers, journalists, store clerks, soldiers, and
doctors. As they danced, they were carefully watched by a well-dressed
group of thieves, muggers, con artists, pickpockets, and burglars. They
engaged the men who came to dance in conversations, bought them
drinks, and took them home when they became drunk. Actually, they
didn't take them home; they took them to some nearby darkened alley
where they beat and robbed them, stabbing and sometimes killing
those who resisted. Back at the dance hall, a disinterested Harry Hill
paid no attention to where the ruffians or the hookers went.[57]

The girls there, not employed by Hill, were hookers, admitted
free through a special entrance. They mingled with the guests, dancing
with as many as they could in order to meet marks and lure them to
their brothel or boardinghouse, wallet in hand. The band played on.
The dance halls, Hill's and others, were emporiums for misbehavior.

"The dives of New York are the hot-beds of its crime. . . . Vice
germinates, grows, buds and yields its bitter fruit [there]. Every stage
of crime is reflected in a true picture of these holes of viciousness,"
wrote NYPD captain George Walling.[58]

Drifting through lower Broadway and the nearby Bowery were two odd
collections of distinctly different men, different from their peers in
New York, different from other men in America, and different from
any other group of men in history—the "sporting man" or "dandy,"
and the "Bowery B'hoy" (boy). In their unusual dress, style of walking
and talking, and clock-defying nightlife, the two brash, sassy classes
could be compared to punk rockers of the twenty-first century.

The sporting man was of any religious or geographic group, young, usually working class, who enjoyed dressing ostentatiously outside of his job. He had fine suits and shoes and was easy to spot because he had a large shiny watch fob dangling from his vest, a diamond stickpin in his shirt or tie or jacket, a smart-looking hat. Sometimes sporting a cane with a gold or brass head, he swaggered through town, easily recognized by all. The dandies were generally aged sixteen to thirty-five and spent a lot of money. They hung out in saloons and theaters; they gossiped with each other on street corners or in the doorway of shops.

They were part of a large mass of young men that lived and partied in the city. "The city at all times contains a large number of strangers, whose evenings are at their own disposal, of young men engaged in trade, who live in boarding houses and hotels, who have plenty of money and no domestic ties. . . . These form a solid phalanx of play-going people," wrote a visitor to Manhattan in 1838.[59]

The sporting man, a glass of beer in his hand and a smile on his face, was a regular fixture at prizefights, casinos, and the racetrack, betting heavily on some tired boxer or some slow horse, ecstatic at victory and demoralized at defeat. These young men made a lot of illegal bets, gambled recklessly, engaged in lawbreaking at illegal fights, and harassed constables. They spent the evening in the alleys of sin, drinking heavily, dancing with loose women, and finishing the day at a house of ill repute, where they lounged not only with bawdy women but with other sporting men in an 1830s fraternity. They were a rare breed with no ambition other than the next girl or next drink, and yet were seen as unique by all. They drifted in and out of a life of sin and crime.

The dandies loved Broadway; it was a second home to them. So did everyone else, especially visitors. "Splendid Broadway, as the avenue is called . . . runs through the whole city. This noble street may vie with any I ever saw, for its length and breadth, its handsome shops, neat awnings, excellent *trottoir*, and well-dressed pedestrians. . . . Were it not so very far from all the old-world things which cling about the heart of an European, I should say that I never saw a city more desirable as a residence," wrote the English-born Frances Trollope in 1832.[60]

Not everybody loved the well-dressed dandies who inhabited the fabled boulevard at night. "Dandies must be exactly the reverse of all the rest of mankind," George Foster wrote, "and as common people see so many beautiful and wonderful and melancholy things as they go through this world that their admiration or their sympathy is constantly in a state of excitement, it of course becomes a necessity of existence with the Dandy that he should admire nothing and sympathize with nothing. . . . A genuine dandy need not have a heart."[61]

Foster admired the street itself, though. "Broadway well deserves its reputation as the centre of fashion and republican aristocracy," he wrote. "The shops are more numerous, more extensive, and filled with more expensive and rarer assortments of goods than those of any other street in America; and this superiority is so unquestionable, that all other cities involuntarily accept the *cue* from the dealers in Broadway." He added that for those who wished to be fashionable, "to be out of Broadway is to be in a vulgar and barbarous state of existence." James McCabe wrote simply, "The most wonderful street in the universe is Broadway."[62]

Broadway was also jammed with basement-level oyster bars, street shops, and cart vendors selling all kinds of food. "Oyster cellars abound; and immense quantities of these luxuries are likewise vended from small waggons in the streets; at which locomotive shops, the pedestrian may be supplied with biscuits, pepper, and ginger beer; in short, for a few pence the carter or mechanic has a whet which might satisfy even a gourmand," said James Boardman in 1833.[63]

The other characters that inhabited the lower section of the city, made famous by playwrights and novelists and, a hundred years later, in black-and-white movies filmed in New York, was the Bowery B'hoy and, to a lesser extent, his lover, the Bowery G'hal. The Bowery B'hoy, a denizen of the night in the Bowery neighborhoods who rarely drifted out of them, was well known for his slang conversations and odd physical appearance and dress. He had his hair cut close at the rear of his head and large curly locks at the front, smeared with an 1840s version of hair gel. He paraded through life, bold as brass, amused all with loud conversation filled with obscure local slang phrases, and spent much of his time with the Bowery G'hal, who was very much like him. The B'hoy wore black jackets and trousers but favored bright red shirts with a cravat tied about the neck and a diamond stickpin. His black hat was firmly tilted on the side of his head. He walked about with a brazen gait, usually holding his coat under his arm. He loved to argue with people and engage in fistfights.

The G'hal dazzled all with loud, bright-colored clothes. She usually sported a pretty bonnet and twirled her parasol around in her tiny hands. She walked the streets of the neighborhood from early morning until midnight. Her skirts went to her ankles and showed off her stockings and colorful shoes. The Bowery B'hoy and his G'hal, always the most raucous couple in New York, frequently engaged in premarital sex, sometimes public sex, that angered the stodgy, conservative moral reformers of the era. Especially criticized were the men who slipped into alleys and masturbated, seen by many, and then returned to their group of friends on the sidewalks. They hung out, as teens do today, in favorite bars, where they drank to excess and purchased illegal lottery tickets; they taunted constables and often consorted with criminals and streetwalkers. The Bowery people, with their odd look, loved to promenade up and down the Bowery, and sometimes Broadway, late at night, greeting their admirers and showing off new bright red handkerchiefs, wild-colored jackets, and high-top shoes. The others promenading at night, strutting with an exaggerated gait, who came and went from their mansions, saw them as genuine New York attractions—walking, talking postcards from Sin City.[64]

George Foster saw the good in the Bowery youth but knew that others did not. "The worst feature in the character of the B'hoy is his dissipation—his worst enemy the grog shop, the three cent cellar [gambling], or the liquor grocery on the corner, . . ." he wrote. "A good strong 'muss' [fight] is the only safety valve through which [the B'hoys] can escape their immense exuberance of animal spirit."[65]

The entire Bowery, about a mile long, was cluttered with pawn-shops, stores that sold cheap goods, and stores that always had some FOR SALE sign in the window, each more desperate for business than the last ("Selling at ruinous prices," bragged many). Newspapers did studies of the prices in the Bowery compared to Broadway and other business districts in town and discovered that the Bowery merchants were right; prices there were some of the lowest in the city. You could buy a woman's dress or man's suit there for much less than in the better shops on Broadway and have money left over to buy addi-tional clothing. It was not just the clothing stores, either. City dwell-ers could buy just about anything cheaper in the Bowery, and in the daytime they crowded stores to take advantage of the low prices.[66]

Shooting galleries filled the neighborhood, too. "Only five cents a shot!" shouted their countermen as every type of fellow lined up to shoot at large targets, such as lions that roared when hit with a bullet and musicians who raised a trumpet and played a tune when struck in the right place. Prizes were boxes of cheap candy and stuffed animals that the sharpshooters gave to their appreciative, smiling dates.

At night, the lamps were lit and the Bowery erupted in a carnival of dance and music. There were a dozen theaters lining the streets, con-cert saloons, huge, two-story-high beer gardens, bar after bar after bar, brothels, bright lights, gambling casinos, lottery parlors, and what would pass today for "dollar stores." Anywhere you went you encoun-tered a small street-corner "Bowery band" sending its slightly off-key, tinny music drifting through the loud night air. It seemed that every street corner had its female fortune-teller, palm reader, or clairvoyant. Moving along with the crowds were tiny street urchins who had become the slickest pickpockets in America and found the pickings easy at night as unsuspecting men with women on their arms surged through the crowded streets and shopped at the overcrowded stores. Members of burglary rings followed well-dressed couples home to case their apart-ments or townhouses. Prostitutes of every kind and every price ap-proached men in the streets, many talking to them right past their wives on their arm. When confronted by an angry wife, the hooker would often give her a price, too, or a two-for-one sex package.[67]

The sporting man and the Bowery B'hoy and G'hal were separate specimens of New Yorkers. They were equal legends but did not hang out with each other. They lived in separate universes, but together, the men and women gave New York a colorful carnival look, its own human circus, the look of which no other city or town in the world could boast.[68]

Some of the women in New York in the pre–Civil War era were almost as criminally minded as the men. They ran counterfeit rings and burglary rings, populated houses of prostitution, worked in illegal casinos, and served as barmaids. They stole as much as the men. One woman was caught stealing enough carpet to cover all the floors of a house and put in jail for thirty days. Another woman was jailed for stealing a single floor rug. Another was put behind bars for beating up her husband. Many midwives were arrested when the mother or baby they attended died. The charges against them were light, and that enraged Bennett at the *Herald*. "It should have been bloody murder," he wrote. Mary Dunn, eighteen, was sent to jail for passing small counterfeit bills at a neighborhood grocery.[69] Mrs. A. E. Brown ran a huge jewelry-theft operation with her husband. It ended when he put $2,000 in stolen jewelry in a trunk and mailed it to her in Baltimore. She did not know that before he mailed it Brown was arrested. She was arrested the moment she walked into the shipping office to claim the trunk.[70]

And then there were the "rascals," as Walt Whitman called them, the wealthy, well-dressed, well-connected men who committed white-collar crimes that nobody seemed to notice but that undercut the foundation of New York life. "New York swarms with rascals of rank," said Whitman in the winter of 1842. "The law, instead of punishing, encourages them. Society's choice circles give them a free pass. They are received pleasantly wherever they go."[71]

And then there were the "butcher boys," gangs of thieves who stole meat from butcher shops. They arrived in front of the store with a wagon pulled by fast horses. One drove the wagon, and the others grabbed huge carcasses of beef from racks in front of the store and tossed them into the open back of the wagon. The boys then leaped on board and sped off into the crowds, dozens of slabs of valuable beef bouncing up and down between their feet. "These robberies opened up to thieves a new field for men of nerve," said Walling. "A few years later watches and other valuables were [similarly] snatched from citizens by men who escaped in wagons."[72]

There was yet another reason for escalating crime by 1842, and that was crime fiction. Many blamed crime writers such as Edgar Allan Poe ("The Murders in the Rue Morgue" and "The Mystery of Marie Roget") and others who wrote books, magazine stories, crime journal tales, and newspaper crime fiction for creating a world of romantic criminals that encouraged young and old to become lawbreakers in real life. Others believed that New Yorkers had become so used to crime, and so disgusted with the police, that in real life, as in crime novels, they had even started to cheer for the burglars and killers. It was "a morbid sympathy for offenders," wrote one editor.[73]

A third major cause of crime in the city in the period 1834 to 1860 was drinking. New Yorkers, like most other Americans, had fallen in love with imbibing during the colonial era. New Yorkers began to drink beer, excessive amounts of it, in the 1750s because water from streams and wells was badly tainted. There was bacteria that caused illnesses in the fabled mountain streams that were the centerpieces of so many paintings that touted the natural beauty of America. Colonists had brought formulas for beer with them from England but soon discovered that they could make the brew from corn, oats, barley, and other ingredients grown outside the villages of early America. People began to drink beer all day long; many imbibed at breakfast. Beer was the main drink at all social functions, from weddings to funerals. Thousands of colonists set up home distilleries. Many soon built large breweries that served their villages. The production of moonshine liquor became a profitable industry, so profitable that Pennsylvania moonshiners decided not to pay taxes on their liquor. An angry President George Washington led an army to put down the "Whiskey Rebellion," and the "moonshine men" surrendered and paid their taxes. City entrepreneurs paid their taxes, too, and rather shortly cities like New York had dozens, and then hundreds, of breweries and taverns.

Prior to the Revolution, almost all liquor came from the West Indies, but in the 1790s and early 1800s the West Indies dramatically raised prices, thinking that in America they had a captive market. They did not. American farmers began producing millions of gallons of liquor and stocked warehouses full of it. They overproduced, and that drove the price down to just a nickel a gallon, cheaper than tea or coffee. American taverns were soon flooded with the liquor and the equally cheap beer. At the same time, the number of bars increased in cities as the population increased. In 1827, New York had 160 taverns; in 1835, it was home to over 3,000. That number, some speculated, climbed to 15,000 by the mid-1850s. You could drink, and drink a lot, anywhere you chose in New York.[74]

The tavern quickly became the community center of small villages in the outer reaches of the colonies and the center of activity in dozens of cities. It was the place to go for drinking, dart games, billiards, food, card playing, gossip mongering, dancing, and all social life. People gathered together and drank. Getting drunk was more American than apple pie.

Beer was popular to wash down food and cool off people on a hot day. Americans drank between six and ten beers a day. By the 1840s, the city was cluttered with bars and drinkers—and drunks. City officials said that by that time New York had one bar for each fifty men and women over the age of fifteen.[75]

Many of the crimes in New York, major as well as minor, were committed by men and women who had been drinking. Men who had too many drinks argued and stumbled into bar fights with each other. Someone pulled a knife and stabbed someone else. Men under the influence of alcohol committed robberies, beat their wives, and raped women. Drunks accidentally knocked over candles and started

fires that destroyed homes. Dozens of crimes emanated from drinking. Whitman wrote of a drunk he saw steal a loaf of bread from the
top of a barrel in front of a grocery store on a crowded street in lower
Manhattan. The store owner chased him, shouting for him to halt,
and caught him, summoned a constable, and watched as the man was
taken to jail. "So the thief was taken off to prison and, being arraigned, a few hours afterward, was summarily convicted and sentenced to the customary place just out of the city, there to remain for
many days at hard labor and confinement," Whitman wrote.[76]

Later, in 1858, Whitman again lamented about alcoholics, who he
said had become an army that surged through saloons in New York and
ended up badly as the hours drained out of the day. "At the station
houses, they are pretty busy providing accommodations for inebriated
Johns, intoxicated Pats and unfortunate Bridgets. A motley set they
are—the debris of the North side, wretched, sodden, degraded, but all
occupying the same dead level. Rum, like poverty, makes strange bed-
fellows," he wrote, adding that the drunks were not just from the lower
classes but from the higher classes, too. In the spring of 1841, a drunken
John Haggerty broke into an apartment where four women lived, snug-
gled up next to them in their bed, and was promptly arrested and jailed.
All of the inebriates were ashamed of their midnight marauding in the
morning when, sober, they had to face a judge and perhaps be carted
off to jail. An informal study showed that 67 percent of all suicides in
New York City were committed by men who were drunk.[77]

Whitman might have added about saloons, too, that many joked that
if you were looking for a cop, that was where to look. One man quipped
that police officers "spent most of their time leaning on bars in corner saloons."[78]

Many men who became drunk added to their lunacy by taking drugs.
The combination of drinks and drugs often killed them. That's what
happened to Barnard Shannery, a grade school teacher in Port Ches-
ter, a suburb of New York. He became very drunk and then took
laudanum. He had been drinking in so many places that day that no
one could name the exact place where he became inebriated.[79]

Many of those who died from drinking were proud of their alcoholic addiction. One man in his twenties simply fell dead in the street one autumn afternoon. The coroner said he died of a combination of lengthy drinking and a case of epilepsy. His love of drinking was attested to by the large tattoo on his arm that read I LOVE RUM.[80]

Patrick Ludwig celebrated one Fourth of July standing in front of a judge as his wife told of how he had come home drunk and beat her. He pulled her hair, then pushed her down to the ground and kicked her repeatedly. It was a common tale, and he was sent off to jail.

Alcoholics had become a part of the city landscape and could be found everywhere, especially at night. One man walking through the Broadway theater district in 1850 wrote that "here and there a lamppost is embellished with a human swine who leans, a statue of drunkenness, against it for support and consigns his undigested supper to his fellow pigs who rise early o'mornings."[81]

Drunks were such a problem in New York that in 1833 the Board of Aldermen asked the city's constables to arrest all of the drunks they could find. Those that had committed a crime could be sent to an almshouse, where, under confinement, they would spend up to six months at hard labor. Repeated drunk offenders could be sent to the penitentiary. The police courts, started in the mid-1820s just to handle crime cases, were filled with drunks and beggars under the new law.[82]

Some of the beggars won police sympathy, but others did not. The police were certain that many of the destitute with their hands held out, whom the cops saw as common criminals, were frauds. "A favorite excuse is that the applicant only needs a nickel or a dime to make up a sufficient amount to pay for his night's lodging, but the chances are that he has more ready cash in his pocket than the person addressed," snorted Captain George Walling.[83]

Hundreds of drunks died when, hopelessly inebriated, they fell and cracked their heads. Lydia Child was walking home late one night and turned a corner onto her street. "Something lay across my path. It was a woman, apparently dead, with garments all draggled in New York gutters, blacker than waves of the infernal rivers. Those who gathered around said she had fallen in intoxication and was rendered senseless by the force of the blow," she told a friend.[84]

Alcoholism was such a problem that in his annual report for 1852, the New York chief of police said it was the number one reason why the crime rate climbed each year and was the highest in the country. He assured the state legislature that if drinking declined, crime would decline with it. Drinking, though, did not decline.[85]

The antidrinking temperance societies arrived in the 1830s and conducted long and loud crusades against the abuse of alcohol and the criminal activity it brought about. They had some effect, but it was minor. These societies had thousands of members in New York, and they held colorful and crowded parades down Broadway and other streets, but they made minimal impact on drinking and had almost no effect in shutting down the strings of bars that they targeted. Drinking was a problem for tens of thousands of men in New York, a problem that often resulted in crime.

New York City was also a town populated by pickpockets who thought nothing of lingering at the most expensive stores on Broadway in order to target wealthy prey. "Look out for the contents of your pockets," wrote Whitman. "It is quite possible that you may be otherwise relieved of your cash."[86]

Many of the pickpockets were ten- and eleven-year-old boys and girls. City fathers had hoped that the establishment of the New York public school system in the 1830s would keep youths off the streets and in the classroom, but the schools did not become popular right away, and by the 1850s only half the children in New York under eighteen went to school; the rest idled their time away on the streets. Many of them turned to crime.[87]

Pickpockets worked alone or in teams of three and four. They roved the streets and squares but found most of their targets in large public halls or on transport vehicles. The hundreds of ferries that provided transportation to Brooklyn, Staten Island, and New Jersey (the fare in 1844 was two cents) were fruitful, as were theaters, omnibuses, hospital lobbies, and crowds at baseball games. The pickpockets easily made off with diamond stickpins from men's shirts, rolled-up wads of paper money, and expensive bracelets slid around ladies' wrists. Some groups of them were so brazen that they went to church and then, mingling with the crowd when it left, preyed on as many religious parishioners as they could. Even bolder pickpockets worked funerals, wearing black suits and moving about teary-eyed as they looted the forlorn members of the family and the dead man's friends and neighbors, pretending to be a relation of the deceased.[88]

Pickpockets were just one of many problems in the city and many residents pointed their fingers at incompetent politicians. Walt Whitman was one. He wrote of one state senator, Judge Scott, that to compare him to Judas would insult the memory of Judas. "We have, in our years, seen examples of slippery, cowardly, sordid politicians," he went on, "but this Scott out Herods Herod. Not one iota of manliness, of honesty, or of patriotism, appears to reside in his character. . . . He sinks below the regard even of his kindred rascals."[89]

The complete moral collapse of New York through prostitution, gambling, and drinking and the subsequent increase of crime because of them was symbolically uncovered in a single visit to the Delevan Temperance Institute by reformer Child. She met a drunken woman in one of the rooms in the as yet unfinished, chilly building. The woman "wept like the rain," said Child, as she told her that her small boy had become a criminal. "He was as good a child as ever lived," she cried, and told her that he had fallen in with a gang of young thieves and they had been arrested and tossed into the house of correction. "He would not have been in their company, ma'am . . . if . . . ," she said, and then began to cry and had to stop speaking. Child, tears in her eyes, nodded in agreement.

He would not have been in the company of the rowdies if he had not been living in the "Sodom and Gomorrah" of the New World and if crime did not wash through the city streets like a thunderstorm, the woman sobbed.[90]

. . .

There was race, too. Nothing sparked trouble in New York City like disputes over it. Antislavery advocate Child was struck by the way that scenes of New York always reminded her of the conditions of slaves—the secret slave trade being conducted on ships that plied the waters in and out of New York Harbor, and the slave catchers that roamed the city looking for runaways. One night she was standing on a lawn at the Battery, her favorite location in the city, watching "the retreating king of day," as she referred to nightfall, when a barge sailed slowly past her. She looked past it and then up to the starlit sky. "I think . . . of the poor fugitive slave, hunted out by mercenary agents, chained on shipboard and perchance looking up, desolate and heartbroken, to the same stars on which I fix my free and happy gaze. Alas, how fearfully solemn must their light be to *him*, in his hopeless sorrow," she wrote in the autumn of 1841.[91]

Child complained bitterly to all that society made the criminal, that no one was born a thief or murderer. She once wrote that there was no difference between the white-collar and blue-collar thief—they both stole—except that only the blue-collar thief was jailed. "Society made both these men thieves, but punished the one, while she rewarded the other. That criminals so universally feel themselves as victims of injustice, is one strong proof that it is true." She added that if society could create so much crime with its injustices, society could cure crime, too, with justice. "The superintendent at Blackwell [Blackwell's Island housed a mental hospital/prison] told me, unasked, that ten years' experience convinced him that the whole system tended to *increase* crime," she wrote.[92]

What annoyed Child, and others, about societal crime was that the city permitted Blackwell's to hire out its mental patients to work in city stores. Hospital officials pocketed the money their patients were paid. They got the jobs because they worked cheaper than the general laborer.[93]

By the winter of 1843, many New Yorkers were fed up with the city, its crime, and its pathetic police force. "The English papers do abuse us shamefully for swindling, repudiation, cheating, and other trifling departures from rectitude, which abuse is all the harder to be borne for the difficulty we have in many of the cases of contradicting the truth of the charges," ex-mayor Hone complained.[94]

The crime rate did not go down in the early 1840s, as people hoped; it went up. The crime wave became so intense that the city was forced to establish extra police courts and assign additional judges to hear crime cases there. Newspapers, especially the penny press, began to send more police reporters to cover all of the courts. Boarders were arrested for robbing fellow boarders. Counterfeit rings succeeded. A man abandoned his pregnant fiancée at the marriage altar and was chased across town by her brother. Respectable middle-class people stayed at New York's swankier hotels for a week or more and then vanished, never paying their bills. Men distributed fake three-dollar bills. A man was stabbed over a hundred times in a bar fight as the others in the bar stood by and watched, not interfering.

Con artists set up innocent citizens by appealing to their greed. In the "horse game," two con men argued loudly about the price of a horse, set at, say, $350. The innocent man would then offer one of them a lesser amount after one of the two arguers walked away. The con man took the money and promised to deliver the horse, but, of course, there was no horse.[95]

New York's numerous residents all seemed to be victims of some game. The "drop game" was another. A con man "found," say, fifty dollars on the street and announced it to the man standing near the money. As the man looked down at the money, another man would walk up to him and say that he, as well as the man who found the fifty dollars should both share in their newfound loot. The con man then gave the mark a hundred-dollar bill, and the man gave him change. The two con men then walked away. The innocent mark had his hundred dollars, but it was counterfeit.

Illegal counterfeit rings were notorious in 1840s New York because America did not yet have a paper-based national monetary system.

Each bank issued its own notes, and criminals with special paper and printing presses duplicated them. The counterfeit rings were so proficient at their trade that in the 1840s one ring had a warehouse full of counterfeit bills from eight different city banks.

A small but profitable criminal industry was shoplifting. By the early 1840s, the city had hundreds of shops, led by huge dry goods emporiums, and they were usually crowded with customers, usually female. The smaller stores had little security protection against shoplifters. The large stores hired private detectives, or off-duty constables, to look out for shoplifters. They arrested some, such as Jane Louisa Reilly, who pilfered forty-three dollars in goods from the Lozee & Mott store and hid them under her clothes, but most went undetected.[96] Security only spotted the very well known thieves; the rest walked right past them. Hundreds of them poured into the stores and, after careful thievery, walked out with goods stuffed into handbags or under large dresses. "The shoplifter carries a bag, with straps fastened around the waist, into which she may easily drop anything she can steal. Some women arrange their skirts so that the whole front top to bottom forms a bag which can be stuffed with feathers, laces, etc, without any outward sign," said one cop.[97]

Frustrated managers said the culprits they feared the most were not the poor women trying to steal clothes to wear to keep warm but the rich women who wanted expensive small things but did not want to pay for them. So the wealthy made petty shoplifting a hobby and departed from the most expensive stores with the priciest goods. Altogether, the wives of the rich merchants and lawyers walked home with as much loot as the poor women thieves in the stores. Many young women, well dressed, helped themselves to clothing they wanted, too. Anne Riley, eighteen, was arrested after leaving a shop because she strolled out the door with a pile of lingerie stuffed under her dress.[98]

They all paled in comparison to robbers, though. Thieves took everything they could and wherever they could. Residents relied on locks, but thieves could jimmy them with bars or open them with false keys. The plunder from robberies was so great in New York that by the mid-1830s, rings of burglars were put together by a mastermind. Normally three to five men worked in a ring. One man got into a house, one man stood guard outside as a watchman, and the others looted the house. They brought large suitcase-style bags or canvas satchels to haul away their loot. Many rings were so busy that they kept calendars, with thievery marked down for particular days and nights.

"One day a robbery uptown, the next downtown, then east, then the west, and then in the center of the city. No band of brigands ever displayed less regard for property which would not pay for carrying away," Captain Walling said of one highly organized ring.[99]

There was so much lawbreaking that people saw criminals everywhere. George Strong said that walking down a street he saw "loafers of the most unquestionable genuineness on the lookout for anything they could lay their hands on."[100]

One editor was so distressed about the increase in thieves that he wrote at the start of one winter that "the honorable society of burglars are now on their usual winter professional tour, and as every attention should be paid to each distinguished guest, we hope that they may be entertained at the public expense."[101]

Bennett of the *Herald* was just as upset about crime and forlornly began one of his columns in the summer of 1841 by writing dismally, "This is the season for murder."[102]

CHAPTER TEN

Five Points and the Boundaries of Hell

[A policeman] was violently attacked by a Five Points thief, nick-named Monkey, who gave him a blow with a sling shot in the mouth, displacing some of his teeth and otherwise injuring him severely.

—*New York Herald*, November 3, 1849

The sleazy centerpiece of crime in New York City was the neighborhood called Five Points, so named because five streets intersected within it—Mulberry, Worth, Park, Baxter, and Little Water (the neighborhood was in today's Chinatown). Five Points had been developed as a haven for criminals in the middle of the 1820s, when young street toughs moved there, and hid there, while they formed powerful street gangs that were the scourge of the city until the Civil War. The street ruffians, nearly always armed with knives, hatchets, and guns, selected exotic names for these gangs, such as the Forty Thieves, Dead Rabbits, Roaches, Plug Uglies, Whyos, Kerryonians, Chinamen, Shirt Tails, Roach Guards, Atlantic Guards, True Blue Americans, Chichesters, Bowery Boys, Eastmans, Gophers, and Five Pointers.

The Forty Thieves was the first, formed in the late 1820s at the back of a grocery store that served as a liquor emporium. The Kerryonians, all men from County Kerry in Ireland, came next. Each gang protected its turf in Five Points through street patrols and, when necessary, all-out warfare in which streets were blocked off with carts and crates, and pitched battles were conducted in which several men were usually killed and many were maimed. Gangs sometimes banded together to fight gangs outside of the Five Points area.[1]

The Dead Rabbits had become so powerful, and so famous, that writers even attached their name to political slogans. The *Brooklyn Daily Times*, as an example, said that because a few evildoers always tried to ruin the United States, America had to be called the "Dead Rabbit Democracy."[2]

British novelist Charles Dickens was appalled when he visited Five Points on a tour of New York in 1842. He wrote, "This is the place; these narrow ways diverging to the right and left, and reeking everywhere with dirt and filth. . . . The coarse and bloated faces at the doors have counterparts back home. Debauchery has made the very houses prematurely old. See how the rotten beams are tumbling down, and how the patched and broken windows seem to scowl dimly like eyes that have been hurt in drunken frays. Many . . . pigs live here. Do they ever wonder why their masters walk upright instead of going on all fours and why they talk instead of grunting?" He concluded that Five Points was representative of all that was "loathsome, drooping and decayed." Even so, he enjoyed his ramble through it. In a dim, noisy subterranean Five Points dance hall he saw a "corpulent black fiddler, and his friend who plays the tambourine, stamp upon the boarding of the small, raised orchestra in which they sit, and play a lively measure," enticing half a dozen couples onto the dance floor.[3]

The British novelist did not have anything good to say about the rest of the city's law-and-order system, either. When he wrote of it he highlighted its "ill-managed lunatic asylum, a bad jail, a dismal workhouse and a perfectly intolerable place of police-imprisonment."[4]

Americans were just as aghast at the depravity of Five Points as the British visitor. George Foster, who roamed the streets of Manhattan at night looking for stories, stopped whenever he entered the Five Points neighborhood. It was, he said, "a sad, an awful sight, a sight to make the blood slowly congeal and the heart to grow fearful and cease its beatings." Foster called the poor and the criminals who resided there "human swine."[5]

Reformer Lydia Child was one of the few women adventuresome enough to explore Five Points. "There you will see nearly every form of human misery, every sign of human degradation. The leer of the licentious, the dull sensualism of the drunkard, the sly glance of the thief—oh, it made my heart ache for many a day. It stunned my senses with the amount of evil and fell upon the strong hopefulness of my character, like a stroke of the palsy," she wrote.[6]

What made Dickens, Foster, and Child really cringe, though, was the outrageous public sex that was conducted right in front of them and the guides who took them on their rambles. On one disconcerting night, Dickens and his friends visited a tavern in which five men and women, completely naked, were having sex on the floor. Dickens, shaken, backed out of the tavern. In other trips, he witnessed other acts of public sex that were probably far more upsetting than anything he had seen in even the most sinful and criminal neighborhoods of London. Those practicing sex were breaking the law, but nobody seemed to mind.[7]

In *Oliver Twist*, Dickens created a London street gang headed by Fagin and populated by teenagers with marvelous names he made up, such as the Artful Dodger. The boys preyed on the public. They were the same type of gang as those that roamed through Five Points.

Some said that while Dickens was quick to illustrate crime, he had no solutions to the problem. He "puts the searing iron to wickedness, whether among poor or rich; and yet when he describes the guilty, poor and oppressed man, we are always in some way reminded how much need there is that certain systems of law and habit which lead to this poverty and consequent crime, should be remedied," said Walt Whitman, who disagreed with Dickens's portrayal of society as all good or all bad people.[8] The editor of the *Sun*, too, nodded his head knowingly when writing about Dickens's visit. He said journalists, both British and American, were making too much out of Boz's (Dickens's pen name) travels to Five Points and other destitute neighborhoods. "A corps of sneaky reporters, most of them fresh from London, are pursuing him like a pack of hounds at his heels to catch every wink of his eye, every motion of his hands, and every word that he speaks . . . to be dished up with embellishment," the *Sun* chief wrote.[9]

Despite the denunciations of Five Points by writers and travelers, the temperance movement saw the conversion to Jesus of the Five Points residents as its holy grail. Every Sunday, for years, a different temperance group would set up a large tent on the street and stage daylong meetings that drew a few disinterested neighborhood dawdlers.[10]

It was an era when hundreds of novelists, short story writers, and playwrights joined Dickens in writing scalding indictments of the New York metropolis and painted it as Sin City on the Hudson, teeming with murderers and robbers in Five Points and other districts. Those works of fiction helped to make New York such a notorious city.

Five Points was a grimy amalgam of urban decay. Colored papers were taped over broken windows. Narrow alleys twisted this way and that, and all seemed to contain saloons, some large and some small. The stench of urine and beer was everywhere. Dozens of tired African Americans slept in piles in some saloons and sailors did the same in others, while dogs slept quietly next to them. Prints of oceangoing ships or George Washington seemed to hang over the liquor bottles in every saloon. Garbage was piled up outside the doors, front and back, and smelled. Those who chose normal sleeping arrangements went to Five Points dives that rented out beds for three cents a night and charged a penny a night to sleep on the floor. Many of them had garbage strewn throughout their rooms. A state investigatory committee reported that in some streets in the neighborhood, piles of garbage were two feet high.[11]

"If some of our disbelieving readers would take a night stroll down into that sickening neighborhood and look around amongst the wretches who hide away during the day and come out at night, reeking with filth and gin fumes, they would think them fit for any crime which the devil could invent," said 1850s writer Ned Buntline.[12]

Other visitors to the neighborhood chronicled filthy, vermin-infested tenements where "rum-degraded human beings lived" and warned readers to watch their step when walking through them. The steps of buildings were covered with garbage, rotted sticks of wood, and torn clothing; on the landings of stairs, people whom one did not know lay dead or dying. One writer called the buildings "dens of death."[13]

James McCabe warned visitors, "It is not safe for a stranger to undertake to explore these places for himself. No respectable man is a match for the villains and sharpers of New York. . . . The city is full of danger."[14]

The street toughs from Five Points had no trouble starting fights. One would simply walk up to someone and say he heard he wanted to fight him. The target would say he did not say that, and the tough would tell him that he had just called him a liar and hit him. It never failed.[15]

The neighborhood of about 3,500 people was anchored by a large, three-story-high abandoned factory called the Old Brewery. It was across the street from Murderer's Alley, named for its killings, and an area of bars called the Den of Thieves. Few outsiders ever went into the Old Brewery, where, it was rumored, hundreds of vagrants lived. Some reports had its population at slightly over a thousand, living either in small family apartments, single and double apartments, or dormitories, sleeping at night and committing crimes in the daytime. (A missionary group purchased it in 1852 and tore it down the following year. Workers who razed it found hundreds of human bones between its walls, said to be the remains of sailors slain in cheap hotels and vagrants killed in the streets.)[16] There were few gaslights on the street corners of Five Points, and the streets and alleys were dimly lit, affording criminals an easy opportunity to strike at visitors. The police had only a single watchman patrolling the beat there, and anyone he sought was swallowed up by the darkness or easily hidden in a cellar hovel or in the back of a dark, twisting alley. The single patrolman was one of the great weaknesses of the early police.

Five Points was filled with prostitutes. The number ranged widely, depending upon whom you talked to and what newspapers you read. Some lived there, and some visited to walk the streets in search of business. The whores in Five Points were different from those in the rest of town, though. In Five Points, whores simply lounged in wide-open saloons and propositioned whoever walked in. Then they left and found a cheap room for a few cents somewhere nearby for sex.[17]

The neighborhood was also full of Irish. Statistics vary, but most indicate that between 60 and 70 percent of Five Points residents were Irish. Ironically, many Irish police officers grew up in the Five Points area; as eyewitnesses to crime there and throughout the city, they had firsthand knowledge of how criminals operated. One of them was Thomas F. Byrnes, son of a saloon bartender, who went on to join the force in 1863 and over the years became one of its most famous members, the hero in several police novels in later years.[18]

Five Points was full of bars, but most were small and sleazy. Nearby, on Hester Street, was McGlory's, one of the most infamous bars in America. The bar, which used Five Points gangsters as bouncers, was a favorite of out-of-town male visitors. You walked through double doors into a long black hallway and then into the two-story-high bar, which was perpetually mobbed with very loud people. Men and men in drag slinking through the table pathways served drinks. Sexual parties were held in second-floor walled-off boxes, liquor flowed, a three-piece band played, and, for a fee, women danced in front of your table. A *Cincinnati Enquirer* reporter spent a night there and was shocked. He said that, much like in today's "red-light" districts, women entered boxes and disrobed if money was placed in their stockings. Five or six women would assault you at once, begging for quarters. Women on the floor danced the cancan, very immodestly, for fifty cents. Men drank until they fell off their chairs, and any rowdies that arrived were taken care of by the bouncers. "Billy McGlory himself is at the bar. . . . A medium sized man, he is neither fleshy nor spare; he has black hair and mustache, and a piercing black eye. He shakes hands all around as if we were obedient subjects come to pay homage to a king," the reporter wrote.[19]

The Five Points residents were night owls. "They are obscene night-birds who flit and howl and hoot by night. . . . Day is hateful to them," wrote Foster.[20]

The Points was full of narrow streets and postage-stamp-sized illegal gambling houses that were open nearly twenty-four hours each day and filled with men losing good money and drinking bad whiskey. Small ground-level shops usually had an apartment or two at the rear for the proprietors. Most of the residents of Five Points were armed with knives, clubs, and, later, revolvers. They smelled of liquor.

One man said of the neighborhood, "No spot of ground on this continent had the reputation of having been the witness of more crime . . . or where want or woe were more apparent. Every house was a brothel, the resort of persons of every age, sex, and color; every store a dram shop where from morning till morning the thieves and abandoned characters of the town whetted their depraved tastes, and concocted future crimes and villainies."[21]

The street gang members all lived here or hung out here. They stayed side by side with a black population separate from the general black population of the city. Within the shadows of Five Points black men and women could do whatever they wanted; many lived with or even married white partners. They steered clear of the street posses, though. The neighborhood vigilantes fought each other within the confines of Five Points and fought any police officers or squadrons who invaded the area looking for a suspect in a crime.

While few willingly stepped into Five Points, all seemed to have an opinion of the people who lived there. Most derided them and called them names, but sociologists were afraid this class of people would beget another generation of criminals just like them, and that generation would beget a third, and in the end these people, not checked by law enforcement, would overwhelm America. "The greatest danger that can confront a country like ours is from the existence of an igno-rant, debased, permanently poor class in the great cities. It is more threatening if this class is of foreign birth and of different habits from those of our own people," wrote Charles Loring Brace, who went to work establishing large homes for wayward boys to keep them out of the clutches of the denizens of the street in Five Points and other New York neighborhoods.[22]

Mayors continually talked about cleaning up Five Points. Mayor William Havemeyer called it "a nest of vipers" in 1845 and urged the Common Council to widen all the streets and add more gas lamps to light the intersections to cut down crime. The councillors did not. It was not until 1849, and the combination of the Astor Place riot and a cholera epidemic in Five Points, that the city government made any moves to sanitize the area, and even then little was accomplished.[23]

Most people took long, circuitous walks to avoid it, and others, when they did walk its filthy, crime-ridden streets, made sure they carried a long, thick wooden club for their own protection. A grand jury report called Five Points "a rendezvous for thieves and prostitutes." Journalist Foster wrote that "nearly every house and cellar was grog-gery below and a brothel above." One reformer said it was "the most notorious precinct of moral leprosy in the city."[24]

The prostitutes in Five Points were raunchy in appearance, but not as bedraggled as the hookers on Water Street, near the shipping docks on the East Side. "Here the prostitutes are generally drunkards. . . . You see the women half exposed at the cellar doors as you pass. Their faces are flushed and pimpled," Walt Whitman wrote of Five Points women.[25]

No one in the city had any respect for the women who resided in the Five Points neighborhood. "Theresa Melionas, an ill-looking, haggard, dissipated creature, 30 years of age, one of those degraded wretches who infest the portion of the Five Points, was brought up under the following circumstances [of criminality]," wrote a police re-porter from the *Herald* about one of them.[26]

Policing of Five Points was lax. Extra policemen assigned there never showed up. One thing they did do was spread the idea that Five Points was a social quicksand, its own universe, and its inhabitants would take care of themselves better than the police ever could. The police feared not only injury but all-out wars with one or more of the street gangs that resided in, and governed, the Five Points area. The cops knew, too, that these gangs were used by Tammany Hall on Election Day to harass the Whig Party and its followers. Why anger the bosses?[27]

And so Five Points, one of America's great cauldrons of crime, rolled along, unmolested by the scared police, its own city in its own country.

CHAPTER ELEVEN

The Brutal Murder of the Beautiful Cigar Girl

The apathy of the great criminal judges, sitting on their own fat for a cushion bench, and the utter inefficiency of their police, are all tending fast to reduce this large city to a savage state of society—without law—without order—and without security of any kind.

—James Gordon Bennett on the Mary Rogers case

The administration of justice in this city has been bringing itself into contempt every year, every week, every day.

—James Gordon Bennett on the Helen Jewett case

On July 25, 1841, Mary Rogers, a beautiful young woman who worked in John Anderson's downtown cigar store, told her fiancé, Daniel Payne, that she was leaving Manhattan to visit her aunt. He never heard from her again. Three days later, Mary's murdered body, in torn clothes with a cord tied around her neck, was found near Elysian Fields, a forested park and entertainment area in Hoboken, on the New Jersey side of the Hudson River. At first, authorities believed she was the victim of street gang violence. Still others said that Rogers's murderer was her fiancé. Still more said it must have been a rival suitor for her affections.

The editor of *The New York Sun* put the blame squarely on the growth of New York and the eagerness of its greedy store owners to make money off the tidal wave of people in town, especially men. He blasted the practice of hiring pretty women to lure men into tobacco shops, or any shops. Mary Rogers had "become the victim of the very passions and vices which her exposure to the public gaze for mercenary gains was so well calculated to engender and encourage," he wrote.[1]

The murder of Mary Rogers struck a chord in the hearts of New Yorkers. Her slaying came on the heels of an ever-rising crime tide and was a sign, yet again, that people could not walk the streets of the city safely anymore. She, or anyone for that matter, was an easy target. Rogers was not a woman who got herself into trouble. She was not a prostitute, did not hang out in saloons or frequent gambling halls. Mary was a typical girl who lived with her mother, harmless, and now she was dead. The homicide shook the Manhattan community to its core.

John Anderson's cigar store in lower Manhattan had substantial competition. Everybody smoked cigars, from refined poets to seasoned dockworkers, and there were dozens of stores that serviced their tobacco addiction. Anderson needed something special to set himself apart from the other stores. That was Mary Cecilia Rogers, a twenty-year-old girl who possessed not only a beautiful, angelic face but also a voluptuous body and, those who knew her said, a smoky sexiness that few women had.

Her father had died in a steamship explosion, and she and her mother left Connecticut and moved to New York, where they opened a small boardinghouse at 126 Nassau Street, just blocks from the hub of the newspaper district and City Hall. Boarders loved her, young men who met her lusted after her, and John Anderson saw a fortune in her. He hired her as his assistant, promising her mother that she would never be left alone in the store and that he would walk her home each evening to provide protection. Men who met her in his store were so smitten they wrote poems about her and lingered in the store talking to her as long as possible, always buying something, and Anderson's business profited.[2]

And then Mary Rogers vanished, in October of 1838 when she was seventeen. A suicide note was found in her room. Her mother went to the press for help, and several newspapers wrote about the disappearance. Some supplied reasons, such as the *Sun*. "The cause of the wayward freak of this young woman is supposed by her friends to be a disappointed love—she having recently received the addresses of a certain widower who, it is said, has deserted her," a *Sun* reporter wrote, adding that the failed love caused her to kill herself. All were certain that she was dead. Then, just a day later, she reappeared, a big smile on her face, and told her mother she had gone to visit a friend in Brooklyn and simply forgot to tell her.[3]

Three years later, in the summer of 1841, she was gone again, this time for good. Mary left her Manhattan boardinghouse home on Sunday, July 25. She wore a white dress, a black shawl, a blue scarf, a leghorn hat, and light-colored shoes and carried a light-colored parasol.[4]

Two days later, fishermen found her body floating in shallow water just off Castle Point, a peninsula north of Hoboken. Dr. Richard Cook performed an autopsy and said she had been gagged, beaten, and raped by three different men and strangled with a torn-off piece of her own dress.

One of her former boarders, said to have been infatuated with her, now a sailor on a ship in the harbor, was grilled on two separate occasions but released by the police. Her fiancé had an alibi and was released by the police, although newspapers suspicious of him would keep his name in the headlines. The newspapers, eager for an arrest, then started to question Dr. Cook's autopsy. He had ruled that she was not pregnant, but pregnancy would fit in with the spurned-suitor theory, and the papers began to suggest it. They also said, and many people agreed, that the autopsy was not thorough and that Cook's suggestion that she was raped and beaten might have been wrong.[5]

There were several reasons why the death of Mary Rogers became one of the most famous murders in United States history, even bigger than the prolonged 1839 trial of Ezra White, finally convicted of stabbing four men to death at a New York party.[6] First, she was beautiful, and slain beautiful women always draw oversized headlines. Second, the death of someone who worked right next door to City Hall, and the police headquarters, drew attention. Third, the girl was not a prostitute, like Helen Jewett, but a simple country girl who lived with her mother and worked to help her meet expenses. Fourth, and most important, numerous journalists, such as Edgar Allan Poe, James Fenimore Cooper, and Washington Irving, whose newspapers were near her cigar store, visited her frequently, as much to see her as to buy cigars. The writers liked her and wanted to avenge her death by getting the constables to arrest someone. These people, who could make a story big, all knew her, probably secretly loved her, and were outraged by her murder.

Then the newspapers also decided that she was noteworthy because she seemed like an ordinary woman who met a horrible fate because of the rising crime tide, from which the city's police offered no protection. She was the classic "girl next door" slain in the dangerous nighttime sordidness of the "big city." News coverage, every single day, became massive, and the story became a national topic of discussion.[7]

The shore area near Elysian Fields where her body was found was jammed with oglers. People picnicked on the spot where she died. Male and female religious zealots brought caravans of people to the spot and gave religious sermons to them all, warning them that if they were not God-fearing they would be killed, too. One of those visitors was reformer Child, who saw Rogers as yet another victim of the crime-infested city. She wrote of how lovely the scene was and what a majestic view anyone there had of Manhattan across the river. "Remembrances of the city haunted me like evil spirits," she said as she surveyed the scene, along with many, many others.[8]

James Gordon Bennett immediately decided who the killers were—the gangs of dandyish ruffians who polluted the neighborhoods of his beloved Manhattan. "The girl was taken by a gang of scraplocks and gamblers," he charged in the *Herald*.

It was the *Herald* that began the mudslinging against the police over the Rogers case. "Nothing tending to elucidate the mystery hanging

over the murder of poor Mary has yet transpired at the police office,"
snickered one of the paper's reporters.

A few days later, Bennett launched a scathing attack on the city's
constables and judges for not immediately solving the case. "The apathy of the criminal judges, sitting on their own fat for a cushion bench,
and the utter inefficiency of their police, are all tending fast to reduce
this large city to a savage state of society—without law—without order—
and without security of any kind," he wrote. "The administration of
justice in this city has been bringing itself into contempt every year,
every week, every day."[9]

Rumors flew through the streets of New York: Mary did not go to
see her aunt when she first disappeared; she was seeing a man other
than her fiancé, Daniel Payne. She was seen in the theater district on
the arm of yet a third man just before she was killed. One rumor had
it that a very well known fourth man had fled the city right after her
body was found, a sure sign that he had killed her.[10]

Editors, especially those in the penny press, saw the crime not just
as a grisly murder of a beautiful woman but as a symbol of the collapse
of the entire world's civilization. The murder coverage was so dominated by the press that witnesses walked into newspaper offices to tell
their story rather than going to the police.

Newspapers held nothing back in reporting the dreadful appearance
of the beautiful girl's body after a week of decomposition. It was, wrote
a reporter for the *New York Journal of Commerce,* "a blackened and decomposed mass of putrefaction, painfully disgusting to sight and smell. Her
skin, which had been unusually fair, was now black. . . . Her eyes so
sunk into her swollen face as to have the appearance of being violently
forced beyond the sockets, and her mouth, which 'no friendly hand
had closed in death,' was distended as wide as the ligaments of the
jaw."[11]

The gang murder theory, advanced by the coroner and reporters,
especially those at the *Herald,* lasted for a few weeks. Then another
theory arose. Could Mary have been killed during an abortion at the

hands of Madame Marie Restell or one of her many surgeons? The *Police Gazette* wrote later that Restell owned a chain of abortion parlors, and one was in Hoboken, where Mary died. It charged that she had killed numerous young women in operations and hinted that Mary was one of them (hounded all of her life by antiabortion zealots, Restell finally slit her own throat in her bathtub years later). "It is well known that females die in healthy childbirth. How many, then, who enter her halls of death may be said to expire under her execrable butchery? Females are daily, no, hourly, missing from our midst who never return."[12]

Others said she had been accidentally murdered by a man who worked for Restell, a well-known New York abortionist who by the winter of 1840–41 had already been indicted sixteen times without any convictions. Each of Restell's appearances in court generated hundreds of news stories, especially in the penny sheets, ever hopeful that she would be incarcerated. Restell had good lawyers who could get indictments quashed; she also had many friends in city government, including the police, to whom she gave valuable gifts at Christmas and at other times of the year. They, in turn, protected her. The abortionist would not be put in prison until the late 1840s, and her sentence then would only be one year.[13]

Restell sold several brands of birth control pills and powders through her establishments, ran ads for them in New York newspapers, and even wrote stories about their powers that were published as "advertorials" in several papers.[14]

Edgar Allan Poe laid the blame for the murder and the failure to solve the case directly at the doorstep of the New York police. "The police seemed blown about, in all directions, by every varying puff of the most ill-considered newspaper opinions. The truth, as an end, appeared to be lost sight of altogether. The magistracy suffered the murderer to escape while they amused themselves by playing court and chopping the technicalities of jurisprudence," he wrote in a letter to the *Columbia Spy* newspaper.[15]

What really angered the newspaper editors and reporters, and all

New York, was the refusal of most police to investigate the case unless they were given substantial rewards to do so. The police in New York had always operated that way and saw no reason to change their tactics in the Rogers case. The press let everybody know about the fee insistence, too. If the investigation was to be solved and the murderer arrested, dozens of police, perhaps hundreds, had to be paid off with extra fees. "It is well known that in the present, inefficiently organized state of our police department, little will be done towards detecting the authors or perpetrators of this awful crime without the promise of a cash bounty," wrote a reporter in *The New York Sun*. "All parties, however much they may differ in other matters, are determined on the reorganization of the police," added the editor of the *Star*.[16]

Officials in Hoboken, and in the entire state of New Jersey, refused to pay any fees and told their police it was their job to investigate the murder. In New York, police, hands out, palms up, wanted extra money. James Gordon Bennett organized a special committee to raise money for them. It collected $1,350 (Mary's boss, Anderson, put in $50), and the city came up with an additional $500, all of which went to the police. The constables, the *Herald* said, were "mere loafers on the public—selling their duties to the highest bidder, and only suppressing crime or catching rogues when private individuals came forward to offer money for the performance of public duties."[17]

A disconsolate Bennett wrote that New York "had been disgraced and dishonored in the eyes of the Christian and civilized world" not only by the crime but also by the high-handed demeanor of the police.[18]

Some police did play small roles in the investigation of the murder, but most insisted on, and were given, extra fees. Then the police made a mess out of the Mary Rogers investigation, from start to finish. Police said at first that she had been killed in New York City and her body tossed into the Hudson. Later, they changed their mind and said she was, or might have been, slain in a thicket of trees in Hoboken. Evidence that turned up later in a forest in Hoboken led all to believe that she was killed there, but the police could not find any suspects. Potential killers that they did find turned out to be completely innocent.

Her fiancé, an early target, committed suicide without telling anyone if he had a role in the murder.[19]

The Mary Rogers case was never solved. People did not remember much about how poor Mary met her end, but they did remember the audacity of paid constables to demand, and receive, extra rewards for working on the investigation. And then, after all of that money was paid to them, they botched the case and never arrested anyone. They were a well-paid and poorly performing police force.

Another reason the case became so famous, and angered so many people, was Poe's tale about it, "The Mystery of Marie Roget." Poe, who reportedly knew Mary, had invented detective fiction as a literary genre with his thriller "The Murders in the Rue Morgue," published the previous year. He created a detective, Auguste Dupin, and had him solve a brutal Paris slaying.

Poe, thirty-two at the time, loved crime writing. He had befriended a reporter in Philadelphia, where he used to live, and the newsman gave him insider information on crime stories he wrote. After Poe moved to New York, he befriended police officers there. They also gave him behind-the-scenes details. The author then took these true stories, changed them a bit, added suspense and intrigue, added or fleshed out characters, and published them as fiction tales. "The Black Cat" was an example of that.

Poe did the same thing with his Roget story. He set it in Paris, brought in detective Dupin, and told the tale as a suspense story. Everyone knew, of course, that it was the Rogers case and that a large amount of the information in his story was taken directly from events in the Rogers investigation. Poe, too, was critical of the police, writing early on that his detective was disgusted with the "extreme remissness" of the local police, who had no idea of what they were doing.[20]

At about the same time the story was published, the case took a new turn when a dying woman was reported to have told the true story of the murder of Rogers, to which she had been an eyewitness, to a judge. The true story was never fully revealed, though. The lingering story, and Poe's tale, and what seemed to be never-ending news accounts of the case for more than a year stoked the public's anger, not just about the murder but about their incompetent and money-hungry constable force. Nothing symbolized the weakness of the constable system more than the Rogers case.[21]

Then, less than a year later, New Yorkers were stunned by another bizarre murder, followed by a heavily publicized trial, and more gross ineptitude on the part of the police.

In late 1841, John C. Colt, the younger brother of the fabled gun maker Samuel Colt, was charged with murdering Samuel Adams, a man who refused to pay him rent money. Colt chopped the man's body into small pieces, stuffed them into a trunk, and tried to have the trunk sent to New Orleans on an oceangoing ship. The vessel's departure was delayed a week, though, and the dreadful smell from the trunk caused seamen to open it and make a grisly discovery.

The Colt case was a wild one, including the digging up of Sam Adams's body and the showing of its cracked skull to the trial jury. The trial also included a shooting demonstration by Samuel Colt himself, half in testimony and half in publicity.

The city newspapers went into overdrive in Colt trial coverage. The *Herald,* as an example, filled its entire first page and several subsequent pages with the daily transcript of the proceedings. Bennett printed special 4:00 P.M. "Colt Trial" special editions every day and had his army of early-morning newsboys work all day to sell them. He startled readers with a huge front-page drawing of the building in which Adams was murdered and then shocked them two days later with an artist's rendition of what Adams's naked body must have looked like after the autopsy, with huge stitched-up cuts on its face.

The *Herald* wrote about everybody involved in the trial and gave graphic descriptions of the crowds of thousands of well-dressed New Yorkers jamming all of the streets leading to the courthouse in an effort to somehow squeeze their way into the tiny courtroom. Every day, *Herald* reporters reminded readers that the trial was unbelievably exciting, a New York City historical event, something they absolutely had to read about.[22]

The trial ran more than a week, with many witnesses. Jurors, tired of public charges of leniency and not intimidated by the defendant's famous brother, sentenced Colt to death by hanging, and the court turned him over to the police who ran the Tombs prison.

In a bizarre finish to the tale, Colt married his lover in his jail cell on the day of his hanging. Suddenly a fire broke out at the Tombs. Guards released all of the prisoners, who scrambled to safety. Colt was found on the floor of his cell, dead by his own hand, a knife plunged into his heart and then twisted for effect. City residents had wanted a hanging. "The tidings were received with . . . fierce mutterings of disappointed rage," wrote Lydia Child. "Those assembled as performers and spectators growled like a hungry bulldog when a bloody bone is plucked from him."[23]

Many people in New York, including public officials and law enforcement leaders, did not believe the suicide story. They argued that Colt's brother and others had visited him, as had his wife, on the day of the fire. Amid all that socializing and all of those visitors, critics argued, someone sneaked in a dead body, perhaps with the knowledge of several police in the prison, and that was the one identified as Colt. "I hear it declared over and over again, by those in a position to know, that Colt did not commit suicide, that the body found in the cell when the Tombs caught fire was only a corpse prepared for the purpose, and that he escaped in the confusion," said officer George Walling, whose sources in the Tombs were well informed. Thousands of New Yorkers believed he escaped, too, but Colt was never heard from again. The mystery remains in the shadows of the Tombs' ruins.[24]

The public, still reeling from the Rogers police debacle, was further angered by the incompetency of the jail guards and the incredible escape, if there was one, of Colt. The public naturally added the Tombs prison police together with the city's constable force and was furious with the one monolithic law enforcement brigade.[25]

All of the city's newspapers lumped the Adams and Rogers deaths together as a one-two combination to show that crime in the city was out of control.[26] Horace Greeley, in an editorial in the *Tribune* later that year, charged that carefully kept and detailed records showed that there was much more crime, and more murder, in 1841 than in previous years. "Murder and assassination are marked by singular atrocity," he complained. Who was responsible? The police.[27]

That Rogers/Colt doubleheader of crime, and the poor performance and galling nerve of the overly greedy police, turned the public's stomach. People were fed up with the police. Something had to be done about them. The public had been alarmed at the death of prostitute Helen Jewett in 1836. Now, five years later, the slayings of Sam Adams and Mary Rogers again rattled the city population. The Jewett murder had been a tragedy, but the Colt and Rogers killings were mileposts of crime. If nothing was done to revolutionize law enforcement, so weak in the hands of the constables, crimes of the magnitude of the double murders would go on and on. Criminals would know that the constables who toiled in the incredibly inefficient police force could not stop them. Beginning in 1842, and over the next few years, the New York City population realized that it was at a critical juncture, not just in law enforcement but in the sprawling metropolis's overall history. The bumbling, corrupt constables with their silly hats and billy clubs had to go, cried politicians from all over the city and the editors of the city's newspapers, especially the leaders of the penny press. A new, professional police force was needed right away.

It was time.

CHAPTER TWELVE

Out with the Old, In with the New

The prevention of crime being the most important object in view, your exertions must be constantly used to accomplish that end. The absence of crime will be considered the best proof of the efficiency of the police.

—Judge Robert Taylor, *Rules and Regulations for Day and Night Police of the City of New-York*, 1848

New York City finally got its professional police force in 1845. That was the same year that a seaman on the *Spencer*, George Walling, with his mates, left the ship to help the New York City fire department and Brooklyn Navy Yard marines, and hundreds of New York residents, battle the Great Fire of 1845, the second worst in city history, which leveled dozens of blocks of stores and offices and destroyed hundreds of homes. Walling liked the city. A few months later, he ended his sailing career and moved to New York to work at a city produce market. In 1847, a friend of his retired from the police force and asked Walling if he would like to take his place. The ex-sailor did and, after an alderman approved, started walking a beat in the Third Ward a few months later. "I certainly never had the slightest idea of becoming a policeman," he said, "but the proposition did not displease me. I had no particular business at the time and decided that I might as well carry a club until something better turned up."[1]

Walling was there at the start, in a cold winter, as the brand-new, professional police force began. He would be a policeman for nearly forty years. He did everything from beating criminals with his night-stick to breaking up robbery rings to battling street gangs, river pirates, and the "butcher boys." He worked as a patrolman, then a captain, then the chief of police. His memories make for a wonderful insider's view of the crime wave that threatened to overwhelm New York City and the efforts of the first police force to maintain law and order in the teeming metropolis.

Many editors and civic reformers wanted the police force replaced with a professional squad not just because of the rising crime wave, but also because some members of the police force did really stupid things and were continually laughed at by the public. A perfect example is the midnight ride of Officer Thomas Doyle on July 24, 1843. The cop was riding his horse down Chatham Street, not paying any attention to where he was going. When he reached the intersection of Tryon Row, he and his steed tumbled down into an open construction pit. There were ropes and signs all around it to warn riders of its existence; Doyle said nothing was there. A disgruntled Doyle said his horse was worth eighty dollars and produced a witness, a friend, who said oh, no, it was worth a good hundred. Because the horse was injured, he had to sell it for just fifteen. Doyle said he lost a twenty-dollar harness in the tumble, too. He wanted a hundred dollars from the city for his losses. The Board of Aldermen, after a few chuckles, gave him eighty.[2]

The Board of Aldermen that compensated the inept Doyle realized that he was not an exception to the watch force; he was a good example of it. The watch department was held in such low regard by the city that in 1843 the Board of Aldermen even had to buy saddles for police horses. One alderman, furious with the police, noted that city had to put up with the watch force "until a more efficient police sys tem shall be adopted."[3]

Right after Mary Rogers's death, Mayor Robert Morris, elected in
1841 as a Democrat, tried to reform the police. "Our system of police
is lamentably defective," he told the Board of Aldermen, with no
structure within it to prevent crime. He argued, too, that the current
system fostered corruption. "Those persons attached to the police department who are honest and vigilant, and there are many such, are
seriously injured by the general bad reputation which the system in-
flicts upon the department."

Mayor Morris's friend William Twell said not only that the officers
were corrupt but that their parallel "could not be found in this country."
He wanted six hundred new patrolmen, a superintendent of police, and
three unsalaried police commissioners. Another plan called for paying
police based on the drop in the crime rate—decrease in crime meant
more pay for officers, but an increase meant less pay. That was defeated.
Yet another proposal calling for a special "super" police magistrate was
turned down. A civic leader insisted that the new chief of police and all
captains had to be elected by the people; that was ignored. Several aldermen threw up their hands and insisted that all that was needed was
another look at the current system. A year dragged by, and the crime
rate continued to climb. During this time, Mayor Morris led a state-
wide campaign to reform the New York police, wrote dozens of letters,
gave numerous speeches, and even traveled to Albany to lobby for his
ideas in the state legislature. His efforts failed.[4]

Then, to everyone's surprise, a new political party, the American
Republicans, also known as the Native Americans, an anti-Catholic,
anti-immigrant, conservative group, just a year old, swept the city elections, winning 48.6 percent of the vote in the three-party race, taking
two-thirds of all the Board of Aldermen and Board of Assistant Aldermen seats, and getting the publishing scion James Harper elected mayor.[5]
They had considerable power and told the people that their number
one priority was law enforcement reform, and right away. Working
with state representatives from their party, they rammed through a new
state bill giving New York City the power to reform its police. The

Native Americans wanted a chief of police, eight hundred officers, a streamlined structure of command, higher law enforcement salaries, and the abolishment of all fees and rewards.

The men who ran Tammany Hall were stunned by the election results, they said, because the American Republicans had bested them at their own game. "Every means of the most disreputable and corrupt character has been resorted to by our opponents. Money has been lavished on the dissolute and indigent without stint, and where intrigue, gold and calumny could not affect the object, *threats* have been resorted to but without avail," wrote up-and-coming Tammany star Fernando Wood to President James K. Polk.[6]

The Native Americans, new and disorganized, then started squabbling among themselves, and the reform never took place, although Harper did appoint two hundred more policemen. Mayor Harper was besieged no matter which way he turned. He was criticized by the people who wanted more and better police and, at his publishing house, lambasted over his editorial stand on slavery. Harper Brothers would not publish any book that raised the slavery issue in a controversial way in the 1840s and even reedited and reprinted books that offended white southerners. They often publicly apologized for doing so, as they did in an 1841 letter to the Charleston, South Carolina, *Mercury*.[7]

Law enforcement reform had to wait until May of 1845, when the Democrats, bitterly unhappy working with the Native Americans, stormed back into power. The Democrats, led by new mayor William Havemeyer, pushed through a new reform bill that contained many elements of Mayor Harper's plan and Morris's, too.

Under the 1845 law, written in the spring of 1844, pushed hard by Havemeyer, and passed by the Democratic Common Council and the state legislature, a force of over one thousand police officers was named to replace all of the old constables (the state legislature cut the size back to nine hundred). A new chain of command was put in place with a police chief, several assistant chiefs, and captains who ran each precinct. Eight new precinct houses were established. The city was broken up into three police districts that covered all seventeen wards. Each of the wards was given its own police court, and extra police judges were hired.

Havemeyer asked Judge Robert Taylor to write a police manual, and in it Taylor, on behalf of the mayor, instructed officers to engage in crime prevention as much as continue the arrest of lawbreakers. "The prevention of crime being the most important object in view, your exertions must be constantly used to accomplish that end. The absence of crime will be considered the best proof of the efficiency of the police," Taylor wrote in the manual.[8]

A point of contention was the one-year term that the police held. Havemeyer argued that it was too short, that it would become political, and that "there is danger that the whole system will be involved in the incessant strifes and annual changes of parties, and its agents precluded from the experience and independence which are indispensable to their usefulness."[9]

The old system of one-year terms was then abolished, and each officer was hired for four years. The state legislature cut that term down to two. The officers were given stars to wear on their jackets to identify them as police. The new officers took over all of the old categories, such as dock police, Sunday police, health wardens, fire wardens, poll watchers, lamplighters, and court police. The hundred or so marshals, who had been around for decades, were downsized and worked administrative jobs or helped maintain courthouse order. The law enforcement squad was asked to wear blue frock coats with the initials M. P. on them (for Municipal Police). They all carried nightsticks. The officers, irritated at the M. P. nickname and a coat that would make them targets of criminals, soon dropped everything except the single copper star-shaped badge and were soon called the "star police." This was soon changed to "coppers" and then to simply "cops."

Most important, the old fee system was eliminated, as the Native Americans had insisted, and the pay of all officers, from chief down to patrolman, was significantly increased to make up for moneys lost in fees. Captain were now paid seven hundred dollars a year and patrolmen five hundred.[10]

The only part of the system that remained intact, criticized by many, was political patronage. Under the new reform law, the Board of Aldermen still hired all of the police officers and named their replacements when they left the force or died. Tammany Hall still controlled the Board of Aldermen. The mayor still had the power to remove any officer without the consent of any police official or the Board of Aldermen. Tammany Hall still controlled the mayor. One writer, looking back on the 1850s, wrote in 1871 that "the better classes of society need that the ultimate control of the police should be out of the reach of municipal politics, as much as if not more than they need that the city budget should be safe from the same influences."[11]

Political patronage was the first order of business when the bill was proposed in March of 1844. In its language, a board consisting of the mayor, three aldermen, and three assistant aldermen would hire and fire all the police. This was amended to give all the aldermen that power, led by the mayor. The legislation also stated that each patrolman appointed by an alderman had to live in that alderman's district. Patrolmen had to have high moral character, be physically able to do the job, and be between the ages of twenty-one and sixty. The new patrolmen had to avoid immoral and licentious conduct. The Board of Aldermen amended the bill some more before, in April 1844, it was sent to Albany, where it was tinkered with by some committees and then passed and put into operation in the spring of 1845.[12]

The new mayor, who would organize the radical new, reformed police department, was, in fact, not only the selection of Tammany Hall but one of the members of its general committee and a trusted man whom Tammany saw as a unifier between its radical and conservative factions. He was also a connection between two rival factions in the party and the Hall, the Hunkers and Barnburners, and was a favorite of former president and fellow New Yorker Martin Van Buren.

At first, Havemeyer did not want the job. He worked hard to get a high-paying job with the federal government that year but was turned down by newly elected President Polk.[13] Then he turned to City Hall. He won the Democratic Tammany nomination on the second ballot, defeating Peter Cooper, the philanthropist and alderman (Cooper's son Edward was later elected mayor). The *Tribune* said that friends of Havemeyer claimed he was "a correct, honest, respectable man" and had, through his mercantile career, amassed "a handsome fortune."[14] The pro-Democratic papers all hailed Havemeyer as a skilled administrator from the private sector who could run the city well. Editors of Whig newspapers said he was a hopeless Tammany lackey.

Havemeyer defeated Mayor Harper, who ran with little assistance from his disoriented Native American party, winning 50 percent of the vote to Harper's 36 percent. Whig Dudley Selden, running as an independent, won 14 percent. More important, the Tammany Democratic ticket swept the Board of Aldermen elections. They won thirty seats, and the Whigs took four. The Natives had none. The new mayor had more clout than any previous chief executive.[15]

That 1845 election did not give Tammany control of the city. That would take another decade. Havemeyer would be followed by four Whig mayors before the emergence of Tammany's Fernando Wood in 1854. Tammany would pick up more members of the Common Council over those ten years, though. It gained so much strength that after Havemeyer's inaugural speech Tammany power brokers fired seventy city workers and within a few weeks let go of the rest. All were replaced by Tammany men. The mayor was glad to have Tammany's support but realized quickly that the Tammanyites in office with him had no experience and little skill. Havemeyer complained that now he had to work with an administration full of men who were not only political appointees but who had never been in those jobs before. The constant turnover of city workers, on a grand scale in the 1830s, '40s, and '50s, made the running of the city, and the administration of the police, more difficult. When Tammany gained complete control in the late 1850s, there would be little turnover, but the city would be run in a far more inefficient manner by department heads with no experience and workers interested only in lining their own pockets. Mayor Have-meyer fought the Common Council, loaded with his own party's men, throughout his term, constantly trying to reform its superstructure and ways of doing city business. He had little success.[16]

Tammany Hall was despised by many. Everyone knew that the people who ran Tammany created a corrupt government in which the politi-cal machine leaders and their friends profited from bribes and em-bezzled moneys. Few knew how to dismantle Tammany or curb its power. In the early 1860s, William "Boss" Tweed would take over com-plete control of Tammany and, it was charged, embezzle close to $200 million from the city in both covert and blatantly open schemes.[17]

Tammany had been around since the end of the eighteenth century. It was allied to the new Democratic-Republican Party of Jefferson and Madison, soon renamed the Democratic Party, because, like the Demo-cratic leaders, it championed the causes of the immigrants, the poor, and the downtrodden. The Democratic Party absorbed huge numbers of laborers, tradesmen, and immigrant workers as it grew. Tammany was the perfect organization for it in New York, where all of its na-tional supporters were represented.[18]

The political organization quickly became riddled with corrup-tion. As early as 1809, New York City newspapers began to criticize Tammany for its crooked management.[19]

No one resented Tammany's chokehold on the city more than the honest cops, who served at the pleasure of Tammany leaders. The police knew the workings and politics of Tammany better than any-one else and realized, by the late 1840s and early 1850s, that the city's political machine had become a monolith and practically unstoppa-ble. The policemen told friends, too, that good men did not step forward to reform the political club because they would be devoured by the machine. Captain George Walling blamed it, and the refusal of others to run against it, for the law enforcement problems of the me-tropolis. "The 'gentleman' is practically debarred from any active par-ticipation in politics," said Walling. "One does not see the merchant princes, nor the great editors in the aldermanic chamber. But we do see the face of the ward 'heeler' and the 'tough.' [This kind of man] rules by brute force rather than intellect."[20]

Many agreed. James McCabe, a bearded journalist and historian, wrote that the Common Council was corrupt, full of very wealthy men who had no visible means of income. "It does not represent the proud intellectual character of New York; for there is scarcely a member who has the intellect or education enough to enable him to utter ten sentences in good English. There was not a man in this important body who possessed the respect or confidence of the citizens of New York. They were elected by bribery and corruption, maintained their positions by the same means, and enjoyed the favor and protection of leaders of their party." McCabe, like many others, was exasperated by local city officials. "The property, rights and safety of the greatest and most important city in the land were entrusted to a band of thieves and swindlers," he added.[21]

This did not surprise anybody. As far back as the first days of the century, aldermen had been enriching themselves through bribery and extortion. In 1806, butchers revealed that they had been paying different aldermen to grant them prime locations in the city for their business.[22]

William "Boss" Tweed chuckled when asked about Common Council corruption. "The fact is New York politics was always dishonest long before my time. There never was a time you could not buy the Board of Alderman."[23]

Reformers charged that Tammany-appointed workers made a fortune. An inspector in the weights and measures department, as an example, was paid fifty cents to inspect any scale he found. Critics said this meant that some of these workers made $200 a day ($6,000 in today's money).[24]

The result was, Walling and others argued, not just corruption in the city government but a general incompetence. Tax money went into general funds, and no one accounted for its expenditure. Streets in poor condition were not fixed, fire departments not improved. The police force was kept small because the funds simply could not be found to hire more men. Courts did not enforce the payment of debts. Private contractors were given enormous amounts of money to provide city services, such as the company that built and ran omnibuses; at one point in that era more than six hundred omnibuses were in operation in the city, at a huge profit to the contractor.[25]

Courthouses were without complete roofs; hundreds of docks were in disrepair. Inadequate public schools dotted the city, and those schools were attended by only half the children in the metropolis. The entire school system was riddled with corruption. As an example, dozens of food emporiums that were paid by the city to supply thousands of lunches for the children pocketed the money and did not send lunches, or, if they did, only a small percentage of the number they were contracted to send.[26]

Another citywide corruption scheme involved employee theft of goods and "fences." Workers in stores with vast quantities of clothing, for example, stole some of it and turned it over to fences for a fee. The fences then sold it to another store. In one case, two attractive shopgirls working at a large clothing store stole thirty-three expensive hats and gave them to a fence, who was arrested. Patrolman William Bell, who uncovered the case, then went to the boardinghouse where the two girls lived, only to find that other members of the theft ring had spirited them away in a carriage. Bell had to go to the Tombs to get an arrest warrant and then went looking for the girls, by then well hidden in the city.[27]

Walling, whose unhappiness with the police force grew even more when he was chief after the Civil War, and had to deal with the Tammany politicians all the time, disdained the men he worked for. "The ruling class in New York has its counterpart in the land of the 'Hindoo' [India], where the 'Thugs' dominate certain portions of the country by the exercise of brute force and criminal violence," he charged.

Those men rose to the top because good men stayed out of politics out of sheer fear. "Even if they are not thrown down stairs or pitched out of windows before the voting commences, the ballot boxes are stuffed with impunity, for the simple reason that the law regarding the proceedings at these gatherings has fallen into a state of 'innocuous desuetude,'" he added.

Walling said that petty thieves were let go because their victims were afraid to testify against them and considered an appearance in court pointless, since the judge would probably release the thief anyway because he was paid off or the thief had some friend at Tammany Hall. The police magistrates were useless, in addition to being corrupt, Walling said after years of dealing with them. He scoffed that they could not spell simple words, did not know the law, were always in a hurry, and were ever on the lookout for a favor or a bribe.

The rich and Tammany politicians could buy justice that the poor could not, Walling added, arguing that rich men who committed murder were often released or, at worst, found "insane" by a judge or jury and committed to a hospital but released after just a few months. He told friends that he had studied the records of those hanged for murder in New York and found that in most cases they were poor or unemployed.[28]

The author of an 1871 report issued by a civic investigatory group, the Committee of Seventy, that reflected back on the 1850s said that "there is not in the history of villainy a parallel for the gigantic crime against property conspired by the Tammany Ring. It was engineered on the complete subversion of government in the very heart of Republicanism. An American city . . . was handed over to a self-appointed oligarchy, to be robbed and plundered by them and their confederates . . . forever."[29]

Critics of Tammany charged that the Hall used street gangs to destroy the campaigns of the Whigs, scared Whig voters away from the polls, bought off voters, or, when unable to do that, simply paid election officials to turn in fraudulent reports of Tammany vote pluralities. They did not care who was elected, as long as it was their man. "No honest man took part in these disgraceful acts, and the public offices passed, almost without exception, into the hands of the most corrupt portion of the population. They were also the most ignorant and brutal. [They were] men whose personal character was infamous; men who were charged by the newspaper press, and some of whom had been branded by courts of justice with felonies, were elected or appointed to responsible offices."[30]

They gained control, critics charged, by bribing state legislators who oversaw the running of New York City. Samuel Tilden, who later ran for president of the United States, said in 1871 that $1 million was spent by Tammany to bribe New York state legislators in 1871. He vowed to lead the reform fight. "According to the strength that is given me, if you will not grow weary and faint, and falter on the way, I will stand by your side not only until civil government shall be reformed in the city of New York, but until the state of New York shall once more have a pure and irreproachable judiciary."[31]

He charged that the state legislature gave the Hall whatever it wanted, including the right to make police officer terms, and all city worker terms, four years, and then renewable each four years. Under one incredible new rule, the mayor, no matter how corrupt or incompetent he was, could be impeached only if he himself recommended it.[32]

One of the reasons that Tammany was able to wield such power, especially after the elections of the early 1850s, was that Albany would not make the New York City government autonomous. It used the state charter to keep running the city government inefficiently. The mayor did not run the city, and neither did the Common Council. Power was split among several parties, different political machines and clubs, and numerous city departments. Control was desperately uncoordinated, and this permitted corruption and unfair use of power by groups such as Tammany.[33]

In a landmark study in 1877, the New York State Commission on Cities blamed the woes of New York City on "the incompetent and unfaithful governing boards, and officials, the introduction of state and national politics into municipal affairs, and the assumption by the state legislature of direct control of city affairs."[34]

This was not news to anyone in Albany or New York City. State legislative domination had been so great that in the 1820s over fourteen thousand municipal jobs in New York and smaller cities, the overwhelming majority, were all political patronage jobs handed out by the state legislature. Part of Tammany Hall's success later was simply bringing jobs back to the city and away from the state.

Nowhere was the hand of Tammany felt more in the 1850s than in the running of the police department. The mayor, the Hall's man, and the aldermen still appointed all of the police. The cops owed their jobs to them, and those politicians owed their jobs to the men who ran Tammany Hall. The leaders of the Hall decided everything involving the police department, and every chief, starting with George Matsell, knew that. To save money, the political organization kept the force small. Police did not bother rowdy customers in certain saloons or brothel customers who were friends of Tammany and paid them off. Police did not investigate contractors who did shoddy work, breaking municipal laws, because Tammany had hired them through the Common Council. Many criminals were never arrested, or were let go when they were, because they were connected to Tammany. Hundreds of Tammany officials, and their friends, committed numerous crimes because they knew they would not be prosecuted or convicted. This increased the crime rate. There was so much corruption in the Common Council in the 1840s and 1850s that the press nicknamed the aldermen "the forty thieves."[35]

Journalists argued that the construction of a new courthouse in New York under Tammany's rule was the perfect example of its corruption. The state legislature originally appropriated $1.4 million for the courthouse. Tammany allowed contractors to file numerous cost-overrun charges for the construction of the building, not checking any and approving all, so that the final price tag was just over $12 million. Conversely, the cost of building Britain's Houses of Parliament, many times the size of the courthouse, was just $10 million.[36]

Another problem Tammany had in the 1840s and early 1850s was the rising success of New York Whig, and later Republican, William Seward, a popular, charismatic senator and former governor. In 1840, Seward, sensing a larger immigrant wave and more and more Irish in New York City, went out of his way to support programs to keep immigrants in America and help them, especially the Irish, because they amounted to a huge voting bloc that he wanted to hold. He did not want any alliance with the nativists because of their anti-Catholic stand,

and that hurt the nativists. He even introduced a bill to the Board of Aldermen to have the city fund parochial schools for Irish Catholics, as the government of Ireland did. The aldermen defeated it, 18–1. Even though they defeated his bill, the leaders of Tammany came to realize Seward was right about the immigrant voting bloc and embraced not just the Irish but any immigrant they could find.[37]

The Irish provided a huge bloc of voters for Tammany in each election. The Irish understood the underhanded, crooked election practices of the Hall because they had lived with those same practices back in Ireland. They knew, as Tammany knew, that victory in the elections was not the approval of political policies but simply victory. They knew how to operate in New York, too, quickly getting Tammany leaders to pressure Irish cops to let Irish suspects go and to cajole Irish police magistrates to throw out cases against Irishmen who voted. All of the Irish understood that what was good for Tammany was good for them, and Tammany understood that what was good for the Irish was good for Tammany.[38]

To the astonishment of the political club, the Whig Party collapsed as a political organization just after the 1852 national elections, a victim of the national antislavery movement. The Whigs were two distinct parties under one roof, the southern and northern blocs. They battled with each other over the slavery question so stridently in the 1840s that they split in the early 1850s and then died. "The Whig Party is dead and will soon be decomposed into its original elements. . . . The Whigs have long been nothing but a hoop to keep northern and southern democracy [Democrats] more or less bound together by fear of the common enemy. . . . If one party dies, the other must perish of inaction," fretted George Templeton Strong, who despised most of the Whigs he knew.[39]

For many residents, the economy of New York City was booming. The economic drought caused by the Panic of 1837 had ended around 1842. The shipping industry had grown dramatically since the middle of the 1830s, and by the late 1840s shipping companies in New York did highly profitable business supplying products from northern manufacturers to buyers in southern slave states. Shipping runs from New York to Richmond, Charleston, Savannah, and even Gulf of Mexico ports such as New Orleans were among the busiest in the world. The city received millions in port fees and shipping taxes. New York had also become home to the shipbuilding industry, which provided not only tax revenue but thousands of jobs, and jobs that grew as the years went by. The number of banks in New York had increased, and many now had branch offices in various American cities. The stock traders on Wall Street had come to dominate the securities business, and the stock market soared. A foreign observer, James Robertson, said in the 1850s that New York was "*the* money market of the states."[40] He put the city's manufacturing industry value at $105 million. Within ten years, its value would climb to $160 million.[41] Real estate had become a thriving industry in the city. The metropolis's population kept moving northward on Manhattan Island, well past Fourteenth Street. Land speculators bought huge chunks of acreage and then cut them up into smaller parcels and sold them. The people who bought the parcels quickly resold them, and the third owners built large houses that they sold for huge profits. Billionaire John Jacob Astor later said, "Could I begin life again knowing what I know now, and had money to invest, I would buy every foot of land on the island of Manhattan." By the late 1840s, hundreds of New Yorkers had snapped up thousands of acres in the gold-strike area of California, too. Others created new businesses in the city selling supplies to the thousands of New Yorkers who sailed to California to prospect for gold. The factories grew in size and number as the northern economy gained strength. On the dark side, burglary rings in New York tracked prospectors from California who made a lot of money in gold and upon their return robbed them as they slept. George Templeton Strong wrote, "I wonder whether we're all going to be ruined and undone by this California business."[42]

However, life for the unskilled laborers did not improve. In fact, in many cases they suffered because the new jobs were all low-paying menial work. The city government, ineffective anyway, cared greatly about the success of the rich and middle class but not very much about the poor and working class. Inattention by city fathers, and no help from Tammany Hall, despite the dazzling speeches of all of its members, meant that the working class did not succeed like the rest of the city. At the same time, the strong economy drove up the prices of land, houses, and rents. The working class was struggling, and many political leaders said that was why many working-class men turned to crime and the crime wave grew yet again.[43]

The thriving economy also left large pockets of men in particular industries out of work or working for low salaries. The groups of men varied, but there were always large numbers left unemployed in New York. Those out of work in winter had it the worst. "Weather cold, but not unkindly, save to the hundreds or rather thousands of men with wives and children to be fed and kept warm, whom this cruel 'pressure' has thrown out of work. They must see with dismay the indications of a severe winter coming," wrote Strong.[44]

At the end of 1854 and start of 1855, there were more and more working-class laborers out of work due to a general economic slump in the country that would lead to the Panic of 1857. "Hard times," mourned George Templeton Strong on New Year's Eve 1854. He wrote that 1854 had "been fruitful of calamity; war in Europe, financial distress here, abundant disaster everywhere. Personally, I have gained nothing, have rather retrograded toward evil." It was a few minutes before midnight. Then he scribbled, "There goes the clock, the old year is out, amid a fusillade [cannon fire] from the distant German region, east of Tompkins Square, that sounds like the preliminary skirmish of a great battle."[45]

The large Common Council usually found it impossible to get anything done. The council rarely raised taxes because that move would be accompanied by criticism from big business, homeowners, and the press. Taxes stayed proportionately low for a large city, and the city never had enough money to build its infrastructure, create job programs, and help the poor. In addition, a series of state supreme court rulings in those years confirmed the concentration of much of the city's local governing power in the hands of the state legislature. And on top of all of that, the members of the state legislature, many of whom lived far away from New York City and despised its residents, continually tinkered with and revised the city's charter, taking away yet more power and giving it to themselves.[46]

New York's great economic boom, then, always included pockets of poverty and was accompanied by chaos in the city government.

There was a general lack of interest in the problems of the cities. In 1850, just 15 percent of the nation's population resided in cities; the rest were farmers and had no interest in policing and crime. So the cities received no national help from anyone and continued to erode.[47]

The nation's political leaders also pushed American nationalism beyond reasonable bounds, determined to push west relentlessly to establish a new and larger country. Hundreds of thousands of individuals, traveling in groups or alone, forged across the Appalachians and into the Mississippi region, building roads, stage depots, villages, and crossroads along the way, leaving the cities behind.[48]

Congress and various national leaders wanted to show the world that America was one large country and that all of its people spoke with one voice. They did not. Ethnic and political groups squabbled throughout the country, especially in cities such as New York. To city dwellers, especially to New Yorkers, crime and the malfunctioning police force were a huge problem, even though America overlooked it. President James Buchanan went even further. He did not want to stop at simply stretching America from coast to coast; he wanted to gobble up as much of the world as he could in a ridiculous attempt at American internationalism. He tried to seize by force, or purchase, Cuba and the upper third of Mexico and in 1857 even nearly blundered his way into a shooting war in Paraguay. American nationalism was a charade.[49]

Besides, ever since the founding of America, a wide gap had been maintained between the federal government and the states. The states did not want the federals intruding on their operation, afraid of what they always perceived as federal power grabbers, and always held them at arm's length, making it nearly impossible for any federal official to provide assistance in fighting crime or reforming the police, even if he wanted to do so.

New York City asked for no help in crime and police matters and received none.

In the days before Havemeyer was sworn in, some of the city's newspapers launched a biting attack on him and said that he was obligated to reform the city government, and that included the police department. Some had little hope that it would be done. "We shall never see the city governed as it should be until its law-observing, God-fearing, vice-hating citizens shall consent to throw national and state politics entirely out of the question and unite in choosing officers who will have no other sins than those of securing an efficient and wholesome city administration," complained Horace Greeley of the *Tribune*, whose circulation would climb to a city/national total of 175,000 by 1857.[50]

Editors were surprised when the new mayor plunged into police reform on his very first day on the job. In his inaugural message, he told the Common Council that the police department was "complicated and inefficient." He said of the police that "the evil should be remedied before its effects are experienced" and asked the council to immediately pass both the state and city bills on police reform.[51]

Reforms such as the elimination of police fees and rewards were well publicized, but, in fact, that system did continue quietly. Grateful property owners would reward police with a bonus for a job well done, and the police would accept it. A number of the new police were members of the old constable force, kept on to train the new arrivals. The old constables did not want to let go of the fee-and-reward system and promoted it when the new force began operations. Constables cajoled rewards out of people who had property stolen from them and persuaded many of the new police to do the same.

A. M. C. Smith, a constable who lingered and joined the new force, earned $1,640 in rewards from 1845 to 1847, or nearly an additional year's salary per year. Many police recovered an amount of stolen money, kept half, and then asked the victim to give them a percentage of the remaining half that they gave to him. He did so just to get some of his money back.

This was a standard illicit practice among the new police. The fees added up, too. One officer, Robert Bowyer, a former constable, in some years in the 1850s earned twice as much in fees as he did in his salary; as the reward for one job, he collected $1,500, or twice his salary for the entire year. Some other police were given rewards to travel somewhere to perform a service for someone. Many of these police, who hid their illegal rewards well, were seen as fine, upstanding members of the force by the press and public. Bowyer, as an example, was hailed as a respectable officer by the *Herald* after he was charged with the vicious clubbing of a man during an arrest.[52]

Citizens, proud of the heroism or extra work of an officer, often banded together and raised money for him. That is what happened to a Patrolman Clarke, of Newburgh, New York. He had been gunned down and nearly killed in a fight with an African American. Grateful and sympathetic citizens raised a hefty $250 reward and gave it to him. Despite this double-dipping system, patrolmen and their captains were always trying to get pay increases from the Common Council, sometimes requesting them every few months.[53]

One step forward was the city's attitude toward police injuries. The city originally did not pay medical expenses but started to do so in critical cases in the 1840s. Patrolman Thomas Lynch died in 1849 as a result of injuries suffered putting down a riot in 1847. He was out of work fourteen months before he passed. He had remained on salary but had no medical coverage. The Common Council voted to give his widow, Ann, a cash bonus when he died, and she paid medical bills with that money. Patrolman Martin Van Nostrand was badly hurt in an 1849 riot and could not work for a year. The city paid his salary for the year and then, at the end of it, voted to pay his medical costs, too. Patrolman William Wilson was badly hurt by a rock propelled by a slingshot as he arrested two men. They got away, and Wilson was put under a doctor's care for six weeks. His wife petitioned the Common Council, and they agreed to pay his salary while he was bedridden and then gave her a lump-sum cash payment to pay his medical costs.[54]

One reason for the many police deaths and injuries in the 1840s was that most police officers carried no weapons except the nightstick. Weapons were at their own discretion and many declined, believing they could enforce the law with their nightstick; that often failed. Many police were injured in the Astor Place riot and other confrontations for that reason. Most police did not carry weapons until the late 1850s.[55]

The continuing problem with the new police department was the same as that of the old. As long as political patronage remained, New York had a law enforcement agency run by the Democratic Party and Tammany Hall. It served the politicians and not the people.

Peter Cooper warned Havemeyer and the Common Council about that right after the election, telling them that under the new ordinance the city had "political police" and not true law enforcers. "It would not be long before the most corrupt party would bid the highest for the spoils of office," he said.[56]

Viscount James Bryce, a British political scholar, was aghast at the influence of political patronage in New York City that he saw on his lengthy visit to America. "The party system . . . has enormously aggravated the patronage and corruption. . . . In great cities we find an ignorant multitude largely composed of recent immigrants un-trained in self-government." He said that good men did not get into politics, leaving the work to "sordid wirepullers and noisy dema-gogues." Bryce added with a sneer that "Satan has turned his heaviest batteries on the weakest part of the ramparts."[57]

Havemeyer paid no attention to Bryce or other critics of political patronage. He told everyone that he would personally interview all eight hundred men who would serve as the patrolmen in the city's first professional police department, and he did. He also kept all of his interviews secret, even the names of those he chose, to prevent politi-cal intervention by others.[58]

He was applauded by the press. Editors wrote that he talked to each candidate in his office, asked others about their character, and told all that they could talk to him whenever they wanted; he would also call them into his office from time to time for reports on the reformation of the police department. He sought men of high moral character as well as men with law enforcement skills and did everything possible to keep politics out of the selections.[59]

The editor of the *Commercial Advertiser* cheered, assuring its readers that the mayor had "worked hard at this business."[60]

What everyone seemed to overlook in their praise, though, was that Havemeyer was the mayor, a politician, and a Tammany champion. Everything he did to avoid political patronage was political patronage. He handpicked the men for the Democrats, not for the city.

Those who applauded the mayor overlooked one other important aspect of his methods, readily admitted by his clerk. Havemeyer wanted tough men. He wanted men who knew how to beat up criminals, use force to subdue those they arrested, and strike fear into the hearts of the lawbreakers in the city. He did not ask for experience in police work or for any training for the job. He just wanted brutal law enforcers. He knew, everybody knew, that the criminals were out of control and had to be reined in, and quickly. The mayor did not seek college professors; he sought, his clerk said, friends of gamblers, prizefighters, and known thieves. It was Havemeyer who coined that famous phrase about the police, "New York's Finest."[61]

Cooper and others feared that the police would be run by Tammany Hall. They were right. The Common Council rejected Havemeyer's first choice for chief of police, experienced and respected magistrate Robert Taylor, solely because he was a Whig, and insisted on a Democrat.

The final choice for the new police chief was an odd one. The mayor and aldermen sought tall, strong, muscular, intimidating patrolmen, yet as their boss they picked the rather dumpy, forlorn-looking George Matsell. The very first chief weighed over three hundred pounds, and his clothes rarely fit him. He had difficulty getting around. He had thick muttonchop-style sideburns that swept down from the hair on his head over his cheeks. He had vision problems and wore thin, iron-framed eyeglasses. He did not look like an action hero at all. He was organized, though, could be tough when he had to be, and, most of all, had a deep and abiding faith in the justice system, understood the problems of the criminal infestation of New York, and had been, for several years, leading small forces of patrolmen out into the city at night to keep the peace. Most important, he was a Tammany Democrat. He seemed guided by something, although no one seemed to know what. Matsell was not someone who had grown up in a law enforcement family, either. His father owned a small bookstore in Manhattan, next to the Metropolitan Hotel. In his twenties, he left his father's business and opened up his own bookstore at the corner of Pearl and Chatham Streets, spending most of his spare time reading, not plotting strategies to guard the people of New York City. He was one of the very last people you would expect to be put in charge of the police force of the largest city in America.[62]

Matsell took over the police department in early August 1845, when the eight hundred new officers began walking the streets. He turned in reports to the mayor and council on a regular basis, worked hard at reorganizing procedures, and met with aldermen and civic leaders. After three months, he felt he had turned the department around.

So did the mayor. Havemeyer was so pleased with the new police that he issued a special report on November 1, 1845, in which he said that he and Matsell had done a splendid job. "The City has been comparatively quiet; we have had no serious riots, and serious offences have not been frequent. The preventive powers of the system have been fully exhibited, and its operation in bringing offenders to justice, and carrying out the other objects for which it was adopted, can be shown fully by the excellent record of persons that have been apprehended by the police of the city," he wrote.[63]

In addition to reforming the police, Mayor Havemeyer was instrumental in the creation of a new immigration policy for the city and state. He also worked hard at increasing the number of streets

and homes connected to a dreadful sewer pipe system. The mayor
also worked hard at improving the transportation system of the city and
increased overall health care.

His new police force, of which he was so proud, did not get off to
a very strong start. The eight hundred cops did not cover the city
well. Nearly 10 percent called in sick each day. Others spent their
time on administrative duty. Three work shifts cut the number of
patrolmen on the streets at any one time down to just a few hundred.

Tough as they were, the new police were afraid to venture inside
the boundaries of the Five Points hellhole in the middle of the Sixth
Ward. In 1846, Mayor Havemeyer assigned thirteen extra policemen
to the Sixth Ward, with specific instructions to patrol Five Points, make
arrests, and break up illegal activities on the streets and alleys, in addition to monitoring the street gangs and gambling dens in the area.
They continued to avoid Five Points, though, and ignored any and all
messages sent to them by the mayor.[64]

Many New Yorkers were not satisfied with the new force and did
not see any distinction between it and the old herd of bumbling constables. As early as 1847, less than two years after the debut of the new
force, public officials were already calling for another reform of the
reformed department. It was very troublesome. The department had
"failed to meet the just expectations of the community," said new
mayor William Brady, who called for an end to it during the two years
that the Whigs controlled the city. "In the opinion of candid and ob-
serving minds the good order and quiet of the city" were not "more
conspicuous than under the former system."

Brady wanted a new force with 1,200 night watchmen and several
hundred day marshals. He was turned down. Mayor Havemeyer had
said that the failure of the system was due to political patronage and
that the two-year appointment should be made an indefinite appointment. Alderman Thomas Tappan said the larger force would be "a
system rendered odious by its inefficiency and disgraceful by its corruption."[65]

Problems with appointments and reappointments under the

continued political patronage system began as soon as the new police started to patrol their beats in 1845 and 1846. Democratic aldermen represented the First Ward in 1846 and named twenty-four
policemen. The Democrats were replaced by two Whigs in 1848, and
only two of those twenty-four officers were reappointed. All nineteen cops appointed by Democrats in 1848 in the Tenth Ward were
fired by the two Whigs who took office as aldermen in 1850. About
99 percent of the officers named by one party were reappointed in the
next election, despite their records, if that party retained the alderman's seat in that ward.[66]

The political patronage of the new police department caused James
Gordon Bennett of the *Herald* to scoff that there was no difference between the new and old departments and that the new cops were only
useful to help the political parties at the polls.[67]

Some policemen knew how to get themselves reappointed even if
they fell out of political favor in their home ward. Officer George
Walling learned that trick early in his career. All you needed to do
was move out of your ward into another, where you could convince
that alderman to give you the job. He was not reappointed in 1849,
so he moved to the next ward and became friendly with an alderman
there, who appointed him to a new term.[68]

The people who put together the first professional police force
bragged that from then on, all of the New York police would be trained,
but that did not happen for years. How could they be? They were the
first. The original requirements were merely that the new cops be U.S.
citizens, be able to read and write in English, never have been convicted
of a crime, and be a one-year resident of the state, under the age of
thirty-five , in good health, of good moral character, and, oddly enough,
taller than 5'8". No professional experience was required, and no skills
in law enforcement were needed, either.[69]

What was required in officers, but never written down, was tough-
ness and attitude. The force was made up of men who had trained
themselves to be rough, at times brutal, and men who could run fast and
wrestle criminals to the ground. There was no rule book to read, no

official instructions to follow. The hiring was not done by trained law enforcement officials, either, but by members of the city's Board of Aldermen. Each alderman or assistant alderman appointed the new policemen who worked in his district. Generally speaking, each district got the same number of patrolmen, so a high-crime area had the same protection as a low-crime area. Residents of high-crime areas complained bitterly that they were being discriminated against and needed far more police than had been assigned to them.

A large number of the first police were of Irish descent, and that number would grow until, in midcentury, nearly three-quarters of all cops would be Irish. Oddly enough, the most-targeted victims of the Irish police were other Irish immigrants. Sociologists of the era said that the Irish police beat up other Irish in New York to make up for old scores and grudges from the days they all lived together in Ireland. Regardless of whom they arrested and beat up, New Yorkers who did not like the Irish, and there were many, complained bitterly that the city was hiring an ethnic police force.[70]

The mayors could interview the candidates but soon halted that practice and turned it over to the ward heelers, managers for the political machine who found work for party people, took care of people's problems, and who did all of the choosing. The new police paid the aldermen who hired them for the privilege, generally about $150. The patrolmen then asked to work with particular captains, usually friends, and each paid his captain $40 for that honor. The captain, in turn, usually paid $200 to the alderman who hired him. All made their payments back rather quickly by performing odd jobs for politicians or simply accepting some of the numerous bribes that floated through the precinct house. The crooked cops enjoyed their work, and the honest police, those few that were honest, were demoralized by the fact that all of the payments and graft swirled about them and that absolutely nothing could be done about it.[71]

One outrage that continued for years was the appointment by captains of friends to serve as precinct house clerks without any prior approval from the city. Hundreds of clerks owed their jobs to their friends the captains.[72]

An enormous cost to the city in the police budget was salary overruns at the end of each year. There was little planning done to determine what the total salaries of patrolmen and captains would be, and each year additional fees had to be paid to cover the salaries of extra police, which critics said were staged so that police and their friends could make more money. As an example, in 1849 the police hired an additional forty-three watchmen during the year, not in the budget, and then had to pay these extra salaries in the early months of 1850. Another civic complaint was that the magistrates approved special, additional fees for police already on salary to transport convicts from the courtroom to the jail for internment, another case of double-dipping.[73] The cost of the new force became so high, and so quickly, that just two years after it was established, in March 1847, several aldermen asked the chief of police if the size of the force could be reduced so that the city could save money. The chief, furious, refused.[74]

The size of the force was not the only problem the new police presented. Captains constantly urged the construction of brand-new precinct houses or vast renovations of the old ones. The precincts also served as refuge houses. Captains let hundreds of indigent citizens and homeless people sleep inside precinct houses at night, especially in winter. There was little control over prisoners. The lack of discipline was so great that in 1847 the city had to order the police to take more steps to stop prisoners from setting their cells on fire to protest their arrests.[75]

The ineffectiveness of the new police, after all of the promises, depressed George Templeton Strong. There was crime, crime, and more crime in the streets, literal death in the air. There seemed to be burglars, killers, and robbers in every neighborhood. It was all people talked about. In just the last ten months of 1840, there had been nineteen riots and twenty-three murders. That summer the editor of the *Commercial Advertiser* complained that the New York police were "wretchedly inadequate" to combat crime. "In a word, lawless violence and fury have full dominion over us whenever it pleases them to rage and it is more owing to the forbearance of the riotous and viciously inclined than to any preventive of repressive means employed." Those complaints were heard from Strong and many others at the end of the summer of 1841 and in the succeeding years.[76]

New Yorkers kept repeating a new joke: "While the city sleeps, the Watch sleeps, too."[77]

One night in the spring of 1845, as the new police force was settling in, Strong stood quietly on a street watching yet another great fire consume an entire block of buildings. He gazed over huge groups of onlookers including whores still putting their clothes back on, disheveled actors, now-homeless tenants, a few curious Bowery B'hoys and their girls, and a large group of suspicious-looking people. "Loafers of most unquestionable genuineness," he called them with disdain, "on the lookout for anything they could lay their hands on."[78]

By the time the new police took over in late 1845, the city had changed. It was "a new kind of city and city life. . . . Something new came into the world," said a historian, "and it had to be endowed with meaningful representation" in newspapers, books, and letters.[79]

The problems of the 1830s and 1840s did not disappear under the new police in the ever-expanding city; they grew. The police were proud that they had developed new systems to arrest criminals, but the criminals were even prouder of the fact that they continually outwitted the police. Banks were a perfect example. In the 1850s, banks started sending messengers to other banks or to the homes of clients. Robbery rings followed these messengers and garroted them, sometimes killing them, when they walked through a desolate neighborhood or past a dark alley. Later, the police rode on bank wagons and trucks to protect the bank shipments, but thieves concocted ways to disable the trucks and the police.[80]

Pauperism was a growing problem in New York City. Laborers who did work earned only two hundred dollars a year, hardly enough to raise a family on. Those women who did work only earned about a hundred a year. The number of poor increased dramatically, as did the number of almshouses funded by the city and civic organizations. People continued to live in hovels burrowed into the basements of the city of stone buildings. "In this one cellar, my father and mother, two brothers and two sisters and myself all lived together—ate, slept, cooked, washed, and ironed and did everything in this one dank and noisome hole. . . . My mother and my father drank whiskey whenever they could get a chance and I early imbibed a passionate fondness for it," said a teenage girl about her childhood in a damp slum in 1850.[81]

Prostitution under the new police was worse than ever, and the ladies of the evening were bolder than before as they walked the streets, come-on smiles on their lips. "Here are two ladies approaching us, magnificently attired," wrote George Foster in 1850, "with their large arms and voluptuous bosoms half naked, and their bright eyes looking invitation at every passer by. . . . Diamonds and bracelets flash from their bosoms and bare arms, and heavily-wrought India shawls of that gorgeous scarlet whose beamy hue intoxicates the eye, hang carelessly from their superb shoulders, almost trailing on the walk. . . . They would be taken for queens or princesses, if such things were ever seen among us. . . . As they pass, they look hard at you and exclaim familiarly, 'How do you do, my dear? Come, won't you go home with me?' "[82]

Many complained that by the 1850s the city and police still had no plan for the treatment of the illegal prostitutes. "[They] cause more guilt, crime and misery than even bad rum," argued Whitman. "We trust that our police, in dealing with this class of offenses, will act on some settled plan—either tolerate such of these places as are quietly kept or steadily suppress them all."[83]

Prostitution was so profitable in the 1850s that one man said that more money changed hands in one day in the prostitution business in New York City than was exchanged at all the banks in Europe in an entire week.[84]

The terror found in the streets was often matched by jubilation, such as on the evening of May 7, 1847, when the city was lit up like a

carnival to celebrate a victory in the Mexican War. George Templeton Strong was caught in the crowd of surging New Yorkers, packed
like fish in cans, who streamed down city streets to set off fireworks,
shout, drink, and holler. "Nearly every building on Chatham Street
and Broadway lit up and glittering. Rockets and Roman Candles
whizzing and popping in every direction, fireworks blazing away on
the Astor and American [hotels], and half a dozen other places, and
every side street that one looked down, glowing, sparkling, as far as
its houses could be seen from the park."[85]

By 1847, most of the city was prospering. Even the grimy old wooden
piers had loveliness to them in the summer of that year, when kids
dove off of them into the rivers. Whitman later spent an afternoon
one summer watching teenagers swimming in the river amid the piers.
"The laughter, voices, calls, responses—the springing and diving of the
bathers from the great string-piece of the decay'd pier, where climb
or stand long ranks of them, naked, rose color'd, with movements,
postures ahead of any sculpture. To all this, the sun, so bright, the
dark-green shadow of the hills the other side, the amber-rolling
waves, changing as the tide comes in to a transparent tea-color—the
frequent splash of the playful boys, sousing—the glittering drops
sparkling, and the good western breeze blowing."[86]

For a few minutes, at least, the beauty of the city overshadowed the
dark hue of the ever-widening crime wave.

CHAPTER THIRTEEN

Police Brutality Raises Its Ugly Head

They were powerful, fearless men, who dispensed the law with
a nightstick, seldom bothering to make arrests.

—Patrolman Cornelius Willemse

Crime in 1856 was far more widespread than it had been years
earlier. The increase in crime was always blamed on the ever-
increasing population of the city, climbing to 629,810 by 1855.[1] The
number of residents approached a million by the very end of the 1860s,
and police chiefs used the population in their reports to the mayor and
Board of Aldermen, constantly whining that the huge number of people
meant more crime. It was not the inept police; it was the population.

In 1855, Walt Whitman called New York "one of the most crime-
haunted and dangerous cities in Christendom." He added that by that
time the criminal element in the city had been joined by new robbers
and murderers who had moved to Gotham from other states, such as
California after the gold rush there. They were, he said, "thieves,
expelled, some of them, from distant San Francisco, vomited back
among us to practice their criminal occupations."

Crime was so prevalent, and the police were still so inept, that Whitman warned visitors to Gotham not to walk around alone at night and
not to trust anybody. "Any affable stranger who makes friendly offers is

very likely to attempt to swindle you as soon as he can get into your confidence. Mind your own business," he wrote.[2]

The *Aurora* editor told tourists, too, of "various kinds of scamps who do business upon the inexperience of strangers . . . sojourners robbed, swindled, and perhaps beaten."[3]

Whitman was one of many in the city who scoffed at newcomers and tourists. He told them all to stay inside their hotel and put their money in the hotel's safe. Those who were robbed, especially those robbed in visits to prostitutes, gained no sympathy, just scorn, from newspaper people who told them that all they did when they reported robberies to the police or got into the newspapers as a victim was give advertising to the brothels where they were robbed.[4]

How to stop all of the crime?

The cops on the first professional police force were told to be tough as soon as they were hired. The old constable had been not only ineffective but weak. Killers, robbers, and gangbangers had gotten away with murder for decades, and the public was sick and tired of it. The new officers were told to use as much force as they felt necessary to apprehend criminals and stem the ever-rising crime wave. A common practice was to crack criminals over the head, or across the back of the neck, with their thick, fourteen-inch-long wooden nightsticks, or billy clubs, regardless of the consequence. Police pushed, shoved, and kicked men down a street. Ears were pulled hard, throats were put in a vise hold, knee pressure was applied to the lower back, ankles were kicked, feet were stomped on. Usually, the nightstick blow to the head knocked men down, or unconscious, and sometimes victims later suffered brain damage.[5]

Police argued that their job often made it impossible to keep the peace without violence. Patrolman Walling found himself the cop on the beat in a neighborhood in which most of the tenants on the east side of the street were English and those on the west side Irish. There were at least a dozen fights per night, and they were nearly impossible to break up. "After dusk the life of a policeman who patrolled the beat alone was not worth much, but by a severe course of discipline, the neighborhood was made safe," he said, referring to cop beatings.[6]

This was the "necessary force" needed to subdue a prisoner and was considered acceptable by police, city officials, and the public. The new police thought nothing of keeping control of a recently arrested prisoner by using their nightsticks. Some refined the technique by wrapping the stick in one or two handkerchiefs so that there would be no marks on it after a beating. Others only hit arrestees in soft places on the body so there would be no bumps or bruises to show violence. Many men were brought to the jail and then, hidden from the public, were beaten badly. Suspects in criminal investigations were often beaten up, kicked down stairs, and shoved against walls in the precinct house and forced to confess to crimes. This was soon dubbed "the third degree," and it became an acceptable form of brutality. Force was often excessive. A Philadelphia woman was beaten to death by one policeman, and a bystander to an arrest who argued with the arresting officers was shot dead.[7]

Police often advised victims of harassment to take matters into their own hands and beat up those bothering them. Captain Walling told one man to beat up the man who was annoying him in order to stop the man's badgering. Walling assured the man that the police would not then arrest him for assault. He beat the man nearly to death; the man never bothered him again. Captain Walling? He said he knew nothing about it.[8]

Sometimes brutality was carried out strictly by the book. A woman who was arrested in New York at her boardinghouse was forced to walk as quickly as possible, almost at a forced-march speed, through dreadful weather and amid streets of mud more than a few inches deep, lifting her ankles and knees up and down, for over a mile to the Tryon Row jail. She said that the walk through the miserable conditions wore her out and made her sick.[9]

Officer Walling said that police supervisors offered few instructions on how to make arrests, disperse a crowd, or bring detainees to the

precinct house. One problem police often had was when they confronted a group of rowdy men alone. Walling mastered the situation
early with a persona of threatened force. He stood up to the group he
was trying to disperse and told them to stop what they were doing or
they would all be arrested. He pulled out his nightstick and held it in
front of him, holding it tight, looking at each man with steely eyes and
a hard-set jaw. There was then a quiet between them until the men
realized that one or more of them was going to be hurt in a confrontation with the cop, even if they won the fight and escaped. "Well?"
Walling would say. The men usually backed off.[10]

Treating criminals brutally had another effect. Lawbreakers began
to tell fellow felons they did not fear the punishment meted out by police courts, often lenient, as much as they feared the violence by the
cop. A criminal could be permanently injured at the overly rough
hands of the police officer, but not harmed at all by a judge. Fear of
the brutal methods of the police began to intimidate criminals by the
late 1840s.[11]

The police also found that the immediate use of force quickly
established their superiority in any confrontation and that the more
criminals knew that, the fewer problems there would be. Police often
plunged into a crowd of street toughs, hitting several over the head with
their nightsticks. This measure often brought success and, overall,
built up the image of all policemen as strict protectors of the law who
got their way. Their captains not only looked the other way in cases of
brutality but encouraged their officers to use whatever force they
thought necessary to achieve their goals. A famous phrase was that the
patrolmen needed to do whatever had to be done to uphold the law.[12]

The public approved. Walling said that "by dint of a few hard licks"
police did their work and that the public was so terrified of crime that
they allowed the police a wide berth in making arrests. Force was a
necessary evil.[13]

There were many who were convinced that cops just had a mean
streak and used their nightsticks, or any weapons they could find, in

order to hurt people they suspected of lawbreaking. One was city political leader Robert Livingston, who testified at a state legislative hearing that "officers of justice, often uneducated or overbearing men, either do not know or designedly exceed the boundaries of their authority. The accused sometimes submits to illegal acts; in others, resists those to whom he ought to submit."[14]

Officers did not accept any verbal abuse, either, whether from those they arrested or bystanders. The cop had to maintain law, and to do that he had to be violent. People soon began smiling at cops as they passed them on the street, or tipping their hats. Men and women wished them a nice day or a good evening. Cop questions were always answered with a "yes, Officer" or "yes, sir" somewhere in the conversation. Within a year, New Yorkers feared the new police and, intimidated, were congenial toward them. "There is no remedy for insulting language," said one New York captain, "but personal chastisement."[15]

The police always defended their tactics, despite some public complaints against the increasing severity of the attacks by the men in blue. "A New York police officer knows he has been sworn in to 'keep the peace' and he keeps it. There's no 'shilly shallying' with him, and he doesn't consider himself half patrolman and half Supreme Court judge," scoffed Officer Walling. "He can and does arrest on suspicion. In times of turbulence or threatened rioting, he keeps people moving."[16]

The police officer often kept them moving, and swiftly, with a few smacks to the back of the head with the billy club. Walling always used the billy club when he had to do so and urged all of his men to do the same.

Criminals who feared the police because of clubbing, it was believed, would not commit crimes. Another reason for the violent clubbing of suspects was the poor image maintained by the New York public of the old constable, who did nothing to rein in criminals or stem the crime wave. The new cops felt that they had to be violent and brutal right away to assure the citizenry that they were tough enough to police the streets. They also faced the time-honored "perp walk" challenge of bringing their suspect from the point of arrest half a mile or so to the nearest police precinct house for incarceration. On the way, friends of the arrested man might attack the police officer and beat him in an effort to get him to release their friend. The new cops, like the old, had to fight for their lives. Their brutality in beating up those who assaulted them was one more sign to all that they were rugged. They may not have yet been New York's Finest, but they were certainly New York's Toughest.[17]

The rougher they were, and the faster they were rough, the better off they were in the eyes of the public. New York residents accepted that as necessary because the people felt safer. The new officers understood early that brutality was just a part of their job and continued to utilize it.[18]

"The New York police have liberty of action—more by far than the London police, who dare not lay a hand on a man unless he is engaged in the very act of violating the law," Walling said, adding that New York's hard-edged policy was far more successful. Walling, who had been to London, said that British police had to stand by while known criminals gathered and prepared for assaults on citizens and hordes of pickpockets roamed the streets. New York's police not only did not allow that, he said, but arrested men, and groups of men, merely on suspicion. They also arrested criminals the department had been looking for if they spotted them in a crowd, something European constables rarely did. The London bobbies did not arrest drunks or prostitutes walking the streets, either, but New York's police did, often manhandling the inebriated men and women drinkers and streetwalkers. A study by the New York Prison Association in 1853 showed that the number of drunk and disorderly people arrested in New York City from 1848 to 1853 rose by 278 percent.[19]

Cops had to be careful. The patrolman who was not careful was often soon a dead patrolman. Charles Baxter was a fine example. He was assigned the East River dock beat, where, one chilly November day, he was scheduled to board the vessel *Thomas Watson* to inspect its cargo, which consisted of six hundred bags of coffee with a value of fourteen dollars per bag. More interested than Baxter was a quartet of young men intent on robbing the *Watson* of its cargo. Thomas Kelly bumped into one of them that morning. He saw William Johnson standing on the dock, eyeing the ship. Johnson wore a straw hat with a red stripe on it. Kelly engaged him in conversation, and Johnson, looking left and right, talked pleasantly to him. He told him that three of his friends were on board, looking to get a cup of coffee, and that he planned to join them, adding that they all might take a cruise on the ship. Later, Johnson got on board (Kelly did not see him), with three other men. They apparently did not know that the watchman, Baxter, was inspecting the ship, and he tried to arrest them when they approached the bags of coffee. There was a melee, and three of the men beat Baxter to death as the fourth stood guard—all over a few bags of coffee. It was one of the first cases in history where a prosecutor convinced a jury that if four men were involved in a murder, then all four had to be hanged; one could not be given a lesser sentence just because he was only the lookout.[20]

The beating of a police officer was highly frowned upon, too. An ex-convict, Ben Waterman, was sent to prison for three months in 1842 for beating up a watchman. New York police were routinely assaulted by people they tried to arrest. One officer went to a home to serve a warrant against a man. The man threatened to punch the officer, and while they were arguing his wife sneaked up on the cop and dumped a large pail of water over his head. Both were arrested and convicted.[21]

Sometimes the judicial tables were turned against the cops. In 1850, two patrolmen arrested a suspect, Bernard Trainor, on the grounds of the Croton Water Works, a state property, where he was employed. He charged them with trespassing, and the state pursued the case against the officers. Incredibly, the patrolmen were fined for doing their job. After much argument, the city then paid their fines and went after Trainor in revenge.[22]

The patrolmen were backed up by their captains and the chief of

police, even though those officials always publicly acknowledged public complaints against police. Each policeman realized that all of his
fellow cops faced the same problems that he did and reacted in the same
way. They defended each other, stood up for each other, and lobbied
for each other. By the early 1850s, the police, under attack by criminals,
newspaper editors, and civic leaders, banded together as "brothers" in
the "blue wall." There were accusations that some police even committed perjury in official investigations or trials to protect their brothers in
blue. Older officers taught rookies the traditions of the police. Squad
rooms were set up as traditional meeting places, decorated with police
notices and photos of retired officers. Stories were swapped between
cops about notorious criminals, or dangerous investigations and arrests. Older officers would instruct their younger colleagues on how to
make an arrest and how much force to use. One generation of officers
groomed another, and part of that grooming was the idea that the police
had to stick together. This sense of blue solidarity was built up with numerous "police parades," in which nearly the entire force marched
down Broadway to remind residents that a powerful and massive group
of officers were protecting them. It was a forerunner of the contemporary "show of force" in which dozens of police cars, sirens blaring, race through city streets to remind residents they are in good hands.
In that era, too, the ceremonial "police funeral" was founded, in which
every officer in the department, in uniform, accompanied by bands,
attended any funeral of a slain officers in a magisterial display of blue
unity. All for one and one for all.[23]

From the early days of the constabulary force through the late 1850s,
the New York police had not only loose street controls but exceedingly
loose authoritative controls from above. The chiefs and captains in
charge of each precinct hailed their patrolmen and detectives, pointed
proudly to the soaring number of arrests, and spent considerable time
publicizing the good civic deeds police routinely performed, such as
caring for lost children and helping elderly ladies cross crowded downtown streets. Families with a low-intelligence relative living with them
often went to the police to beg them to find the relative, who had fled.

The officers did so happily.[24] Police also patched up differences between feuding store owners, or told street vendors who sold certain goods not to sell them in front of stores that sold the same goods. Businessmen all appreciated these efforts.

The New York police force never had serious oversight from its administrators—the internal affairs division did not come until generations later—or figures of authority. Leadership did little to punish recalcitrant police or to arrest police who were bribed or participated in illegal schemes. The city was growing too fast and criminality becoming too professional for captains and chiefs to keep up. They did not try, either, and because of that, the force always had a difficult time maintaining law and order.[25]

The men in blue sometimes turned out to be a motley crew, however. Many of those first officers did not meet the height requirements or even approach any of the physical requirements that made them "able-bodied men." In 1847, after medical exams were finally given two years after the new force's debut, police doctors found fifty men, or 6 percent of the force, unfit for duty even though they drew full pay. Cops were not in good health generally, and many reported sick, frequently. All police were not the strapping young men the force bragged about. A British tourist wrote in 1852 that the police were "of all ages and sizes including little withered old men, five foot nothing high."[26]

Officer Walling wrote in his memoirs that her remarks were common. He reminisced about his own hiring. "It is amusing to me to recall the ease with which the appointment was secured. The men at that time owed their appointments to entirely political preferences; there were no surgeons' inspections, not any civil service examinations. As a matter of fact, no attention was paid to the physique or mental requirements of the applicant. . . . I received no special instructions as to what were my duties [either]," said Walling.[27]

Walling was told to be tough, as were all of the police. Why? The criminals were tough. Cops began to feel like they were targets of rowdies, robbers, killers, and street gangs. They did not have enough brethren to win skirmishes against street toughs, so they turned vigilante.

Many men were killed by the new police, who waited for them to walk down a street and then attacked them out of an alley and beat them to death. Men were killed by gun-wielding patrolmen who waited for hours for them to walk down a certain street. The cops would then assassinate the criminals. Why? They felt that they were losing the war against crime and needed a sneak-attack mentality to win it.

In his 1915 memoir, officer Cornelius Willemse said of nineteenth-century cops, "They were powerful, fearless men, who dispensed the law with a nightstick, seldom bothering to make arrests."[28]

They knew that the magistrates, even the new police magistrates, would most likely toss their charges against criminals out of court or assess them fines instead. In one heatedly debated case in 1850, a magistrate found a man guilty of a crime and ordered him sent to prison. Then, suddenly, he asked him to pay fifteen dollars in bail money. The man did so, and the judge released him; he never went to jail. This was a common occurrence.[29]

Mayors themselves did the same thing. Anybody of importance who was arrested could plead his case to the mayor and have his conviction overturned. In the fall of 1835, three French noblemen got drunk and scuffled with constables. They were arrested and tossed into a cell at a local watch house. Word of the arrests reached City Hall, and the next morning the mayor came down and had them released. They thanked him profusely and went on their way. The mayor's intervention annoyed many, but it was rather commonplace.[30]

The police took justice into their own hands and were very careful to cover their tracks so the finger of blame would not be pointed at them. These men knew, too, that criminals were as likely to kill them as they were likely to murder criminals. They believed it was better to strike first and try to avoid detection, or if caught say their actions were nothing more than self-defense in a city soaked in crime. The police magistrates worried, too. They were so afraid of the criminals in their courts that several were armed. In one unforgettable courtroom in St. Louis, related in a story in the *Herald,* an angry magistrate stood up behind his bench, drew a long sword from the belt of his trousers, flashed it in the air menacingly, and threatened to stab anybody who came near him.[31]

There were complaints against the men in blue. From January 1 to July 1 of 1854, as an example, citizens filed 239 complaints against police. Nineteen cops were fired and seven retired after these complaints were filed. One hundred and thirty-eight were suspended without pay. Seventy-five of the complaints were dismissed.[32]

Some citizens were so irate at the way they were treated that they published pamphlets to tell their story and point fingers at policemen. Frances Connor was one. In 1848, she wrote a letter that was part of a case against someone else. The police arrested Connor at her boardinghouse and put her in jail for several days, and then she went to trial. She wrote that everything possible was done to harass her and wreck her reputation over a very minor incident. "Conspiracy, false pretense, false imprisonment, my moral character has been grossly abused, health injured, intellect impeached and my name forged," she wrote bitterly in the pamphlet. "If crime and misrule be supported, as in the present case, and individuals robbed of their claim, there can be no discipline to be supported in society."[33]

Many residents kept away from the police, fearing consequences. Later, Jacob Cantor told a state legislative hearing that "it seemed in fact that every interest, every occupation, almost every citizen, was dominated by an all controlling and overshadowing dread of the police department," and added that the 95 percent of middle- and working-class New Yorkers knew that they did not have the money or influence to be free of persecution, as did the rich.[34]

The arrest of criminals was one goal of the "new" police force. The other was crime prevention. Over eight hundred men in blue had to be able to stop criminals, no matter how many there were, from attacking citizens or robbing stores. Crime prevention was necessary. Captains told their officers to keep notes on how long it took them to walk their beat, how many stores they passed, how many residences. They were told to keep a record of the number of unlocked houses or stores they found and records of whom they talked to and for what reason. Lists of suspicious-looking people and of men who lounged on street corners were required. Cops wrote down physical descriptions of people they were looking for so that others could arrest them if they spotted them in their neighborhood. Each cop was asked to point out lawbreakers to other cops so that they would be known on sight. Police kept records of criminals who were visiting New York from other cities, with notes on local criminals with whom they met. The notes were turned over to all patrolmen to increase surveillance.[35]

In the late 1850s, police went so far as to round up suspected criminals, several dozen of them at a time, and hold a mass police lineup of them. The police got newspapers to run stories asking anyone who had been robbed lately to come into the station house for a viewing of the lineup of suspected robbers to make identification.[36]

When photography arrived in the late 1850s (there were seventy-seven photography galleries in 1854), New York was the first to establish the infamous "Rogues Gallery," a series of books of pictures of known criminals, with descriptions, that police studied at their precinct houses for street familiarity. They were quite detailed. One man was described thus: "smooth shaven and wears a dark brown wig, reaching over the forehead. He squints a great deal and is constantly chewing tobacco . . . complexion sallow, with hollow cheeks, receding chin, prominent nose, on the left side of which are two prominent warts, stoops considerably and has a halting gait."[37]

The crude 1857 Rogues Gallery would later lead to the enormous lists of criminals maintained by large urban police departments and the Federal Bureau of Investigation, the CIA and Homeland Security, national lists of fingerprints and DNA samples would follow.[38]

The new New York City police, like the old, always deferred to the rich. Wealthy men and women were rarely arrested for anything, even when they were drunk or disorderly. The police determined who was well off strictly by their clothes. If you made enough money to buy expensive clothes, you were a member of society and not a common criminal. If you did commit a crime, your clothes kept you out of the dock and the jail. Those dressed shabbily, police believed, clearly belonged to the lower classes, and as such committed thefts and robbed people. The "floater" or "drifter" or "idler" was always a target of the police. The idler had no job and therefore, police believed, would rob individuals to pay his bills and obtain food.

"An idler . . . has no right to complain . . . if the eyes of the police follow him wherever he roams or rests," said one editor. "His very idleness is an offense against all social laws. He wrongs somebody and only wants a faint impulse to push him into a league with burglars and incendiaries."[39]

The entire nation was awash, one editor said, in a "carnival of murder." The story of two Massachusetts men, Weeks and Whitney, who had held grudges against each other for years, was typical. Whitney told Weeks that if he could pick him up and throw him a few feet he would be judged the stronger of the two, and Weeks agreed. As he moved in to pick Weeks up, though, Whitney, the father of four small children, punched him a few times and then pulled out a long jackknife and stabbed him several times, killing him.

Murders were so frequent, and so infuriated the public, that many longtime anti-capital-punishment champions changed their mind on the subject and now called for executions. Walt Whitman was one. After an 1857 murder, he feared that a jury would be lenient with the killer, a man named Rogers. "We hope not. An example and a warning are imperatively demanded. The extreme penalty of the law should be inflicted. Let him hang!" Whitman said.[40]

The police targeted teenagers. Young men were seen as capable of anything. Youthful, headstrong, and jobless, they preyed on all. What really appalled the residents of New York was that the crime wave swept up young children, aged eight to sixteen, and most were the children of dirt-poor immigrants. "Nineteen out of twenty of these mendicants are foreigners cast upon our shores, indigent and helpless, having spent the last shilling in paying their passage money, deceived by the misrepresentation of unscrupulous agents and left to starve amongst strangers who, finding it impossible to extend relief to all, are deterred from assisting any," wrote Philip Hone.[41]

Many of the kids were asked to steal food and money by parents who lived in shantytowns or one-room hovels in tenements. Few suspected theft by children, and the kids usually got away with it. Many were taken in by street gangs and small robbery rings because magistrates always felt sorry for children brought before them and rarely put wide-eyed children in jail. These New York robbery gangs' use of children was similar to the way that Dickens's Fagin-led London street gang utilized them.

The little girls were especially useful. Gangs had them working as thieves in the daytime and then dressed them up and used them as prostitutes in the evening. "Most of the girls who sell fruit at the different offices are in the daily habit of practicing the most beastly and immoral things," said one police captain.[42]

The world of prostitutes changed in the 1850s. In previous decades, whoredom was finding its place in the city, cooperating with the flash newspapers, aligning itself with the police and judges and expanding the market as far as it could go. The problem the prostitution business had in the 1840s was brothels in run-down neighborhoods that were not that attractive, a clientele that was too working-class, and not enough wealthy patrons. That all changed in the 1850s when madams, and everybody else, realized that New York's population was growing rapidly and that more and more men visited the city on business or on vacation. The market of men was becoming enormous. The brothels thrived.

Many of them moved to what is now the Soho section of lower Manhattan, the area bounded by the Bowery, Canal, Laurens, and Houston. These were neighborhoods with few poor and working-class people, plenty of wealthy johns, and well-built, attractive apartment-style housing for larger and more comfortable brothels. "Not only did the felon and fancy female [prostitutes] hold forth in this district, but likewise the so-called sporting element, which was then made up of 'shoulder hitters,' dog fighters, gamblers, actors and politicians," said the *Police Gazette*. This neighborhood was also right next door to Broadway, which was booming in the 1850s. Broadway's entertainment district was getting enormous, and the spillover crowd from its theaters, night-clubs, and saloons created a surplus of business for the brothels.[43]

The hotel business was booming in the 1850s, and by the end of the decade New York had over forty hotels, most of them large and expensive. They were a natural oasis for sex. "Fallen women of the higher classes abound at the hotels," wrote McCabe.[44]

The prostitutes of the 1850s seemed to look better and dress better, many observers said. They patrolled the hotel lobbies and theater balconies, as usual, but now could also be found loitering in the best restaurants, which were the most likely place to meet men with money. "Almost without exception, they seem in the faint light of the street to be dressed with elegance and taste, to be handsome in feature and form, and to have left in them something of womanly reserve and modesty," wrote journalist Edward Crapsey.[45]

The houses of prostitution were run by madams but owned by the wealthy real estate developers, such as Amos Eno, who ran half a dozen. These men gave the whorehouses respectability, better health and sanitation conditions, and a better public image. The legal business invaded many brothels. Lawyers, detectives, and patrolmen arrived to ask questions about johns and obtain information in divorce cases. The madams and women were forthcoming, and in return, the police did not arrest anyone. It was a nice arrangement, and it lasted for decades.[46]

In the 1850s, sex of all types flourished. The first "model art shows" arrived and did a solid business. In these shows, partially or completely naked women took part in "shows" in front of a crowd of men. They were advertised as "art" to get around obscenity laws and not inter-rupted by police. Teenage boys sold photos of naked women at the doors to these theaters, and all over town, and police did not arrest any of them. Concert saloons opened. They were standard saloons with singers and dancers who put on a show while a dozen or so women sang along in the audience and solicited men while they did so. Brothels held large, elaborate costume and masquerade balls in an effort to attract more men in a more commercial way.

Guidebooks replaced the flash newspapers in the mid-1850s. These pamphlets were very detailed guides to the brothels of New York, with descriptions of acts of "service" the women performed, street addresses, and descriptions of the houses. The editors often editorialized about the luxuries of the brothel and, from time to time, criticized city policies on sex. The guidebooks also helped the madams solicit women as sex workers, reminding them in editorials that they were safe in the brothels but very unsafe in the violent streets of New York.[47]

Many complained about the expansion of the prostitution and sex trade, and police refusal to crack down on it, as the 1850s rolled on, but most just scoffed. "There are certain propensities and passions inherent in our nature which will have vent in one shape or another, despite all the combined legislative wisdom of communities," wrote Whitman. "It has always been so, it is now so, and until some radical change takes place in frail human nature, it will always be so."[48]

Why didn't the police do something about the extension of the prostitution business, and all crimes? Some thought that the police needed better salaries in order to function efficiently and so the government could attract better people to the force. "We have no right to look for saintliness in blue uniforms and pewter badges when their wearers receive but $25 to $35 a week," wrote one man.[49]

The first professional police were always criticized.[50]

In 1895, Jacob Cantor testified before a state senate hearing against the police. He cited their overly close ties to Tammany and said what many had said about the illicit relationship between the cops and politicians back in the 1840s and 1850s. The officers were guilty, Cantor said, of "arrest and brutal treatment of [Whig] voters, watchers and workers; open violations of the election laws, canvassing for Tammany Hall candidates, invasion of election booths, forcing of Tammany Hall posters upon [Whig] voters (and) denial to Republican voters and election district officers of their legal rights."

Cantor added that "a cloud of witnesses" agreed with him and had testified "that the police conducted themselves at the several polling places upon the principle that they were there not as guardians of the public peace to enforce law and order, but for the purpose of acting as agents for Tammany Hall in securing to the candidates of that organization by means fair or foul the largest possible majority."[51]

Mayor Havemeyer, out of office after his first term, was back in City Hall again in 1848 as Tammany's choice for mayor. The Hall preferred Barnburner Havemeyer over Hunker candidates. The former mayor won reelection, but most of the aldermanic posts went to the Democratic Hunkers. Near the end of his second term, Havemeyer recognized all of the complaints against the police, every single one of which he investigated, but stood firm in his belief that law enforcement was better than under the old system and that no system is perfect. "So fully are those benefits recognized by the whole community, that the complaints of the inefficiency of the police, which were formerly so incessant and universal, are now seldom if ever heard," the mayor told the increasingly unhappy residents of New York.[52]

Havemeyer was one of the few Tammany mayors in the late 1840s. All of the factions in the Hall tried to work together to regain City Hall, the mayor's office as well as the Common Council, in order to give themselves a permanent grip on city government and the lucrative New York patronage. All of that would coalesce shortly under the fabulous Fernando Wood, a former congressman and survivor of a notorious sex scandal who was idling in the political shadows in the late 1840s, trying to avoid trouble and make a fortune in city real estate.[53]

One of the main faults of New York's City government in the 1850s was the continued failure to recognize the rapid growth of the city's population and to develop a plan to accommodate the hundreds of thousands of new arrivals. The problem was not just that New York City was growing but that Brooklyn was experiencing a surge in growth, too, as were the surrounding cities of Jersey City and Newark, in New

Jersey. From 1840 to 1870, New York's population grew to nearly 900,000, a 300 percent jump. Brooklyn's population in that same thirty-year period soared from 47,613 to 280,000, a 600 percent increase. Newark climbed from 17,000 to 71,000, a leap of more than 400 percent. Jersey City rose from 3,072 to 29,000, a 900 percent jump. Conversely, Philadelphia's population only rose to 565,000, a 100 percent jump, and Baltimore from 102,000 to 212,000 a 100 percent increase. Boston's residency went from 93,000 to 177,000, a doubling. Taken together, all of metropolitan New York saw an increase of more than 400 percent, a far bigger jump than any other metropolitan area in the world. Those numbers would not level off for decades as the city grew. As an example, in the next few years, from 1870 to 1890, New York's population doubled again, and the size of cities around it, such as Brooklyn and Jersey City, grew by two and a half times. From 1880 to 1920, the United States' population jumped from 50 million to just over 100 million people, but New York City's percentage increase was still larger than the nation's.[54]

"We cannot all live in cities, yet nearly all seem determined to do so," wrote Horace Greeley of the *Tribune*.[55]

At the same time, New York's imports and exports jumped from $94 million to $400 million and represented one-quarter of all American trade imports and exports. In 1852, a writer for *Banker's Magazine* wrote that "it is fully conceded that New York is now the grand center of commercial and monetary movement in this country."[56]

` Visitors to the city were dazzled by the unrelenting surge in population and the speed with which everything moved. "New York is certainly altogether the most bustling, cheerful, lifefull, restless city I have yet seen in the United States. Nothing and nobody seems to stand still for half a moment in New York," wrote Lady Emmeline Stuart-Wortley, a British noblewoman who visited the city in 1850 with her thirteen-year-old daughter.[57]

That was no secret, and yet, when city fathers started to plan the development of the remainder of Manhattan Island, in studies that started in 1807 and became more intense in 1811, they ignored the pleas for parks, tree-shaded streets, waterfront esplanades, height limits on buildings, leisure areas, band shells, outdoor amphitheaters, and forested walkways and, instead, decided that the entire island would one day be a city just for residences, stores, and warehouses, clogged and congested from one river to the other, the perfect landscape for crime.[58]

No one profited more in that 1850s era than the owners of the city's burgeoning stores, some of the largest in the nation. "Most extraordinary dimensions," sighed Scottish journalist William Chambers on an 1853 visit. The size and number of stores raised the eyebrows of another British visitor, Edward Watkin. "Great length of 'cassimeres and woolens goods stores,' here, few hundred yards of 'straw bonnet stores,' and there a whole street devoted to 'leather stores.' . . . It seemed as if almost every kind of supply had its chief quarter in the city. . . . Quite startling to a stranger accustomed to more quiet waters."[59]

New York women flocked to these stores and emerged as the best-dressed ladies on earth. British author William Thackeray, who had traveled the world, wrote that "Solomon in all his glory, or the Queen of Sheba when she came to visit him in state, was not arrayed so magnificently as these New York damsels."[60]

In the corridors of New York's high society in the early part of the decade, though, there was a great deal of nervous energy being expanded in every direction. The clubby relationships were at an all-time high for tensions. Men continually tried to impress each other with their wealth, and women with their ostentatious style of living. Many began to loathe some of society's pushy members. George Templeton Strong, a very visible member of that club, was angry at many of them, especially the Stevenses of Bleecker Street. "There's a painful sense of arduous exertion that I feel whenever I meet them. They are always in a state of effort, like the statue of an athlete with every muscle in the anatomy straining and turgid, gasping to maintain or to establish the exalted social and intellectual position of the family and all its members, that unparalleled brute Master Austin included."[61]

Strong was irritated by many of the wealthy women he knew, too.

A friend of his, David Graham, became very ill, and the diarist was angry at Graham's wife's behavior in the crisis. "A handsome, negligent, extravagant, heartless harridan of a wife has aggravated the case sadly. She has the bad blood of the female Hyslops in her veins, has spent her husband's property, run him into debt and left him in his suffering in the arms of hirelings."[62]

Strong, and many others, complained that the pace of life in New York was becoming too fast in the 1850s. "In the morning hours, when the New York business population . . . pours out into the main artery, Broadway, and descends hurriedly downtown, nothing in the world could stop or divert the torrent. Even if Sebastopol had been in their way, those men would have run over it at one rush," wrote Adam de Gurowski.[63]

The ineptitude of the new police was apparent to all in the spring of 1849, when the feud between two prominent actors and their followers came to a head at the Astor Place Opera House. William Macready, British, and Edwin Forrest, American, two temperamental performers, had been rivals for fame and attention in England and America for years. Both were working at competing theaters in the same play, *Macbeth*. Macready starred in the production at the Astor Place Opera House and Forrest headlined in the play at a Brooklyn stage. Philip Hone, an ardent theatergoer, wrote in his diary that Forrest was "a vulgar, arrogant loafer, with a pack of kindred rowdies at his heels." Forrest's supporters crammed the opera house and when Macready first took the stage pelted him with missiles, programs, books, rotten eggs, and a few large chairs hurled down from the balcony. They screamed and yelled at him and then turned on the patrons, driving them from the theater. It was "a mob," wrote Hone, who predicted that a riot would soon follow, if not on the next day, sometime that week.

He was right. Three nights later, Macready was persuaded to return to the theater to continue his performances. Sailors from a nearby British ship, *America,* arrived carrying large placards that announced that if there was trouble they could get guns. Again, hundreds of "Forresters" jammed the theater, and again, when Macready appeared, they threw anything they could find at him. Officer George Walling was one of the police who, fearing disorder, positioned themselves in the balcony, their eyes constantly scanning the theater for trouble. He tried to halt the riot when it started but was beaten down to the ground by a group of angry troublemakers and watched hopelessly as a man threw a chair that nearly hit Macready onstage. The barrage of chairs and missiles increased as Walling struggled to get up. Other police arrested a number of rioters inside the crowded theater and maintained order, barely, but it was a very different story outside in the streets that surrounded the playhouse. There, hundreds of rioters attacked the theater, tossing paving stones that had earlier been torn up by work crews fixing a sewer line. The paving blocks and smaller stones destroyed windows and doors. Thousands of shards of sharp glass flew through the night air, striking area residents. "The stones came from the mob in volleys. . . . All was terror and confusion," said Walling, who had moved outside with six other cops. "The audience was positively terror stricken."

The hapless police, half of them unarmed, had their hands full inside the theater, where they were joined by the mayor and other city officials. Fearful of trouble, the mayor had asked the state militia, the 7th Regiment (there were city militias and private militias in the area, too), to be present at the performance, and they were, in full force, ready for action. Two units of the militia, totaling three hundred men, accompanied by sixty cavalrymen, blocked off several streets and then surrounded the mob that had grown to several thousand people. Some militiamen escorted straggling theatergoers around the mob to safety. There was much shouting, jeering, and cheering and finally, on the mayor's instructions, a loudly shouted order to disperse by the head of the militia. The crowd did not move, and the militiamen, on foot and horseback, opened fire with their rifles, at first deliberately aiming over the heads of the people in the crowd to scare them. Many of the bullets hit the walls of buildings and ricocheted into the crowd, though, wounding a dozen or more. This caused the crowd to rebel, not disperse. "The scene was now one of the wildest excitements and the fury of the mob became uncontrollable," said Walling.

The police and militia feared that the unhappy mob would over-run them, and the militia leader then ordered his men to fire directly into the crowd. "There was a flash, a deafening roar, and then were heard the cries of the wounded and the groans of the dying. The effect of the volley was awful," said Walling. "Scores lay upon the ground, writhing with pain. Terror stricken, the cowardly rioters rushed from the scene, trampling upon the prostrate forms of those who had fallen."[64]

There was more firing.

"Three or four volleys were discharged and about 20 people were killed and a large number wounded," wrote Hone, who was there at the theater and had walked outside to see what was going on. "It is to be lamented that among those killed were several innocent persons, as is always the case in such affairs. A large proportion of the mob being lookers-on, who, putting no faith in the declaration of the magistrates that the fatal order was about to be given, refused to retire and shared the fate of the rioters."[65]

Many in the theater, and in the neighborhood, feared that clash. George Templeton Strong stood on a nearby corner with his father-in-law and a judge and watched as the militia prepared for a confrontation. "Everything looked much in earnest—guns loaded and matches lighted—everything ready to sweep the streets with grape at a minute's notice, and the police and troops very well disposed to do it whenever they should be told. The mob were in a bitter, bad humor, but a good deal frightened," he wrote in his diary.[66]

City officials blamed the riot on the spontaneous anger of the crowd, but others were not so sure. Walling, who had been in the middle of it, said, "My experience has satisfied me that the concerted actions of a mob have rarely anything spontaneous about them. In many cases. the so-called 'uprising' has much premeditation in its composition." The cop added that throughout the day people had been trying to set up disputes between native-born New Yorkers and immigrants, and thousands of handbills urging a demonstration at the opera house had been handed out.[67]

Other riots followed the Astor Place melee. In 1852, a horde of thirty drunk men roared into the Bowery Street Theater, refusing to buy tickets, and rumbled down the aisles. Several police in the theater tried to push them back into the lobby but failed. A full-scale riot was stopped because a ticket seller ran to the nearest precinct house, and the captain there dispatched a squad of men to the theater. They put down the disturbance and arrested all of the men in front of a very shaken crowd. From time to time, in the early 1850s, there were riots involving a half-dozen men or fewer, often drunk, and in most cases the rioters evaded arrest.[68]

The Astor Place riot was the perfect example, right at the end of the decade, that the new police were just as ineffective as the old constable corps and that the city was hurtling blindly into the 1850s, which promised to be yet another decade of law and disorder. The new police had been on the streets for seven years by 1852. Crime was up, and residents were afraid to walk through neighborhoods at night. One man called police in New York in the early 1850s "the worst in the world," and most residents agreed.[69]

At the end of the 1840s, blame was being placed all over New York for bad police, riots, drunkenness, whores, illegal gamblers, and, especially, criminals. Many people had made up their minds that the city had spawned a criminal class, similar to the tawdry underworld portrayed in some of Dickens's novels. Many others argued that since statistics showed that an overwhelming percentage of men in prison and city jails were immigrants, and that many street gangs were ethnic in composition, all criminals had to be immigrants. The Protestants said all the criminals were Irish Catholics, and the Irish Catholics said they were all Protestants.[70]

One New York judge on the bench in 1855 was so convinced that all criminals were immigrants that he joked that all murders, riots, and violent assaults were committed by the Irish, daring burglaries and highway robberies were the work of the British, and petty theft, larceny, and forgeries were crimes of native Americans.[71]

Police Chief Matsell? He did not listen to anybody. When he looked out of his office window, or strolled down the avenues of New York, all he saw was police triumph. "The discipline of the department has been steadily improving during the past year, and it may be fairly anticipated that, under the operations of the amended law, the department will become what its original projectors intended it should be—an efficient organization for the prevention and detection of crime," he said.[72]

Matsell had statistics, too. He pointed out that in the year 1852 there were approximately 38,000 arrests, a 3.5 percent increase from 1851. He had deployed far more policemen on the streets and out of the office in 1852. There were more patrolmen to make arrests and, he said proudly, a police presence that deterred crime. What he did not say, and knew, was that many of those arrested were, for a few dollars shoved into the palm of a patrolman, allowed to escape. One pair of policemen went to a jail one night in 1851 to find it empty, the cell never locked by the police officer who "incarcerated" the men.[73]

Matsell admitted, too, that despite the increase of police in the department over the previous five years, and more cops on the street, actual crime prevention was quite low because so many officers were working in administrative capacities. A study of the police force that year shows that there were 903 police. One hundred and seventy-eight were on special detail that did not involve patrolling the streets—civil court personnel, police court workers, and administrative assistants. That left 36 men in each district at night, but half of them were sleeping in precinct house dormitories, resulting in just 18 cops on the streets in each district. That meant that one man had to oversee fifteen blocks of city turf, a nearly impossible task. Each cop realized, too, that hard work would not bring promotion; that was all political.

There was no incentive for hard work, and, consequently, the officers worked little, spending much time having coffee in street shops, chatting with passersby, and complaining about their jobs. Little crime prevention was undertaken.

CHAPTER FOURTEEN

Blood in the Streets

Probably in no city in the civilized world is life so fearfully insecure.

—Isabella Bird Bishop

The police department could not stem the crime wave or stop riots, and by the late winter of 1853 its leaders were admitting that things were just about out of control. The chief told the state legislature in his annual report on crime the previous year that "offenses against the person became of such frequent occurrence that peaceable citizens became alarmed and were afraid to venture beyond their domicile after a certain hour in the evening, while it was evident that many of the policemen were careless, if not indolent, and rather preferred to turn away from places where they were likely to get hard usage and but little honor, than to interfere with such evil disposed persons."[1]

James Gerard, a police reformer, conducted a study that showed that crimes against people were three times as high as property crimes in the late 1840s and six times as high as in the late 1830s. Foreign visitors said they did not feel safe in the city. "Probably in no city in the civilized world is life so fearfully insecure," said Isabella Bird Bishop, a visitor from England.[2]

The three main causes of crime in the 1830s and '40s—prostitution, drinking, and gambling—were even more prevalent in the 1850s. The swelling size of New York meant far more customers for those trades. More and more women drifted into prostitution, and they made more money. Their appearance was seen by some as sexual and romantic, but many, such as Whitman, had only scorn for them. "Dirty finery, excessively plentiful; paint, both red and white, draggle-tailed dress, ill-fitting, coarse features, un-intelligent, bold glance, questioning, shameless, perceptibly anxious, hideous croak or dry, brazen ring in voice, affected, but awkward, mincing, waggling gait," he said of the whores.[3]

By the early 1850s, the way the police ignored the problem of prostitution, and all of its crimes, was obvious to everybody, and public officials and newspaper editors often complained about it. All realized, too, that many police officers were in collusion with madams who paid them to look the other way. The involvement of the police with whores and madams was greater, and deeper, in the early 1850s than it had been in the last quarter of a century. One man said in 1852 that the cops were too involved with brothels and bars to do their job. Later, looking back, New York City police critic Reverend Charles Parkhurst said that "the guilt of the proprietors [of vice] is not nearly so great as the guilt of a police system that tolerates and fosters guilty proprietorship. It is our police system that is the supreme culprit."[4]

A continuing problem for the new police, one that escalated in the 1850s, was the old harbor pirates, small gangs that had been preying on ships docked in New York Harbor, generally East River docks. The total value of cargo on the ships was probably the highest of any harbor in the world. In the early 1850s, police estimated that about $400 million in cargo was in the holds of the ships at the docks that ringed Manhattan each year—attractive targets. There were several small gangs in the city, totaling a hundred or so men, who slipped out from underneath piers in small, wide boats in their home Fourth Ward and quietly moved up or down the river after midnight, unseen by anybody in the dimly lit waterway. They boarded a berthed vessel that had few security guards and when the crew was sound asleep. The guards were overwhelmed quickly and quietly, tied up, and gagged, and the ship was looted. Men carried off whatever they could that was worth something and could be put on their boat. Gold, silver, and jewelry were best because they were small items and could easily be concealed. They also raided the cargo areas of ships and stole coffee, tea, sugar, and other foodstuffs. The loot and cargo were taken out of the bags they came in and put into bags the thieves brought with them to eliminate any sign of ownership by the vessels. Then the men sailed back into the darkened waters, still unseen. If they were captured, they were put in jail and arraigned in the morning. The problem the police and judges had, though, was that the property that was confiscated was never in vessel bags, just nondescript brown bags or canvas sacks carried by the pirates, who claimed the goods were theirs. Few were incarcerated.

The river bandits infuriated the police. "The river pirates pursue their nefarious operations with the most systematic perseverance and manifest a shrewdness and adroitness which can only be attained by long practice. Nothing comes amiss to them. In their boats, under cover of night, they prowl around the wharves and vessels in a stream and dexterously snatch up every piece of loose property left for a moment unguarded," said Chief Matsell.[5]

Another group of harbor pirates, mostly children below the age of twelve, were the "daybreak boys," who boarded ships between 5:00 and 6:00 A.M., just as the sun rose, and stole whatever they could find that was small. Then they rifled the bags and pockets of sailors still sleeping and got away in small boats, like the older harbor pirates. They were not as organized as the older thieves, though, and sometimes wounded or killed their victims.

An example of their violence was an encounter in the 1840s. Several daybreak boys were rowing up the East River and noticed a rowboat with three teenagers in it who were dressed like sons of wealthy parents. The daybreak boys sailed up next to them and, brandishing long knives, boarded the boat. The three victims, trying to resist, were beaten up and robbed of all their money and watches.[6]

Merchant-ship owners and dockworkers begged the police to attack the harbor pirates, but the constables had neither the resources nor the inclination to do so. It would not be until the eve of the Civil War, and a generation of controversy and turmoil within the police department, that special units would be formed just to patrol the harbor and its hundreds of docks to cut down on the waterway robberies.[7]

A perfect example of how crime escalated, in public, with no law enforcement to stop it, was the melee that took place at Cozzens', a restaurant at the docks on the Hudson River. Several boatloads of boys from New Jersey street gangs, the Jersey City Riflemen, Short Boys, and others, landed and went directly to Cozzens' to get drinks. Upon seeing them, and recognizing them, the owner refused to let them stand at the bar or even walk into the restaurant. "[They] thereupon proceeded to break windows, pull up the planks of the piazza, smash chairs, etc. broke Cozzens's head, and hurt his two sons badly. It was a melee of the fiercest sort for a few minutes; the three Cozzenses, five workers and Mrs. Connolly . . . against some sixty blackguards, the latter finally beaten off," wrote an irritated George Templeton Strong, who knew Mrs. Connolly and the Cozzenses. There were no police anywhere in the vicinity of the restaurant to save those who were nearly killed. The gang members got back on their boats and disappeared over the water.[8]

New York had a brand-new journal in the early 1850s, *The New York Times*. The *Times* had a lot of money behind it, and its editor, Henry Raymond, thought nothing of spending huge sums of cash to get the news. The *Times* quickly became successful, and one of the reasons was its crime coverage. In its "Police News" each day, it covered most of the courts in the city and kept up with the *Herald* and *Sun* in crime news. It kept up with the *Sun* in the citywide criticism of James Gordon Bennett, too, calling his *Herald,* a newspaper with a heavy concentration of medicinal ads, "the recognized organ of quack doctors."[9]

The trouble the police had in fighting crime, too, was that the criminals simply became better at what they did, especially the burglars. The small burglary rings had become well-oiled crime machines by the middle of the 1850s; their members were far more skilled and experienced than they were in the early '40s, when burglary first became a significant problem in the city. By the md-1850s, burglars not only had smoothly operating teams but carried whatever tools, oils, greases, crowbars, and explosives they needed to succeed.

Burglars scared residents. One man woke up in the middle of an early-morning robbery and panicked. He yelled and then ran for the bedroom window. Still in his underwear, he flung open the window and jumped out of it. He fell on several flagpoles that jutted out over the front of the building and then hit the ground. He was terrified, but still alive.[10]

Many patrolmen called them the "princes of larceny" because they were so good and difficult to catch. "A 'second story' man is required to be shrewd, have an absolute knowledge of police methods, be an 'A-1' judge of human nature, know the ways of servants, profound in divining feminine artifices in concealing valuables, expert in judging the value of precious stones, and, but rarely, furs and garments," said Walling, who chased burglars all of his career. Walling added, too, that burglars knew what to look for, did not waste time on objects that were not worth a good deal of money, and got out of an apartment or house in less than two minutes to prevent suspicion or capture.[11]

The burglars' success always came at the expense of Walling and his fellow officers, but there did not seem to be much they could do to halt the tide of carefully planned and executed thefts. "The complete prevention of their depredations has always seemed to me to be impossible, and the only safeguard against their operations is incessant vigilance on the part of store-keepers and householders," added Walling.[12]

The police in the 1850s continued to be targets of those who said they were still corrupt, perhaps more corrupt than the constable force of the 1830s. Critics had plenty of evidence. Stories abounded of police taking money from gamblers, whores, unlicensed tavern owners, pickpockets, and burglars. Police were often accused of shaking down street vendors whom they were about to arrest for operating without a license. Sometimes those who were arrested were brought to court by the dozens and usually paid a fine of fifty-nine dollars. The police were often accused of being afraid to grapple with armed criminals or break up fights, instead padding their arrest totals with useless arrests of cart vendors who peddled food or clothes without a license. Some cops, like William Bell, arrested a dozen frazzled vendors at a time, each counting as a separate arrest for him to add to the totals for the month.[13]

Chief George Matsell was seen as crooked from the first day he left his beloved bookstore and took charge of the country's largest police force. He helped slave catchers find and capture runaways under the terms of the 1850 Fugitive Slave Act. Horace Greeley called him a "slave catcher" himself.[14] He was rumored to be in the pay of Madame Marie Restell, the ill-famed head of a large city abortion ring. Ever since the Mary Rogers murder in 1840, directly connected to Restell and her abortionists, critics had accused Matsell of taking money from her to protect her operations and interfere with investigations of her (she avoided jail despite nearly twenty investigations and indictments). Some said he was paid a salary by her, and others said he received a cut of her income. He was said to have sent some under arrest to particular lawyers for representation and collected a percentage of the legal fee. Others said he steered friends of his who were arrested to the courts of friendly magistrates. Sometimes, it was charged, he even directly interfered, getting friendly aldermen or magistrates to release his friends, for a fee.

Many pointed fingers at his estate in Viola, Iowa. Somehow, on his moderate police salary, and with no second job, Matsell had earned enough money to build a twenty-room mansion, with an impressive wine cellar, that sat on three thousand acres of lush, rolling land. He and his wife entertained there as if they were European royalty. Where did that money come from?

The only thing the aldermen did prove was that Matsell was an alien. They said he had not been born in the United States but had moved here from England. An investigator was sent to England, and he brought back records proving that charge. "[He] has monstrously bamboozled the people. He has . . . lobbied law through the legislature through which he ha[s] retained his office for life, palpably against the spirit of our institutions. He is the source of the bloody strife at primary and legal elections and continues, through brute force and his own police satellites, to elect nearly all the heads of departments, judiciary and who, in return, are his abject slaves," read the report.[15]

The aldermen then fired him, but an independent board, led by new mayor Fernando Wood, exonerated Matsell, finding that since his father had become a naturalized citizen in New York, so, then, had his son.[16]

Matsell just shrugged his shoulders at the torrent of charges against him over the years. He blamed all inquiries on "evil disposed persons, seeking the advancement of their own ends. If any abuses exist, they are unknown to me," he said, and added that after his retirement he had become editor of the *Police Gazette* and earned a comfortable income there to fund his home in Iowa.[17]

Captain Walling and his fellow officers had a new look in the early 1850s—an official uniform. The police had rebelled against persistent orders to adopt a uniform since 1844, when the law authorizing the new force called for a silver star badge to be worn at all times (the badge was soon made of copper). Most police did not wear it for fear of being attacked by street thugs or of being asked to work by civilians.[18] They railed against it even more in the 1850s when police reformer James Gerard suggested it. Gerard, who studied the police of the country and the world, told the Common Council that part of the effectiveness of the police in London was their uniform. It suggested authority and made it easy for people in trouble to summon an officer. The New York cops wanted nothing to do with it; in addition to previous defenses, they argued that nearly a thousand uniformed policemen would send the message to New Yorkers that they were, indeed, the mayor's army and that the city was occupied by the enemy. The "police" on their caps would make them targets for underworld bandits, they wailed. The Common Council disagreed and, despite several public protests and a court battle by the police, ordered them to adopt a new uniform. It included a smart dark blue, double-breasted wool coat with a stand-up collar and two rows of eight gold buttons in front. The collar and cuffs were made of blue velvet. The cop wore a gold badge on his coat and a navy blue cap with gold leaf braiding on the front and sides, a starched white shirt and single-breasted blue vest, striped blue pants, and a thick leather belt. The city fathers were certain that the uniformed police would be more successful.

The police not only looked official but looked good. One man said of a cop in that era that in his uniform he was "a handsome man, large and powerful in every sense of the word."[19]

Not only did the patrolmen have to wear the new uniforms, but they had to pay for them out of their own pocket, which angered them even more. The London police did not have to pay for their uniforms, they argued, so why should those in New York? They wrote letters to the newspapers to protest. Many claimed that they had now lost their freedom as men and that they were no different from the slaves in the South. They lost again because, the Common Council and newspapers argued, they were already making more money than the average laborer in New York and could afford it. Paying for their uniform would also encourage them to become more devoted to the force because they had to pay for the privilege of working in it.[20]

The police force neatly got around paying for uniforms, thanks to the generosity of stores and businesses in the city. They donated money for "prizes" of forty dollars for victory in special police marksmanship contests. Strangely enough, all of the police, all one thousand of them, won first prize and walked home with forty dollars each, which was more than enough to cover the cost of a uniform.[21]

No sooner had the battle over the uniform ended than Chief Matsell started a primitive, ad hoc "police Academy." He hired military drill instructors and firearms experts to train the police in physical conditioning, fighting, and revolver marksmanship. In a classroom, they were trained in the rules of the police department and given some instructions on how to act with not just criminals but the general public. The training was short, but it was a step in the right direction and the beginning of the road to one of the best police academies in America, which began in the 1890s. When they finished the new training, the 1,102 New York City cops on patrol in 1853 were ready to hit the streets.[22]

Officer requirements had increased. A policeman still had to be of high moral character and sober but now also had to know the first four rules of arithmetic in addition to being able to read and write. He now also had to have a doctor's note and the written backing of at least twenty-five residents of his ward who had known him for five years. However, there was still no requirement for physical conditioning or any skill at apprehending or arresting criminals. No skill in firing weapons, using knives, wielding nightsticks, or wrestling people to the ground was required. The 5'8" height requirement, scoffed at by all, was dropped. The four-year appointment was eliminated, and police were allowed to work as long as they wanted to, pending character and performance reviews. Under the new rules, hailed by all the politicians in the city, a cop still did not have to be qualified to be a cop.[23]

The brand-new Police Commission board, charged with hiring and firing all officers and monitoring the operations of the department, now consisted only of the mayor, the city recorder, and one of the city judges. It was hoped that the elimination of the aldermen would remove the politics and all of the patronage from the police department. The new, independent board was one of several instituted under new state laws to decentralize the city government and take power away from the huge Common Council—the "forty thieves," controlled by Tammany—and redistribute it to the wards and neighborhoods. The mayor was still the head of the board, still had hiring and firing power, and continued to exert considerable control over the other two members of the board. Reformers were elated because the first mayor to serve on the board was Jacob Westervelt, for a year. The first recorder and judge were city liberals who had led one of the reform movements and criticized police corruption. All three were directly elected by the people. The new board seemed perfect to many.

Others objected to it because the use of the new board meant continued domination over the city by the state legislature. Later, Seth
Low, a mayor of Brooklyn, said that "it is a dangerous thing, in wholly
democratic communities, to make the legislative body supreme over
the executive [the mayor]."[24]

Things changed rapidly, however. The second mayor on the commission, who would serve two terms, was Fernando Wood, the politically manipulative representative of Tammany, who had big plans for
the future of the city and even larger plans for the future of Fernando
Wood.

The police earned more money under the new, streamlined 1853
board. The men in blue lobbied for salary increases all the time, and
the patrolmen did it jointly with the captains to have more strength
when they bargained with the city. They pleaded that they were in dangerous work, were often overworked, and had to work both nights
and days. At one point, a small group even threatened to go on strike
if they did not obtain a pay increase. Between 1844 and 1848, in fact,
the captains and patrolmen realized a substantial 40 percent pay increase in their yearly salaries (up to $700 for patrolmen). The new
Common Council in 1855 upped that another $100, to $800 for patrolmen, but had to withdraw the offer when the Panic of 1857 hit the
city.[25]

Religious animosity in the city increased. The strife between
Catholics and Protestants increased in the early 1850s, a grim state of
affairs that no one thought possible because the animosity between
the two groups was so high in the 1840s, as the number of Irish in the
community skyrocketed. By the middle 1850s, nearly two million
Irish, a quarter of that nation's population, had fled to America, and
nearly one million settled in New York, giving it the highest Irish
population of any city in North America. The rush of the Irish to
New York was so great that in the year 1850 alone, more than 117,000
Irish arrived on its streets. Thirty thousand abandoned children in
the city were Irish. Nearly three-quarters of the residents of Five
Points were Irish.[26] Catholics would taunt Protestants in speeches and

in handbills, and Protestants would do the same to them. One Native American, anti-Catholic ruffian gave a talk standing on top of a wooden barrel on a street corner and had to be saved from a loud mob of Catholics by the police, who hustled him away. He thought nothing of it and advertised that he would be preaching again the following Sunday. "He sets up for a Protestant martyr on the strength of his detention," wrote Strong, who said of the man's vow to preach again that "there will be a mob originating with the Irish and German parishes if he's not arrested, and with the Order of United Americans and the Godly butcher boys of the Hook and First Avenue if he is."[27]

Living conditions deteriorated in the 1850s. Everybody suffered from the hot summer weather, and city fathers did nothing about it, such as urging window ventilations in homes and businesses and seeing to it that those who fell ill from heat stroke were treated. The police were not dispatched into neighborhoods to find those who fell ill with heat exhaustion and get them to a doctor.

The dirt streets became filled with mud after rainstorms, and everybody complained about it. "State of the streets defies description," wrote Strong in May of 1852. "You can hardly get into an omnibus without going ankle deep in juicy black mud." He and other New Yorkers were so fed up with mud and dirt that even the beauty of a glistening white snowfall was lost in their sure knowledge of what would follow. "Snowdrifts and banks . . . are very beautiful. But the lovely whiteness and purity of their soft complex curves of surface will soon be polluted and degenerate into mire and gutter water and mud broth," Strong added.[28]

A much larger problem was the justice system, as it had been in the 1830s and 1840s. It sadly featured a poorly trained, ineffective, and often corrupt system of police court magistrates. They were appointed in the 1830s and 1840s and elected by the people in the 1850s. The men were lawyers with little administrative or judicial experience, knew almost nothing about police work or the prison system, and owed their jobs to the political leaders who helped them get elected and re-elected, especially the men who ran Tammany Hall. Since they owed their jobs to these men, they did what they were told and took extreme advantage of legal loopholes to do so.

As an example, an alderman would tell a police magistrate to make certain that nothing happened to a friend of his who had just been arrested. Under the law, the police magistrate simply dismissed the charges against the man. The law then was written in such a way that the alderman, using the power of his office, could also throw out the charge even before it went to the police court. Magistrates could also drop charges if the accused merely posted bail, which often was later unaccounted for.

Even in properly run courts, the overwhelming number of cases meant that defendants would have a swift and not very comprehensive hearing. In 1855, the number of police magistrates was the same as it had been ten years earlier, even though the city population had grown by about 50 percent. All cases were rushed through the system, and little attention was paid to them. In fact, the police courts had always been set up for hearings every other week, so in the early 1850s the judges had 50 percent more cases with no extra time to hear them. Many charges were simply ignored because policemen provided little evidence, and the judge did not want to be bothered with a case brought to trial on circumstantial evidence and the word of a cop.

An incompetent or corrupt magistrate could be removed, but to do that the city had to get the legislature to pass an act to remove one single man, and that was nearly impossible. Magistrates could also be indicted by state and city grand juries, and some were, but not many. Whenever a judge was indicted, newspaper editors would applaud, but their joy would not last long because there were so many other judges.[29]

Judicial practices were outdated, too. In that era, witnesses to a crime were forced to remain in a jail cell all day, or overnight, in order to testify against someone, amid vicious criminals, so few witnesses offered to do so, and criminals were let go. It was not until

1841 that the Common Council ruled that witnesses had to be held in separate rooms from criminals and had to be supplied with snacks and drinks throughout the day to make their court appearances a little easier to bear. Property crimes were just as troublesome. In 1850, Simeon Fagan had twenty-two dollars of his money stolen from the police property office, where it was held as evidence in a counterfeit case. Someone had passed the bad bills to Fagan, and he was on trial. The evidence was stolen so that there would not be anything offered in court to incriminate the counterfeiter. A court ordered the police to pay back Fagan just three dollars, not twenty-two, because a magistrate determined that the other nineteen dollars was counterfeit. Fagan fumed.[30]

George Walling, who had many cases dismissed due to incompetent judges himself, said that the shabby judicial system was a major reason the crime wave in New York was so substantial. "The accused is [often] discharged from custody, a fact which, I have no doubt, encourages others in the commission of crime in the expectation of similar leniency. A man should be compelled to prosecute in such cases. A magistrate should not allow any compromise in his court, but should enforce the attendance of witnesses on behalf of the people. In not doing so, he is simply permitting what, under other circumstances, would be a criminal offense—the compounding of a felony," Walling said. "That is what it is, morally, if not legally, and that is constantly winked at by our judges. We cannot expect the laws to be properly enforced."

Walling had no praise for the prosecutors, either. He said that all of them were under such pressure in the community, and often threatened, that they believed, and their wives believed, that their lives were in danger. And so they backed off on arrests and trials and let judges dismiss criminals without filing complaints about the practice.

Prosecutors also had to bow to politicians. "The politician also peremptorily demands the discharge of a culprit after he has been proved guilty beyond the shadow of a doubt, and not infrequently a prisoner is allowed to walk out of the court room a free man, even after he has

been committed to the Island [jail] for a term of months," Walling
complained.

The cop, Walling said, was seen not as the upholder of justice but
as "the public enemy." "The police are by no means supported by
the authorities in the enforcement of the law, and as a natural consequence, are sometimes dilatory in bringing culprits to justice, or, as has
happened time and again, mete out punishment themselves," he said.

Captain Walling loved to tell the story about a procession he had
attended for the queen of England in London. A man in a carriage
broke through the line of Coldstream Guards lining the parade route.
He was chased, beaten up, and tossed in jail. At a parade in New York,
a bit later, a well-known gambler and a friend in a carriage broke
through a police line to cross the street. The gambler berated the police who tried to stop him and beat one with his whip. The police
relented, backed off, and let the man through. Walling said it was the
perfect example of good and bad police work. He fumed. "As a nation, we have the best form of government in the world. Under our
municipal system here in New York there is less liberty and protection to person and property than in any city in Europe."[31]

White-collar crime soared as the city's financial markets boomed
in the 1850s and stores began to realize significant profits. Smart men
realized they could make more money through thievery than through
hard work. One was James McIlveen, the bookkeeper for J. Beck &
Co., a large department store downtown. It went out of business,
and a police investigation showed that for years McIlveen had been
embezzling money from the store. He had balanced the books perfectly, and no one was ever aware of his thievery. All told, the bookkeeper stole $130,000 in funds, with which he purchased an expensive
city lot and built a large home on it.[32]

White-collar crime increased like every other kind until the end of
1852, when all of crime burst open like a dam collapsing from the torrent of a raging river. After a long string of weekend burglaries in

November, Bennett wrote in the *Herald*, "Where are the police! There was, last week, a burglary on Fourth Street, another on Broadway, one on Fifth Street and one on almost every street in the city. Six hundred dollars in property were carried away from one house alone, yet no arrests were made. We therefore ask where are the police? The inefficiency of the police of this city, and the irregular manner in which the duties of that branch of the executive are carried out must have attracted the attention of the most superficial observer. Unless some plan is adopted for the better organization of this body, that immense injury and loss of property and life will be entailed upon the citizens of this metropolis."

Bennett said that the rising immigrant population and high unemployment had led to more crime but that, in fact, a "vicious portion of the population will be triumphant unless something is done, and right away." The editor knew who the culprits were, too. "The first and greatest end to be obtained is the entire separation of police from political and party influence."

In a scathing denunciation of the police, he argued that a cop needed to be skilled at chasing criminals, and not just someone who was capable at "hunting up barroom votes to secure his election." Bennett had always argued that officers should not hold two-year terms renewable by Tammany Hall but should enjoy lengthy terms in order to gain skills. They needed to wear a uniform and be devoted to the prevention of crime, not the party success on Election Day. "Thief catching is a trade or art which requires sagacity penetration and skill," he added.

At the end of his long and blistering piece, Bennett said that New York needed to adopt the practices of Boston, Philadelphia, and, especially, London. His cry for a better police force, and an honest one, was taken up by most editors in the city as well as civic leaders. It had been nearly eight years since the establishment of the new force, and it was worse than the old one.[33]

All one man did to get himself murdered was ask for directions. He was alone, lost, and looking for a certain street and house. He asked a man seated on a stoop to help him. The man walked with him for several blocks and then shoved him between two homes, robbed him, and killed him.[34]

White-collar crime grew even more quickly than street crime in the 1850s. In one week in the middle of January 1852, 135 men who worked in the financial district were arrested for various forgeries in their businesses. That followed a wave of forgeries of $1,000 bonds and securities the previous winter.[35]

Domestic crime grew in the 1850s, too. In the previous two decades, disputes between married people had been few, but the pressures of life in New York caused a lot of domestic strife. There were numerous attacks by husbands on wives and wives on husbands. Love triangles boomed as women got out of the house more to work and met men. New York had a huge influx of young, single men and unhappy married and single women. Trouble naturally followed. One of the saddest cases on the police blotter was that of Barnard and Catherine Rogers of Newark, New Jersey. Catherine was having a love affair behind her husband's back with a man named Dana in New York. He wrote her numerous love letters, and Catherine mistakenly left one on the kitchen table. Her husband read it and flew into a fury. She told him that she couldn't stand him and had fallen in love with Dana. She was going to leave her husband to marry Dana, she said. Barnard pulled a double-barreled revolver out of a drawer and shot her dead, then took his own life. The *Herald* not only did a big story on the murder/ suicide, telling its readers that Barnard's body was "infested with vermin" when found, but shocked readers by printing the entire love letter from Dana to Catherine that was left on the table.[36]

Men paid no attention to court orders to stay away from their wives. Frequently a woman obtained a "separate domicile" decree from a judge allowing her to separate from her husband and live in a different home or apartment and start a new life. Men did have the right to visit their estranged wives if they let them. One man obtained approval from his wife, told her he was looking forward to seeing her, and then, when he arrived, pulled out a revolver and shot her in the heart, killing her.[37]

More lovers became involved in disputes, too. William Gillian, "a good kind fellow" and former *Herald* newsboy, got into a fight with another young man over the affections of a woman and killed him.[38]

Domestic disputes were not limited to the working class. Dozens of wealthy members of the city establishment beat their wives, too. One of the most severe cases was that of William Morgan. His wife had been confined to a hospital for a month in 1853, and upon her return home her husband began not only slapping her but kicking her. Terrified, she went to the police.[39]

Other wives were ruined by a husband's illegal financial activities. Man-about-town George Davenport embezzled thousands of dollars from friends and neighbors, and embezzled thousands more from his financial business, creating a scandal. His shaken wife left him and went home to her parents' house in Connecticut. She was "thinking of her dirty, little swindling scamp of a husband," wrote a friend of the family.[40]

Domestic conflicts started appearing in numerous cities in the 1850s. A man in Baltimore came home early and caught his wife in bed with another man. He ran into the kitchen, got a large knife, and stabbed his wife to death by plunging the knife into her back several times. He stabbed the other man several times, too, but he did not die and escaped.[41]

Racial crimes grew throughout the 1850s as tensions between blacks and whites mounted across the nation due to the enormous pressure being put on the slave states by those in the growing abolitionist movement and northern congressmen. One crime covered by nearly all of the New York papers was the racial dispute at the Elysian Fields Hotel in Hoboken, across the Hudson River, a town visited by thousands of New Yorkers for its parks and spectacular view of Manhattan. Mrs. McCarthy, the owner of the hotel, tired of her all-black waiter staff and fired them, replacing them with fellow Irish. The Irishmen turned out to be good countrymen but poor waiters, so she fired all of them and rehired the black staff. The Irishmen and the blacks clashed, and one of the black waiters was stabbed to death in the melee. This happened on the eve of one of the country's largest abolitionist conventions, held in Worcester, Massachusetts. Racial discrimination was evident in press coverage of crime, too. All crimes committed by African Americans were noted as "colored" crimes. Blacks who robbed blacks were written of as "colored" criminals assaulting "colored" victims. There was no such labeling for any other minority in New York.[42]

There were so many homicides committed in New York City by the middle of the 1850s that the *Herald* and other papers simply put a generic ANOTHER MURDER headline on most of the stories.

One of the worst nights for murder in the city in the 1850s, and in the century, was August 2, 1855. A wealthy doctor visiting New York from New Orleans, staying at the St. Nicholas Hotel, became drunk in the hotel's handsomely appointed bar. A cop tried to stop him from drinking. The doctor pulled out a knife and tried to stab the watchman but missed. The doctor was put in jail. Someone bailed him out in an hour, though, and he returned to the hotel bar and continued to drink. A few hours later he grabbed a bell in the lobby and walked through the hallways, ringing it. A Colonel Loring, visiting town from California with his sick wife, tried to stop the man but failed. Loring then scuffled with the man, who again pulled out a knife and stabbed him to death. At the same time, in a Brooklyn apartment, Patrick McMahon, who returned home drunk, killed his wife by stomping her to death with his boots. And within a few hours, a drunk man in New York returned home in a rage, pulled his three-year-old son out of bed, sat down on the floor with him, and, holding him tight, slashed him to death with a knife. While all of this was going on, another man, in Brooklyn, tried to murder his wife but only wounded her.[43]

By the middle of the 1850s, too, residents of New York, and all of the states, were psychologically torn because they did not really know to what country they belonged. It had been eighty years since the first shots of the American Revolution were fired, and what had been achieved, they asked. The northerners despised the southerners; half

the nation was mired in the immoral mud of slavery; promised won-
ders of the machine age often blew up. Catholic fought Protestant,
and Jews were ignored and/or detested by all. Less than 5 percent of
Americans had much money, and most were desperately poor. Fewer
than half went to school; epidemics such as yellow fever, smallpox, and
cholera killed tens of thousands (in New York City, hundreds of residents kept disease-spreading pigs in their homes), and most doctors
were quacks. Women had no rights; kids did not respect their elders.
Americans kept stumbling into wars—the Revolution, the War of 1812,
the Mexican War. The U.S. Army kept waging war on Indian tribes. Political parties were corrupt. People were murdered in their beds, and
priests stole from their own poor boxes. Whenever they were in trouble,
Europeans looked back at the history of their countries and found sta-
bility and purpose. New Yorkers, and Americans, could not. "We are so
young a people that we feel the want of nationality. . . . We crave a
history, instinctively," lamented George Templeton Strong.[44]

And, too, as the 1850s dragged on, North and South slowly divided. "South and North were by 1857 rapidly becoming separate
peoples," lamented historian Allan Nevins in one of his books about
the Civil War.[45]

Southerners' fear of the big city was so great that in the early 1850s,
Augustus Longstreet hesitated to become the president of the College
of South Carolina because it was located in a big city, Columbia, which
had only six thousand residents.[46]

Despite all of this, Chief Matsell told all that 1853 had been a great
success. In the first six months of the "new, new" police, he said, twenty-
five thousand arrests were made, an impressive seven thousand over
the first six months of the previous year. That success prompted Chief
Matsell to ask the city to hire architects to design new and better
precinct houses and to request city workers to clean out all existing
precinct houses, plus make renovations. The world was beautiful, the
chief said.

CHAPTER FIFTEEN

The Fabulous Fernando Wood

I have made myself useful in the office of Mayor. My success in removing many evils, and in the introduction of reforms of great benefit, has exceeded my expectations.

—Fernando Wood

There is nothing to explain the complicated New York mayor Fernando Wood better than the biography published just fifteen months after he took office. The highly laudatory book, written by Donald MacLeod, presented Wood as the latest in a long line of distinguished Woods, hailing back to the 1600s. He was, MacLeod said, not only a highly successful mayor loved by all New Yorkers but a man who would soon be president. New Yorkers who loved Wood, and those who hated him, read the book to find out more about the fabulous Fernando, the man who had won the mayor's race, consolidated the warring factions in Tammany Hall, pledged an end to crime and prostitution, and promised to reform the police and reconfigure the entire New York City government. The tall, thin, strikingly handsome new city leader, who had become a millionaire in the real estate market, seemed too good to be true.

The Wood in the book *was* too good to be true. What New Yorkers did not know was that Wood had not only paid MacLeod to write the book but had paid a publishing house to print and distribute it. He might even have written chapters of it himself. It was typical Wood: If you can't get people to love you, just say they do and hope that everybody believes you. If you can't make history, just tell everybody that you did.[1]

Mayor Wood barely won the election, garnering just 44.6 percent of the vote in a five-way race. Yet he believed that everybody in the city supported him and admired him. He was a man of enormous self-confidence who in 1840 had skyrocketed to fame at the young age of twenty-eight as a first-term congressman, fell back to earth when he lost reelection to the House, stumbled through several careers, and finally plunged into New York City real estate and moved his second wife and their children into a large mansion. The Woods would eventually have seven children, and Mrs. Wood spent most of her time raising them. She also served as her husband's official mayoral hostess and, as the years passed, became exhausted from her dual city and familial responsibilities.

People loved him and loathed him, but always wanted to know what was going on in his headline-grabbing life and chaotic world of perpetual scandals. The scandals started when he discovered that his first wife cheated on him. Angry that he paid more attention to politics than to her, she fell into a series of sexual affairs, some with his aides, which brought about a first-class scandal and a well-publicized divorce. Her bedroom antics dogged him for years. It was the first of many scandals, political, cultural, and financial, that plagued his otherwise high-flying career.

Mayor Wood's enduring self-confidence came from a belief that he was chosen by Providence to be a leader, and everybody should know that. All should support him and hold him in the high esteem in which he held himself. The mayor was a driving social force, a political hurricane, and he would do great things, he said, because it was his destiny to do them. He had a deep, loving relationship with his brother, who had served as his top political adviser for years and whom he trusted completely. His brother also helped him through his laudatory columns in the influential newspaper of which he was the editor, the *New York Daily Times.*

When he became the mayor, one of the first things Wood did was establish a good working relationship with Police Chief Matsell and several of the city's most trusted police captains, led by Captain George Walling, famed for his recent work in cracking down belligerent criminals and gangs that had terrorized New Yorkers for more than a decade.

At the same time that Wood rose to power by winning the election and rather speedily putting the entire police force under his thumb, Walling bloomed as a policeman. Walling had joined the force in 1847 and rose in the ranks swiftly, making captain in 1853. Walling was a hard-nosed tough guy who swung his billy club freely and agreed with the New York police philosophy that necessary force was needed to maintain law and order. Walling worked at first as a patrolman and then as a detective, bringing fresh ideas to detective work and establishing a name for himself as one of the city's premier investigators. He had substantial administrative skills and was a driving force in the organization of the early police department. Bosses and patrolmen liked him, trusted him, and admired his tenacity for work and his fairness to all. He was disciplined, organized, and useful to others in the force. He told all that new leadership was necessary in the city, leadership that buried the old alderman/assistant-alderman patronage kingdom in blue. Political independence and strict adherence to a belief in hard work were necessary in order for the police to grow and prosper. Walling believed that if the force could be free of political influence, and the entire nefarious skulduggery that brought with it, the NYPD could become the best department in the nation, in the world. He truly believed that and told it to all the New Yorkers he knew and met.

He believed strongly in blunt force. "No shilly-shallying" was his motto. Strong police were elementary in the new force in order to strike fear into the hearts of criminals. It was also necessary to show citizens, all so tired of an ineffective police, that the new men in blue meant business. He began to enforce a new tough cop policy as soon

as he became a captain and sold that policy to all of his superiors in
the department, the city council, and the mayor. Tough police were
good police, he said.

He proved that in his treatment of the new, colorful, and brazen
Honeymooners street gang, which had for weeks been terrorizing
anyone living in the Madison Avenue area of lower Manhattan in
1854. The Honeymooners put one man at the corner of Madison
Avenue and East Twenty-ninth Street each night to monitor the intersection. The criminal knocked down, or out, anyone he pleased
and robbed him. If he saw any cops, he simply drifted back into the
shadows and fled. Walling, a captain by that time, came up with a bold
plan. He selected a dozen of his roughest and toughest officers, called
them the Strong Arm Squad, and sent them out to Madison Avenue in
plainclothes when the sun set. Their target was the Honeymooners
gang. The police crept up on the Honeymoon men, from the front or
rear, and, without warning, pulled out their heavy wooden billy clubs
and hit them over the head repeatedly, until they fell to the ground,
bleeding badly. Then each was arrested. This rough practice, repeated
nightly, became so successful that Walling soon sent his men throughout the district, disguised as citizens, and they beat up all of the Honeymooners they could find. The Honeymoon was soon over. The
gang, its members brutally maimed, soon broke up. An emboldened
Walling then sent all of his men, in uniform and out of it, to break up
battles between immigrants in tenement blocks who had been warring
with each other. Hundreds of them were beaten up, too, and sent to
the hospital. Hundreds of squatters crowded into abandoned buildings, and numerous fights broke out there. The Strong Arm Squad
soon arrived; the strife soon stopped. Walling's reputation grew, and
so did that of the Strong Arm Squad, which was soon replicated in the
other police precincts of the city. The police, all of them, were every
bit as thuggish as the thugs they chased. The criminals in the city soon
feared them. Walling believed that clubbing and overt brutality were
necessary and that if you allowed some criminality, you would not be
able to stop any criminality.

Right at the same time Walling was establishing his credentials as a strict disciplinarian and sending his men throughout the city to enforce his new get-tough policy, Fernando Wood was elected to his first term as mayor. No one was happier with Wood's election and rapid takeover of City Hall than Walling. Wood announced on his first day as mayor that he was going to reform the crooked police force and root out prostitutes, illegal tavern keepers, and casino moguls from the dark corners of the city in which they hid. He was going to sweep all the crime, sin, and human garbage off the streets of New York. He was going to do this by personally stepping in to take over the police department. No timid police chiefs or corrupt captains were going to stop him. He would wave his magic wand with one hand and with the other smite the devil. Walling and all the clean cops in the city were thrilled.

To do all of that, Wood needed Walling and other strong, resourceful police leaders like him. He sought them out, called them into City Hall for long meetings, and, day after day, told them all that a new era was on its way for the NYPD. Fernando Wood would work miracles, Walling and the others believed. From that autumn when Walling crushed the Honeymooners and Wood ran for mayor, the lives of the two would be tightly intertwined. Wood would oversee Walling's rise, and Walling would help Wood clean up the police department, restore law and order in the streets, and make New York the most magnificent city in the world. They were two kindred souls, two blood brothers.

But something went wrong. Something went very wrong.

New York City was a carnival of ice and snow in the wintertime. Some thought that the snow made the metropolis look gorgeous, and others thought it was an endless source of trouble. "One has to walk warily over the slippery sidewalks and to plunge madly over crossings ankle-deep in snow, in order to get uptown and down . . . [but walking] is not so bad as the great crowded sleigh-caravans that have taken the place

of the omnibus. These insane vehicles carry each [a] hundred suffer-
ers, of whom about half have to stand in the wet straw with their feet
freezing and occasionally stamped on by their fellow travelers, their
ears and noses tingling in a bitter wind, their hats always on the point
of being blown off. . . . On Broadway, the Bowery, and other great
thoroughfares, there is an orgasm of locomotion. It is more than a
carnival; it's a wintery dionysiaca," complained George Templeton
Strong.[2]

Regardless of the season, Broadway by the late 1850s rivaled Paris's Champs-Élysées as the grand boulevard of the world. Broadway
"when lighted at night makes the street seem as bright as day," Whitman said. Visitors to the town were amazed at the glitter of the street
after the sun went down. "The light in the rooms of the houses shining
through the glass windows at night is so wonderful and is such a surprise
to us that I cannot describe it," said one man.[3]

By the late 1850s, New York had grown into an entertainment
mecca. It was jammed with saloons, casinos, theaters, symphony halls,
opera houses, and clubs. Castle Garden and the Crystal Palace were
two of the largest entertainment structures in the world. Visitors called
it "the gayest city in the United States." One added that Broadway and
its neighborhood had "more places of amusement than perhaps any
district of equal size in the world."[4]

The metropolis's bars and restaurants had gained world renown.
Many of the bars on lower Broadway and the Bowery were still a bit
scruffy, but the bars in the large, elegant hotels were beautiful. The
restaurants in town were superb, too. The eatery at the St. Nicholas
Hotel offered two soups, two kinds of fish, ten boiled dishes, nine roast
dishes, six relishes, seventeen entrees, three cold dishes, five varieties
of game, thirteen varieties of vegetables, seven pastries, seven fruits;
and ice cream and coffee.[5]

The rich lived very well. As the years passed, the wealthy built
larger and larger mansions, first downtown and later on the upper
reaches of Fifth Avenue, toward what would later be Forty-second

Street. The homes of the rich were full of expensive furniture, lush
satin and velvet drapes, Axminster carpets, marble and inlaid tables,
large looking glasses, extensive libraries filled with first-edition books,
oak tables, dozens of chairs in the dining rooms, and large closets
lined with the finest clothes from both America and Europe. "The
furnishings and interior ornaments of these dwellings, particularly
those on Fifth Avenue, are of a superb kind; no expense being apparently spared as regards either comfort or elegance," wrote William
Chambers, a visitor from Scotland.[6]

Throughout the 1830s, '40s, and '50s, New Yorkers spent money
recklessly to live the high life, attend sporting events, and purchase
houses. No one in the world earned money faster, or spent it quicker,
than the residents of Gotham. "New Yorkers seem to live to make
money and spend it," said one man.[7]

That glitter and glamour were just illusions, though.

The more beautiful the city became, the more difficult it was to
manage, and the magnificence of the town's appearance began to take
on dark hues. Despite its marvelous façade, the city's plunge into chaos
continued in the 1850s. Gotham did have six hundred omnibuses, but
they ran without a permanent schedule, were very overcrowded, and
often broke down. Ten years after it was created, the city's water system, supplied by Croton Reservoir, was still mismanaged and insuf-
ficient, dockworkers still engaged in fisticuffs with each other, fire
department crews still battled other crews at blazes that caused hundreds of thousands of dollars in damage, shoplifters still looted the
towns' department stores, people still starved. Garbage still piled up
in front of restaurants, bars, and residences, and its foul odor wafted
through the air of the congested neighborhoods. The city's street-
cleaning service was so poor that businessmen pooled their money
and hired their own street cleaners. Fewer than half the city's children
went to schools; many of the rest turned into lawless street urchins.
New steamships blew up; trains jumped off their tracks; horses bolted
and raced through city streets. Abortionists still flourished, brothels

made a fortune, and diseases still swept through the city's neighborhoods, killing hundreds. The economy was up and down, and the poor
felt seething animosity toward the rich.

Yet none of these troubles had any impact at all on the inefficiency
of the police and the rising crime wave.

Crime was a separate world in New York City. Poverty or unemployment did not affect it. Civic measures did not curb it. The complete mismatch between crime and all other city issues was a historical
aberration. This worried Captain George Walling, who had grown a
beard and was now in charge of one of the city's most overcrowded
police precincts. To make the force work better, he streamlined his
chain of command, became a micromanager who oversaw the work of
his men, instituted new law enforcement practices, cracked down as
hard as he could on illegal businesses such as loan sharking and prostitution, and worked with neighborhood and religious leaders to curb
crime. He believed in the reforms started by Mayor Wood and told
his men to do so, too. Like all the police, though, overworked and
overworried, Walling was concerned about the crime tide.

All of the police captains, such as Walling, and politicians, such as
Wood, were constantly under pressure from civic organizations to
eliminate crime. Residents of the city complained bitterly that they did
not just fear being mugged, robbed, or perhaps killed but feared the
way that crime was overcoming them and their families, like some dense
poisonous gas spreading through the streets and claiming everybody.
Their complaints were endless. They wanted to know why the police
did not try a second and third method of cracking down on crime if
the first did not work. Why didn't the police keep in touch with law
enforcement officials in other cities to get ideas on how to curb crime?
Why did the police ignore prostitution, gambling, and drinking? Why
were little children allowed to become part of criminal gangs and leaders of pickpocket rings? Why did the police and the city council per-
mit women to form counterfeit rings and theft rings? Why no
prosecution of abortionists? Was there no morality at all in New York

City? Why couldn't Captain Walling, or Mayor Wood, with his considerable powers, end crime?

Everyone who visited the city seemed to have been warned about thieves and murderers. The police force could not seem to catch anybody; the patrolmen all had their hands outstretched for a bribe. Stories filled the newspapers every day about crime. People who were in no danger at all always sensed that they were. One woman visiting the city disembarked from a train and waited for her bags to be taken into a hotel by a porter. She stood next to a huffing horse and watched the porter intently, as did the other hotel arrivals. "I saw people making distracted attempts, and futile ones, as it appeared, to protect their effects from the clutches of numerous porters, many of them probably thieves," she said.[8]

In the late 1850s, crime was everywhere. Mayor Wood held all power over the police department; the police chief did not. That annoyed Captain Walling, who otherwise admired Wood. The inability of the chief to run his department, always bowing to the mayor or state legislature, continued for years and became a fatal weakness. When he retired, Walling said that "time and time again have I attempted, one way or another, to have fuller power placed in my hands, but for the last four years during which I was superintendent, my position was that of a mere figure-head. . . . A man who is held responsible for the actions of certain subordinates in any public department, should have absolute control over those under him."[9]

Why did the city's crime problem grow? Many pointed their fingers at corruption and incompetence at City Hall. Visiting Scotsman William Chambers asked many New Yorkers what the causes of the city's problems were. "One uniform answer—maladministration in civic affairs. You could not take up a newspaper without seeing accounts of unchecked disorders, or reading sarcasm on official delinquencies," he wrote in 1853, the year before Wood was first elected mayor.[10]

Criminals seemed to be able to do whatever they wanted and planned their escapades in the shadowy alleys of downtown bars or on the busy docks. Four or five of them planned a daily series of robberies of stores, vendors, and passersby. Street gangs outlined an entire weekend of activities at their favorite tenement hovel. Some designed strategies for robbery and murder, and others collected guns and knives. Women put together theft rings in neighborhoods or stores. Burglary rings of three, four, five, and more men designed careful robberies. Ten-year-old pickpockets decided what type of civilian to target, and twelve-year-old whores wrapped their dresses as tightly around their breasts as they could. Farther downtown, over expensive drinks, elegantly dressed Wall Street brokers dawdled over lunch, planning stock fraud and securities theft.

And nobody seemed able to stop them.

Fernando Wood paid little attention to his critics. He saw himself not only as the city's chief administrator but as its goodwill ambassador and head cheerleader. He began the day before dawn, answering mail and making schedules by candlelight at his lavish mansion. He arrived at work promptly at 9:00 A.M. and faced a crowd of job seekers and aides at his City Hall office. All commented on how crowded the mayor's office always was, full of city workers, press, lobbyists, and supplicants. He talked to all of them and then read stacks of letters from job seekers, such as one from a Brooklyn man who swore to his brother-in-law's patriotism ("an upholder of democracy") and veneration of Wood in an effort to get a patrolman's job but never mentioned any police skills in a very long letter. Other job seekers complained of the lines of people to see the mayor and asked to meet him in bars late at night. He had always made it a practice to attempt to meet people at night because he believed there was too little time in the day to finish his work. That practice extended back to the 1830s, before he had served in any public office. Sometimes Wood made it to the meetings and sometimes he did not. "Waited for you until 11 O'clock last night," wrote one man whom Wood stood up.[11]

Those whom he did meet in the evening were always grateful. "Our interview last night has only increased my respect for your independent and dignified perseverance in carrying out what you believe to be right and just," gushed John Sichnbishop, a friend of the mayor's, in 1859.[12]

At night he was off to dinners with Tammany leaders, meetings with police officials, and various receptions, balls, and festivals. He was the chief speaker at the George Washington Day dinner, the Abraham Lincoln Day dinner, and anybody else's dinner. He went to the Tammany New Orleans Ball one night, the Typographers Ball the next. He not only attended the huge nighttime police parades but led them, waving to the crowds and bowing to their enormous cheers.

He tackled the problems of the police the way he tackled all others—with panache. He hired a team of doctors and nurses to work full-time for the police to keep his men healthy and on the job. He streamlined the chain of command in the police force, visited captains on a regular basis, listened to complaints from cops and citizens, and read all newspaper accounts of police activity. He wanted to reward police who did good work with medals, but there were none. So he created his own set of medals and handed them out frequently.

One thing he did not get, and wanted badly, was the elimination of the police board, established in 1853, and the installation of himself as the sole head of the police. He argued, unsuccessfully, that two of the men on the board were judges and therefore incapable of running that board. As a politician, he incredibly maintained, he alone was objective and qualified to do that. He tried to get the Board of Aldermen to elect him the lone autocrat in the police department, vowing to clean up the department once and for all. They refused.

Wood did not see New York City as others did. To the mayor, New York was an Emerald City, a fabulous urban mecca, a real-life Babylon. It was full of glamour and elegance and money. It featured hundreds of tall, trimasted sailing ships, powerful locomotives, sleek omnibuses and carriages, lavish parties, rich receptions, gaudy weddings, and picnics in the park involving the best-dressed people in the world sipping varieties of champagne. It was a massive collection of fabulous building blocks, and on top of them all, by himself, a big smile on his face, his arms outstretched, he stood, the emperor of it all.

The public was just as leery of Wood as the head of the police force as it had been of all previous mayors. He was worse, they thought, because he not only lied about his intentions, which was obvious to all, but was sneaky. His entire administration was full of secret meetings, closed-door meetings, and unannounced meetings. He would hold a meeting and then lie about what happened at it or, walking out of the meeting, say that there had been no meeting. People liked him, but no one trusted him, despite all of his posing, waving, and bowing.[13]

Politically, Wood backed immigrants running for any office to snare the immigrant vote for himself. He backed one man who had few qualifications for a post because the man was related to *Herald* editor James Gordon Bennett and Wood was certain that his endorsement would bring Bennett's endorsement for him as mayor. All of these maneuvers paled in comparison to his duplicitous work with the police department, though. He assessed hundreds of policemen a percentage of their salaries as "donations" to his campaign fund. He raised over $10,000. He again solicited the services of street gang rowdies who wrecked his opponents' campaigns. He furloughed hundreds of police on Election Day so that there would be no law enforcement on the streets to hold back his disruptive street gangs. Someone should have complained about this, right? They did. The complainants were none other than the members of the Police Commission. To answer them, Wood simply suspended the entire commission for several days prior to the election, Election Day, and a few days after ballots were cast.

Wood was enormously popular, but there were people who complained about the way he campaigned and charged that he won the election by fraudulent means. His defense? He wrote later that "the dissatisfaction towards myself has almost entirely subsided."[14]

He was a visionary, the mayor argued, and as such asked the city for huge increases in spending for street paving, hospitals, public education, and the police department. The police department deserved more money than anybody else, he said with unrestrained passion, because its record was flawless. It provided excellent service to a city of some 600,000 people, made tens of thousands of arrests, and was far better organized and productive than it had been five years earlier. Critics said the extra budget money would go into somebody's pocket, most likely Wood's.

Wood said that these increases were natural and obvious to anyone who had lived in New York for more than a few years. The population was growing rapidly, and more people meant more services, and that meant higher costs. "The increases in people have been so rapid that local legislation has hitherto been unable to keep pace with progress," he said.

As mayor, he asked the citizens of New York to start a grassroots movement to abolish the city charter and return all political power in the city to the city—and to him, as the mayor. "The object of government is simple," he told the city at meeting after meeting. "It is to govern in the public interest, for aiding the many without threatening the few."

And as for the charges that he was trying to make himself the emperor of New York City? The humble mayor responded that only if he was given full power could he correct "every municipal wrong."[15]

By the end of 1856, Wood had become not just the mayor but the political strongman in the city. He achieved the seemingly impossible in early 1857 when he became, at the same time and for the first time in history, the mayor and the head of Tammany Hall. He was, on any day of the week, the most powerful man in the history of New York City.

And he never forgot to remind the people of that.

Wood was a figure of great controversy, Tammany Hall was constantly criticized, taxes soared, the police were corrupt, and the crime rate rose rapidly; yet New York and its mayor seemed to be islands of calm compared to other metropolises. San Francisco did not have a

mayor until 1850, and had no police force. The city was run by vigilantes for several years. When Mayor Ephraim Burr was elected in
1850, ten thousand heavily armed vigilantes guarded voting booths to
ensure his success.

The people of Boston were unable to elect a mayor at all. There
were seven elections from mid-1844 to mid-1845 to select one, but
nobody won. Finally, Thomas Aspinwall Davis squeaked into office,
but he became ill soon after his inauguration. He resigned due to poor
health, but the city council would not let him leave and insisted he
remain in office. He did, but the work of being mayor killed him several months later. The city council then had to rush out to conduct
its eighth election for mayor. Davis's death left disorder throughout
the city.

In Baltimore, Mayor George William Brown told all he was a rock-
solid supporter of the Confederacy when it was founded in 1861. The
Union army arrested him, his entire city council, and the police chief
and tossed them all into prison, where they remained until the war
was over four years later. The city had to scramble to elect a whole new
government to run a town riddled with robberies, political crises,
and financial troubles.

In New York, Wood had a big problem, though, and that was
the newly elected, heavily Republican state legislature, most of whose
members hated him and were determined to do all that they could to
drastically cut his power or, if possible, make him completely powerless. There was no better way to do that than through the police
department, whose members the mayor saw as his personal army.

Governor John A. King started that pogrom right way, in his inaugural address, in which he stated that "experience renders it quite
certain that the Legislature will hesitate to entrust the management of
that [New York] system to the Mayor alone."[16]

Wood said those measures would "materially affect the municipal
interests of the city—not only the public, but the Democratic Party is
to be made the victim."[17]

Wood delivered a strident inaugural address of his own and told the crowd, obviously targeting state legislators, that "if the ship must go down, let those who drive her on the rocks take the helm and command—I will not."[18]

The mayor had his work cut out for him.

One of Wood's major reform movements was the curbing of the city's prostitution industry, something for which he needed the police department.

Prostitution had spread throughout the late 1840s and 1850s, and the police had done little to stop it. Mayor Wood did not think it possible to eliminate all prostitution. It seemed safe and secure within private homes; he just wanted to stop the public nature of it. The city was awash in hookers. Whores populated just about every street corner, hotel lobby, and theater in the city. They sashayed throughout town and drummed up business as the police watched. Just stopping the public solicitation of whores would help rid the city of something that tarnished it in the eyes of tourists and visitors, and residents, too. So, in 1855, he urged the police to pick up and jail any single woman they thought looked like a prostitute.

The decree started a firestorm.

"I think his policy dangerous and bad," Strong told friends. He said that the new policy meant that any woman waiting for her husband, or on her way to meet a friend, could be arrested and incarcerated. "If the policeman did make a mistake, the morning would find her in disgrace for life, maddened perhaps by shame and mortification," he wrote.[19]

Wood soon abandoned his plan.

The mayor's plan might have been short-sighted, but his goal was not, said Captain Walling, He and his fellow captains were as exasperated as the mayor every time they saw whores roaming the streets or smiling at them in the theater. No matter how hard the captains told their men to crack down on prostitutes, they did not. They were paid off, and the captains could not seem to stop the bribes.

In Wood's first administration, the police had to fight the sexual war not only against the prostitutes but against some of the most noted men and women in the city, who formed the bizarre "Free Love League," also called the Progressive Union Club, an organization whose leaders were in favor of open sexuality wherever people found it. The society met biweekly. It won much press attention but attracted the police, too, who raided the meetings and arrested many of the six hundred members of the league. It faded within a year.[20]

The always ebullient Wood was all things to all people. In his first inaugural address, the new mayor described himself as "a man of honor, a friend of labor and industry and a protector of the poor." He was, he told his audiences, not the politician the voters believed him to be at all. "My mind & time is so occupied with municipal affairs that politics is almost forgotten," he wrote William Marcy, and he promised the public that one of his major programs was a complete reform of the police department.[21]

That reform, though, did nothing except give Wood more power over the police than any mayor in the recent history of the city. Many within the police department fumed about his power and his use of it. "He . . . assumed full control of the force, which resulted in its being used for political purposes. He failed to give satisfaction and was ridiculed and condemned," wrote Captain Walling.[22]

The mayor had his critics, but he also had supporters, and many of them were influential city leaders. John Bigelow, a powerful Democrat who left the party to become a Free Soiler and then a Republican, told his many friends that Mayor Wood was the handsomest and most brilliant man he ever met. E. L. Godkin, the editor of *The Nation*, said he was the Julius Caesar of New York City politics. Many political stars of the 1860s and '70s owed their success to Wood. "It was in Wood's school that most Tammany leaders of the next generation learned their politics," Godkin wrote.[23]

James Gordon Bennett loved him, at first. "People said he was to be the rowdy's man, the rum Mayor, the blackguard's friend and many other things. What a blunder was here," he wrote in the *Herald*.[24] Regardless of the status of their friendship, which had its ups and downs, the mayor and the editor kept up a busy correspondence over the years, even if their notes were just a paragraph or two long.[25]

One of Wood's goals as mayor was to do what was best for the future of the city. Another was to do what was best for Tammany Hall, his political home. The third, and most important, goal was to do what was best for Fernando Wood. He was a politician with seemingly endless visions of himself in high office. His job as mayor could lead him to wherever he wanted to go, he believed. Wood constantly played one power group off against another, took people, organizations, and whole states to court, and politicked from the moment he woke up until the moment he laid his head down on the pillow to sleep late at night.

None of this was easy. Tammany itself, his big supporter, had been torn apart with factional warfare between the hards (liberals) and softs (conservatives), financial groups, the old party base and the new one. Only a master puppeteer could corral all of them as one large political base and stand on it smiling. Wood could do that, at least temporarily. For the moment, in the late 1850s, Tammany appeared to be losing its power. The political organization, like most in the country, was pressured by the pro- and antislavery factions. Many of the antislavery Tammanyites left the organization over the issue and joined the Republicans. Some of the more liberal members joined the Free Soilers. In the very late 1850s, Wood pulled away, too, and formed his own powerhouse, Mozart Hall. In addition to that, the Republican-controlled state legislature crippled Tammany with the new charter revisions of 1857.[26]

Tammany also suffered because in the late 1850s thousands of New Yorkers had swung over to the antislavery crusade and voted Republican in the city, not Democratic. The Democratic Party had always been able to control the state legislature because of the heavy New York City vote that put so many of its legislators in office. Now they lost numerous state legislative elections to Republicans, and the new Republicans, with a sudden majority, took over the state government.[27]

The first test of Wood's political strength and police supremacy came in the spring of 1855, just after he was sworn in, when, under considerable pressure from temperance groups, the state legislature passed a bill shutting down bars and banning the sale of liquor on Sundays, a more formal decree than the previous Sunday closing laws. Wood opposed the laws because so many immigrant groups in the city visited bars on Sunday, their lone day off from work. He also opposed the closing of taverns and liquor stores because many were run by the Irish. As an example, in the Second Ward there were 111 bars and liquor stores, and almost all of them were owned by the Irish. Wood did not want his mostly Irish cops shutting down mostly Irish bars, which would result in Wood losing tens of thousands of mostly Irish votes.[28] The immigrants and the Irish had elected him. He said the law was not clear in its enforcement provisions and had the city's district attorney go to court to challenge it. He won, and the law was nullified. Smiles, and beer, flowed.[29]

Right in the middle of all of these arguments, Wood suddenly announced that even though the police did not make any arrests or shut any bars on Sunday, it turned out that in 1856 the cops mysteriously made three times as many arrests for violation of the Sunday bar laws as in 1854, a "documented" 878 to 338. His supporters were pleased, and his critics were, naturally, not at all surprised at the phantom statistics.[30]

Wood had to work with city officials battling health epidemics. Yellow fever struck again in the summer of 1855 and killed hundreds. "Men and women die deserted and without aid," wrote Strong in his diary. "Corpses rot unburied in desolate houses. . . . [Even the] wealthy have to strive to procure the interment of wife or child, in a pine box, carried off with others, on a cart and thrown into a common trench."[31]

Wood's wild first term did not gain him the universal love he had expected from Tammany or the Democratic Party. Different groups in Tammany merged in an attempt to prevent his nomination to a second term as mayor. They had succeeded in their efforts to deny him the nomination for governor that year, a job he desperately wanted because he believed that it would catapult him to the presidency. No city mayor had ever been elected president. To get to the White House, Wood felt, he had to run the state. Getting control of the state from City Hall was quite a problem, but it did not intimidate him. Nothing intimidated him. He just had to work harder, that's all. That ultimate goal, the White House, was too big and too fabulous to ignore.

The political wings of the party fought hard to end Wood's career but failed. The indefatigable Wood worked hard to merge all the groups in Tammany and at the same time build a large, personal political machine that he was convinced could override the power of Tammany and carry him first to the governor's mansion in Albany and then to 1600 Pennsylvania Avenue.

Summing up his first few years in office, he modestly proclaimed that "I have made myself useful in the office of Mayor. My success in removing many evils, and in the introduction of reforms of great benefit, has exceeded my expectations."[32]

Wood had considerable support in his bid to be the first man ever elected to two consecutive terms as mayor. Immigrants, especially the Irish, loved him. He was a reformer and had, in fact, reformed numerous parts of the city's political machinery. Nationally, he was pro-South, and city businessmen, especially in shipping, admired him for that because the antislavery crusaders, the new Republicans and old Whigs, now dead or dying, were trying to build hurdles to northern trade with the southern states.[33]

And, too, he had his brother, Ben, who adored him and had since childhood. Ben's never-ending support for his brother, personally and in the pages of his newspaper, helped him retain power and hold off those Tammanyites who wanted to destroy him.[34]

One big reason for Wood's overall popularity with Tammany and the city Democrats, though, was his remarkable ability to rig an election. He sent his thugs to the Tammany primary conclave, and they won support. Then he employed street toughs, including rowdy street gangs, to campaign against his foes, spent money for influence and bribes, and mastered all the forms of skulduggery in political life.

He had help from above, too. In the middle of the 1856 campaign, the well-connected Lorenzo Shepard died at the age of thirty-six. Shepard was a major power broker within Tammany and a man who might have steered James Libby, Wood's foe, to victory. The other Tammany leaders, including the newly elected William Tweed, were considered too young and too powerless. Shepard's death "has created an entirely new phase in city politics, and gives Mayor Wood the vantage ground and position," wrote someone at the *Herald*.[35]

Wood ran a hard campaign and won with 44.5 percent of the vote in a five-way race. Wood not only was reelected mayor but carried into office a large number of Democrats. The Tammanyites won eleven Common Council seats to the Republicans' five. The American Party won none. The Democrats captured a solid majority of seats in the city's Common Council for the first time in years and helped Democratic presidential candidate James Buchanan win the state's electoral votes with a big plurality in New York City. Those state electoral votes carried him to victory in a three-way presidential race. On top of all of that, the Democratic candidate for governor, the one whom the party preferred over Wood, lost, bringing a smile to Wood's face.[36]

As always, Wood had been overly nervous about the election, as he was about any contest in which he was involved. As an example, in his 1861 race he was sure the Republicans, who hated him, were getting both President Abraham Lincoln and Secretary of State William Seward to mount a national movement against him. Seward's son had to calm him down. "The administration . . . does not in any way interfere in the popular elections. [Your letter] affords him [Seward] much pleasure to be assured of your support of the Union which, in the present alarming crisis, is the cause of the country itself," Fred Seward wrote to the mayor.[37]

On the day after the election, Fernando Wood had complete control of the Common Council, the Democratic Party, and Tammany Hall. Tammany would hold general control for two more decades, making itself not only the country's most powerful political machine but the most powerful city political machine in American history.

It was a machine, though, that did not want to give up its control of the police to the new, reformed police commission. Everybody wanted to reform the police. Tammany and the mayor would reform the police department, all right, but reform it in a way that did not give the police less power but gave them more.

Wood had an odd view of the New York police department. He not only saw it as a department of law enforcers who worked for the city, not the state; he saw it as a department of law enforcers who worked explicitly for him. They were his personal bodyguard. He told everybody this throughout his terms as mayor and told those who disagreed that they were wrong and not fit to be New Yorkers. He expressed it best on the first day he took office, in his inaugural speech. "This [police] department of the city government is placed more directly under the supervision of the Mayor than [any] others. With the restricted power of appointment and removal, I feel much responsibility and concern. . . . There is an apparent want of efficiency and energy which must arise . . . from want of nerve and vigilance from those who direct it. It shall be my aim to remedy these omissions."

Two months later, in a lengthy letter to reformer James Gerard, the mayor again held his ground and told Gerard that "New York can only be saved from a rule of corruption engendered by the devotees of the three great vices—namely intemperance, gambling and debauchery, but by the strong one-man power [leader] who, with a bold and fearless hand [makes rules]." He told Gerard, as he told others, that the mayor would not share police power with anyone.[38]

Just two weeks earlier, Wood, in a packed auditorium at Tammany Hall, told his supporters, jammed into each row and standing in the aisles, who wildly cheered him on, that "the Mayor ought to be the active head of the police. Why? He executes the laws, as the police execute the laws." He scoffed at the new police commissioners, telling the crowd that dozens of unqualified men were trying to land those jobs only because they received a hefty $8,000 salary. The mayor alone, he said, should be in charge, "without hindrance or molestation." The crowd roared its approval.[39]

He also told New Yorkers that the courts were getting in the way of how he wanted to run the police department and the city. "The judiciary is not the proper authority for determining police matters; nor are its members qualified," he said.[40]

The mayor told the Common Council that the city should not have to pay for all of the salaries of its policemen. Hundreds of policemen patrolled the docks to protect shipping, and so the shipping companies should pay their salaries. The railroads were very profitable, he said, because the police protected all of them. The railroad moguls should pay the salaries of those police, the mayor argued. Those industries refused to pay police salaries, despite several pleas from the mayor.[41]

Wood not only took complete control of the police but started numerous new protocols in the department. As an example, he reorganized each of the precincts to make all of them directly responsible to him. He created a complaint book in which any New Yorker, anonymously, could file police corruption or brutality charges against any patrolman (Wood never really read it, though). The mayor knew about all the complaints from the populace about law enforcement. "There is dissatisfaction in the public mind with the inefficiency of the police. Let there be none!" he shouted, adding that "good police are destructive of disorder, vice and crime."[42]

He would not give in an inch to anyone who tried to take his police power away from him. Once, the Common Council demanded that he release the names of all the police he hired and all those he dismissed, certain that if they had a chance to study the list they would find numerous examples of corruption and cronyism. The mayor refused to deliver it, citing his "executive privilege" to withhold important documents.[43]

And whenever members of the Common Council, or civic leaders, tried to talk to him about reform in the police department he simply told them, with great pride, that "each policeman is a sentinel" and then walked away from them.[44]

If all of that failed, he bragged that he had to "protect the department" from all in the state and national government who were trying to wreck it and that he "did it for the people, not myself." He knew, and everyone knew, that nothing symbolized the city more than the police, and that if Wood could control the force, and make it better, all would appreciate it, and him. It was always one of his chief priorities.[45]

All of those frustrated by his stand fumed about him. He blithely answered that none of them knew what they were talking about, except him. "No man but myself could appreciate the critical state of our social condition," he continually told people.[46]

Captain George Walling cringed at remarks such as that from the mayor. Walling knew, and all the police knew, that the mayor had made himself the dictator of the police force, assuming all control, despite the newly created commission. Walling, especially, did not like the political overtones of the police administration. Walling said, though, that there was nothing they could do about it. As the years went by, many other officers, like Walling, began to fear Wood's intense control of the police.

One of Wood's more outrageous ideas was to have New York City secede from the United States and form its own country. City merchants had lengthy and very close ties to the South because they sold millions of dollars' worth of merchandise to southerners. The political strife between the northern and southern states was driven by the slavery issue. It was very bad for business. So the mayor tried to get the Common Council to declare New York a separate country so it could continue to do business with the South as a nonaligned nation and, at the same time, continue its prosperous business with the North. He was voted down.[47]

The mayor of New York had tens of thousands of supporters and just as many critics. His opponents were astounded by some of his policies and often wrote critical pamphlets about him, accusing him of everything from common misdemeanors to grand conspiracies to defrauding the public. One was Abijah Ingraham. He did not gloss over his feelings of hatred for the mayor, titling his pamphlet *A Biography of Fernando Wood: A History of the Forgeries, Perjuries, and Other Crimes of Our "Model Mayor."* In it, Ingraham charged Wood with conspiring with others to commit fraud in the sales of eggs, ducks, turkeys, oysters, beef, pork, cigars, brooms, paper, tobacco, glass, and even matches. "He is a merciless shylock," wrote Ingraham.

Wood's tormentor, without veiling his language, called the mayor a crook. "If ever existed a criminal whose coolness surpassed his crimes, it is the hero of these pages. If there ever lived a culprit whose callousness exceeded his criminality, it is our 'model Mayor.' . . . Fernando Wood has been a depredator in the bank, in the counting house, at the merchant's desk and in the mayoralty chair," he said.[48]

The mayor paid no attention to charges such as these because they got in the way of his drive to be the president. That drive was a strenuous one. Wood worked hard to ingratiate himself with President Buchanan, but none of it made any impression on the president or people in his cabinet. Wood told Buchanan he had supported him and rounded up tens of thousands of votes for him in the 1856 elections. He then expected Buchanan to back him for governor, but the president did not. Wood then decided to run for reelection to City Hall and told all who would listen that he had a letter from the president urging him to do so. When asked to produce it, Wood told all that he had "lost" the phantom letter.

Wood ignored Buchanan's snubs and moved right on, setting his sights on the presidency and writing Buchanan that he could control all of New York City for him and had enormous influence with the city's newspapers and would woo their editors in order to gain their support for the president.

He did not know that Henry Wikoff, an old friend of Buchanan's, had sent the president scathing denunciations of Wood. In one of his letters, Wikoff charged that the mayor was a cheat. In a second, he said he was a liar, and in a third, he said that Wood had "vaulting ambitions" for his own sake.[49]

His goal of running the country seemed very reachable to the mayor. Buchanan was elected in a three-way race in 1856 and appeared to be quite weak as a national leader and certain not to be renominated. The Republicans in 1860 would surely nominate New York senator William Seward for president. The Democrats seemed to be leaning toward Illinois senator Stephen Douglas, the popular "Little Giant" of American politics. Wood believed that Douglas's support would fade if he was ever challenged on his fabled Kansas-Nebraska Act, which declared that if the people wanted slavery in the midwestern territories, they should have it. That idea made Douglas wildly popular in the slave-ridden South. What if the people voted against slavery in those same referendums, though? What would Douglas say about that? And wouldn't the Democrats want a strong urban candidate from the Northeast such as Wood? He had a chance, and he would do all he could to grab it.

The creation of the Republican Party and its immediate success in the 1856 city, state, and national elections gave Wood new woes. Walling, by 1857 unhappy with Wood's domination of the police department, and the loss of much of his own power because of that, chafed. What would happen to him, to the department, if Wood became president? What would happen if he did not and remained in the mayor's office, angry and frustrated?

Waiting on the sidelines to derail any political ambitions Wood had were the Republican governor of New York and the Republican state legislature, all of whom knew he feared them. They decided that the most effective way to undercut Wood, and destroy any drive for the presidency, was to cripple his beloved police force. That would surely ruin him.

But what started out as a campaign by the state power brokers to weaken the mayor flooded beyond its boundaries and caused an epic riot that thrust the unprepared mayor and an unsuspecting Captain George Walling into the middle of a historic political battle that dramatically changed the course of New York City and law enforcement in the United States.

CHAPTER SIXTEEN

Blue Blood: The 1857 Police Riots

The old police being disbanded and the new police as yet inexperienced and imperfectly organized, we are in an insecure and unsettled state at present . . . a state of siege.

—George Templeton Strong

The year of 1857, a watershed in the history of the NYPD and New York City, began quite naturally, with a flood of stories about crime and bumbling police in the New York newspapers during the very first week of the year. On January 1, New Year's Day, many of the papers carried the story of a man beaten and stabbed to death in an alley in Philadelphia. It resembled numerous slayings in New York. Homicides were so frequent in New York that an early 1857 crime story began, "Another atrocious murder was perpetrated. . . ." Right next to that story was a narrative about Hiram Barnes, who with a friend was convicted of a scheme to burn down Barnes's store in an arson plot.[1]

Worst of all, at the end of his term in December 1856, Governor Myron Clark freed nineteen convicts, among them men convicted of murder, burglary, and forgery, in a clemency proclamation that drew the fire of many New York newspapers. They said it was all part of the incompetent police/court system where even when an arrest was made the perpetrator was freed. Some went as far as to say that prostitutes and criminals' girlfriends were persuaded by those in jail to use sexual favors to soften up the hearts of judges and politicians to gain a release. "It is very hard to get a rogue convicted and still harder to keep him in prison with an executive who yields to the most delicate outside pressure. There's no protection for society except in revolvers, which will immediately rise in value as each new batch of convicts in Sing Sing is released. Governor Clark merits a statue from the fraternity of thieves," wailed James Gordon Bennett over the release of the criminals in the *Herald*.[2]

In that first week of January, when the convicts arrived in New York, police also faced a new wrinkle in the criminal world. Many crooks now stayed in brothels and then went out to commit crimes. They returned to the brothels and paid off madams and prostitutes to tell an investigating police officer that they had been there in the whorehouse all day.[3]

It was getting harder to make arrests on sex crimes in the late 1850s, too. Not only did women not report rapes, but those raped said that they had initiated the sex. In even more bizarre cases, many women began telling police that they and their boyfriends were engaging in rough sex games, that the forced penetration was not rape at all. Judges were perplexed and usually let the suspect go. Police captains such as George Walling did not know how to proceed when confronted with rapes and sex games, and they received no instructions from the mayor or the courts.[4]

Sex-game investigations led to bizarre marital cases. One man arrested by police had led two lives for nearly twenty years. He married one woman and lived with her for twelve years, fathering two children. He then disappeared. It turned out that he had moved in with another woman, lived with her for five years, and died. She went to court as his legal beneficiary, but the first wife showed up, too, with all of her kids. The court ruled in favor of the second wife, infuriating the first.[5]

By the first week of January 1857, steal-to-order theft rings had become an industry. People throughout New York told stories of theft rings taking orders for goods and then sending a division of burglars out to procure them and a battalion of fences to sell them.[6]

But all of those crimes together did not generate one-hundredth the press coverage of the brutal, bloody murder of high-society dentist Dr. Harvey Burdell, massacred in his office on Bond Street in the final act of a long sex scandal that had New Yorkers talking all winter and spring. It was a high-profile murder that once again put the New York police, who let it happen right under their noses, in a very bad light.

Burdell was a rascal. He was one of the city's most successful dentists, catering to wealthy residents, but made most of his fortune in banking and real estate speculation. One of the homes he bought was a townhome at 31 Bond Street. Burdell, who spent a lot of time in Bowery gambling halls and whorehouses, treated prostitutes at his office at 31 Bond, letting them pay for their dental care with sex rather than cash.

Burdell had started a sexual relationship with Emma Cunningham, a thirty-three-year-old widow with five children, in 1854. He bought the Bond Street townhome for her. She turned it into a boardinghouse, and Burdell took two rooms, one for a bedroom and one for an office. He and Emma quarreled constantly, and their fights became genuinely hostile after his attractive twenty-four-year-old female cousin, Dimis Hubbard, began to spend long periods of time living in the boardinghouse as his guest. Emma also learned, through conversations with the maids, that Burdell was having numerous sexual trysts with women in his office. On January 31, 1857, Burdell's badly mutilated body was found on the floor of his office, with blood splattered over five feet high on the walls. He had been strangled with a garrote and then stabbed fifteen times with a long knife.

The press ballyhooed everything turned up in the two-week inquest, including an "official" marriage certificate produced by Emma Cunningham that stated she was married to Burdell, who she said had told her to keep their union a secret. Then there was George Snodgrass, eighteen, one of the suspects, who had a dresser full of underwear belonging to Emma Cunningham's fifteen-year-old daughter. Another boarder, John J. Eckel, often argued with the dentist. The maids testified that the entire boardinghouse was a sexual carnival and added that one day Emma told them that she did not think Burdell would live until summer. Emma, Eckel, and young Snodgrass were all charged with murder.

Nearly ten thousand people attended the highly publicized funeral of Burdell. Emma was not allowed to go but was permitted to view Burdell's body in the coffin. She broke down, wailed that she wished she knew who killed him, and nearly fainted. The numerous witnesses to the event said they believed she was in genuine misery over his death and seemed innocent.

At the trial, held in a packed courtroom, the defense shredded the character of Harvey Burdell, portraying him as a sexually insatiable predator. Dimis, his beautiful cousin, was described as not only a homewrecker and harlot but an incestuous one at that. Emma's marriage certificate seemed to exonerate her. Why would she kill her own husband and lose all of his, and her, fortune? It made no sense.

It made no sense to the jury, either; they acquitted Cunningham. That did not end the ribald story, though. It turned out that while imprisoned in the Tombs awaiting the trial, Emma told numerous other prisoners that she was pregnant with her "husband's" baby. After she was acquitted, she concocted an elaborate ruse in which a doctor she hired would find a baby and give it to her to present to the world as Dr. Burdell's heir and solidify her claim to his money and houses. The doctor she hired to assist her in her elaborate hoax, a Dr. Uhl, went to the police, though, and told them of her scheme. Emma wound up with nothing.

People had no idea who the killer was, but all thought the police had done a poor job in the investigation and the prosecutors a shabby one in the courtroom. "The Burdell trial seems to bring out no stronger evidence than was disclosed on the inquest. If the prosecution can prove nothing further, its case is one of strong suspicion and nothing more, and should never have been brought to trial," said George Templeton Strong.[7]

The New York state legislature was pushed hard by the new Republican Party to reform the government of New York City, crush Tammany Hall, and fix the badly damaged police force. The state cut down the size of the Common Council to twelve, renamed it the Board of Supervisors, ordered that the Democrats and Republicans each had to have five members on it, and gave it power, for the first time ever, to veto the mayor's decisions. The state also eliminated the old three-man police commission, in power for just three years, and replaced it with a seven-man commission to run the newly created Metropolitan Police District, which now included Kings, Westchester, and Richmond Counties, in addition to New York. The legislators deliberately brought in the other counties in order to get around the standard "home rule" defense of city authority to which Fernando Wood always resorted to stop state legislation from affecting his iron-fisted mayoral rule (whenever he began the "home rule" defense he brought out "watch charters" from the 1790s). The commission included five members appointed by the governor and approved by the state senate, plus the mayors of Brooklyn and New York. Mayor Wood's power over the police ended, and abruptly, too.[8]

The primary reason the state took charge, though, was not the murders, robberies, and rapes. It was Wood's continued refusal to obey the new state law that forbade drinking on Sunday. Wood told his men to ignore it, and they did. When anyone questioned him on it he launched into his standard speech on "home rule" or insisted that the law was unconstitutional. The Republicans had not just been lobbied by the antidrinking crusaders; they had nearly been strangled by them. The temperance leaders had been raising a storm over the Sunday drinking law for years and finally got their way. Wood never thought the group had that much power over any political party.[9]

Wood was outraged. He told all that the loss of control over the police meant total loss of control for the city, and many agreed with him. Former mayor Havemeyer said that New York officials alone should hold power over the New York City police. What did people in faraway Albany know about the problems of New York? Mayor Wood was said to have spent over $100,000 to lobby state legislators in the state capital to kill the proposal. Whenever he went to Albany, he was on the inside out for blood and on the outside extremely courteous to all, even his worst enemies. He thanked those he did see for their time and apologized for not meeting others ("I owe you an apology for not seeing you," he started one note). He dressed immaculately, often with a bow tie adorning his expensive suit.

He signed all of his letters in a high, florid style, "Fernando Wood." Sometimes his charm worked and sometimes it did not, such as in the case of the police bills.[10]

Wood took the police issue all the way to the state supreme court, where he lost in late May 1857. At the beginning of May, the mayor, deeply wounded, went to his police and told them that if they worked for the new commissioners and Wood eventually won a court decision, they would all be fired. About 80 percent stayed on, as did all of his captains, including George Walling. In late May, all of the police in Manhattan refused to work for the new commission and were dismissed for insubordination. The men, supported by Mayor Wood, refused to leave their posts. The mayor refused to turn over any police property. The new commission, furious, appointed a whole new police force of eight hundred men. The mayor told the old force to keep patrolling. New York City suddenly had two police departments.[11]

The public was confused. Suspects arrested by one force were freed by the other. One force would refuse to conduct sweeps ordered by the mayor, but the other force would undertake them. Walling and the other captains of the mayor's force battled over who had control of the precinct houses and the patrols on the streets. The criminals did not know whom to fear, whom to obey, or whom to bribe. Chaos reigned.[12]

"Public peace and security of person and property in Brooklyn, New York and their enormous suburban villages have been of late injuriously affected. Murders have increased and an inattention from the police authorities accompanied their fatal circumstances. Highway robberies have multiplied. The escaped convicts from other states, cities, countries and foreign lands have been allowed to congregate together," read that part of the act that expressed a need for sweeping changes in the police department in New York City.[13]

The police were confused and angry, too. Captain Walling, part of the old troop, wrote that "there were two complete sets of policemen on duty, covering the same beats throughout the city. Collisions were frequent."[14]

The New York Times agreed. One of its editorial writers said that crime had increased dramatically from the spring of 1856 to the spring of 1857, "only to be accounted for under a system when the police force is perverted from its proper calling and made the political machine that it notoriously has been and still is." The *Times* blamed Wood and his fabled "one man rule" for that. So did Horace Greeley. In one of his rougher editorials, he said in the *Tribune* that Wood was "a bold, bad man."[15]

Many city newspapers and magazines published in New York applauded the state's intervention to reorder city business and reform the police department, which many said was the most corrupt in the United States' history. Wood had promised all that the police, under his leadership, would shut down brothels and illegal bars; they did not. He said that the administration of the department would be clean and honest, but when he took over he gave himself the power to fire cops for any reason at all. He was ordered by the legislature to command the police to close bars on Sunday; he never did so. He fired police who were not members of his party. Police were ordered to contribute money to his 1856 campaign fund and asked to harass his political enemies. Only Democrats were allowed to hold jobs as police officers. On Election Day, the police allowed the street-gang toughs in Wood's employ to run roughshod over polling places, beat up voters, and disrupt the entire election, which Wood won. Throughout the year, Wood and some of his City Hall cronies would hold top-secret, all-day meetings with the police commissioner and captains to evaluate the patrolmen to determine whether or not they would keep their jobs.[16]

Crime had become the ruination of New York and had to stop. "The truth is that the misgovernment or no-government . . . must inevitably force upon the minds of our people the fact that cities of the size of ours . . . cannot be governed on the pure Republican plan of frequent election and universal suffrage, unless some new check or element of discipline is introduced," said one man.[17]

The Democrats chortled at the new police force. Since the Republicans were the dominant party in the state legislature, New Yorkers saw the elimination of the old force and installation of the new as a way in which the Republican Party could control New York City and make the police the standing army of the party (they skipped over the fact that for decades it had been the "standing army" of the Democratic Party). "The mass of our people will see in the change only an adroit trick by which the police department ceases to be the tool of one party only to become the tool of another," argued a writer in *The New York Times*.[18]

The Democrats all said they had reformed the city. They had decentralized many departments and taken the government out of City Hall and brought it to the people. The Republicans countered that they did not diffuse power but scattered it about so carefully that it could not be found—but was always there. James Parton, a reformer, asked in 1866, "Was there ever such a hodgepodge of a government before in the world?"[19]

Tammany leaders said that reformers like Parton had missed the point. The point was, they argued emphatically, that New York was governed the way it was, had to be governed the way it was, because the huge metropolis had become a great democracy. In a great democracy, power and influence belonged to all, so the carving up and distribution of power by Tammany made sense. "New York City . . . is the hot bed of American democracy," said the editor of the *Democratic Review*.[20]

And, too, Tammany leaders all said, using other words, to the victor belong the spoils. "We are not answerable for the conduct of those who either from malice or because they are irretrievably bad, or because they desire to occupy the offices which we now hold, circulate stories calculated to injure those among us who are known to be among the best and firmest of our citizens," said William "Boss" Tweed, looking back on the Wood mayoralty in 1871.[21]

In 1857, crime was nearly completely out of control in New York City. The murder rate had nearly doubled over the last ten years, as had the overall crime rate. The power of the street gangs in Five Points had grown considerably. There were more whores and drunks than ever, and illegal gambling casinos dotted the streets. Everybody was frustrated by crime and the inability of the police to curb it.

"Mobs and murderers appear to rule the hour. Everybody who feels himself aggrieved takes the law into his own hands and appeals to the revolver. The revolver rules; the revolver is triumphant. Juries discharge, without leaving their seats, the gallant and lion-hearted fellows who fire revolvers at unarmed men, and avenge their wrongs without the bore and expense of a criminal trial. . . . No punishment follows crime," wrote a disheartened Walt Whitman.[22]

And so the new, new Metropolitan Police were appointed by the state legislature. Mayor Wood, who controlled almost all of the city's patronage and ran the police with an iron fist, objected. He charged that only the city could administer a police force and that state interference was blatantly unconstitutional. The state insisted it was correct. Wood refused to acknowledge the new force and supported the old one.

In June, Joseph Taylor, the city street commissioner, died. Wood had a man in place to replace him, but the new governor, John King, overruled Wood and appointed Daniel Conover, whom one longtime New Yorker called a "dirty politician." Wood had the police eject Conover from his office and boot him out of City Hall. The cops held

Conover by the neck and arms and dragged him down the steps outside the building. An infuriated Conover obtained a warrant for Wood's arrest and, surrounded by fifty of the new Metropolitan Policemen, stormed across the park toward Wood's office, only to find that the mayor had locked all the doors to the building. Inside City Hall were about eight hundred of Wood's Municipal policemen, nearly the entire force, ready to do battle if need be.

And battle they did.

The new police managed to get into the building and confront the old cops, who were already there. The old cops had been joined by a hundred or so Wood hangers-on, street thugs from the Plug Ugly gang, ward heelers, and a horde of Irishmen intent on protecting their beloved mayor. Fistfights broke out between the two battalions of police, and within minutes some of them hauled out their nightsticks and began to strike the others with them, delivering hard, vicious blows to their arms, backs, and even heads. Rumors flew that several had been killed on each side, but that was not true. Several cops, on both sides, had been badly injured, and many were taken to the office of the city recorder, where volunteer doctors treated their wounds.

Captain George Walling was there at the recorder's office. He was trying to find out, from any city official he could locate, what was going on before he stepped in with his men. At that time, all he knew was that there was a riot going on between the two police forces. He did not know why or what had to be done, or if he was supposed to step in to restore order. All was confusion around him. In that same office were a lawyer for Conover and the sheriff. The lawyer told the sheriff that he had to serve the arrest warrant that had been obtained on the mayor. The sheriff told Conover's attorney, Brown, and Walling that they had to go with him, Brown because he had obtained the warrant and Walling for official police protection. Captain Walling knew Mayor Wood well and was unhappy that he had suddenly been thrust into the middle of the dispute and had to arrest his boss. He managed to worm his way through the loud and raucous mob of new police and old police into the mayor's office, the lawyer and sheriff behind him.

There, Walling spoke for them all. He told the mayor that he had to arrest him because Conover had obtained a warrant. He carefully told him that if the tables had been turned, if some other man had been mayor and Wood the head of the new police, with an official warrant, he would have had to arrest that mayor, too. He was just doing his job, Walling told the furious mayor. "Mr. Mayor, here is an order for your arrest. It is in the hands of the sheriff of this county. I warn you that it is your duty as a law-abiding citizen to quietly submit to arrest," he said to Wood.

Wood, a smirk on his lips, walked around the desk to confront Walling. He grabbed his staff of office, which was leaning against a wall, and slammed it down on the floor with a loud thud. "I will never submit!" he yelled at the police captain, standing directly in front of him. "You only want to humiliate me. I will never let you arrest me." The mayor, shouting some epithets, then threw Walling out of his office.[23]

Conover's lawyer, Brown, told the mayor that the battle between the police outside City Hall and in its corridors had resulted in many injuries, and the number would grow if he did not submit to arrest. Then, a moment later, Police Chief Matsell arrived and excitedly told the mayor that the old Municipals had driven the new Metropolitans out of City Hall and into the park that surrounded it.[24]

The news of the arrival of the new police and Conover had flown through the city. Hundreds of New Yorkers surrounded the building and wandered through the park, eager to watch what promised to be an event without precedent in American history.

Then, coincidentally, at the exact moment that the police began to clash inside City Hall, the National Guard's 7th Regiment, composed of several hundred guardsmen, was parading in perfect formation on a street near City Hall, flags unfurled and its band playing military music. The guardsmen stopped when told of the police fracas, then moved on, uncertain what their role was, headed for ships that would take them to a prearranged visit to Boston. Then they stopped again, with the hundreds in the crowd watching intently. The leaders had a discussion about the police battle, and then the troops marched away, toward the docks, their band continuing to play. George Templeton Strong, one of many across the street from City Hall, observed the scene and followed the soldiers down the street with his eyes. They began to disappear from view, and their music seemed farther and farther away. Then something happened. "The drums that were dying away began to grow louder and to draw nearer and the National Guard re-appeared, defiling through the park gates and stationing themselves in hollow squares on the south front of City Hall," he wrote.[25]

Once the 7th Regiment had formed a ring around City Hall, its leader, General Charles Sandford, accompanied by Conover, walked calmly into the building and to the mayor's office. He told the mayor that Conover had a legitimate arrest warrant and that it had to be served on him by the police or, now, Sandford. Wood looked out the window and saw that he was surrounded by a small army of guardsmen. Matsell nodded to him that he should submit to arrest.

Wood, in a huff, agreed to accompany Matsell to a nearby courthouse. There, with friends, he arranged for his case to be heard by a magistrate very friendly to him. The magistrate said there was no cause for arrest, and the case was thrown out. The mayor returned to City Hall. By that time, the 7th Regiment had calmed down the feelings of police on both sides, the inquisitive public, and the press and formed a circle around City Hall.[26] The confrontation had ended, and most of the police from both sides had left, as did the hundreds of spectators.

The new and old police jammed City Hall, and poured out into the park, all day as negotiators moved back and forth within the building to resolve the dispute between the two police forces. New Yorkers were intrigued by the unfolding Shakespearean scene.

George Templeton Strong saw the mayor as the perfect symbol of New York City corruption. "He is an egregious demagogue and scoundrel and it's a great pity that his opponents are nearly as bad," he said the next day as he again lingered in the park with hundreds of others to see how the police riot would end.[27]

It ended very badly for Wood.

On July 3, 1857, following court approval of the new Metropolitan force, all of Wood's Municipal Police were let go, leaving the new Metropolitan force to maintain order in the city, and to do it with the annual drunkenness of the Fourth of July on its doorstep. Wood challenged the state legislature. He also told the Common Council that the new Metropolitan Police could not keep the peace on the Fourth of July, and, in fact, the new force was very disorganized as of the day the court decision was handed down. It was so disorganized that no one had bothered to legally swear in any of the new police. This was done hastily, and by late afternoon only about eighty of the eight hundred were sworn in. No one on either force knew who was technically in charge of the precinct houses, police weapons, and property that day. The next day, certain that the loss of the old force and installation of the new authorities as the sole force would cause massive police chaos, the Dead Rabbits street gang struck.[28]

What no one in charge of either police force, with one waiting on line to be appointed and the other still lingering, powerless, in the precinct houses, or Mayor Wood, knew was that the leaders of the largest city street gangs saw the divided police force as the opportunity to satisfy old grudges, and they did so, armed to the teeth. This surprised no one. "The old police being disbanded and the new police as yet inexperienced and imperfectly organized, we are in an insecure and unsettled state at present," warned diarist Strong, who later described the following riots as "a state of siege."[29]

Early on the evening of July 4, 1857, while most city residents were still celebrating the national holiday, and drinking considerable amounts of beer, the Dead Rabbits organized several other street gangs and led them in an attack on the rival Bowery Boys gang, most of whose members were in their clubhouse in the Bowery, unaware of what was about to happen. The Dead Rabbits' coalition marched down the street toward the clubhouse and encountered several dozen surprised Bowery Boys. One of them raced back to the clubhouse to alert the rest of the gang, who promptly poured out into the street, armed with clubs, chains, and knives. The two groups clashed in front of hundreds of stunned and frightened bystanders who alerted the police, as the gangs knew someone would.[30]

The gangs also knew that the splintered police force would have to scramble to halt the street riot. In the previous week, in separate incidents, street gangs had beaten up several of the new Metropolitan cops. Each of the leaders of the two police forces decided that the gang fight was the jurisdiction of the other and did not send any patrolmen to break up the men. By 9:00 P.M., the sky black, the disturbance had become a huge riot that covered several large city blocks. Unencumbered by police or any other figure of authority, the rioters engaged in mayhem. Hundreds of gang members were beaten up, and stores in the neighborhood were looted. Some residents were harassed and beaten up in their dwellings. The fighting lasted through most of the night of July 4.[31]

In the morning, the Rabbits attacked the Bowery Boys at another building and began the battle all over again. They burst into a bar run by the Bowery Boys and destroyed it, hurling rocks through the windows and shattering mirrors. Other, smaller gangs, who had held grudges against the Dead Rabbits from back in the early days of the 1830s, then joined the Bowery Boys and attacked the Dead Rabbits' coalition on Bayard Street. A few patrolmen on the new force, and several from the old force who were still working, were swept up into the battle and badly beaten. One cop tried to edge his way through the crowd to the leaders of the Rabbits, but he was battered. He was disarmed, knocked about with his own nightstick, and then stripped of his clothes. He crawled away through the crowd of battlers in his shorts and made it to a precinct house on White Street. The captain there sent several dozen cops into the neighborhood to break up the riot, but they were pushed back on their first assault. They regrouped and charged again; this time they broke through the lines of street-gang brawlers and reached some gang leaders, arresting them. They tried to pull them out of the melee and take them to a police station, but rioters raced to the rooftops and hurled hundreds of paving stones and iron bars down at the police, forcing them to run away and leave the gang leaders behind. The police were also assaulted by hundreds of bystanders caught up in the riot. The bystanders mistakenly believed that the police were out to get them, not the street thugs, and hurled hundreds of rocks and missiles at them in a rage.[32]

A Sergeant Hicks, who had been in the melee, told reporters later that "a strong malignant feeling was manifested in my district last night by a large gang of rowdies residing therein, [especially] against the Metropolitan Police. . . . [There was] considerable fighting during a latter part of the night between those rowdies and a party of men in the Bowery."[33]

Witnesses to the riot said it was "indescribable confusion." A *Herald* reporter wrote that "the crowding, fighting mass in the streets—the howling, shrieking women and children in the upper floors busily engaged in showering every description of missile on the heads of those below, hitting indiscriminately friends and foes, the explosions of firearms amid the shrieks of the wounded and dying, rendered the scene one of horror and terror."[34]

That night Captain Isaiah Rynders, who also served as political boss of the Sixth Ward, arrived at the scene around 7:00 P.M. He stood on top of a barricade that had been built across one of the city streets and asked all of the men to cease and desist and go home. He was immediately attacked, hit several times in a hail of rocks and projectiles thrown at him, and forced out of the neighborhood. He left as fires were set in the lobbies of several buildings and in stores. The blaze grew higher and higher as Rynders walked as fast as he could to police headquarters. He told the captain that the city needed all of the men and firepower available to settle the riot. The 8th and 71st Regiments of the state militia, under General Charles Sandford, were called in to disperse the rioters.[35]

The militia, as always, arrived quickly, and its members were heavily armed. Sandford led several hundred men down the street, bayonets at the ready, revolvers in their belts, and rifles slung over their shoulders. They were joined by nearly two hundred police from both departments. This army charged into the rioters, beating them and pushing them back. The leaders of the street gangs, seeing so many National Guardsmen and fearing even more rumored to be on their way, retreated out of the neighborhoods, leaving dozens of broken storefront windows, hundreds of tossed paving stones, and smoldering fires behind them. News soon arrived that about five hundred more guardsmen and police had secured City Hall and the park in front of it and were ready for any fight that anybody wanted. The rioters pulled back, and peace was restored.

Twelve men had been killed in the fighting, but both sides claimed that there were several more deaths and that those corpses had been pulled out of the fracas and buried secretly in neighborhood backyards and basements. Over three hundred rioters were injured, and half of them were sent to local hospitals. The *Herald* and other papers printed the names of those killed and wounded for several days but never reached a complete total. Police said just over one thousand men from all of the gangs participated in the two-day riot, making it the largest in New York history up to that time.[36]

Everyone in New York City was shaken by the riots. It was the worst melee since the fabled Astor Place riot of 1849. Residents and city officials were appalled that no police were at first sent to break up the disturbance, that the lack of police permitted the riots to spiral out of control, and that those police who did arrive later had no effect on the disorders and were driven back, rather hastily. If it was not for the National Guard, the street gangs would have run roughshod all over New York. Gotham was, all realized, a city without a real police force even though it had two on the payroll.

That squabble was followed just a week later by another outburst of riotous violence. A group of the new Metropolitan Police encountered a crowd of Germans in the Seventeenth Ward on July 12, and a melee broke out. One man was killed by a single gunshot. No one ever discovered who fired the gun. The death triggered an outpouring of anger from the German community. The Metropolitans left but that night came back in force, nearly four hundred of them, and battled the Germans again. The next night, genuinely scared that the police—both forces—were out of control, several thousand Germans met at a large outdoor public meeting. There, leaders got them to cease the civil disturbances and to pledge not to harass the police. The German leaders also complained loud and long, though, about police brutality on the part of the new Metropolitan Police, who charged into the crowd of their friends and neighbors without much warning. The Irish in the city, no friends to the Germans, allied themselves with the Germans in protesting police violence. Those two ethnic groups, and others, began to complain that the new Metropolitan Police had become the standing army of the state, just as all Americans had feared for years. Within days, New Yorkers had a dim view of the new police, a worse view than they had of the old Municipal force. They argued, too, that the new police were given their jobs as patronage by the Republican Party, just as the old police had benefited so heavily from the Democrats. Nothing had changed at all; New Yorkers just had a different political machine to worry about. It had been promised that many of the Municipal Police would be rehired for the Metropolitan force because of their experience. They were not; the Republicans in the statehouse wanted to keep them out. As an example, in one ward, there were twenty-eight new Metropolitan policemen, and just one of them was from the old Municipal force. The new force was not heavily composed of the Irish, either, and the Irish in the city saw it as discrimination.

Some applauded the changeover to the new force and the lessening of power in the mayor's office, and some condemned it. In Brooklyn, there were celebrations hailing the takeover of the new Metropolitan Police force. Candles were put into the windows of precinct houses, and there were rifle salutes. In the Wall Street area of Manhattan, there was disappointment. The businessmen had become close to the old police force and cherished it; they were also reluctant to deal with a new police department.[37]

The city newspapers urged everyone to obey the new law and the new police force, given substantial legitimacy by the courts. The editor at

Harper's Weekly urged all to "rally bodily to support the Albany Commissioners, and help them, honestly, fearlessly, like good citizens, preserve the peace and enforce the laws."[38]

Slowly, in the following week, the civil disorders ceased, order was restored, and New York City's law enforcement contingent settled in. But then, in 1858, the criminals came out of their abodes and the crime wave began all over again.

EPILOGUE

Crime patterns did not change much when the new, state-appointed
Metropolitan Police settled into their jobs in New York City.
The street gangs continued fighting each other, bank frauds remained
routine, muggers and robbers continued their practices, the number
of drunks on street corners increased, prostitutes carried on as usual,
and gambling remained uncontrollable. The new police did not do
much more than the old Municipal force. That was illustrated one
night a week after the Dead Rabbits riot when George Templeton
Strong took a walk downtown to get more information for his daily
diary. He headed for the area around Tompkins Square Park on the
Lower East Side because there had been a small riot there the night
before, and another the day before that. The disturbances were played
up in all the newspapers. Some of the papers even suggested the chaos
was started by the retired Municipal policemen in an effort to get their
jobs back. Strong did not find the trouble. There were no "mobs" of
ruffians, as he had expected. "I saw nothing more alarming than sun-
dry groups of Teutons jabbering gutterals with vehemence and smelled
no gunpowder," he wrote. One thing he did notice was the lax behavior of the police. "The new police seem very inefficient from want of
organization and a couple of regiments [National Guard] were under
arms last night. Should there be occasion for their active intervention,

I trust they will fire low and give the blackguardism of the city a sharp lesson."

He went to a nearby police precinct and talked to patrolmen there. He learned, as he had been told by terrified residents of the neighborhood, that the new police were afraid to venture into high-crime neighborhoods or the enclaves of the street gangs, just like the members of the old force. "Police scarcely venture east of it," Strong wrote of the area and noted that the neighborhood had been without any police protection for three days.[1]

But the most remarkable event of the post-riot summer was the resuscitation of defrocked mayor Fernando Wood. Arrested, brought to court, stripped of power, humiliated, and made to look ridiculous, the crafty politician had somehow emerged stronger than ever. Wood did not hide, cower, or bow to his superiors in Albany. He went back to his mayor's office and developed a whole new strategy toward the police and his personal power. Wood, with a wide smile on his face, not only took his seat on the new Police Commission, along with the mayor of Brooklyn, his friend, stunning all, but spent the month of July working to get one of his men appointed to a seat already vacated by one of the new commissioners. "It may lead to the very unexpected result of giving Wood and his friends the control which the police bill was expressly intended to take from them," chuckled Strong, adding that he still thought Wood was "a scoundrel."[2]

Wood would be turned out of office because of the widely publicized police riot, but he would be back. The feisty mayor formed his own political machine, Mozart Hall, put together a coalition of immigrants and southern sympathizers, employed his old street gang thugs to disrupt elections, and won the mayor's office for a third time in 1859. Two days later, his wife, Annie, died, leaving him with seven children to care for, as well as the ever-growing city.[3]

In 1860, Wood headed for the Democratic Convention in Charleston, South Carolina, intent on becoming the party's nominee for vice president, or perhaps president if the convention collapsed into chaos, as Wood believed it surely would. He arrived as a political hero, the wealthy and flamboyant three-time mayor of the biggest city in the country. The southerners loved him for his pro-South stands on issues. He went to Charleston in a special, lavish train car, put up all of his slate's delegates in expensive, elegant hotels, paid all of their bills, and oversaw party after party, signing everybody's bar bill as he did so. He received substantial press attention, and his speeches were printed in their entirety in the local newspaper. His plan was to capture New York's delegate seats for his National Democrats, battling to oust the Tammany Hall slate. He lost.

The Democratic Convention did tumble into confusion, as he predicted. The southerners, unwilling to nominate Senator Stephen Douglas of Illinois, who they felt betrayed them with his shifting stand on the Kansas-Nebraska Act, stormed out of the convention and went home. Douglas could not get enough votes to win the nomination. The convention was shut down and reopened a month later in Baltimore. There Wood again failed to have his delegation seated but made many speeches and met with numerous party leaders, still hopeful of a vice presidential nod. He did not get it and went home, highly disappointed.

Back in New York, Captain George Walling watched the "Wood for President" saga with delight. Nothing fazed the mayor. Wood was soon out of office, and Walling worked with the new mayor, advancing all of his ideas and receiving little support. Walling continued as a captain throughout the Civil War, directing his men in the famous New York City draft riots of 1863. He went on to be named police chief in 1874 and served until 1885.

Following his third and final term as mayor, Wood served five consecutive terms as a congressman and died in 1881. When he died, the population of New York City was 1.9 million people. When he was born in 1812, it was just 96,000. During his lifetime and his political career, New York City grew into the largest, richest, and most culturally renowned city in the world—thanks to him, for better or worse.

. . .

As the year 1859 drew to a close, three extraordinary events took place at the same time to form a fitting end to the era. First, the brand-new, oversized, and elegant Fifth Avenue Hotel opened in August at the northwest corner of Fifth Avenue and Twenty-third Street. The hotel boasted of rooms for eight hundred guests, all of whom were welcome to use one of the very first passenger elevators in the country, and of course to marvel at the establishment's majestic architecture, spacious lobby, and superior restaurants. The debut of the hotel marked the success of the city as a world business hub, architectural mecca, and tourist attraction. The hotel made the metropolis the worthy rival of Paris, London, and Rome.

At the same time that summer, construction was well under way for St. Patrick's Cathedral at Fifth Avenue and Fiftieth Street, an imposing edifice that would solidify the power of the Roman Catholic Church in New York and, with it, the power and influence of the Irish Catholics, who by then made up nearly one-quarter of the city's ever-growing population.

Both of these successes were met in that very hot August of 1859 with a raging river of crime that flooded the city. There were murders, robberies, and felonies just about everywhere. Police statistics for 1859 showed that there were more than ninety thousand arrests, about triple the number in the mid-1840s. Roughly a hundred men and women were murdered that year, more than twice the murder rate in the mid-1840s. Crime was everywhere. The progress in the city in so many areas, such as religion, entertainment, and business, was met with no progress anywhere in law enforcement. The new Metropolitan Police were as ineffective as the old Municipals. The crime rate did not plunge when the Civil War started, either, as so many hoped it would with numerous criminals joining the army. It rose.

The crime wave in New York would not subside until the late 1870s, after civil service was finally established. In the 1870s, there were more

police, honest police, to patrol the streets, and crime and corruption
declined. As an example, the murder rate in New York at the end of
the 1850s was somewhere between 10 and 13 per 100,000 people, but
tougher police work caused it to drop to just 5 per 100,000 by 1880
and remain at about 5 per 100,000 each year through the start of the
1920s. The rate for crime in general dropped significantly in the 1880s
and remained steadily low for forty years.

In the 1860s and early 1870s, William "Boss" Tweed would run
Tammany Hall and the city with an iron fist and steal millions from
city coffers, but after he went to prison the power of Tammany subsided somewhat. It was still in business through the 1920s, but never
again controlled the city the way it did in the middle of the nineteenth
century.

Over the next few decades, *Tribune* editor Horace Greeley grew to
be the most famous newspaperman in the United States, became heavily
invested in politics, and was the nominee of both the Democratic and
Liberal Republican parties in 1872 against President Grant (Greeley
died shortly after being trounced at the polls). *Herald* editor James Gordon Bennett was named the U.S. ambassador to England by President Lincoln. George Templeton Strong became the head of the U.S.
Sanitary Commission when the Civil War broke out. Editor Walt
Whitman wrote *Leaves of Grass*, published in 1855, and went on to become one of the country's most celebrated poets.

The New York City Police Department served as a model for other
urban law enforcement agencies in America throughout the nineteenth
century. Departments in Philadelphia, Boston, Baltimore, Richmond,
Cincinnati, Chicago, Cleveland, Pittsburgh, Washington, D.C., and
other urban areas replicated what they saw in New York. They all
had problems with state interference, political patronage, government
corruption, lack of funds, riot control, and use of weapons, as well as
difficulty with the courts and neighborhood associations. They all had
their successes and failures, but they turned out pretty much the same
as the police in New York. Everything in New York was bigger, more
complicated, more problematic, and more expensive. The gambling,

prostitution, and drinking difficulties were the same in most of the large cities, but always smaller than in New York because of its size and ever-increasing population. All the other cities had street gangs and faced the same woes in controlling them, as did New York, but in time, as in New York, the street gangs disappeared. The success of the NYPD, over the long run, after all of its troubles, paved the way for good policing in America. All of the city police departments made America a safer place to live, despite problems, big and small, that arose from time to time.

During the rest of the nineteenth century, New York grew in its splendor. Residents saw the construction of several large sports stadiums, the development of Central Park and numerous others, the growth of the boroughs, the building of the Brooklyn Bridge, and the rise of vaudeville and the Broadway theaters. Walt Whitman wrote of the city and its harbor in the summer of 1878, "First-class New York sloop or schooner yachts, sailing, this fine day, the free sea in a good wind. And rising out of the midst, tall-top't, ship-hemm'd, modern, American, yet strangely oriental, V-shaped Manhattan, with its compact mass, its spires, its cloud-touching edifices, group'd at the centre, the green of the trees and all the white, brown and gray of the architecture, well blended, as I see it, under its miracle of limpid sky, delicious light of heaven, above and June haze on the surface below."[4]

And walking the streets, docks, alleys, promenades, and avenues, watching it all, in rain or shine, summer splendor or winter snow, was a cop on the beat.

Notes

Chapter One

1. George Templeton Strong, *The Diary of George Templeton Strong*, ed. Allan Nevins and Milton Thomas, 4 vols. (New York: Macmillan, 1952), 1:104, May 9, 1836.
2. Kenneth Holcomb Dunshee, *As You Pass By* (New York: Hastings House, 1952), 75.
3. Philip Hone, *The Diary of Philip Hone*, ed. Allan Nevins, 2 vols. (New York: Dodd, Mead, 1927), 1:46, September 7, 1831.
4. Edwin Burrows and Mike Wallace, *Gotham: A History of New York City to 1898* (New York: Oxford University Press, 1999), 479.
5. Hone, *Diary* 1:133–35, July 10, 1834.
6. *Boston Post,* July 15, 1834.
7. *New York Times,* August 8, 1834.
8. *Journal of Commerce*, July 6, 1834.
9. Strong, *Diary* 1:94, November 5, 1838; Hone, *Diary* 1:46, September 7, 1831.
10. *New York Evening Post,* July 9, 1836.
11. John Quincy Adams, *Diary,* in *Memoirs of John Quincy Adams*, ed. Charles Francis Adams, 12 vols. (Philadelphia, 1876), 9:162.
12. Hone, *Diary* 1:viii.
13. Ibid., 1:xv.
14. Strong, *Diary* 1:233, May 8, 1844.
15. Burrows and Wallace, *Gotham,* 473.
16. Frank O'Brien, *The Story of the Sun* (New York, D. Appleton, 1928), 71.
17. Hone, *Diary* 1:241–42.

18. Lydia Maria Child, *Letters from New York* (New York: Columbia University Press, 1998), 93.

19. Hone, *Diary* 1:199-200, February 24, 1836.

20. George Walling, *Recollections of a New York City Chief of Police* (New York: Caxton Book Concern, 1887), 32.

21. Larry Whiteaker, *Seduction, Prostitution and Moral Reform in New York, 1830–1860* (New York: Garland, 1997), 24–25.

22. David Johnson, *Policing the Urban Underworld: The Impact of Crime on the Development of the Urban American Police, 1800–1887* (Philadelphia: Temple University Press, 1942), 48–49.

23. Carl Bridenbaugh, *Cities in Revolt: Urban Life in America, 1743–1776* (New York: Knopf, 1955), 108–9.

24. James Richardson, *The New York Police: Colonial Times to 1901* (New York: Oxford University Press, 1970) 13; Augustin Costello, *Our Police Protectors: A History of the New York Police* (1885; Montclair, NJ: Patterson Smith, 1972), 51.

25. Proceedings of the Board of Alderman of the Municipal Assembly of the City of New York Proceedings of the Council of the Municipal Assembly of the City of New York (New York: Board of Alderman, 1902–1935), 120 vols; Proceedings, Board of Aldermen, Minutes, September 5, 1842, 24:276.

26. Michael Feldberg, *The Turbulent Era: Riot and Disorder in Jacksonian America* (New York: Oxford University Press, 1980), 42.

27. Patricia Cline Cohen, Timothy Gilfoyle, and Helen Lefkowitz Horowitz, *The Flash Press: Sporting Male Weeklies in 1840s New York* (Chicago: University of Chicago Press, 2008), 73.

28. Feldberg, *Turbulent Era,* 55–62.

29. New York City Common Council report for 1841.

30. Willard A. Heaps, *Riots, U.S.A., 1765–1970* (New York, Seabury Press, 1966), 17–18; James Richardson, *Urban Police in the United States* (Port Washington, NY: Kennikat Press, 1974), 21.

31. Strong, *Diary* 1:118, December 10, 1838.

32. John Schneider, "Mob Violence and Public Order in the American City" (Ph.D. dissertation, University of Minnesota, 1971), quoted in Richard Maxwell Brown, *Strain of Violence: Historical Studies of American Violence and Vigilantism* (New York: Oxford University Press, 1977), 3, 7; Abraham Lincoln, *Abraham Lincoln: Selected Speeches, Messages, and Letters,* ed. T. Harry Williams (New York: Rinehart, 1957), 7.

33. Charles Dickens, *American Notes for General Circulation* (London, 1892; Reprint, New York: Barnes and Noble, 2005), 127–28.

34. John Runcie, "'Hunting the Nigs' in Philadelphia: The Race Riot of August 1834," *Pennsylvania History Magazine* 39, no. 2 (April 1972): 191–92.

35. Eric Homberger, *The Historical Atlas of New York City: A Visual Celebration of 400 Years of New York City's History* (New York: Henry Holt, 1994), 65.

36. Hone, *Diary* 1:30, November 27, 1830.

37. James Fenimore Cooper, "From *Notions of the Americans in New York*," in *Empire City: New York Through the Centuries*, ed. Kenneth Jackson and David Dunbar (New York: Columbia University Press, 2002), 142.

38. Brown, *Strains of Violence*, 95.

39. Feldberg, *Turbulent Era*, 12.

40. Ibid., 14.

41. Strong, *Diary* 1:177–78, April 12, 1842.

42. Leonard Richards, *Gentlemen of Property and Standing: Anti-Abolition Mobs in Jacksonian America* (New York: Oxford University Press, 1970), 86–87, 90, 92.

43. Quoted in Feldberg, *Turbulent Era*, 20.

44. J. M. Matthews, *Fifty Years in New York: A Semi-Centennial Discourse Preached in the South Dutch Church* (New York: D. Fanshaw, 1858), 32.

45. Hone, *Diary* 1:169–70, August 2, 1835.

46. Feldberg, *Turbulent Era*, 81.

47. Ralph Waldo Emerson, *Essays and Journals* (Garden City, NY: International Collectors Library, 1968), 634.

48. Cohen, Gilfoyle, and Horowitz, *The Flash Press*, 125.

49. Sidney George Fisher, *A Philadelphia Perspective: The Diary of Sidney George Fisher, Covering the Years 1834–1871*, ed. Nicholas B. Wainwright (Philadelphia: Historical Society of Pennsylvania, 1967), 169.

50. Michael Gordon, *The Orange Riots: Irish Political Violence in New York City, 1870 and 1871* (Ithaca, NY: Cornell University Press, 1993), 211.

51. Strong, *Diary* 1:336, December 2, 1848; Hone, *Diary* 1:49–50, October 15 and 17, 1831.

52. *Niles' Weekly Register*, August 23, 1834; Hone, *Diary* 1:136–37.

53. Richardson, *Urban Police in the United States*, 21–23.

54. Hone, *Diary* 1:452, January 2, 1840.

55. *New York Herald*, July 14, 1842.

56. Cohen, Gilfoyle, and Horowitz, *The Flash Press*, 182.

57. Feldberg, *Turbulent Era*, 106–9.

58. Ibid.

Chapter Two

1. Oliver Carlson, *The Man Who Made News: James Gordon Bennett* (New York: Duell, Sloan and Pearce, 1942), 142.

2. Hone, *Diary* 1:32, December 1, 1830; Mark Caldwell, *New York Night: The Mystique and Its History* (New York: Scribner, 2005), 104–5; O'Brien, *The Story of the Sun*, 58–59, 93.

3. Timothy Gilfoyle, *City of Eros: New York City, Prostitution, and the Commercialization of Sex, 1790–1920* (New York: Norton, 1992), 287.

4. George Foster, *New York in "Slices," by an Experienced Carver* (New York: Dick and Fitzgerald, 1848), 37.

5. *New York Evangelist*, December 8, 1832.

6. David Montgomery, "The Working Classes of the Pre-Industrial City," in *Urban America in Historical Perspective*, ed. Raymond K. Mohl and Neil Betten (New York: Weybright and Talley, 1970), 110.

7. Strong, *Diary* 1:15, April 12, 1836.

8. Caldwell, *New York Night*, 110–11.

9. *New York Herald*, April 11, 12, 1836; Patricia Cline Cohen, *The Murder of Helen Jewett: The Life and Death of a Prostitute in Nineteenth-Century New York* (New York: Knopf, 1998), 6–7, 20.

10. Carlson, *The Man Who Made News*, 151.

11. *New York Herald*, April 13, 1836.

12. Carlson, *The Man Who Made News*, 157.

13. *New York Sun*, April 13, 1836.

14. *Boston Post*, April 16, 1836; Cohen, *The Murder of Helen Jewett*, 32–33.

15. *New York Herald*, April 17, 1836; Strong, *Diary* 1:15, April 12, 1836.

16. Hone, *Diary* 1:210–11, June 4, 1836.

17. Cohen, *The Murder of Helen Jewett*, 302–5.

18. Ibid., 211.

19. *New York Herald,* June 9, 1836.

20. Cohen, *The Murder of Helen Jewett*, 322–23.

21. Hone, *Diary* 1:372, December 9, 1838.

22. Strong, *Diary* 1:23, June 8, 1836.

Chapter Three

1. *American Annual Cyclopedia for 1861* (New York: D. Appleton, 1862), 525.

2. Foster, *New York in "Slices,"* 104–5.

3. James D. McCabe Jr., *Lights and Shadows of New York Life; or, The Sights and Sensations of the Great City* (1872; New York: Farrar, Straus & Giroux, 1970), 738, 73.

4. Thomas Floyd-Jones, *Backward Glances: Reminiscences of an Old New-Yorker* (Somerville, NJ: Unionist Gazette Association, 1914), 2–5.

5. *New York Sun,* November 9, 1833, June 28, 1838.

6. *New York Aurora,* March 26, 1842; David S. Reynolds, *Walt Whitman's America: A Cultural Biography* (New York: Knopf, 1995), 98.

7. Catherine McNeur, *Taming Manhattan: Environmental Battles in the Antebellum City* (Cambridge, MA: Harvard University Press, 2014), 129; Daniel Ray Papke, *Framing the Criminal: Crime, Cultural Work and the Loss of Critical Perspective, 1830–1900* (Hamden, CT: Archon Books, 1987), 37; O'Brien, *The Story of the Sun,* 2, 8.

8. John Stevens, *Sensationalism and the New York Press* (New York: Columbia University Press, 1991), 26; *New York Sun,* July 21, 1834.

9. O'Brien, *The Story of the Sun,* 11, 86.

10. Horace Greeley Papers, New York Public Library.

11. *New York Herald,* May 6, 1835.

12. Douglas Fermer, *James Gordon Bennett and the* New York Herald: *A Study of Editorial Opinion in the Civil War Era, 1854–1867* (New York: St. Martin's Press, 1986), 44.

13. Ibid., 72.

14. *New York Herald,* March 26, 1842; *New York Aurora,* March 26, 1842.

15. Carlson, *The Man Who Made News,* 125.

16. *New York Herald,* July 28, 1841.

17. Ibid., January 13, 1840.

18. Carlson, *The Man Who Made News,* 65–67; Frederic Hudson, *The History of Journalism in the United States, from 1690 to 1872* (New York: Harper Brothers, 1873), 429.

19. Lambert Wilmer, *Our Press Gang; or, A Complete Exposition of the Corruption and Crimes of the American Newspapers* (Philadelphia: J. T. Lloyd, 1859), 79.

20. Papke, *Framing the Criminal,* 38; George Payne, *History of Journalism in the United States* (1920; Westport, CT: Greenwood Press, 1970), 258–59.

21. *New York Aurora,* April 18, 1842; Daniel Stashower, *The Beautiful Cigar Girl: Mary Rogers, Edgar Allan Poe, and the Invention of Murder* (New York: Penguin Group, 2006), 94.

22. Catherine Mitchell, *Margaret Fuller's New York Journalism: A Biographical Essay and Key Writings* (Knoxville: University of Tennessee Press, 1995), 9.

23. Hone, *Diary* 1:195, January 20, 1836.

24. P. T. Barnum, *The Struggles and Triumphs of P. T. Barnum, by Himself,* ed. John G. O'Leary (1882; London: MacGibbon and Kee, 1967), 668; Fermer, *James Gordon Bennett and the* New York Herald, 22–23.

25. Fermer, *James Gordon Bennett and the* New York Herald, 83; James Buchanan to James Henry, May 17, 1861, in ibid., 104; Frederick Moore Binder, *James Buchanan and the American Empire* (Selinsgrove, PA: Susquehanna University Press, 1994), 216, 219; Elbert Smith, *The Presidency of James Buchanan* (Lawrence: University Press of Kansas, 1975), 120, 146.

26. George Wilkes, *Mysteries of the Tombs: A Journal of Thirty Days Imprisonment in the New York City Prison for Libel* (New York, George Wilkes, 1844), 55; *Natchez Trader,* July 3, 1841.

27. William H. Seward, *The Works of William H. Seward*, ed. George Baker, vol. 2 (New York: Redfield Press, 1853), 38–39.

28. Frank Luther Mott, *American Journalism,* 3rd ed. (New York: Macmillan, 1962), 215; *New York Herald,* October 31, 1835.

29. Ibid., August 2, 1841.

30. Caldwell, *New York Night,* 90; Foster, *New York in "Slices,"* 68–69.

31. Papke, *Framing the Criminal,* 48–49.

32. *Brooklyn Daily Times,* December 2, 1858.

33. Walt Whitman, "Advice to Strangers," *Life Illustrated,* August 23, 1856, available online at the Walt Whitman Archive, http://www.whitmanarchive.org/published /periodical/journalism/tei/per.00274.html.

Chapter Four

1. Augustin Costello, *Our Police Protectors: A History of the New York Police* (1885; Montclair, NJ: Patterson Smith, 1972), vii.

 2. George William Curtis, "Editor's Easy Chair," *Harper's New Monthly Magazine*, February 1862, 409.

 3. Ramon de la Sagra, "From *Five Months in the United States of North America,*" in *Empire City: New York Through the Centuries,* ed. Kenneth Jackson and David Dunbar (New York: Columbia University Press, 1992), 172.

 4. Archibald Prentice, *A Tour in the United* States (London, 1848), 10.

 5. Carolyn Karcher, *Lydia Maria Child Reader* (Durham: Duke University Press, 1997), 312.

 6. Walt Whitman, *Prose Works: 1892,* ed. Floyd Stovall, 2 vols. (New York: New York University Press, 1963–64), 1:16.

 7. Ibid., 172.

 8. *New York Aurora,* March 8, 1842.

 9. George Foster, *New York by Gas-Light and Other Urban Sketches*, ed. Stuart Blumin (Berkeley: University of California Press, 1990), 8–9; Alan Pred, *Urban Growth and City-Systems in the United States, 1840–1860* (Cambridge, MA: Harvard University Press, 1980), A43, A45, A50.

10. Isabella Bird Bishop, "New York Panorama: 1854," in Bayrd Still, *Mirror for Gotham: New York as Seen by Contemporaries from the Dutch Days to the Present* (New York: New York University Press, 1956), 155.

11. J. North Conway, *The Big Policeman: The Rise and Fall of America's First, Most Ruthless, and Greatest Detective* (Guilford, CT: Lyons Press, 2010), 164–81.

12. *Brooklyn Eagle,* September 30, 1846.

13. *The Stranger's Hand Book for the City of New York; or, What to See and How to See It* (New York: C. S. Francis & Co., 1853).

14. Lydia Maria Child, *Letters from New-York: Lydia Maria Child,* ed. Bruce Mills (Athens: University of Georgia Press, 1998), 55.

15. Foster, *New York by Gas-Light,* 132–33.

16. Susan Elizabeth Lyman, *The Story of New York: An Informal History of the City from the First Settlement to the Present Day* (New York: Crown Publishers, 1975), 119, 122.

17. Hone, *Diary* 1:11–12, March 25, 1829.

18. Bishop, "New York Panorama: 1854," 158.

19. *New York Herald,* January 2, 1842.

20. Basil Hall, "From *Travels in North America in the Years 1827 and 1828,*" in *Empire City: New York Through the Centuries,* ed. Kenneth Jackson and David Dunbar (New York: Columbia University Press, 1992), 154.

21. Whitman, *Prose Works, 1892* 1:17.

22. *New York Aurora,* March 14, 1842.

23. Whitman, *Prose Works, 1892* 1:166–67.

24. Child, *Letters,* 9.

25. Robert Ernst, "Immigrants and Tenements in New York City, 1825–1863," in *Urban America in Historical Perspective,* ed. Raymond A. Mohl and Neil Betten (New York: Weybright and Talley, 1970), 114–16.

26. "Selected Writings of African-Americans in Brooklyn (1849 to 1928)," in *Empire City: New York Through the Centuries,* ed. Kenneth Jackson and David Dunbar (New York: Columbia University Press, 1992), 262–63.

27. Oscar Handlin, *The Newcomers: Negroes and Puerto Ricans in a Changing Metropolis,* New York Metropolitan Region Study (Cambridge, MA: Harvard University Press, 1959), 12–16; McNeur, *Taming Manhattan,* 98–99; Burrows and Wallace, *Gotham,* 476, 378; Peter Hall, *Cities in Civilization: Culture, Innovation and Urban Order* (London: Weidenfeld and Nicolson, 1998), 761.

28. Ernst, "Immigrants and Tenements in New York City, 1825–1863," 117.

29. Rayond A. Mohl and Neil Betten, eds., Introduction, Pre-Industrial City, *Urban America in Historical Perspective* (New York: Weybright and Talley, 1970), 94.

30. *New York Times,* May 16, 1856; McCabe, *Lights and Shadows of New York Life,* 63; Foster, *New York in "Slices,"* 86.

31. Thomas Jefferson to anonymous [William Short], *The Writings of Thomas Jefferson,* vol. 15 (Washington, DC: Thomas Jefferson Memorial Association, 1907), 469.

32. William Bell, *The Diary of William Bell, Policeman, New York City, 1850–51*, microfilm, New-York Historical Society.

33. Charles Dickens, "American Notes for General Circulation," in Jackson and Dunbar, 193.

34. McNeur, *Taming of Manhattan*, 190; Bell, *Diary*, October 7, 11, 1850.

35. *New York Daily Times*, January 12, 1853.

36. *New York Times*, July 15, 1867; Reynolds, *Walt Whitman's America*, 109.

37. Reynolds, *Walt Whitman's America*, 108; *New York Sun*, December 1, 1842.

38. Richardson, *Urban Police in the United States*, 21.

39. *New York Tribune*, December 21, 1842.

40. Costello, *Our Police Protectors*, vii; Bridenbaugh, *Cities in Revolt*, 297–98.

Chapter Five

1. Wilbur Miller, ed., *The Social History of Crime and Punishment in America* (Los Angeles: Sage Publications, 2012), 17.

2. *New York Times*, January 9, 1862, February 15, 1855; Gerald Astor, *The New York Cops* (New York: Charles Scribner's Sons, 1971), 7; Costello, *Our Police Protectors*, 131; McCabe, *Lights and Shadows of New York Life*, 178. An article about the annual New York prison numbers in the year 1855 (published in *The New York Times* on February 21, 1856) showed that the crime totals had climbed to nearly thirty-seven thousand a year already.

3. New York Secretary of State study of murders over twenty years, submitted by the Board of Aldermen of New York City, 1905. The Board of Alderman Documents (these are reports put together by the New York City Board of Aldermen, usually papers with statistics, and then submitted to the state as part of the annual record of New York City governmental and law enforcement activity), 22 (1855), 6–8, shows 86 murders in 1854, National Science Foundation report, February 26, 2015. Statistics were not kept very well in the mid-nineteenth century, and that is why the number of murders, and crimes, varies. In his book *The Collapse of American Criminal Justice* (Cambridge, MA: Harvard University Press, 2011, 17), William Stuntz puts the 1840s murder rate at 4.4 per 100,000 residents and states that it more than doubled, to 10.2, by 1859. Eric Monkkonen, in his book *Crime, Justice, History* (Columbus: Ohio State University Press, 2002, 64–66), states that the rate was about 5.0 per 100,000 in the 1840s, 7.5 in the 1850s, and just over 10.0 in 1859, or twice the 1840s rate. In another of Monkkonen's books, *Murder in New York City* (Berkeley and Los Angeles: University of California Press, 2001, 16), he puts the 1859 and 1860

numbers higher, close to 110 per year. A study of murders in 1843 written about in the *Herald,* which probably did not record all of them, showed 43 slayings, or a rate of 10.0 per year. A study Randolph Roth did in his *American Homicide* showed the murder rate between 1840 and 1860 steady at that the murder rate tripled to about 13.0 by 1860, or Monkkonen's numbers were from an investigation of over 1,700 cases documented by the New York City Coroner's Office as well as newspapers. The Board of Aldermen numbers, reported by that same Coroner's Office to the city, were the most official available at that time. So, in general, the murder rate of somewhere from 86 to 110 a year in the late 1850s is the most accurate one can put together. It stayed high through the Civil War. In 1864, there were 80 murders in the city, according to a city report to the state legislature written about in *The New York Times* on January 5, 1865; Johnson, *Policing the Urban Underworld,* 127.

4. John C. Van Dyke, *The New New York: A Commentary on the Place and the People* (New York: Macmillan, 1909), 175–76.

5. *New York Sun,* October 16, 1841.

6. James Lardner and Thomas Reppetto, *NYPD: A City and Its Police* (New York: Henry Holt, 2000), 7.

7. *New York Herald,* April 20, 1841.

8. Ibid., various issues, January 1842.

9. Johnson, *Policing the Urban Underworld,* 58; *New York Herald,* January 5, 1842.

10. McCabe, *Lights and Shadows of New York Life,* 354.

11. Edward Spann, *The New Metropolis: New York City, 1840–1857* (New York: Columbia University Press, 1981), 251.

12. Roth, *American Homicide,* 302; McCabe, *Lights and Shadows of New York Life,* 818, 839–42; Robert Dykstra, *The Cattle Towns* (New York: Atheneum, 1970), 123–33, 291–93.

13. McCabe, *Lights and Shadows of New York Life,* 56.

14. *New York American,* May 4, 1841.

15. *Brooklyn Daily Times,* December 2, 1858.

16. Ibid., July 21, 1857.

17. Roger Lane, *Murder in America: A History* (Columbus: Ohio State University Press, 1997), 114–15, 117; *New York Herald,* March 13, 1841.

18. Walling, *Recollections of a New York City Chief of Police,* 432.

19. Johnson, *Policing the Urban Underworld,* 53–54; *New York Herald,* January 3, 1842.

20. Walling, *Recollections of a New York City Chief of Police,* 461.

21. Ernst, "Immigrants and Tenements in New York City, 1825–1863," 124.

22. Lane, *Murder in America,* 129–30; Stuntz, *The Collapse of American Criminal Justice,* 30.

23. *New York Tribune,* April 10, 1857; Lawrence Friedman, *Crime and Punishment in*

American History (New York: Basic Books, 1993), 150: *Brooklyn Evening Star*, January 12, 1846.

24. Spann, *The New Metropolis*, 249–50.

25. McCabe, *Lights and Shadows of New York Life*, 525–26.

26. *New York Aurora*, July 20, 1857.

27. Monkkonen, *Murder in New York City*, 22–23.

28. Johnson, *Policing the Urban Underworld*, 4–6; Philadelphia mayor Matthew Clarkson, "An Address to the Citizens of Philadelphia Concerning the Better Government of Youth," *Philadelphia Gazette*, June 6, 1795.

29. J. C. Myers, *Sketches on a Tour Through the Northern and Eastern States, the Canadas and Nova Scotia* (Harrisburg, VA: J. H. Wartmann and Brothers, 1849), 50–51.

30. *New York Spectator*, April 30, 1835.

31. Conway, *The Big Policeman*, 40; Astor, *The New York Cops*, 18; Child, *Letters*, 44.

32. McNeur, *Taming Manhattan*, 231.

33. Strong, *Diary* 2:149, January 14, 1854.

34. Foster, *New York in "Slices,"* 20.

35. Dickens, *American Notes*, 125.

36. Seward, *Works* 2:301.

37. *New York Tribune*, April 11, January 8, 1857.

38. Child, *Letters*, 18.

39. *New York Herald*, April 20, 1841.

40. Foster, *New York in "Slices,"* 22.

41. Proceedings, Board of Aldermen, Minutes, 1789–1859, June 28, 1841, 21:114.

42. McCabe, *Lights and Shadows of New York Life*, 242–43.

43. O'Brien, *The Story of the* Sun, 29.

44. Lane, *Murder in America*, 102.

45. *Brooklyn Eagle and Kings County Democrat*, September 2, 1846; *New York Sun*, March 27, 1843.

46. *New York Tribune*, March 1846.

47. Richardson, *The New York Police*, 76; *New York Herald*, January 12, 1842, February 4, 1852.

48. *New York Herald*, January 8, 12, 1842.

49. Ibid., January 12, 1842.

50. Ibid., April 25, March 13, May 17, 1841, January 8, 1842; David Rothman, "Perfecting the Prison: United States, 1789–1865," in *The Oxford History of the Prison: The Practice of Punishment in Western Society*, ed. Norval Morris and David Rothman (New York: Oxford University Press, 1995), 113.

51. *New York Herald*, March 25, 1841.

52. Ibid., January 3, 1842.

53. David Scobey, *Empire City: The Making and Meaning of the New York City Landscape* (Philadelphia: Temple University Press, 2002), 151.

54. Charles Loring Brace, "The Dangerous Classes of New York," in *The American Way of Crime*, ed. Wayne Moquin and Charles Van Doren (New York: Prager, 1976), 15–16.

55. *Harper's Weekly*, May 20, 1871.

56. John Pintard's letter to his daughter, March 1, 1833, in Kenneth Jackson and David Dunbar, *Empire City: New York Through the Centuries* (New York: Columbia University Press, 2002), 162.

57. *New York Times*, January 9, 1862; Hall, *Travels in North America in the Years 1827 and 1828*, 155.

58. Bell, *Diary*, October 11, 1850.

59. Strong, *Diary* 1:150, October 11, 1840.

60. *New York Tribune*, July 10, 1852.

61. *New York Herald*, January 8, 1842.

62. Monkkonen, *Murder in New York City*, 16, 28–29, 32, 34.

63. *Brooklyn Eagle*, October 26, 1846; *New York Herald*, July 6, 1852.

64. *New York Herald*, January 3, 1842.

65. Miller, *The Social History of Crime and Punishment in America*, 154.

66. Walling, *Recollections*, 48–49; Whitman, *Brooklyn Daily Times*, October 22, 1858.

67. Child, *Letters*, 61; Lane, *Murder in America*, 126–27.

68. *Chicago Tribune*, November 24, 1865.

69. David Reynolds, *Walt Whitman's America: A Cultural Biography* (New York: Columbia University Press, 2002), 162.

70. Walt Whitman, *New York Dissected* (New York: Rufus Rockwell Wilson, 1936), 130.

71. *New York Aurora*, April 22, 1842.

72. Introduction to Walt Whitman, *The Journalism of Walt Whitman*, vol. 1, ed. Herbert Bergman, Douglas A. Noverr, and Edward J. Recchia (New York: Peter Lang, 1998), xvi–xvii; *Brooklyn Daily Eagle*, September 29, 1846, June 12, 13, 1846; Reynolds, *Walt Whitman's America*, 106.

73. Whitman, *Prose Works, 1892* 1:286–89.

74. Reynolds, *Walt Whitman's America*, 99–100.

75. Whitman, *Journalism* 1:lxx.

76. *New York Aurora*, March 28, 1842.

77. McNeur, *Taming Manhattan*, 199.

78. Burrows and Wallace, *Gotham*, 493.

79. Costello, *Our Police Protectors*, 131; Johnson, *Policing the Urban Underworld*, 127; *Philadelphia Public Ledger*, January 21, 1859; Robert Gray Gunderson, *The Log-Cabin Campaign* (Lexington: University of Kentucky Press, 1957), 143.

80. Hone, *Diary* 1:235–36, January 3, 1837.

81. Ibid., 1:127, May 12, 1834.

82. *Brooklyn Daily Times*, January 15, 1858.

83. Hone, *Diary* 1:508, November 3, 1840.

84. Richardson, *The New York Police*, 18, Jerome Hall, "Legal and Social Aspects of Arrest Without a Warrant," 49 *Harvard Law Review* 566 (1936).

Chapter Six

1. *McDowall's Journal,* January, April, February, and September 1833,

2. Gilfoyle, *City of Eros,* 252; memo to Police Commissioner, April 12, 1915, MP-MJP, 41 (his reference was to the prostitutes and police of the pre–Civil War era), Moss testimony in Lexow Commission report 4:4495–98; Van Dyke, *The New New York,* 278.

3. Herbert Asbury, *The Gangs of New York* (Garden City, NY: Garden City Publishing, 1927), 249–50.

4. *Brooklyn Daily Times,* June 20, 1859.

5. Carolyn Karcher, *The First Woman in the Republic: A Cultural Biography of Lydia Maria Child* (Raleigh, NC: Duke University Press, 1994), 328–29.

6. Child, quoted in Karcher, *The First Woman in the Republic,* 328.

7. Karcher, *The First Woman in the Republic,* 328, 329.

8. McNeur, *Taming Manhattan,* 180–81.

9. Child, *Letters,* 128.

10. Richardson, *Urban Police in the United States,* 19–20; Hone, *Diary* 1:209, June 2, 1836.

11. Jean Ampère, *Promenade en Amérique,* 2 vols. (Paris, 1855), 1:388.

12. Bishop, "New York Panorama: 1854," 160.

13. Anonymous resident to Francis Grund, in Junius Browne, *The Great Metropolis: A Mirror of New York* (Hartford, CT: American Publishing, 1869), 71.

14. Walling, *Recollections,* 141.

15. Lyman, *The Story of New York,* 136; Still, *Mirror for Gotham,* 129, James Weldon Johnson, *Black Manhattan* (1930; New York: New York Times and Arno Press, 1968), 45.

16. Chris McNickle, *To Be Mayor of New York: Ethnic Politics in the City* (New York: Columbia University Press, 1993), 45; Conway, *The Big Policeman,* 44–46; Lardner and Reppetto, *NYPD,* 10.

17. Stevens, *Sensationalism and the New York Press,* 14.

18. Still, *Mirror for Gotham,* 131.

19. Lewis Mumford, *The City in History: Its Origins, Its Transformations and Its Prospects* (New York: MIF Books, 1961), 46–50.

20. Walt Whitman, "The Latest Raw Head and Bloody Bones," *Brooklyn Eagle and Kings County Democrat,* January 22, 1847.

21. Strong, *Diary* 4:96. August 6, 1866.

22. Rothman, "Perfecting the Prison," 104–5.

Chapter Seven

1. Costello, *Our Police Protectors,* 58–59.

2. Stuntz, *The Collapse of American Criminal Justice,* 91; Gulick, *The Metropolitan Problem and American Ideas,* 32–33, 46–47.

3. Richardson, *The New York Police,* 15.

4. Costello, *Our Police Protectors,* 78.

5. Child, *Letters,* 61.

6. *New York Tribune,* July 10, 1852.

7. Hone, *Diary* 1:421, September 10, 1839; de la Sagra, *Five Months in the United States of North America,* 172.

8. Frederick Marryat, *A Diary in America, with Remarks on Its Institutions,* 2 vols. (Philadelphia: Carey and Hart, 1839), 1:26.

9. Child, *Letters,* 63–73.

10. *New York Aurora,* March 8, 1842.

11. Child, *Letters,* 63.

12. Proceedings, Board of Aldermen, Minutes, December 27, 1842, 24:86–87; December 5, 1842, 24:74–75.

13. Proceedings, Board of Aldermen, Subcommittee Report, January 1843.

14. Richardson, *Urban Police in the United States,* 20–21.

15. Lane, *Murder in America,* 125.

16. Roth, *American Homicide,* 310–30.

17. *New York American,* August 17, 1840.

18. *New York Herald,* January 2, 1842.

19. Roth, *American Homicide,* 310–30; Lyman, *The Story of New York,* 156.

20. Astor, *The New York Cops,* 6; Reynolds, *Walt Whitman's America,* 102; Marilynn Johnson, *Street Justice: A History of Violence in New York City* (Boston: Beacon Press, 2003), 16.

21. McCabe, *Lights and Shadows of New York Life,* 572–74.

22. Strong, *Diary* 1:273, January 8, 1846.

23. McCabe, *Lights and Shadows of New York Life,* 162–66.

24. Hone, *Diary* 1:451, January 1, 1840.

Chapter Eight

1. Child, *Letters*, 44.

2. *Pittsburgh Gazette*, November 28, 1823.

3. *Hazard's Register* 5 (February 6, 1830): 87.

4. Statistics from Roth, *American Homicide*, supplemental volume chart; Costello, ix, 144.

5. Lane, *Murder in America*, 126–27.

6. Frederick Seward, *Autobiography of William H. Seward from 1801 to 1834, with a Memoir of His Life, and Selections from His Letters from 1841 to 1846* (New York: D. Appleton, 1877), 785–86.

7. *Brooklyn Daily Eagle*, May 5, 1847.

8. *Commercial Advertiser*, August 20, 1840.

9. Board of Assistant Aldermen Procedures, Documents, 19:56, 188.

10. Robert Collyer, *Lights and Shadows of American Life* (Boston: Redding, 1844), 10–13.

11. *Evening Tattler*, December 27, 1841.

12. Costello, *Our Police Protectors*, vii.

13. *New York Tribune*, April 11, 1857.

14. Ibid.

15. Walling, *Recollections*, 32.

16. Costello, *Our Police Protectors*, 80–81.

17. Ibid., 81–83, 36–37, 85.

18. *Philadelphia Public Ledger*, June 17, 1840.

19. Proceedings, Board of Aldermen, Documents, 3, no. 25, 140–141, no. 888, 570.

20. Lardner and Reppetto, *NYPD*, 17.

21. "Police Report," *Hazard's Register* 12 (November 2, 1833): 281.

22. Walling, *Recollections*, 38–39.

23. Ebenezer Burling to the New York Humane Society, box 4, John Jay Papers, New-York Historical Society; Diary of Robert Taylor, August 16, 1846, New York Public Library; Costello, *Our Police Protectors*, 229; *New York Herald*, January 28, 1840.

24. Walling, *Recollections*, 603.

25. Bell, *Diary*, October 5, 1850.

26. Costello, *Our Police Protectors*, 147.

27. Brace, "The Dangerous Classes of New York," 14–15.

28. Strong, *Diary* 1:27, July 3, 1836.

29. Child, *Letters*, 11.

30. Dunshee, *As You Pass By*, 75–77.

Chapter Nine

1. Asbury, *The Gangs of New York*, 88–90; O'Brien, *The Story of the Sun*, 23.

2. *New York Herald*, January 28, 1852.

3. Foster, *New York in "Slices,"* 28.

4. Ibid., 28–29.

5. Asbury, *The Gangs of New York*, 14, 161.

6. Jack Lait and Lee Mortimer, *New York Confidential* (New York: Crown Publishers, 1948), 222; Edward W. Martir, *The Secrets of the Great City: A Work Descriptive of the Virtues and Vices, the Mysteries, Miseries and Crimes of New York City* (Philadelphia: Jones, Brothers, 1868), 518.

7. Richardson, *The New York Police*, 57.

8. Whiteaker, *Seduction, Prostitution and Moral Reform in New York*, 26; Johnson, *Policing the Urban Underworld*, 150.

9. Gilfoyle, *City of Eros*, 291.

10. Foster, *New York by Gas-Light*, 94.

11. Johnson, *Policing the Urban Underworld*, 156–57.

12. Whiteaker, *Seduction, Prostitution and Moral Reform in New York*, 26–27, 31; Caldwell, *New York Night*, 131; Cohen, Gilfoyle, and Horowitz, *The Flash Press*, 139.

13. Gilfoyle, *City of Eros*, 289.

14. Burrows and Wallace, *Gotham*, 484–85; Gilfoyle, *City of Eros*, 255.

15. Foster, *New York by Gas-Light*, 75.

16. Ibid., 74.

17. *New York Herald*, February 10, 1842.

18. William Duer, *Reminiscences of an Old New Yorker* (New York: W. L. Andrews, 1867), 10.

19. Bridenbaugh, *Cities in Revolt*, 318.

20. Gilfoyle, *City of Eros*, 29–31.

21. Edgar Allan Poe, *"Doings in Gotham, Letters III and V,"* in *Empire City: New York Through the Centuries*, ed. Kenneth Jackson and David Dunbar (New York: Columbia University Press, 1992), 199–200.

22. Herman Melville, "From *Moby-Dick*," in *Empire City: New York Through the Centuries*, ed. Kenneth Jackson and David Dunbar (New York: Columbia University Press, 2002), 223.

23. Philip Hauser and Leo Schnore, eds., *The Study of Urbanization in New York* (New York: John Wiley and Sons, 1967), 82–84, 86–98.

24. Cohen, Gilfoyle, and Horowitz, *The Flash Press*, 20–21.

25. *New York Times*, June 1, 2008.

26. *New York Herald*, January 2, 5, 1842.

27. *New York Spectator,* September 24, 1842; Cohen, Gilfoyle, and Horowitz, *The Flash Press,* 24–25.

28. *New York Times,* June 1, 2008.

29. *Subterranean,* September 20, 1845.

30. Cohen, Gilfoyle, and Horowitz, *The Flash Press,* 50–51.

31. *Whip and Satirist of New York and Brooklyn,* April 9, 1842.

32. *Sunday Flash,* February 12, 1842.

33. Cohen, Gilfoyle, and Horowitz, *The Flash Press,* 67, 167.

34. Ibid., *The Flash Press,* 2.

35. Ann Buttenwieser, *Manhattan, Water-Bound: Planning and Developing Manhattan's Waterfront from the Seventeenth Century to the Present* (New York: New York University Press, 1987), 39–48: Gilfoyle, *City of Eros,* 34; Caldwell, *New York Night,* 112–14; *Flash,* August 14, 1842.

36. *Whip and Satirist,* April 9, 1842.

37. *Gazette Extraordinary,* August 27, 1842, including *Philadelphia Journal* quote.

38. Child, *Letters,* 121–24.

39. Cohen, *The Murder of Helen Jewett,* 75.

40. Arthur Cole, *The Irrepressible Conflict, 1850–1865* (New York: Macmillan, 1934), 158.

41. Proceedings, Board of Aldermen, Minutes, September 29, 1834, 6:71; Proceedings, Board of Aldermen, Documents, vol. 1, no. 20.

42. Gilfoyle, *City of Eros,* 82; Cohen, *The Murder of Helen Jewett,* 84–86.

43. Whiteaker, *Seduction, Prostitution and Moral Reform in New York,* 34.

44. *New York Herald,* February 15, 1841.

45. *New York Tribune,* April 10, 1857.

46. Wilbur Miller, *Cops and Bobbies: Police Authority in New York and London, 1830–1870* (Columbus: Ohio State University Press, 1973), 5; *Journal of Commerce,* August 26, 1836.

47. New York Magdalen Society, first annual report, 3, Larry Whiteaker, *Seduction, Prostitution and Moral Reform in New York* (New York: Garland Pub., 1997), 47.

48. *Whip,* August 6, 1842.

49. Female Benevolent Society, first annual report, 13.

50. *Advocate of Moral Reform,* May 1, 1841.

51. Gilfoyle, *City of Eros,* 49.

52. Johnson, *Policing the Urban Underworld,* 178–79.

53. *Advocate,* April 15, 1843, 63; *New York Herald,* March 13, 1841; Bell, *Diary,* October 14, 1850.

54. *New York World,* date unknown, in McCabe, *Lights and Shadows of New York Life,* 594–95.

55. Ibid., 597–98.

56. Ibid., 600–604.

57. Ibid.

58. Walling, *Recollections*, 479.

59. George Combe, *Notes on the United States of North America, During a Phrenological Visit in 1838–9–40*, 3 vols. (Philadelphia: Carey and Hart, 1841), 1:28–29.

60. Frances Trollope, "From *The Domestic Manners of the Americans*," in *Empire City: New York Through the Centuries*, ed. Kenneth Jackson and David Dunbar (New York: Columbia University Press, 1992), 157.

61. Foster, *New York in "Slices,"* 76.

62. Ibid., 8; McCabe, *Lights and Shadows of New York Life*, 123.

63. James Boardman, "From *America and the Americans*," in *Empire City: New York Through the Centuries*, ed. Kenneth Jackson and David Dunbar (New York: Columbia University Press, 1992), 160.

64. *Flash*, July 10, 1842; McCabe, *Lights and Shadows of New York Life*, 186–88.

65. Foster, *New York in "Slices,"* 15.

66. Ibid., 120–22; Foster wrote stories in his paper, the *Tribune*, based on his own visits to stores in the Bowery and Broadway in the mid-1840s.

67. McCabe, *Lights and Shadows of New York Life*, 188–93.

68. Whiteaker, *Seduction, Prostitution and Moral Reform in New York*, 160–61.

69. *New York Herald*, January 8, 1842, January 28, 1852, January 20, 1852; *New York Tribune*, April 12, 1857.

70. *New York Tribune*, November 15, 1852.

71. *New York Aurora*, February 28, 1842.

72. Walling, *Recollections*, 497.

73. *New York Tribune*, December 21, 1841.

74. Burrows and Wallace, *Gotham*, 485; Cole, *The Irrepressible Conflict*, 160.

75. Richardson, *The New York Police*, 27.

76. *New York Aurora*, February 28, 1842.

77. Ibid., December 6, 1858; *New York Herald*, March 13, April 20, 1841.

78. Van Dyke, *The New New York*, 281.

79. *New York Tribune*, April 11, 1857; *New York Herald*, November 21, 1852.

80. *New York Herald*, April 10, 1857.

81. Foster, *New York by Gas-Light*, 75.

82. *New York Sun*, July 4, 1834; Costello, *Our Police Protectors*, 78–79.

83. Walling, *Recollections*, 449.

84. Child, *Letters*, 62.

85. Annual Crime Report, *New York Times*, March 10, 1853.

86. *New York Aurora*, March 8, 1842.

87. Lane, *Murder in America*, 98.

88. McCabe, *Lights and Shadows of New York Life*, 532; Johnson, *Policing the Urban Under-world*, 54.

89. *New York Aurora*, April 12, 1842.

90. Child, *Letters*, 187 (notes).

91. Ibid., 76.

92. Ibid., 129–32.

93. Proceedings, Board of Aldermen, Minutes, November 23, 1842, 24:6.

94. Hone, *Diary* 2:171, January 17, 1843.

95. *New York Herald*, April 11, 1852.

96. Ibid., March 13, 1841.

97. Walling, *Recollections*, 463.

98. McCabe, *Lights and Shadows of New York Life*, 376–77; *New York Herald*, January 3, 1842.

99. Waling, *Recollections*, 456.

100. Strong, *Diary* 1:260, April 25, 1845.

101. *Philadelphia Public Ledger*, November 15, 1836.

102. *New York Herald*, July 22, 1841.

Chapter Ten

1. Asbury, *The Gangs of New York*, 30–31, 17.

2. *Brooklyn Daily Times*, July 8, 1857.

3. Dickens, "American Notes for General Circulation," 186–94.

4. Ibid., 123–31.

5. Foster, *New York by Gas-Light*, 120; McNeur, *Taming Manhattan*, 192–93.

6. Child, *Letters*, 19.

7. Caldwell, *New York Night*, 130.

8. *Brother Jonathan*, February 26, 1842.

9. O'Brien, *The Story of the Sun*, 105–6.

10. *New York Herald*, November 22, 1852.

11. Dickens, in Asbury, *The Gangs of New York*, 10–11; Tyler Anbinder, *Five Points: The 19th-Century New York City Neighborhood That Invented Tap Dance, Stole Elections, and Became the World's Most Notorious Slum* (New York: Free Press, 2001), 79, 82–83.

12. *New York Post* history article on Five Points, February 26, 2012.

13. Ibid., 12–13

14. McCabe, *Lights and Shadows of New York Life*, 15.

15. *Brooklyn Eagle*, September 12, 1846.

16. Asbury, *The Gangs of New York*, 14–15, 19.

17. Anbinder, *Five Points*, 213.

18. Conway, *The Big Policeman*, viii–ix.

19. Article in the *Cincinnati Enquirer*, late 1830s, in Asbury, *The Gangs of New York*, 187–88.

20. Foster, *New York by Gas-Light*, 123.

21. Costello, *Our Police Protectors*, 77.

22. Charles Loring Brace, *New York Children's Aid Society, Second Annual Report* (New York: A. B. Wynkoop, 1855), 3–7.

23. *New York Post*, January 30, 1846.

24. Gilfoyle, *City of Eros*, 38.

25. Whitman, *New York Dissected*, 6.

26. *New York Herald*, March 17, 1836.

27. Costello, *Our Police Protectors*, 77.

Chapter Eleven

1. *New York Sun*, July 29, 1841.

2. Stashower, *The Beautiful Cigar Girl*, 16–17.

3. *New York Sun*, October 3, 1838; *Commercial Advertiser*, October 3, 1838.

4. *Commercial Advertiser*, July 28, 1841.

5. *New York Herald*, August 13, 1841.

6. *New York American*, February 15, 1839.

7. Jan Whitt, *Settling the Borderland: Other Voices in Literary Journalism* (Lanham, MD: University Press of America, 2008), 69; Helena Katz, *Cold Cases: Famous Unsolved Mysteries, Crimes, and Disappearances in America* (Santa Barbara, CA: Greenwood, 2010), 5.

8. Child, *Letters*, 27–32.

9. *New York Herald*, July 1841; Stashower, *The Beautiful Cigar Girl*, 125.

10. Stashower, *The Beautiful Cigar Girl*, 95.

11. *New York Sun*, July 1841, in Stashower, *The Beautiful Cigar Girl*, 89–90.

12. Stashower, *The Beautiful Cigar Girl*, 213.

13. *New York Herald*, March 13, 1841; *New York Sun*, November 19, 1840; Furer, 66–68.

14. *New York Sun*, November 19, 1840.

15. Stashower, *The Beautiful Cigar Girl*, 260.

16. Ibid., 88; Richardson, *The New York Police*, 90.

17. Richardson, *The New York Police*, 80.

18. Ibid., 287.

19. *New York Globe,* October 13, 1841.

20. John Walsh, *Poe the Detective: The Curious Circumstances Behind "The Mystery of Marie Roget"* (New Brunswick, NJ: Rutgers University Press, 1968), 42–45.

21. *New York Morning Courier,* November 18, 1842; Walsh, *Poe the Detective,* 56–57.

22. *New York Herald,* January 19–24, 1842.

23. Child, *Letters,* 81, 137–43.

24. Walling, *Recollections,* 15.

25. Child, *Letters,* 241 (notes).

26. *New York Tribune,* October 15, 1841.

27. Ibid., December 21, 1842.

Chapter Twelve

1. Walling, *Recollections,* 33.

2. Proceedings, Board of Aldermen, Minutes, December 4, 1843, 24:47–48.

3. Ibid., November 17, 1843, 24:18.

4. *New York Herald,* January 9, 17, 1843; Proceedings, Board of Aldermen, Documents, XXI, 188, 195–96, May 31, 1843.

5. *New York Tribune,* April 12, 1844.

6. Fernando Wood to James Polk, November 5, 1844, Polk Papers.

7. Mushkat, *Reconstruction,* 216–17, Karcher, *The First Woman in the Republic,* 688n39.

8. Robert Taylor, *Rules and Regulations for Day and Night Police of the City of New-York: With Instructions as to the Legal Powers and Duties of Policemen* (New York, 1848), 25–26.

9. Proceedings, Board of Aldermen, Documents, XII, no. 21, 384–94, no. 35, 549–56.

10. Costello, *Our Police Protectors,* 103.

11. T. D. Woolsey, "Nature and Sphere of Police Power," *Journal of Social Science* 3 (1871): 113.

12. Proceedings, Board of Aldermen, Minutes, March 13 and 18, 1844, 24: 433–36.

13. Howard Furer, dissertation, New York University, 1963.

14. *New York Tribune,* March 22, 1845.

15. Mushkat, *Reconstruction,* 224; *New York Sun,* April 12, 1845.

16. *New York Evening Post,* May 13, 1845.

17. Conway, *The Big Policeman,* 54.

18. Lyman, *The Story of New York,* 128.

19. Jerome Mushkat, *Tammany: The Evolution of a Political Machine* (Syracuse, NY: Syracuse University Press, 1971), vii.

20. Walling, *Recollections*, 598.

21. McCabe, *Lights and Shadows of New York Life*, 66–68, 76.

22. Mushkat, *Tammany*, 5.

23. Kenneth Ackerman, *Boss Tweed: The Rise and Fall of the Corrupt Pol Who Conceived the Soul of Modern New York* (New York: Carroll and Graf, 2005), 37.

24. Ibid., 71.

25. Walling, *Recollections*, 598–99.

26. Bell, *Diary*, October 16, 1850.

27. Ibid., October 1850.

28. Walling, *Recollections*, 597–600.

29. Quoted in McCabe, *Lights and Shadows of New York Life*, 78–79.

30. Ibid., 76.

31. Samuel J. Tilden, *Writings and Speeches of Samuel J. Tilden*, ed. John Bigelow, 2 vols. (New York: Harper and Brothers, 1885), 556–606; *New York Evening Post*, November 2, 1871.

32. McCabe, *Lights and Shadows of New York Life*, 79.

33. Mushkat, *Tammany*, 6–7.

34. Hauser and Schnore, *The Study of Urbanization*, 116–18.

35. The nickname appeared in numerous New York newspapers.

36. McCabe, *Lights and Shadows of New York Life*, 82.

37. Glyndon Van Deusen, *William H. Seward* (New York: Oxford University Press, 1967), 72; Walter Stahr, *Seward: Lincoln's Indispensable Man* (New York Simon and Schuster, 2012), 97; Terry Golway, *Machine Made: Tammany Hall and the Creation of Modern American Politics* (New York: Norton, 2014), 37–39; Mushkat, *Tammany*, 3.

38. McNickle, *To Be Mayor of New York*, 7–9.

39. Strong, *Diary* 2:109, November 6, 1852.

40. James Robertson, *A Few Months in America: Containing Remarks on Some of Its Industrial and Commercial Interests* (London: Longman, 1855), 14.

41. Still, *Mirror for Gotham*, 133.

42. Astor quote from Conway, *The Big Policeman*, 35; *New York Herald*, November 22, 1852; Strong, *Diary* 1:347, March 27, 1849.

43. Mushkat, *Wood*, 37–39.

44. Strong, *Diary* 2:201, December 13, 1854.

45. Ibid., 2:205, December 31, 1854.

46. Mushkat, *Feman Wood*, 40.

47. Larry Gara, *The Presidency of Franklin Pierce* (Lawrence: University Press of Kansas, 1991), 84–85; Eugene McCormac, *James K. Polk: A Political Biography, 1845–1849*

(New York: Russell and Russell, 1965), 616–20; Allan Nevins, *The Ordeal of the Union*, 2 vols. (New York: Charles Scribner's Sons, 1947), 2:430–32, 470; David Potter, *The Impending Crisis, 1848–1861* (New York: Harper and Row, 1976), 89; Bureau of the Census, *Sixteenth Census of the United States*, 4 vols. (Washington, DC: GPO, 1942), vol. 1, illustrated tables 7 and 8.

48. Edward Shepard, *Martin Van Buren* (Boston: Houghton Mifflin, 1899), 289.

49. Potter, *The Impending Crisis*, 68–69; Binder, *James Buchanan and the American Empire*, 260–61.

50. *New York Tribune*, April 12, 1845.

51. William F. Havemeyer, *Annual Message*, New York, May 13, 1845; Furer, dissertation, 33–34.

52. Richardson, *The New York Police*, 62–63; *New York Herald*, July 14, 1848.

53. *New York Tribune*, April 4, 1857; Proceedings, Board of Aldermen, Minutes, February 18, 1850, 37:219.

54. Proceedings, Board of Aldermen, Minutes, May 9, 1850, 21:661–62; November 19, 1849, 21:318, 312–13.

55. Richardson, *The New York Police*, 68.

56. Peter Cooper to the Common Council, May 18, 1845, in *Reminiscences* (New York, 1882), 152–54.

57. James Bryce, "The American Commonwealth," 1888, quoted in Hauser and Schnore, *The Study of Urbanization*, 116–18.

58. *New York Herald*, July 1, 1845; *New York Sun*, July 1, 1845.

59. *Commercial Advertiser*, July 3, 1845; *New York Tribune*, July 19, 1845.

60. *Commercial Advertiser*, August 1, 1845.

61. Howard B. Furer, *William Frederick Havemeyer: A Political Biography* (New York: American Press, 1965), 40–41.

62. Costello, *Our Police Protectors*, 101.

63. Message of the Mayor in Relation to the Police of the City of New York, November 1, 1845, document 21, 1845.

64. *Valentine's Manual*, 1859, 55.

65. Richardson, *The New York Police*, 59; Proceedings, Board of Alderman, Documents, 14, no. 1, 10–11, no. 35, 520–29, no. 37, 547–65.

66. *Valentine's Manual*, 1848, 69–70; "Quarterly Reports of the Police Captain of the Tenth Patrol District." October 1, 1850, Municipal Archives.

67. Richardson, *The New York Police*, 56.

68. Walling, *Recollections*, 47–48.

69. McCabe, *Lights and Shadows of New York Life*, 177.

70. Floyd-Jones, *Backward Glances*, 6; Miller, *Cops and Boppies*, 155.

71. Asbury, *The Gangs of New York*, 103.

72. Proceedings, Board of Aldermen, Minutes, February 15, 1847, 32:317; April 22, 1850, 32:590.

73. Ibid., February 7, 1844, 37:238–39; July 26, 1841, 21:177.

74. Ibid., March 1, 1847, 32:352.

75. Ibid., December 16, 1850, 37:574–75; February 8, 1847, 32:279.

76. *Commercial Advertiser,* August 20, 1840.

77. Richardson, *The New York Police,* 35.

78. Strong, *Diary* 1:260, April 25, 1845.

79. Thomas Bender, "The Culture of the Metropolis," *Journal of Urban History* 14 (1988): 494.

80. Ishbel Ross, *Crusades and Crinolines: The Life and Times of Ellen Curtis Demorest and William Jennings Demorest* (New York: Harper and Row, 1963), 166–68.

81. Conway, *The Big Policeman,* 34; Foster, *New York by Gas-Light,* 100–1.

82. Foster, *New York by Gas-Light,* 70.

83. *Brooklyn Daily Times,* June 19, 1859.

84. Cole, *The Irrepressible Conflict,* 156.

85. Strong, *Diary* 1:293, May 7, 1847.

86. Floyd Stovall, ed., *Prose Works, 1892,* 2 vols. (New York: New York University Press, 1963–64), 1:273–75.

Chapter Thirteen

1. Mushkat, *The Ruin of New York Democracy,* 3.

2. Whitman, "Advice to Strangers," in *New York Dissected,* 141.

3. Whitman, "Depot to Stopping Place," in ibid., 136.

4. *New York Atlas,* June 15, 1856.

5. Papke, *Framing the Criminal,* 127.

6. Walling, *Recollections,* 48.

7. Benjamin Sewell, *Sorrow's Circuit; or, Five Years' Experience in the Bedford Street Mission* (Philadelphia: Jaspar Harding and Son, 1859), 333; *Philadelphia Public Ledger,* August 11, 1855.

8. Walling, *Recollections,* 359.

9. Frances Connor, *The Vindication of Frances Connor: The Report of Her Late Case Against George Matsell, the Chief of Police,* pamphlet (New York, 1848), 12.

10. Costello, *Our Police Protectors,* 120.

11. Johnson, *Policing the Urban Underworld,* 185.

12. Ibid.

13. Walling, *Recollections,* 507, 509.

14. Robert Livingston, New York State Assembly documents, 1855, vol. 7, no. 150.

15. *New York Times,* July 18, 1866; Johnson, *Policing the Urban Underworld,* 144–45.

16. Walling, *Recollections,* 194.

17. Richardson, *Policing the Underworld,* 136–37.

18. *Chicago Tribune,* October 28, 1857; *Philadelphia Public Ledger,* July 21, 1854; Richardson, *Urban Police in the United States,* 51, 134–35, 193.

19. *New York Tribune,* March 17, 1853.

20. *New York Herald,* April 11, 1852.

21. *New York Herald,* January 8, 1842; *New York Tribune,* April 10, 1857.

22. Proceedings, Board of Aldermen, Minutes, February 11, 1850, 37:142–43.

23. James Richardson, "To Control the City: The New York Police in Historical Perspective," in *Cities in American History,* ed. Kenneth Jackson and Stanley Schultz (New York: Knopf, 1972), 272, 283; Richardson, *Urban Police in the United States,* 49–50.

24. Bell, *Diary,* November 18, 1850.

25. Richard Wade, "Violence in the Cities: A Historical View," in *Cities in American History,* ed. Kenneth Jackson and Stanley Schultz (New York: Knopf, 1972), 477.

26. Lothrop Stoddard, *Master of Manhattan: The Life of Richard Croker* (New York and Toronto: Longmans, Green, 1931), 10.

27. Walling, *Recollections,* 31–32.

28. Cornelius Willemse, with George Lemmer and Jack Kofoed, *Behind the Green Lights* (Garden City, NY: Garden City Press, 1931), 20.

29. Proceedings, Board of Aldermen, Minutes, March 1, 1847, 32:317.

30. Hone, *Diary* 1:179, October 3, 1835.

31. *New York Herald,* March 13, 1841, January 2, 1842.

32. Costello, *Our Police Protectors,* 133.

33. Connor, *The Vindication of Frances Connor,* 12, 14.

34. Jacob Cantor at an 1895 New York Senate hearing, describing New York life at midcentury. His testimony was republished in Ross Sandler, ed., *Police Corruption, Municipal Corruption: Cures at What Cost?* (New York: New York Law School and the New York Law Review, 1995), 24.

35. Bell, *Diary,* December 22, 1850, January 1, 1851.

36. *New York Herald,* January 10, 1857.

37. Walling, *Recollections,* 567.

38. Conway, *The Big Policeman,* 47; Johnson, *Policing the Underworld,* 95.

39. *Journal of Prison Discipline* 6, no. 1 (January 1851): 103.

40. *Brooklyn Daily Times,* November 16, 1857.

41. Hone, *Diary,* January 29, 1847, 1:785.

42. Richardson, *The New York Police,* 53; Brace, *The Dangerous Classes of New York,* passim.

43. Edward Van Every, *Sins of New York, as "Exposed" by the* Police Gazette (New York: Frederick A. Stokes, 1930), 74–79; Gilfoyle, *City of Eros,* 120.

44. McCabe, *Lights and Shadows of New York Life,* 201–2.

45. Edward Crapsey, *The Nether Side of New York* (New York: Sheldon, 1872), 138–39.

46. Gilfoyle, *City of Eros,* 124–26.

47. Ibid., 130–31.

48. Whitman, *Journalism,* "On Vice," 7.

49. Browne, *The Great Metropolis,* 50–51.

50. David Potter, *The Impending Crisis, 1848–1861* (New York: Harper and Row, 1976), 229–30.

51. Cantor in Sandler, *Police Corruption, Municipal Corruption,* 13.

52. Mushkat, *Tammany,* 238; Richardson, *The New York Police,* 60; Proceedings, Board of Alderman, Document, 1856, II, No. 97, 170.

53. Mushkat, *Tammany,* 259.

54. Spann, *The New Metropolis,* 430; Hall, *Cities in Civilization,* 746; John Reader, *Cities* (New York: Atlantic Monthly Press, 2004), 161.

55. Mohl and Betten, Introduction, Pre-Industrial Cities, 94.

56. Spann, *The New Metropolis,* 436n7.

57. Emmeline Stuart-Wortley, "From *Travels in the United States,*" in *Empire City: New York Through the Centuries,* ed. Kenneth Jackson and David Dunbar (New York: Columbia University Press, 1992), 209.

58. Reader, *Cities,* 151.

59. William Chambers, *Things as They Are in America* (London and Edinburgh: W. R. Chambers, 1854), 177; Edward Watkin, *A Trip to the United States and Canada, in a Series of Letters* (London: W. H. Smith, 1852), 11.

60. James Wilson, *Thackeray in the United States, 1852–3, 1855–6,* 2 vols. (New York: Dodd, Mead, 1904), 1:146, 149.

61. Strong, *Diary* 2:81, January 3, 1852.

62. Ibid., 2:87, March 13, 1852.

63. Adam de Gurowski, *America and Europe* (New York: D. Appleton, 1857), 371–72.

64. Walling, *Recollections,* 46.

65. Hone, *Diary* 2:360–61.

66. Strong, *Diary* 1:351–53, May 12, 1849.

67. Walling, *Recollections,* 46.

68. *New York Herald,* November 22, 1852.

69. Thomas James, *Rambles in the United States and Canada During the Year 1845, with a Short Account of Oregon* (London: J. Ollivier, 1846), 43.

70. Jerome Mushkat, *Fernando Wood: A Political Biography* (Kent, OH: Kent State University Press, 1990), 41.

71. *New York Herald,* April 1, 1855.
72. Costello, *Our Police Protectors,* 116.
73. Bell, *Diary,* February 27, 1851.

Chapter Fourteen

1. Annual Report of the Board of Police Commissioners for 1852, *New York Times,* March 18, 1853.
2. J. W. Gerard, *London and New York: Their Crime and Police* (New York: W. C. Bryant, 1853), 9–10; Isabella Bird Bishop, *The Englishwoman in America* (1856; Chicago: Lakeside Press, 2012), 339–40.
3. Whitman, "Street Yarn," in *New York Dissected,* 120.
4. Parkhurst to Police Commissioners, January 16, 1894, Gilfoyle, *City of Eros,* 185.
5. Asbury, *The Gangs of New York,* 66.
6. Walling, *Recollections,* 141.
7. *Valentine's Manual,* 1859, 171–72.
8. Strong, *Diary* 2:61, August 12, 1851.
9. Carlson, *The Man Who Made News,* 238.
10. *New York Herald,* November 22, 1852.
11. Walling, *Recollections,* 454–55.
12. Ibid., 209.
13. Bell, *Diary,* October 16, 1850; Ernst, "Immigrants and Tenements in New York City, 1825–1863," 125.
14. *New York Tribune,* April 10, 1851.
15. *New York Times,* December 8, 1855.
16. Ibid.; Richardson, *The New York Police,* 68.
17. Richardson, *The New York Police,* 70.
18. Cole, *The Irrepressible Conflict, 1850–1865,* 156.
19. Julian Hawthorne description, in Conway, *The Big Policeman,* 69.
20. Carlson, *The Man Who Made News,* 254.
21. Costello, *Our Police Protectors,* 129.
22. Richardson, *The New York Police,* 68.
23. Costello, *Our Police Protectors,* 126.
24. Seth Low, in Hauser and Schnore, *The Study of Urbanization,* 118.
25. Richardson, *The New York Police,* 86.
26. Conway, *The Big Policeman,* 31.
27. Lyman, *The Story of New York,* 136; Strong, *Diary* 2:140, December 15, 1853.
28. Strong, *Diary* 2:91, May 1, 1852; 2:127, August 17, 1853; 2:159, February 21, 1854.

29. Richardson, *The New York Police,* 74–75.

30. Proceedings, Board of Aldermen, Minutes, September 20, 1841, 21:235, February 11, 1850, 37:141–42.

31. Wallling, *Recollections,* 599–601.

32. *New York Tribune,* April 22, 1857

33. *New York Herald,* November 22, 1852.

34. Ibid., February 3, 1852.

35. Ibid., January 24, 1852, January 2, 1842.

36. Ibid., November 15, 1852.

37. Ibid.

38. Ibid., November 20, 1852.

39. Strong, *Diary* 2:130, September 8, 1853.

40. Ibid., 2:178, June 20, 1854.

41. *New York Herald,* July 3, 6, 1852.

42. Ibid., July 4, 7, 1852, January 12, 1842, numerous other editions also.

43. *New York Times,* August 3, 1855; Strong, *Diary* 2:180, August 3, 1855.

44. Strong, *Diary,* 1:196–97, November 8, 1854.

45. Nevins, *Ordeal of the Union* 2:553.

46. Ibid., 588.

Chapter Fifteen

1. Mushkat, *Fernando Wood,* 1.

2. Strong, *Diary* 2:250–51, January 5, 1856.

3. Still, *Mirror for Gotham,* 167.

4. Ibid., 138.

5. William Ferguson, *America by River and Rail; or, Notes by the Way on the New World and Its People* (London: J. Nisbet, 1856), 49–52; Still, *Mirror for Gotham,* 139.

6. Charles Lyell, *A Second Visit to the United States of America,* 2 vols. (New York: Harper and Brothers, 1849), 2:248–49; Chambers, *Things as They Are in America,* 173–204.

7. Still, *Mirror for Gotham,* 141.

8. Bishop, *The Englishwoman in America,* 332–33.

9. Walling, *Recollections,* 577–78.

10. Chambers, *Things as They Are in America,* 173–204; Still, *Mirror for Gotham,* 148.

11. S. L. Nasing to Fernando Wood, January 2, 1859; Charles Stuart to Fernando Wood, December 28, 1859; Thomas Barr to Fernando Wood, December 30, 1839, Wood Papers.

12. John Bichnbishop to Fernando Wood, December 16, 1859, Wood Papers.

13. Mushkat, *Fernando Wood,* 42–43.

14. Wood to Joseph Moore, May 3, 1878, Wood Papers.

15. Various issues of city newspapers in the summer of 1855, Mushkat, *Fernando Wood*, 52.

16. *New York Times*, January 27, 1857.

17. Wood to Erasmus Corning, November 30, 1850, Gratz Collection, in Mushkat, *Fernando Wood*, 62.

18. Mushkat, *Fernando Wood*, 61; *New York Times*, January 6, 1857.

19. Strong, *Diary* 2:217–18, March 31, 1855.

20. Ibid. 2:234, October 17, 1855, note.

21. *New York Times*, March 6, 1855; Wood to William Marcy, March 10, 1855, Wood Papers.

22. Walling, *Recollections*, 54.

23. Alexander Callow Jr., *The Tweed Ring* (New York: Oxford University Press, 1966), 18; E. L. Godkin, "The Moral of Tweed's Career," *Nation*, November 7, 1878, 280, in *History of the State of New York*, vol. 7, ed. Alexander Flick (New York: Columbia University Press, 1937), 144.

24. *New York Herald*, March 31, 1855.

25. James Gordon Bennett to Fernando Wood, April 16, 1861, Wood Papers.

26. Jerome Mushkat, *The Reconstruction of the New York Democracy, 1861–74* (Rutherford, NJ: Fairleigh Dickinson University Press, 1981), 17, 18.

27. Ibid., 22.

28. Paul Weinbaum, "Temperance, Politics and the New York City Riots of 1857," *New-York Historical Society Quarterly* 59, no. 3 (July 1975): 267.

29. Mushkat, *Fernando Wood*, 44.

30. Xavier Donald MacLeod, *Biography of Hon. Fernando Wood, Mayor of the City of New York* (New York: G. F. Parsons, 1858), 216.

31. Strong, *Diary* 2:231, September 9, 1855.

32. MacLeod, *Biography of Hon. Fernando Wood*, 217.

33. Mushkat, *The Reconstruction of the New York Democracy*, 297.

34. Ibid., 23.

35. *New York Herald*, September 20, 1856.

36. Mushkat, *The Reconstruction of the New York Democracy*, 299.

37. Fred Seward to Fernando Wood, November 29, 1861, Wood Papers.

38. Mayor Fernando Wood to James Gerard, April 5, 1855, in MacLeod, *Biography of Hon. Fernando Wood*, 229.

39. Fernando Wood speech at Tammany Hall, March 22, 1855, in ibid., 229.

40. *New York Herald*, January 2, 1855.

41. MacLeod, *Biography of Hon. Fernando Wood*, 207.

42. Ibid., 211.

43. Ibid., 233.

44. Ibid., 235.

45. Ibid., 232.

46. Ibid., 236.

47. Mushkat, *The Reconstruction of the New York City Democracy*, 23.

48. Abijah Ingraham, *A Biography of Fernando Wood: A History of the Forgeries, Perjuries, and Other Crimes of Our "Model Mayor,"* pamphlet (New York, 1850s).

49. Henry Wikoff to James Buchanan, December 31, 1856, James Buchanan Papers, Historical Society of Pennsylvania, Philadelphia.

Chapter Sixteen

1. *New York Herald,* January 15, 1857.

2. Ibid., January 3, 1857.

3. Ibid., January 5, 1857.

4. Ibid., January 10, 1857.

5. Ibid.

6. Ibid., January 12, 1857.

7. Strong, *Diary* 2:333, May 6, 1857.

8. *New York Tribune,* April 16, 1857; Weinbaum, "Temperance, Politics and the New York City Riots of 1857," 246.

9. Ibid., 246–47.

10. Fernando Wood to unknown recipient, May 23, 1855, Wood Papers; *New York Evening Times,* April 23, 1857; Richardson, "To Control the City," 274–75.

11. *Brooklyn Eagle,* May 30, 1857.

12. Richardson, *Urban Police in the United States,* 38–39.

13. Proceedings, Board of Aldermen, Assembly docs (June 1857), no. 127, 2–5; *New York Times.* March 24, 1857.

14. Walling, *Recollections,* 56.

15. *New York Times,* May 12, 1857; Spann, *The New Metropolis,* 391.

16. James Richardson, *Urban Police in the United States,* 37–38.

17. *Harper's Weekly* 1 (1857): 225.

18. *New York Times,* April 16, May 1, 13.

19. Spann, *The New Metropolis,* 388.

20. *Democratic Review,* May 7, 1857.

21. *New York Times,* August 22, 1871.

22. *Brooklyn Daily Times,* November 7, 1857.

23. *Frank Leslie's Illustrated Newspaper,* June 27, 1857.

24. Walling, *Recollections,* 59–61.

25. Strong, *Diary* 2:323–45, September 17, 1857.

26. Mushkat, 74.

27. Ibid., 342.

28. Wood, Board of Aldermen Proclamation, LXVII, 1857, 11; *New York Herald,* July 5, 1857.

29. Strong, *Diary* 2:346–47, July 5, 1857.

30. *Harper's Weekly,* July 11, 1857.

31. A good general description of the riots is given in Weinbaum, "Temperance, Politics and the New York City Riots of 1857," 246–57; the story of the cop beatings is on 256.

32. *New York Herald,* July 6, 1857.

33. Ibid.

34. Ibid.

35. Ibid.; *New York Daily Times,* July 6, 1857.

36. *New York Herald,* July 6–8, 1857; there was an inquest. Stories on the inquest were in the *New York Daily Times* on July 7, 8, 10, 11, and 13 and the *New York Journal of Commerce* on July 8.

37. *Frank Leslie's Illustrated Newspaper,* June 27, 1857.

38. *Harper's Weekly,* mid-July 1857.

Epilogue

1. Strong, *Diary* 2:349, July 14, 1857.

2. Ibid.

3. Callow, *The Tweed Ring,* 24.

4. *New York Tribune,* July 4, 1878.

Bibliography

Historical Papers

Fernando Wood Papers, New York Public Library

Horace Greeley Papers, New York Public Library

Hudson Family Papers, Concord Free Library, Concord, Massachusetts

James K. Polk Papers, Library of Congress

John Jay Papers, New-York Historical Society

Proceedings of the Board of Alderman of the Municipal Assembly of the City of New York Proceedings of the Council of the Municipal Assembly of the City of New York (New York: Board of Alderman, 1902–1935), 120 vols., New York Municipal Archives

William Bell Papers, New-York Historical Society

Journals, Pamphlets, and Book Chapters

Bender, Thomas. "The Culture of the Metropolis." *Journal of Urban History* 14 (1988): 492–502.

Bishop, Isabella Bird. "New York Panorama: 1854." In Bayrd Still, *Mirror for Gotham: New York as Seen by Contemporaries from the Dutch Days to the Present*. New York: New York University Press, 1956.

Boardman, James. "From *America and the Americans*." In *Empire City: New York Through the*

Centuries. Edited by Kenneth Jackson and David Dunbar. New York: Columbia University Press, 1992.

Brace, Charles Loring. "The Dangerous Classes of New York." In *The American Way of Crime*. Edited by Wayne Moquin and Charles Van Doren. New York: Prager, 1976.

Connor, Frances. *The Vindication of Frances Connor: The Report of Her Late Case Against George Matsell, the Chief of Police*. New York, 1848.

Cooper, James Fenimore. "From *Notions of the Americans in New York*." In *Empire City: New York Through the Centuries*. Edited by Kenneth Jackson and David Dunbar. New York: Columbia University Press, 1992.

Curtis, George William. "Editor's Easy Chair." *Harper's New Monthly Magazine*, February 1862.

De la Sagra, Ramon. "From *Five Months in the United States of North America*." In *Empire City: New York Through the Centuries*. Edited by Kenneth Jackson and David Dunbar. New York: Columbia University Press, 1992.

Ernst, Robert. "Immigrants and Tenements in New York City, 1825–1863." In *Urban America in Historical Perspective*. Edited by Raymond A. Mohl and Neil Betten. New York: Weybright and Talley, 1970.

Godkin, E. L. "The Moral of Tweed's Career." *Nation*, November 7, 1878. In *History of the State of New York*, vol. 7. Edited by Alexander Flick. New York: Columbia University Press, 1937.

Hall, Jerome. "Legal and Social Aspects of Arrest Without a Warrant." 49 *Harvard Law Review* 566 (1936).

Havemeyer, William. *Annual Message*. New York, May 13, 1845.

Journal of Prison Discipline 6, no. 1 (January 1851).

Melville, Herman. "From *Moby-Dick*." In *Empire City: New York Through the Centuries*. Edited by Kenneth Jackson and David Dunbar. New York: Columbia University Press, 1992.

Montgomery, David. "The Working Classes of the Pre-Industrial City." In *Urban America in Historical Perspective*. Edited by Raymond K. Mohl and Neil Betten. New York: Weybright and Talley, 1970.

Poe, Edgar Allan. "*Doings in Gotham*, Letters III and V." In *Empire City: New York Through the Centuries*. Edited by Kenneth Jackson and David Dunbar. New York: Columbia University Press, 1992.

Prince, Carl. "The Great 'Riot Year': Jacksonian Democracy and Patterns of Violence in 1834." *Journal of the Early Republic* 5, no. 1 (Spring 1985): 1–19.

Richardson, James. "To Control the City: The New York Police in Historical Perspective." In *Cities in American History*. Edited by Kenneth Jackson and Stanley Schultz. New York: Knopf, 1972.

Rothman, David. "Perfecting the Prison: United States, 1789–1865." In *The Oxford*

History of the Prison: The Practice of Punishment in Western Society. Edited by Norval Morris and David Rothman. New York: Oxford University Press, 1995.

Runcie, John. " 'Hunting the Nigs' in Philadelphia: The Race Riot of August 1834." *Pennsylvania History* 39, no. 2 (April 1972): 187–218.

"Selected Writings of African-Americans in Brooklyn (1849–1928)." In *Empire City: New York Through the Centuries.* Edited by Kenneth Jackson and David Dunbar. New York: Columbia University Press, 1992.

Stuart-Wortley, Emmeline. "From *Travels in the United States.*" In *Empire City: New York Through the Centuries.* Edited by Kenneth Jackson and David Dunbar. New York: Columbia University Press, 1992.

Taylor, Robert. *Rules and Regulations for Day and Night Police of the City of New-York: With Instructions as to the Legal Powers and Duties of Policemen.* New York, 1848.

Trollope, Frances. "From *The Domestic Manners of the Americans.*" In *Empire City: New York Through the Centuries.* Edited by Kenneth Jackson and David Dunbar. New York: Columbia University Press, 1992.

Valentine's Manual. New York, 1859.

Wade, Richard. "Violence in the Cities: A Historical View." In *Cities in American History.* Edited by Kenneth Jackson and Charles Schultz. New York: Knopf, 1972.

Weinbaum, Paul. "Temperance, Politics and the New York City Riots of 1857." *New-York Historical Society Quarterly* 59, no. 3 (July 1975): 246–70.

Whitman, Walt. "Advice to Strangers." *Life Illustrated,* August 23, 1856, available online at the Walt Whitman Archive, http://www.whitmanarchive.org/published /periodical/journalism/tei/per.00274.html.

Woolsey, T. D. "Nature and Sphere of Police Power." *Journal of Social Science* 3 (1871).

Books

Ackerman, Kenneth. *Boss Tweed: The Rise and Fall of the Corrupt Pol Who Conceived the Soul of Modern New York.* New York: Carroll and Graf, 2005.

Adams, John Quincy. *Diary.* In *Memoirs of John Quincy Adams.* Edited by Charles Francis Adams. 12 vols. Philadelphia, 1876.

American Annual Cyclopedia for 1861. New York: D. Appleton, 1862.

Ampère, Jean. *Promenade en Amérique.* 2 vols. Paris, 1855.

Anbinder, Tyler. *Five Points: The 19th-Century New York City Neighborhood That Invented Tap Dance, Stole Elections, and Became the World's Most Notorious Slum.* New York: Free Press, 2001.

Asbury, Herbert. *The Gangs of New York.* Garden City, NY: Garden City Publishing, 1927.

Ashworth, John. *The Republic in Crisis, 1818–1861.* New York. Cambridge University Press, 2012.

Astor, Gerald. *The New York Cops*. New York: Charles Scribner's Sons, 1971.

Barnum, P. T. *Struggles and Triumphs of P. T. Barnum, Told by Himself*. Edited by John G. O'Leary. 1882; London: MacGibbon and Kee, 1967.

Bauer, K. Jack. *Zachary Taylor: Soldier, Planter, Statesman of the Old Southwest*. Baton Rouge: Louisiana State University Press, 1985.

Bell, William. *The Diary of William Bell, Policeman, New York City, 1850–51*. Microfilm, New-York Historical Society.

Binder, Frederick Moore. *James Buchanan and the American Empire*. Selinsgrove, PA: Susquehanna University Press, 1994.

Bishop, Isabella Bird. *The Englishwoman in America*. 1856; Chicago: Lakeside Press, 2012.

Boles, Henry. *Prisoners and Paupers: A Study of the Abnormal Increase of Criminals, and the Public Burden of Pauperism in the United States; the Causes and Remedies*. 2 vols. New York: G. P. Putnam's Sons, 1893.

Brace, Charles Loring. *New York Children's Aid Society, Second Annual Report*. New York: A. B. Wynkoop, 1855.

Bradley, Patricia. *Women and the Press: The Struggle for Equality*. Chicago: Northwestern University Press, 2005.

Bridenbaugh, Carl. *Cities in Revolt: Urban Life in America, 1743–1776*. New York: Knopf, 1955.

Brown, Richard Maxwell. *Strain of Violence: Historical Studies of American Violence and Vigilantism*. New York: Oxford University Press, 1977.

Browne, Junius. *The Great Metropolis: A Mirror of New York*. Hartford, CT: American Publishing, 1869.

Bryce, James. *The American Commonwealth*. London, 1888; Indianapolis: Liberty Fund, 1995.

Bureau of the Census. *Sixteenth Census of the United States*. 4 vols. Washington, DC: GPO, 1942.

Burrows, Edwin, and Mike Wallace. *Gotham: A History of New York City to 1898*. New York: Oxford University Press, 1999.

Buttenwieser, Ann. *Manhattan, Water-Bound: Planning and Developing Manhattan's Waterfront from the Seventeenth Century to the Present*. New York: New York University Press, 1987.

Caldwell, Mark. *New York Night: The Mystique and Its History*. New York: Scribner, 2005.

Callow, Alexander, Jr. *The Tweed Ring*. New York: Oxford University Press, 1966.

Carlson, Oliver. *The Man Who Made News: James Gordon Bennett*. New York: Duell, Sloan and Pearce, 1942.

Chambers, William. *Things as They Are in America*. London, 1855; New York: Negro Universities Press, 1968.

Child, Lydia Maria. *Letters from New-York: Lydia Maria Child*. Edited by Bruce Mills. Athens: University of Georgia Press, 1998.

Chitwood, Oliver Perry. *John Tyler: Champion of the Old South*. Newtown, CT: American Political Biography Press, 1990.

Cohen, Patricia Cline. *The Murder of Helen Jewett: The Life and Death of a Prostitute in Nineteenth-Century New York*. New York: Knopf, 1998.

Cohen, Patricia Cline, Timothy Gilfoyle, and Helen Lefkowitz Horowitz. *The Flash Press: Sporting Male Weeklies in 1840s New York*. Chicago: University of Chicago Press, 2008.

Cole, Arthur. *The Irrepressible Conflict, 1850–1865*. New York: Macmillan, 1934.

Collyer, Robert. *Lights and Shadows of American Life*. Boston: Redding, 1844.

Combe, George. *Notes on the United States of North America, During a Phrenological Visit in 1838–9–40*. 3 vols. Philadelphia: Carey and Hart, 1841.

Conway, J. North. *The Big Policeman: The Rise and Fall of America's First, Most Ruthless, and Greatest Detective*. Guilford, CT: Lyons Press, 2010.

Cooper, Peter. *Reminiscences*. New York, 1882.

Costello, Augustin. *Our Police Protectors: A History of the New York Police*. 1885; Montclair, NJ: Patterson Smith, 1972.

Crapsey, Edward. *The Nether Side of New York; or, The Vice, Crime and Poverty of the Great Metropolis*. New York: Sheldon, 1872.

Dickens, Charles. *American Notes for General Circulation*. London, 1892; New York: Barnes and Noble, 2005.

Duer, William. *Reminiscences of an Old New Yorker*. New York: W. L. Andrews, 1867.

Dunshee, Kenneth Holcomb. *As You Pass By*. New York: Hastings House, 1952.

Dykstra, Robert. *The Cattle Towns*. New York: Atheneum, 1968.

Emerson, Ralph Waldo. *Essays and Journals*. Garden City, NY: International Collectors Library, 1968.

Feldberg, Michael. *The Turbulent Era: Riot and Disorder in Jacksonian America*. New York: Oxford University Press, 1980.

Ferguson, William. *America by River and Rail; or, Notes by the Way on the New World and Its People*. London: J. Nisbet, 1856.

Fermer, Douglas. *James Gordon Bennett and the New York Herald: A Study of Editorial Opinion in the Civil War Era, 1854–1867*. New York: St. Martin's Press, 1986.

Fisher, Sidney George. *A Philadelphia Perspective: The Diary of Sidney George Fisher, Covering the Years 1834–1871*. Edited by Nicholas B. Wainwright. Philadelphia: Historical Society of Pennsylvania, 1967.

Floyd-Jones, Thomas. *Backward Glances: Reminiscences of an Old New-Yorker*. Somerville, NJ: Unionist Gazette Association, 1914.

Foster, George. *New York by Gas-Light and Other Urban Sketches*. Edited by Stuart Blumin. 1856; Berkeley: University of California Press, 1990.

———. *New York in "Slices," by an Experienced Carver*. New York: Dick and Fitzgerald, 1848.

Friedman, Lawrence. *Crime and Punishment in American History*. New York: Basic Books, 1993.

Gara, Larry. *The Presidency of Franklin Pierce*. Lawrence: University Press of Kansas, 1991.

Gerard, J. W. *London and New York: Their Crime and Police*. New York: W. C. Bryant, 1853.

Gilfoyle, Timothy. *City of Eros: New York City, Prostitution, and the Commercialization of Sex, 1790–1920*. New York: Norton, 1992.

Golway, Terry. *Machine Made: Tammany Hall and the Creation of Modern American Politics*. New York: Norton, 2014.

Gordon, Michael. *The Orange Riots: Irish Political Violence in New York City, 1870 and 1871*. Ithaca, NY: Cornell University Press, 1993.

Greeley, Horace. *Recollections of a Busy Life*. New York: Arno, 1868.

Gulick, Luther. *The Metropolitan Problem and American Ideas*. New York: Knopf, 1962.

Gunderson, Robert Gray. *The Log-Cabin Campaign*. Lexington: University of Kentucky Press, 1957.

Gurowski, Adam de. *America and Europe*. New York: D. Appleton, 1857.

Hall, Peter. *Cities in Civilization: Culture, Innovation and Urban Order*. New York: Pantheon Books, 1998.

Handlin, Oscar. *The Newcomers: Negroes and Puerto Ricans in a Changing Metropolis*. New York Metropolitan Region Study. Cambridge, MA: Harvard University Press, 1959.

Hauser, Philip, and Leo Schnore, eds. *The Study of Urbanization*. New York: John Wiley and Sons, 1967.

Heaps, Willard. *Riots, U.S.A., 1765–1970*. New York: Seabury Press, 1966.

Homberger, Eric. *The Historical Atlas of New York City: A Visual Celebration of 400 Years of New York City's History*. New York: Henry Holt, 1994.

Hone, Philip. *The Diary of Philip Hone, 1828–1851*. Edited by Allan Nevins. 2 vols. New York: Dodd, Mead, 1927.

Hudson, Frederic. *The History of Journalism in the United States, from 1690 to 1872*. New York: Harper Brothers, 1973.

Ingraham, Abijah. *A Biography of Fernando Wood: A History of the Forgeries, Perjuries, and Other Crimes of Our "Model Mayor."* New York, 1856.

James, Thomas. *Rambles in the United States and Canada During the Year 1845, with a Short Account of Oregon*. London: J. Ollivier, 1846.

Jefferson, Thomas. *The Writings of Thomas Jefferson*, vol. 15. Washington, DC: Thomas Jefferson Memorial Association, 1907.

Johnson, David. *Policing the Urban Underworld: The Impact of Crime on the Development of the American Police, 1800–1887*. Philadelphia: Temple University Press, 1942.

Johnson, James Weldon. *Black Manhattan*. 1930; New York: New York Times and Arno Press, 1968.

Johnson, Marilynn. *Street Justice: A History of Violence in New York City*. Boston: Beacon Press, 2003.

Karcher, Carolyn. *The First Woman in the Republic: A Cultural Biography of Lydia Maria Child*. Raleigh, NC: Duke University Press, 1994.

Katz, Helena. *Cold Cases: Famous Unsolved Mysteries, Crimes, and Disappearances in America*. Santa Barbara, CA: Greenwood, 2010.

Lait, Jack, and Lee Mortimer. *New York Confidential*. New York: Crown, 1948.

Lane, Roger. *Murder in America: A History*. Columbus: Ohio State University Press, 1997.

Lardner, James, and Thomas Reppetto. *NYPD: A City and Its Police*. New York: Henry Holt, 2000.

Lincoln, Abraham. *Abraham Lincoln: Selected Speeches, Messages, and Letters*. Edited by T. Harry Williams. New York: Rinehart, 1957.

Lyell, Charles. *A Second Visit to the United States of America*. 2 vols. New York: Harper Brothers; London: J. Murray, 1849.

Lyman, Susan Elizabeth. *The Story of New York: An Informal History of the City from the First Settlement to the Present Day*. New York: Crown, 1975.

MacLeod, Xavier Donald. *Biography of Hon. Fernando Wood, Mayor of the City of New York*. New York: G. F. Parsons, 1858.

Marryat, Frederick. *A Diary in America, with Remarks on Its Institutions*. 2 vols. Philadelphia: Carey and Hart, 1839.

Martin, Edward. *Secrets of the Great City: A Work Descriptive of the Virtues and Vices, the Mysteries, Miseries and Crimes of New York City*. Philadelphia: Jones, Brothers, 1868.

Matteson, John. *The Lives of Margaret Fuller: A Biography*. New York: Norton, 2012.

Matthews, J. M. *Fifty Years in New York: A Semi-Centennial Discourse Preached in the South Dutch Church*. New York: D. Fanshaw, 1858.

McCabe, James D., Jr. *Lights and Shadows of New York Life; or, The Sights and Sensations of the Great City*. 1872; New York: Farrar, Straus and Giroux, 1970.

McCormac, Eugene. *James K. Polk: A Political Biography, 1845–1849*. New York: Russell and Russell, 1965.

McNeur, Catherine. *Taming Manhattan: Environmental Battles in the Antebellum City*. Cambridge, MA: Harvard University Press, 2014.

McNickle, Chris. *To Be Mayor of New York: Ethnic Politics in the City*. New York: Columbia University Press, 1993.

McPherson, James. *Battle Cry of Freedom*. New York: Oxford University Press, 1988.

Miller, Wilbur. *Cops and Bobbies: Police Authority in New York and London, 1830–1870*. Columbus: Ohio State University Press, 1973.

——, ed. *The Social History of Crime and Punishment in America*. Los Angeles: Sage Publications, 2012.

Mitchell, Catherine. *Margaret Fuller's New York Journalism: A Biographical Essay and Key Writings*. Knoxville: University of Tennessee Press, 1995.

Monkkonen, Eric. *Crime, Justice, History*. Columbus: Ohio State University Press, 2002.

———. *Murder in New York City*: Berkeley and Los Angeles: University of California Press, 2001.

Mohl, Raymond and Neil Betten. *Urban America in Historical Perspective*. New York: Weybright and Talley, 1970.

Mott, Frank Luther. *American Journalism*. 3rd ed. New York: Macmillan, 1962.

Mumford, Lewis. *The City in History: Its Origins, Its Transformations and Its Prospects*. New York: MIF Books, 1961.

Mushkat, Jerome. *Fernando Wood: A Political Biography*. Kent, OH: Kent State University Press, 1990.

———. *The Reconstruction of the New York Democracy, 1861–74*. Rutherford, NJ: Fairleigh Dickinson University Press, 1981.

———. *Tammany: The Evolution of a Political Machine*. Syracuse, NY: Syracuse University Press, 1971.

Myers, J. C. *Sketches on a Tour Through the Northern and Eastern States, the Canadas and Nova Scotia*. Harrisburg, VA: J. H. Wartmann and Brothers, 1849.

Nevins, Allan. *The Ordeal of the Union*. 2 vols. New York: Charles Scribner's Sons, 1947.

O'Brien, Frank. *The Story of the Sun*. New York: D. Appleton, 1928.

Oxford History of the Prison: The Practice of Punishment in Western Society. Edited by Norval Morris and David Rothman. New York: Oxford University Press, 1995.

Papke, Daniel Ray. *Framing the Criminal: Crime, Cultural Work and the Loss of Critical Perspective, 1830–1900*. Hamden, CT: Archon Books, 1987.

Payne, George. *History of Journalism in the United States*. 1920; Westport, CT: Greenwood Press, 1970.

Poe, Edgar Allan. *The Works of Edgar Allan Poe*. Vol. 8, *Literary Criticism III: The Literati—Minor Contemporaries, Etc.* Edited by Edward Clarence Stedman and George Edward Woodberry. New York, 1895; Freeport, NY: Books for Libraries, 1971.

Potter, David. *The Impending Crisis, 1848–1861*. New York: Harper and Row, 1976.

Pray, Isaac. *Memoirs of J. G. Bennett and His Times*. New York: Stringer and Townsend, 1855.

Pred, Alan. *Urban Growth and City-Systems in the United States, 1840–1860*. Cambridge, MA: Harvard University Press, 1980.

Prentice, Archibald. *A Tour in the United States*. London: C. Gilpin, 1848.

Reader, John. *Cities*. New York: Atlantic Monthly Press, 2004.

Reynolds, David. *Walt Whitman's America: A Cultural Biography*. New York: Knopf, 1995.

Richards, Leonard. *Gentlemen of Property and Standing: Anti-Abolition Mobs in Jacksonian America*. New York: Oxford University Press, 1970.

Richardson, James. *The New York Police: Colonial Times to 1901*. New York: Oxford University Press, 1970.

———. *Urban Police in the United States*. Port Washington, NY: Kennikat Press, 1974.

Robertson, James. *A Few Months in America: Containing Remarks on Some of Its Industrial and Commercial Interests*. London: Longman, 1855.

Ross, Ishbel. *Crusades and Crinolines: The Life and Times of Ellen Curtis Demorest and William Jennings Demorest*. New York: Harper and Row, 1963.

Roth, Randolph. *American Homicide*. Cambridge, MA: Belknap Press, 2009. *American Homicide Supplemental Volume* (statistical supplement) is online at Historical Violence Database, https://cjrc.osu.edu/research/interdisciplinary/hvd.

Sandler, Ross, ed. *Police Corruption, Municipal Corruption: Cures at What Cost?* New York: New York Law School and the New York Law Review, 1995.

Scobey, David. *Empire City: The Making and Meaning of the New York City Landscape*. Philadelphia: Temple University Press, 2002.

Seward, Frederick. *Autobiography of William H. Seward from 1801 to 1834, with a Memoir of His Life, and Selections from His Letters from 1841 to 1846*. New York: D. Appleton, 1877.

Seward, William H. *The Works of William H. Seward*, vol. 2. Edited by George Baker. New York: Redfield Press, 1853.

Sewell, Benjamin. *Sorrow's Circuit; or, Five Years' Experience in the Bedford Street Mission*. Philadelphia: Jaspar Harding and Son, 1859.

Shaw, David. *The Sea Shall Embrace Them*. New York: Free Press, 2002.

Shepard, Edward. *Martin Van Buren*. Boston: Houghton Mifflin, 1899.

Still, Bayrd. *Mirror for Gotham: New York as Seen by Contemporaries from the Dutch Days to the Present*. New York: New York University Press, 1956.

Smith, Elbert. *The Presidency of James Buchanan*. Lawrence: University Press of Kansas, 1975.

Spann, Edward. *The New Metropolis: New York City, 1840–1857*. New York: Columbia University Press, 1981.

Stahr, Walter. *Seward: Lincoln's Indispensable Man*. New York: Simon and Schuster, 2012.

Stanton, Elizabeth Cady, Susan B. Anthony, and Matilda Gage. *History of Woman Suffrage*. 6 vols. 1881–1922; New York: Source Book Press, 1970.

Stashower, Daniel. *The Beautiful Cigar Girl: Mary Rogers, Edgar Allan Poe, and the Invention of Murder*. New York: Penguin Group, 2006.

Stevens, John. *Sensationalism and the New York Press*. New York: Columbia University Press, 1991.

Stoddard, Lothrop. *Master of Manhattan: The Life of Richard Croker*. New York and Toronto: Longmans, Green, 1931.

Stranger's Handbook for the City of New York; or, What to See and How to See It. New York: C. S. Francis, 1853.

Strong, George Templeton. *The Diary of George Templeton Strong*. Edited by Allan Nevins and Milton Thomas. 4 vols. New York: Macmillan, 1952.

Stuntz, William. *The Collapse of American Criminal Justice*. Cambridge, MA: Harvard University Press, 2011.

Taylor, Robert. *Diary*. New York Historical Society.

Tilden, Samuel J. *Writings and Speeches of Samuel J. Tilden*. Edited by John Bigelow. 2 vols. New York: Harper and Brothers, 1885.

Tyler, Lyon G. *The Letters and Times of the Tylers*. 2 vols. 1884; New York: Da Capo Press, 1970.

Van Deusen, Glyndon. *William H. Seward*. New York: Oxford University Press, 1967.

Van Dyke, John C. *The New New York: A Commentary on the Place and the People*. New York: Macmillan, 1909.

Van Every, Edward. *Sins of New York, as "Exposed" by the* Police Gazette. New York: Frederick A. Stokes, 1930.

Walling, George. *Recollections of a New York City Chief of Police*. New York: Caxton Book Concern, 1887.

Walsh, John. *Poe the Detective: The Curious Circumstances Behind "The Mystery of Marie Roget."* New Brunswick, NJ: Rutgers University Press, 1968.

Watkin, Edward. *A Trip to the United States and Canada, in a Series of Letters*. London: W. H. Smith, 1852.

White, George. *From Boniface to Bank Burglar*. Bellows Falls, VT: Truax Printing, 1905.

Whiteaker, Larry. *Seduction, Prostitution and Moral Reform in New York, 1830–1860*. New York: Garland, 1997.

Whitman, Walt. *The Journalism of Walt Whitman*, vol. 1. Edited by Herbert Bergman, Douglas A. Noverr, and Edward J. Recchia. New York: Peter Lang, 1998.

———. *New York Dissected*. New York: Rufus Rockwell Wilson, 1936.

———. *Prose Works, 1892*. Edited by Floyd Stovall. 2 vols. New York: New York University Press, 1963–64.

Whitt, Jan. *Settling the Borderland: Other Voices in Literary Journalism*. Lanham, MD: University Press of America, 2008.

Wilkes, George. *Mysteries of the Tombs: A Journal of Thirty Days Imprisonment in the New York City Prison for Libel*. New York: George Wilkes, 1844.

Willemse, Cornelius, with George Lemmer and Jack Kofoed. *Behind the Green Lights*. Garden City, NY: Garden City Publishing, 1931.

Wilmer, Lambert. *Our Press Gang; or, A Complete Exposition of the Corruption and Crimes of the American Newspapers*. Philadelphia: J. T. Lloyd, 1859.

Wilson, James. *Thackeray in the United States*. 2 vols. New York: Dodd, Mead, 1904.

Index